Constitutions, Markets and Law

NEW THINKING IN POLITICAL ECONOMY

Series Editor: Peter J. Boettke
George Mason University, USA

New Thinking in Political Economy aims to encourage scholarship in the intersection of the disciplines of politics, philosophy and economics. It has the ambitious purpose of reinvigorating political economy as a progressive force for understanding social and economic change.

The series is an important forum for the publication of new work analysing the social world from a multi-disciplinary perspective. With increased specialisation (and professionalisation) within universities, interdisciplinary work has become increasingly uncommon. Indeed, during the 20th century, the process of disciplinary specialisation has reduced the intersection between economics, philosophy and politics and impoverished our understanding of society. Modern economics in particular has become increasingly mathematical and largely ignores the role of institutions and the contribution of moral philosophy and politics.

New Thinking in Political Economy will stimulate new work that combines technical knowledge provided by the dismal science and the wisdom gleaned from the serious study of the worldly philosophy. The series will reinvigorate our understanding of the social world by encouraging a multidisciplinary approach to the challenges confronting society in the new century.

Recent titles in the series include:

Explaining Constitutional Change
A Positive Economics Approach
Stefan Voigt

Ethics as Social Science
The Moral Philosophy of Social Cooperation
Leland B. Yeager

Markets, Planning and Democracy
Essays after the Collapse of Communism
David L. Prychitko

Governance and Economic Development
A Comparative Institutional Approach
Joachim Ahrens

Constitutions, Markets and Law
Recent Experiences in Transition Economies
Edited by Stefan Voigt and Hans-Jürgen Wagener

Constitutions, Markets and Law

Recent Experiences in Transition Economies

Edited by

Stefan Voigt

Professor of Economics, Ruhr-University Bochum, Germany

Hans-Jürgen Wagener

Professor of Economics, Europa University Viadrina Frankfurt (Oder) and Head, Frankfurt Institute for Transformation Studies, Germany

NEW THINKING IN POLITICAL ECONOMY

Edward Elgar
Cheltenham, UK • Northampton, MA, USA

Published by
Edward Elgar Publishing Limited
Glensanda House
Montpellier Parade
Cheltenham
Glos GL50 1UA
UK

Edward Elgar Publishing, Inc.
136 West Street
Suite 202
Northampton
Massachusetts 01060
USA

A catalogue record for this book
is available from the British Library

Library of Congress Cataloguing in Publication Data
Constitutions, markets and law : recent experiences in transition economies / edited by Stefan Voigt, Hans-Jürgen Wagener.
    p.cm. — (New thinking in political economy)
Includes index.
    1. Europe, Eastern—Economic conditions—1989—Congresses. 2. Constitutional law—Europe, Eastern—Congress. I. Voigt, Stefan. II. Wagener, Hans-Jürgen. III Series.

HC244 .C66 2002
2002017913
324.47—dc21

ISBN 1 84064 791 4
Printed and bound in Great Britain by MPG Books Ltd, Bodmin, Cornwall

Contents

Tables

Contributors

Anne van Aaken is a Senior Lecturer at the faculty of Law at Humboldt University Berlin.

Ivan Baron Adamovich is Lecturer in Economics at the University of Fribourg in Switzerland.

Frank Bönker is a Senior Lecturer at the European University Viadrina at Frankfurt (Oder).

Laszlo Bruszt is Associate Professor of Political Science at Central European University in Budapest.

Ruth Gavison is Full Professor at the Faculty of Law at Hebrew University in Jerusalem.

Dieter Grimm is rector of the German Institute of Advanced Study and a former member of the German Constitutional Court.

Horst Hegmann is a Senior Lecturer at the Private University Witten-Herdecke in Germany.

Christian Kirchner is Professor of Law and Economics at the Humboldt University Berlin.

Ivan Krastev, Co-founder and director of the Center for Liberal Strategies in Sofia.

Mark Oelmann is a Lecturer in Economics at the University of Cologne.

Claus Offe is Professor of Political Science at Humboldt-University Berlin.

Peter Ordeshook is Professor of Political Science at the California Institute of Technology in Pasadena.

Stephan Panther is Associate Professor at the University of Kassel.

Ralitsa Peeva is a researcher with the Center for Liberal Strategies, Sofia.

Katharina Pistor is Associate Professor of Law at Columbia Law School, New York.

Gerard C. Rowe is Professor of Law at European University Viadrina at Frankfurt (Oder).

Eli Salzberger is Professor of Law at the University of Haifa.

Hanna Suchocka is a former Prime Minister and Minister of Justice of Poland.

Imre Vörös is Professor of Law and head of department, former Constitutional Court judge.

Stefan Voigt is Professor of Economics at Ruhr-University Bochum.

Hans-Jürgen Wagener is Professor at the European University Viadrina at Frankfurt (Oder) and Director of the Frankfurt Institute for Transformation Studies.

Preface

Stefan Voigt and Hans-Jürgen Wagener

By now, more than a decade has passed since the beginning of the transition processes in Central and Eastern Europe which brought about the necessity for entirely new political and economic systems and, hence, also constitutions. Although representatives of Constitutional Political Economy might seem to be 'natural advisors' of the concerned societies, their role in advising seems to have been rather marginal. It is conjectured that this irrelevance can be explained by two facts, little available positive knowledge on the working properties of alternative constitutional rules on the one hand and an underestimation of the role of the state in the transformation process on the other. Until now, constitutional economics has been concerned primarily with legitimising the state in terms of fairness, justice, or efficiency. In order to advise societies on how to write their constitutions on a more concrete level, solid knowledge of the functional requirements and the working properties of constitutional rules is, however, crucial.

The recent experiences with constitution–making in Central and Eastern Europe might have made this necessity clearer. In order to find out whether the transition processes – and the constitutional design processes coming along with them – have led to any new insights in positive constitutional economics or have at least helped to formulate the relevant questions more precisely and have thus led to a sharper description of the research program, the editors convened a workshop in Berlin. It took place at the Institute for Advanced Study from June 28 to July 2, 2000.

Beyond the participants of the workshop we owe thanks to a number of people. These include the permanent fellows of the Institute as well as its administrative head, namely Yehuda Elkana, Jürgen Kocka and Wolf Lepenies as well as Joachim Nettelbeck who were immediately supportive of the idea of the workshop. They further include the immensely hospitable staff of the Institute who helped us to carry out the workshop. Andrea Friedrich spent lots of time with the project and secured its smooth functioning. Mitch Cohen did style–editing on some of the papers, Uta Lange did the formatting.

Again, Edward Elgar and his staff proved to be very efficient publishers. Last, but not least, thanks are due to the German Ministry of Education and Research (Bundesministerium für Bildung und Forschung) who financed the project.

This volume is more than a simple documentation of the workshop. Some papers were substantially modified or even rewritten entirely. Some of those who actively participated in the workshop did not produce written papers. Among them are Alexander Blankenagel from Berlin's Humboldt–University and Stephen Holmes from New York University. Unfortunately, health reasons prevented Ulrich K. Preuss from delivering a written version of his oral comment on Ruth Gavison given at the workshop. We are especially grateful to Horst Hegmann for filling the gap. The concluding remarks delivered by Christian Kirchner were not modified, they thus refer to the papers as given during the conference.

Introduction

Stefan Voigt and Hans-Jürgen Wagener

CONSTITUTIONS IN TRANSITION – CONSTITUTIONAL
POLITICAL ECONOMY'S STATE OF THE ART IN LIGHT
OF RECENT EXPERIENCES IN REAL-WORLD
CONSTITUTION-MAKING

The transition processes in Central and Eastern Europe are equivalent to
radical modifications in political and economic systems. More than ten years
after they began, it seems to make sense to pause for asking very simple
questions on two levels: on the empirical level, we can ask how far transition
has progressed, whether establishing simultaneously rule of law in the
political and market economy in the economic sphere was indeed impossible
as predicted and feared by some observers (Elster 1991a), and how the
various transition countries fare against each other, etc. On a second, more
theoretical, level, we can try to take these experiences explicitly into account
and reflect upon the adequacy of various disciplines: did transition reveal
theoretical shortcomings to explain the developments in the region? Are there
indications that such shortcomings have been used to modify or extend the
theoretical content of various disciplines? Do we identify new necessities for
interdisciplinary approaches? Questions with regard to this second level were
the main concern of the colloquium on 'Constitutions in Transition' that took
place at the Institute for Advanced Study in Berlin in June 2000 and they
form the basis for this volume.

Before talking about constitutions in transition proper and the research
program that has evolved in economics over the last few years to analyse
constitutional choice and constitutional change, we would like to mention
some deficiencies of economics in general that have become more apparent
during the transition processes. Especially in welfare economics, economists
took pride in the so-called 'institutional neutrality' of their analysis with
regard to allocation and distribution (see Furubotn and Richter 1997 with

numerous examples). The fundamental theorems were supposed to hold regardless of the concrete institutional structure. In principle, then, it was assumed of no import whether one was operating within a market economy or a centrally planned one.

The unwillingness, or inability, to take concrete circumstances – context – explicitly into account had long been criticised by various economists who did not manage to become mainstream, however. This is certainly not the right place to discuss how issues of political economy, which stood at the beginning of the discipline in the 18ᵗʰ century, moved more and more to backstage until they were hardly noticed at all. Coincidence or causality, over the last ten years, approaches that do take context explicitly into account have experienced a veritable boost. Here, we are not only thinking of the New Institutional Economics and the New Economic History, but also of Political Economy proper to which many mainstream thinkers have paid renewed attention. It will be hard to prove, but our conjecture is that neglecting context has caused inadequate theoretical analysis and some unrealistic advice in the first phase of the transition process.

Taking institutions explicitly into account surely is an important advance. But things can still go wrong: many of those who presently take institutions explicitly into account come from highly formalised backgrounds such as contract theory and mechanism design. Often, they seem to fall prey to the assumption that institutions can induce pretty much any equilibrium, as long as they are designed in a clever fashion. In other words: the conception of being able to steer entire societies with precision has been shifted from the level of individual choices to the level of institutional choice. In many cases, the restrictions that traditions, mores, norms etc. constitute are neglected. Those who try to incorporate them under headings such as informal or internal institutions (see, e.g., North 1990; Voigt and Engerer 2000 is an overview over the NIE and the transition processes) are often highly sceptical with regard to the possibility of transforming basic rule systems deliberately and radically within a short period of time. A prominent hypothesis reads that formal institutions can only be implemented effectively if they are not conflicting with the informal ones. But if the informal ones are not compatible with the rule of law, democracy, and a market economy, one ends up in a mess. This may explain different transformation successes like the Polish and the Russian.

We were pointing at some deficiencies of economics in general. It might be worth noting that other scholars are even more critical with regard to other disciplines. Joel Hellman, in his review of *Institutional Design in Post-Communist Societies* by Jon Elster, Claus Offe and Ulrich Preuß, writes (1998): 'However, nearly a decade after the Autumn of the People in 1989, we would appear to be headed toward another 'dismal failure': this time, the failure to understand the dynamics of postcommunist transitions and to draw lessons from these transitions for the broader concerns of our respective disciplines. Perhaps with the exception of the economics of transition, the literature to date has not yet met the early expectations; truly comparative work is still rare.' Stephen Holmes complains in a similar fashion (1999, 72): 'But the greatest failing, in the end, is the absence of serious policy research. There is no 'Legal Reform Strategy Center' devoted to the subject... . In some sense, Western donors have more money than they have ideas.' And, more than merely verging onto the cynical (ibid.): 'Where laws are not enforced, legislative drafting can be donated as an amusement park for foreign lawyers.'

Constitutional political economy starts from the assumption that economics – here defined as a specific approach to analyse behaviour – cannot only be applied to choice situations within exogenously given rules but also to the choice of rules. Until a few years ago, constitutional political economy was primarily a normative endeavour interested in legitimising the state and its actions in terms of fairness, justice, or efficiency. Moreover, most of the research program's representatives were conceptualising the constitution as a social contract (e.g. Buchanan 1975). This has changed in the meantime: more and more papers on what can be dubbed positive constitutional economics are published (Voigt 1997 is a first survey) and the constitution-as-contract paradigm has been challenged by scholars who prefer to interpret it as a coordination or equilibrium-selection device such as Russell Hardin (1989) or Peter Ordeshook (1992). Both of these developments promise to be highly relevant for explaining the constitutional changes that have taken place in Central and Eastern Europe. For the description and explanation of change, the positive branch of constitutional political economy is an obvious precondition. The constitution as coordination-device view might have some advantages over the constitution-as-contract view when the difficulties of the process of changing constitutional reality are analysed. In a concrete historical situation, the implicit assumption of social contract theory that society can agree on pretty much any set of rules and subsequently implement them becomes obviously problematic.

One may ask the question: do constitutions matter? If England can do for centuries without, why should they be important for transition countries in Central and Eastern Europe? If England does not have a written constitution, however, it does not imply that she has no constitution at all. A market economy will operate at low transactions costs if the domain of individual activity and rights is clearly defined and contracts are observed. Due to multi-varied externalities it needs a state to support it. But the state should not interfere arbitrarily with individual rights and freedom. Civil law and constitutional law are the two legal pillars upon which rest complex modern democratic societies. As long as the rules are known, observed, or enforceable at low cost, it does not matter whether they are codified or not.

The experience of the transition processes has made the necessity of positive constitutional economics more apparent. Our knowledge concerning the working properties of alternative constitutional rules and the possibilities and limits to choose among a bundle of theoretically possible ones that can subsequently be implemented has proven to be insufficient. More solid knowledge concerning the working properties of constitutional rules is also a precondition for giving well-founded advice to societies in transition. In that sense, normative and positive constitutional economics should be seen as complements and not as competitors.

As part of economics, positive constitutional economics is based on the rational choice-paradigm. Three research areas can readily be distinguished:

(1) Constitutional rules could be used as explanantes for differential outcomes. At the end of the day, economic growth rates will be most interesting to economists, but variables such as political and economic stability, the distribution of gains that can be attributed to modified constitutional rules etc. might also be of interest because they will have an intermediate impact on the rate of economic growth that a society achieves. Alternative constitutional rules that could be compared for the impact on the variables of interest include representative vs. direct democracy, the separation of powers – especially the vertical separation, i.e., federalism – and the effects of two or more chambers compared to just one.

(2) Constitutional rules could be considered as explananda, i.e. their emergence and modification should be explained drawing on individual action based on individual interest. With regard to Central and Eastern Europe, it could be asked to what degree the preferences of those

directly involved in the process of constitution-writing are reflected within the rules of the final constitutional document (see McGuire and Ohsfeldt [e.g. 1989] for numerous studies in that vein on the ratification of the US Constitution). Slightly more subtle, the effects of the procedural rules for the deliberations of the constitutional conventions should be analysed. Possible questions are what effects time-limits have on constitutional assemblies, how constitutional assemblies that serve as legislatures at the same time allocate their resources between the two tasks, what consequences the regular information of the public concerning the state of discussion has, and how various decision-rules affect the outcome of the deliberations (Elster 1991b). It is tempting to propose an empirical test of the use of what Riker (1983, 1984) termed heresthetics, i.e. the art of political strategy.

(3) Whereas normative constitutional economics is based on some concept of social contract theory, the way the constitution is conceptualised in positive constitutional economics is much more open to debate. The social contract conception usually implies substantial optimism concerning the possibility to make societies choose equilibria vastly different from those its members had chosen had they had a different set of constitutional rules (Ordeshook 1992 is rather critical concerning this view). Representatives of the New Institutional Economics are much more critical with regard to the possibilities to reach radically different equilibria by 'institutional politics'; they point toward path-dependency, political transaction costs, inertia and the like (North 1990). With regard to Central and Eastern Europe, it could be asked whether any factors – such as internal or informal institutions – can be identified that prevent those societies from setting and enforcing constitutional rules that have proven to be welfare-enhancing in other environments.

In this volume, Ruth Gavison sets the scene by asking a very fundamental question regarding any theory of the constitution or constitutional design, namely 'what belongs in a constitution?' According to Sunstein (1991, 635), the theory of what belongs and what does not belong in a constitution 'remains in a surprisingly primitive state'. Candidates certainly include basic human rights (does an extensive list serve anything?), and – closely related – the right to individual exit and/or collective secession (on this, see Chen and Ordeshook 1994), the fiscal and monetary constitution as well as election laws. It would have to be inquired whether any lessons can be drawn from recent constitution-writing experiences in Central and Eastern Europe.

Hans-Jürgen Wagener deals with the question where and how the basic principles of a desired economic order are to be institutionalised. Freedom of contract, freedom of trade, and private property rights are often found in constitutional texts which begs the question how they are secured. In general, the role of the state in the economy has to be defined, but how rigidly lest historical contingencies become unmanageable?

Hans-Jürgen Wagener's contribution is closely connected to that of Laszlo Bruszt who also deals with the interdependence between markets and states. According to him, there are three important state functions that remain severely undersupplied in some of the transition countries. These are (1) the creation of secure expectations especially with regard to private property, (2) the capacity of the representatives not to give in to rent-seeking demands even to groups who are powerful, and (3) the capacity to deal with the competing interests of various groups in a balanced fashion. He observes that some markets as well as some states have been captured by special interest groups so that two functions that would have to be secured in order to be able to speak of a functioning market – firstly to be able to profit from rational enterprise and secondly that profit can *only* be realised from rational enterprise – are not sufficiently secured in some states. It is his central hypothesis that the characteristics of constitution-making played an important role of what he calls the corruption of states and markets.

Peter Ordeshook deals with the question whether 'Western' constitutions are relevant for anything other than the countries they serve, namely whether they can be made relevant for the countries of Central and Eastern Europe. He insists that the constitution-as-coordination view is clearly superior over the constitution-as-contract notion. Subsequently, he develops a couple of principles that any constitution-maker should follow if she is interested in the constitution leading to coordinating the behaviour of actors in fundamental ways. In that sense, the experiences made in the West are seen as universalizable by Ordeshook.

Countries can be divided into those that developed their formal legal system internally and those that copied it from abroad. Recent empirical research with regard to civil and commercial codes shows that *de jure* and *de facto* law is much more congruent in the former group of countries than in the latter. In her contribution, Katharina Pistor asks whether this holds also true for constitutional law. Her hypothesis is that the effectiveness of constitutional law depends on the demand for it. Demand can be expressed by either of two variables, namely whether law was passed as the result of a free choice from within the country combined with an adaptation of the imported law to the specific needs of the country or whether at least parts of the population were familiar with the fundamental principles of an imported legal system.

Former Polish Prime Minister Hanna Suchocka deals with the concept of the separation of powers. She recounts how it was first used as a slogan and then gained more precise meaning little by little. The constitutional changes of April 1989 that were brought about as a consequence of the roundtable talks did not lead to the explicit mentioning of the concept in the constitution. Yet, they did away with the unity-of-power concept that had been dominant for so long. Therefore, from the point of view of the separation of powers, the amended constitution was full of inconsistencies. First explicit mention of the concept was integrated into the so-called 'small constitution' that was passed in 1992 but only with the new constitution of 1997 was it explicitly formulated. According to Suchocka, political actors are still in the process of defining its precise meaning for Poland, an exercise that will still take lots of time.

Ivan Krastev is one of the contributors to this volume who has actively participated in the process of writing, discussing, and proposing a new constitution. In the paper jointly authored with Ralitsa Peeva, he contributes to the demystification of constitutions. They can be enacted and changed at will, and sometimes, the reasons for choosing one rather than another possible solution are very arbitrary, earthly reasons. Krastev and Peeva illustrate their critical position towards the 'Chicago view of constitutional choice' with five examples: why was Bulgaria the first country in Central and Eastern Europe to adopt a new constitution? Why does the constitution contain an article prohibiting parties based on ethnic or religious principle? Why was a vice-president introduced? Why did the Constituent Assembly have 400 members? How can the three preconditions for becoming a candidate for presidency (age, place of birth, country of residency) be explained? Lawrence Lessig, who belongs to the Chicago School criticised by the authors, answers Krastev and Peeva by pointing out how much they really agree with the positions that they set out to doubt.

Imre Vörös who used to be member of the Hungarian Constitutional Court reflects on the observation that constitutional change does not necessarily have to take place in an explicit fashion in which the text of the constitutional document is modified, but can also be brought about implicitly, e.g.

by modified interpretation of the unchanged document by the judiciary (Voigt 1999). In his contribution, Vörös shows that the role of the Hungarian Constitutional Court in bringing such changes about have been quite substantial.

Eli Salzberger and Stefan Voigt are interested in the decisions of constitution-makers and legislators to delegate power. More specifically, they analyse under what conditions one can expect internal (domestic) delegation to occur and under what circumstances one should rather expect external (international) delegation. They conjecture that societies trying to establish radically different political and economic systems will have a higher propensity to delegate because that might give some of their policies higher credibility. In principle, one should expect a comprehensive set of powers to be delegated onto the international plane because credibility can be enhanced even more than by delegation on the national one. But giving sovereign rights away might appear especially costly to societies who have just (re-)gained their sovereignty.

Dieter Grimm, a former member of the German Constitutional Court, asks how the concept of constitutionalism can and should be modified if one does not confine it to the borders of the nation-state but if one takes supranational entities – and especially the European Union – explicitly into account.

Christian Kirchner completes the volume by critically reviewing the discussions that took place during the Berlin Workshop and by pointing towards the possible future development of constitutional economics.

REFERENCES

Buchanan, J. (1975), *The Limits of Liberty – Between Anarchy and Leviathan*, Chicago: University of Chicago Press.

Chen, Y. and P. C. Ordeshook (1994), 'Constitutional Secession Clauses', *Constitutional Political Economy*, **5** (1), 45-60.

Elster, J. (1991a), *The Necessity and Impossibility of Simultaneous Economic and Political Reform*, manuscript: University of Chicago.

Elster, J. (1991b), *Arguing and Bargaining in two Constituent Assemblies*, The Storrs Lectures.

Furubotn, E. and R. Richter, R. (1997), *Institutions and Economic Theory: An Introduction to and Assessment of the New Institutional Economics*, Ann Arbort: University of Michigan Press.

Hardin, R. (1989), 'Why a Constitution?' in B. Grofman and D. Wittman (eds), *The Federalist Papers and the New Institutionalism*, New York: Agathon Press, pp. 100-20.

Hellman, J. (1998), 'Constitutional Reviews: Institutional Design in Post-communist Societies: Rebuilding the Ship at Sea', by Jon Elster, Claus Offe, and Ulrich K. Preuss (Cambridge University Press, 1997), in: *East European Constitutional Review*, **7** (3).

Holmes, S. (1999), 'Can Foreign Aid Promote the Rule of Law?', *Eastern European Constitutional Review*, **8** (4).

McGuire, R. A. and R. L. Ohsfeldt,. (1989), 'Self-Interest, Agency Theory, and Political Voting Behaviour: The Ratification of the United States Constitution', *American Economic Review*, **79** (1), 219-34.

North, D. C. (1990), *Institutions, Institutional Change and Economic Performance*, Cambridge: Cambridge University Press.

Ordeshook, P. C. (1992), 'Constitutional Stability', *Constitutional Political Economy*, **3** (2), 137-75.

Riker, W. H. (1983), 'Political Theory and the Art of Heresthetics', in A. Finifter (ed), *Political Science: The State of the Discipline*, Washington, D.C.: American Political Science Association, pp. 47-67.

Riker, W. H. (1984), 'The Heresthetics of Constitution-Making: The Presidency in 1787, with Comments on Determinism and Rational Choice', *American Political Science Review*, **78**, 1-16.

Sunstein, C. (1991), 'Constitutionalism and Secession', *University of Chicago Law Review*, **58** (2), 633-70.

Voigt, S. (1997), 'Positive Constitutional Economics - A Survey', *Public Choice*, **90**, 11-53.

Voigt, S. (1999), 'Implicit Constitutional Change - Changing the Meaning of the Constitution Without Changing the Text of the Document', *European Journal of Law and Economics*, **7** (3), 197-224.

Voigt, S. and H. Engerer (2000*), Institutions and Transition*, survey for the German Federal Ministry of Finance within the project 'New Trends in Economics', mimeo.

1. What Belongs in a Constitution?

Ruth Gavison[1]

For this question to be intelligible at all, we must use 'constitution' in the sense of a formal written document, which enjoys some form of superiority over regular law-making, and some form of entrenchment. In other words, arrangements will be considered constitutional for my purposes only if they are taken away, so to speak, from the realm of 'ordinary politics' and from the standard discretion of regular legislatures. The level of entrenchment may differ in the same document for various provisions,[2] and modes of entrenchment may vary among constitutions,[3] but the question I will consider will not take these detailed features into account.[4]

There are three standard candidates for inclusion in a constitution: basic governmental structures and the relations between the main powers and functions of government; basic values and commitments; and human rights. Some constitutions describe language and flags and other symbols.[5] These may either be seen as an additional group, or be seen as a part of the main commitments of the state. In addition, a constitution usually specifies the mechanisms for its own amendment and enforcement, and proposed constitutions often contain provisions about the mechanisms of their adoption.

The title question presupposes that we have made a decision that we want or need a constitution, and the question we face is what should be included in it. However, as we shall see, it is not always possible to follow this sequence. It may well be that we start out wanting a constitution, but that we can then see that it is impossible to get a good one, because too many important elements of the desired constitution cannot in fact be enacted. Under such circumstances, it may well be rational to decide to prefer the regulation of constitutional issues by regular laws or even by convention, and let the formal constitution await better times. I will return to this question below, after I discuss the three clusters of issues which naturally 'belong' in constitutions.

Before I turn to each of these groups, some general comments are in place. Constitutions are required neither by logic nor by legal theory. Similarly, they are not indicated by universal human and political experience.

They are not even dictated by democracy or by the idea(l)s of limited government and human rights. England is an example supporting all these claims. Nonetheless, most modern countries, and most modern democracies, have Constitutions. This in itself suggests that there is nothing logical or conceptual, that makes the idea of formal, entrenched, constitutions inconsistent with democracy.[6] In fact, political experience suggests that democracy and constitutionalism are a good pair, with a tendency of democracy and constitutions to reinforce each other.

It is important to notice that it is not always easy to separate the three clusters of issues. A commitment to democracy, for example, is often a central part of the credo of a state.[7] But it has important implications for the structure of the regime. Democracies may be parliamentary or presidential or a combination thereof, but they must have regular elections for the legislature and an effective multi-party system. Similarly, democracy, even under the thinnest, most formal, characterisation requires some civil and political rights such as the rights to vote and to be elected, and some freedom of speech and association. Similarly, a commitment to a 'social' state may require some protection of social and economic rights. But if these are merely declaratory, and do not involve effective mechanisms of enforcement, they may be a part of the credo, rather than 'real' affirmation of 'rights'.

The main purposes and functions of constitutions are at least three. First, to both authorise, and to create limits on, the powers of political authorities. Second, to enhance the legitimacy and the stability of the political order. Third, to institutionalise a distinction between 'regular politics' and 'the rules of the game' and other constraints (such as human rights) within which ordinary politics must be played. The rules of the games are the shared part, which gives society some coherence and identity. This shared framework can then facilitate a robust democratic debate between different conceptions of the good life, and between different interest groups. These purposes will suggest guidelines for answering the question of exclusion and inclusion of provisions within the constitution.

Questions about constitutions can never be answered for all societies and states, for all times. Constitutions are designed to solve the problems of the societies under consideration. The need for a constitution itself, and its structure and content, should thus be discussed against the background of the social and political problems facing that society. Since these problems are different, importation of constitutional arrangements should be done, if at all, extremely cautiously.[8] On the other hand, comparative studies are extremely important. There are aspects of the study of human societies, which are indeed 'universal' in important ways. These do indicate some implications in terms of immanent and persistent problems and the structural ways to deal with them. This attitude gives credence to enterprises such as universal human rights, and to 'public choice' models of constitution. These indications, however, are often incomplete and underdetermined.[9] Comparative studies, which stress both similarities and differences among societies, may thus provide a very illuminating source of learning from the experience of others.[10]

A major question is that of the enforcement of the supremacy of the constitution. In the framework of my concerns, the question is whether such enforcement mechanism should be explicitly included in the constitution. As we shall see below, this question relates both to the form of the institutional arrangements adopted in given societies, but also to the effectiveness of the constitutional order as a whole, especially that of protecting human rights against the legislature.

The last two decades have given us very rich material about processes of constitution making and amendments: It has been a time of dissolution and of birth of nations, and in many cases these transformations had significant 'constitutional moments'. Constitutional moments are those in which there is a change in the basic framework of government, not just in the content of specific political arrangements within it. Some such changes take the form of the adoption of new constitutions, or of significant amendments of existing ones.[11] In other cases, serious constitutional changes take place through either a radical re-interpretation of the constitution by the courts, or through apparently minor changes in an existing constitution.[12] In addition to the former USSR and Eastern Europe, interesting constitutional developments took place in South Africa, Canada and Israel. In addition, older constitutional systems show interesting signs of reflection and modification. Notably, England has made a first step towards a Bill of Rights with semi-constitutional significance. I will draw on this rich experience in the comments that follow, but this reliance will be impressionistic rather then systematic and comprehensive.

One last general caveat is called for. No one likes to discuss unimportant questions. Hence, my discussion of the question what should be in a constitution implies that I see it as an important one. Nevertheless, I want to warn us against taking it too seriously. Constitutions affect social and political reality, and this is why they are important. Their impact on these realities is, however, indirect and limited. Often, the question of the *content* of an arrangement is more important than the question whether it is included in a constitution or in regular legislation or even in a convention.[13] Always, the reality of societies is more important than the relationships and values declared in a constitution. Nonetheless, since constitutions do help in making social realities, it is important to attend to the special contribution they may make to good government.

GOVERNMENTAL STRUCTURES

Only unitary states have the luxury (or burden) of debating the question whether governmental structure should be included in the constitution. All states must have provisions regulating these subjects, but in unitary states these may evolve, and be enforced in part as constitutional conventions. This is precisely what has happened in England, and Dicey is still a powerful spokesperson for the desirability of this way of regulating the structure of government. However, federal governments cannot make this choice, since it is a central issue of such governments that the division of powers between sub-units and the central government is determined in a way that will be beyond the unilateral change of either states or the central government.[14] Even in federal governments, however, major differences are apparent in the scope, and clearly in the content and arrangements, of the constitutions. In addition, unitary states do not need constitutions, but many of them do have them.

This obvious point highlights the important distinction between formal and material constitutions. The decision whether the state should be a federal state or a unitary one is itself a major constitutional decision. If the state is a federal one – the relations between central and local government must be made in a formal constitution, which cannot be changed unilaterally by the member parts.[15] However, if the state is unitary, its (material) constitutional arrangements need not be included in a formal constitution at all.

In federal states we must have a constitution which is beyond the powers of change of the parts thereof, but many questions remain. Should the federal constitution discuss the arrangements and the powers of the sub-units, or should it be confined to the powers and structure of the central government? Who should be the arbiter between the national government and the parts? Should the constitution include provisions concerning cessation? What should these provisions be? These are normative questions, but this fact should not mislead us into thinking that the only relevant premises for their resolution are general and universal normative principles. Both the comparative study of constitutions and a closer analysis of how these questions ought to be answered in particular states suggest that the answer to this question is dictated by historical and not by theoretical considerations. The US federal constitution was a document seeking to form a union whose members were fully established. It is thus confined to the federal powers. The German Basic Law, on the other hand, discusses in detail both the federal government and the lander. Moreover, it is quite clear in the latter that the Bill of Rights part applies to all lander, and that the constitutional court deals with all matters arising under it. It took a long development and a civil war until the federal Bill of Rights was seen as 'incorporated' into States' constitutions. The *necessity* to incorporate governmental structures into the federal or national constitution applies only to the central government. As mentioned above, that structure must be protected against unilateral changes by one or more of the member states (or by the central government on its own). The internal constitutional arrangements of the sub-units may, in principle, be regulated by the states as they choose. In fact, it may be seen as a part of their autonomy that their own internal affairs are controlled by them. This would suggest a reason *against* including the *details* of such arrangements in the central, federal constitution. On the other hand, it is also quite clear that member states should obey some structural constraints if the federation is to be stable and viable. These general constraints on both the structure of member states and on the relationships between them should of course be included in the federal constitution.[16]

Another possible difference between constitutions is illustrated by this observation. Some constitutions mainly entrench the political status quo. Constitutionalisation is meant to achieve unity and the additional stability allowed by entrenchment. In these constitutions, at least for the short term, there is no need for great detail. The details will be provided by the experience of the past. Very different are the constitutions erecting a new political order, especially ones that want to make a statement of a break with tradition and the past.

In unitary states, the most important question is whether the structural details of the regime should be constitutionalised. Once an affirmative answer is given, which of the basic governmental arrangements should be included in the constitution, and which should be left to regular legislation or to constitutional conventions? The answers to all these questions depend on the functions constitutionalisation is supposed to serve, and on the special conditions of the society and legal system under consideration. A general reason for entrenchment is the need for *institutional stability*. Clearly, a special, burdensome mechanism of change would make it harder to amend the basic institutional structure, and this will generate the stability. Some stability of basic governmental structures is a crucial condition of governability. Many decisions require long-term planning. The ability to plan long-term legislative and policy initiatives depends, among other things, on constitutional stability. Moreover, stability is very important in creating the sense of tradition and continuity, which are important elements of the legitimacy of government.[17]

We glimpsed another reason in the explanation of the reason why federal states require an entrenched constitution: entrenchment is necessary when there is a wish to prevent a unilateral change or a change by a transitory or non-representative majority. Finally, entrenchment is crucial when the constitution is a complex package deal, and the partners to it (states or segments of the population) make their agreement to the package deal dependent on the entrenchment of a provision that is deemed crucial to them and is their incentive for going into the deal. Entrenchment in such cases is needed to give the arrangement the stability it requires, and minimises the chance that some political players will gain the benefit of the compromise, but will undermine it to their own advantage whenever an opportunity presents itself.[18] In the same vein, entrenchment is crucial when the structure of government is a complex set of checks-and-balances. A structure like this should be amended with care, since one apparently local change may frustrate the effectiveness of the system as a whole.[19]

These comments suggest that an entrenchment is indicated strongly when the constitutional arrangement is the product of a serious compromise, and when the structures include a complex set of checks and balances, so that it is important that elements of the whole will not be changed randomly and easily.

Effective federalism also requires that there is an authoritative way to resolve controversies about relations between central government and provinces. This was one of the main purposes of creating a federal Supreme Court under Article III of the US constitution, and this function is among the ones explicitly given to the German Constitutional Court. However, even this is not totally true. In Canada, relations between central government and provinces are evolving slowly, and it is not clear whether the involvement of the Canadian Supreme Court has been either effective or desirable.[20]

It is important to note that, in distinction with the situation concerning rights and credos, there is no serious argument against judicial review of the 'institutional' part of constitutions. This consensus is based on the fact that the provisions of the constitution in these matters are relatively clear, and that there is a necessity that there will be an authoritative arbiter of the disputes that do arise. Moreover, while decision of issues of these sorts may have tremendous political impact, institutional questions are usually not as emotionally charged and as controversial as matters of basic values and of human rights.[21]

This part of constitutions always includes details of the legislative, executive and judicial powers. For these, it often includes both a specification of their powers and modes of their election or appointment. It also provides some account of their relationships. There is some variety on other elements which belong to the structural part of constitutions. I will consider just one group of such elements. In all countries, institutions such as the law enforcement agencies, the state controller, and the central bank may develop great significance because they enjoy a middle-of-the road position. On the one hand, they do form a part of the executive branch. On the other, it is recognised that they need a measure of independence from the executive to fulfil their tasks effectively. This delicate balance of accountability and independence is sometimes achieved by statutory (or even conventional) arrangements. But at times, especially in 'younger' constitutions, the need is felt to include these institutions within the constitution itself, so that the power of the executive, and even the legislature, to reduce their independence, will be limited. In general, this tendency to include within the constitution the structure of institutions whose independence requires special protection seems desirable. However, we should also remember that in these matters, as in all others, the realities are at least as important as the constitutional provisions. At times, the de facto reality does not give independence despite constitutional entrenchment.[22] At other times, these institutions may develop in a way that gives them too much independence, and the necessary constraints of accountability are weakened. Such phenomena may happen even if the institutions are not regulated in the constitution, or even by statute.[23]

Not surprisingly, the main debate on this part of constitutions relates to the *content* of the arrangements and the balances of powers. These fascinating debates go way beyond the realm of this paper. One feature needs a special discussion, however: the stringency of the amendment process. How flexible, or how immune from change, should the structural elements of a regime be? It is often claimed that the US federal constitution is too hard to amend. The sensitivity to particular circumstances led Sunstein and Elster to recommend that in the new post-Soviet regimes, arrangements should be flexible, and allow relatively easy amendment by the regular political branches. Recent events in Syria suggest that constitutional flexibility may indeed be an asset.[24]

I cannot leave this issue without reminding ourselves that the decisions incorporated in the constitutional text itself are only a part of the picture. Constitutions are living documents, and much of their practical import is the function of the way they are used, interpreted and implemented. It may well be the case that very stringent rules of amendment will give legitimacy to more creative interpretive attitudes by both courts and by the political players themselves.[25]

It is hard to specify a general recommendation for the balance between stability and flexibility of constitutional arrangements concerning regime structure. The fact that social realities at times do not 'obey' constitutional mandates may mean that the practical implications of over-stringency may not be disastrous, but this does not free us from the need to try and specify considerations for the right balance.[26] When the reasons for entrenchment are stronger – the amendment mechanism should also be stronger. I mentioned above the case of the 'historic compromise' or the delicate system of checks and balances, which should not be upset and undermined easily. In such cases, the incentive to make changes may be great, and the consequences for the viability and stability of government may be high. A stringent mechanism of amendment may then be required.

While one principle of amendment for the whole constitution has the benefit of simplicity and elegance, it may not always be a good idea to use a uniform requirement. A more nuanced amendment mechanism may be more suitable. At least two types of differentiated amendment procedure come to mind. One is that of the German Basic Law, which specifies that the Bill of Rights part is beyond amendment, while allowing amendment of the other parts. The other is a differentiation within the structural regime part itself: the senate provision and the pro-slavery interim arrangements in the US Constitution were more protected than other parts of the constitution. Clearly, the reasons behind the different treatment of constitutional arrangements in the two cases are very different. The first one is primarily symbolic and declaratory, and relates to the nature of human rights and to the historical circumstances of the enactment of the German Basic Law. Bills of Rights do not enjoy special immunity in other constitutional systems, but it is almost inconceivable that any state will derogate from the constitutional guarantee of rights such as human dignity or freedom. Changes in the actual protection will be made by legislation, adjudication or social practices. The second case, on the other hand, reflects the special need for entrenchment for 'great compromises'. A differentiated amendment procedure may be indicated when the constitution marks a great break with the past. On the one hand, commitments to democracy and to human rights may seem to require great entrenchment. On the other hand, the political system may be very volatile, and there is a need for trial and error in some structures, calling for flexibility.[27]

One thing should be clear – the more stringent the amendment procedure is, the shorter the constitution should be. In some new constitutions, the arrangements are specified in very great detail. A stringent amendment mechanism may then mean that it will be very hard to adapt the *details* of the regime structure to changing circumstances. We saw that there may be good reasons for making such changes difficult in some contexts, and for the principles of separation of powers and their structures. On the details, flexibility should be the rule.

BILLS OF RIGHTS

All new constitutions contain detailed Bills of Rights.[28] Moreover, in many of them this section of the constitution is given pride of place, and gets to be the first chapter, preceding the description of the main organs of government and their respective powers. This attitude is quite natural when the societies making their new constitutions want to stress the difference between the old regime, which did not protect human rights, and the new one they are now initiating. Nonetheless, as we shall see, the idea that states should constitutionalise Bills of Rights is not free of controversy.

It is important to remember that the inclusion of detailed Bills of Rights does not guarantee an adequate protection of human rights. This is true for both democracies and non-democracies: the presence of glorious Bills of Rights in a country's constitution does not, in itself, guarantee their actual protection.[29]

Nonetheless, as a matter of general principle, there are good structural and expressive reasons to give Bills of Rights constitutional status. The high visibility and solemn nature of most constitutions help in making the commitment to human rights a part of 'civil religion' and civil-shared culture.[30] A deep acceptance of this ethos is required if protection of human rights is to be effective. Moreover, there is an obvious reason for taking the protection of human rights away from the realm of regular politics. We believe one's entitlement to basic human rights does not depend on the arrangements adopted by one's society. Human rights are those that persons have because of their humanity. Their states are obligated to protect them, but they do not have the power to deny them. Today, these commitments are stemming from both moral theory and from international law.[31] It is thus sensible to make the protection of such rights be superior to the acts of government and even legislatures. This is especially the case if the society in question is rifted, and if it contains 'chronic' minorities, who cannot defend their interests through the regular political channels.[32] Even if Bills of Rights are neither necessary nor sufficient for adequate protection of rights, there are obvious reasons for including such Bills in constitutions, or even of entrenching Bills of Rights independently.[33] Even if Bills of Rights and judicial review have not guaranteed adequate protection, on the whole the existence of such documents and institutions permitted processes and developments that increased protection of human rights. Bills of Rights very rarely have been invoked to frustrate progressive legislation, and they have often been invoked to invalidate oppressive laws.[34] It is thus not surprising that some scholars have argued that the best institutional defense of human rights is judicial review.

Against this background, it is interesting to note that people, whose commitment to human rights is unquestionable, have also argued forcefully *against* constitutional Bills of Rights, and especially against judicial review of legislation which allegedly violates them.[35]

The objections to Bills of Rights are very rarely phrased as objection to the idea of rights.[36] Critics often support the educational force of declarations of rights. What they object to is the discourse of rights, which, according to them, destabilises the fabric of life in society, which is built on a combination of rights and duties. In addition the critics say that Bills of Rights tend to underestimate the fact that in many cases rights conflict with other rights and with other interests, so that often the mere fact that an action or a law infringe a right is not very significant. We need to know if the infringement is justified, and to do that we need more than rights discourse. Often, the critics claim, a rights-discourse leads to an underestimation of conflicting interests, and may thus lead to either wrong decisions, or to frustrated expectations, or both. It is better, the critics say, to specify the social arrangements in more detail, and not to derive them in an unmediated way from general declarations of rights.

Most critics would probably have accepted that the educational benefits of declarations of rights easily overcome these drawbacks had it not been for the *institutional* implications of constitutional rights: the fact that they often transfer the power to make ultimate decisions on matters concerning rights away from the political process. Judicial review and invalidation of laws allegedly violating human rights is a frequent way of giving rights the 'teeth' they require to effectively protect individuals. On the other hand, such review raises the counter-majoritarian difficulty, and may create serious backlashes when the court is perceived to declare laws unconstitutional when they deviate from their own partisan ideology or conception of the good life.

In states with constitutional Bills of Rights and judicial review, the debates usually center around the desirable *scope* of judicial review. Naturally, these countries do not consider the possibility of abolishing their Bills of Rights or of judicial review. In countries where these institutions do not exist at present, I believe these questions should be raised and discussed before a constitutional decision is made. The mere fact that most countries live well with constitutionalised Bills of Rights and with judicial review does not mean that all countries should have them. I have indicated above that the main problem is not the inclusion of a Bill of Rights in a constitution, or even entrenching it. It is the nature of the enforcement agency and its powers. I shall return to this question below.

BASIC VALUES AND COMMITMENTS

The third cluster of candidates for inclusion in constitutions is a declaration of basic values and commitments. Frequent commitments declared in such contexts are to a republic (or monarchy), to social justice, to happiness, democracy, freedom or a national character of the state. Some states declare their religious (or secular) identity. Many believe that these elements are the least important parts of the constitutional arrangement. Often, they are just expressive, and it is hard to find any practical implication that follows from them. Yet the inclusion of these elements may be extremely significant in highlighting one of the main features of constitutions, suggesting a source of either strength or weakness, as the case may be. It indicates clearly the degree to which the society governed by the constitution has an inner cohesion and civic identity that is in fact accepted by the large majority of citizens. And, in some cases, these declaratory parts are used, by courts or other state organs, to derive important practical implications as well.

We said above that constitutions seek to give special visibility, legitimacy and stability to the shared framework of political life. The importance of this declaration is often a matter of historical contingency. Homogenous nation states, not involved in a conflict or a challenge of their distinctness, do not ordinarily need this function of constitutions. They gain their cohesiveness from the homogeneity in fact of their population. But modernity means, among other things, that this form of nation-state becomes less likely. Even in non-democratic states, effective government includes the need to deal with the fact that there are serious conflicts of interests among parts of the population, as well as between the state and other groups and individuals who are their citizens or members. In democracies, and especially in divided democracies, the constitutional framework facilitates the inevitable negotiations and compromises of effective government.[37] It is extremely helpful when these negotiations and campaigns, which can at times be extremely divisive, are conducted against the background of a secure and wide acceptance of a shared framework, affirming and declaring the shared commitment and allegiance of all to the welfare of this shared entity. If the shared framework is successful, the debates are debates about different conceptions of the public good of the whole, and on the meaning of distributive justice within it, not a challenge to the political and social order as a whole.

Often, these declarations are so broad that they do not have much practical import. This may be the status of the French commitment to 'Freedom, Equality and Fraternity'. Yet even declarations of this sort have been interpreted in some manner. Thus, the commitment in the US constitution to liberty and happiness, and the absence of a commitment to equality from it, were used by some to argue that the ideal of substantive equality is foreign to the American national ideals.

At times, the ideals specified in the solemn and festive openings of constitutions are universal ideas. When this is the case, they function in ways similar to human rights. The declaration is an affirmation of an ideal, which is supposed to be shared by all. The declaration itself does not add a particularistic characterisation to the society in question, and so does not raise debates about the essence of that society.[38] At other times, these declarations simply reflect the types of regime choices articulated in the part of governmental arrangements (e.g. the declaration that the state is a democracy). The most interesting – and controversial – ideals are those that are neither. They reflect a particular choice, which is not universal, and is not a choice of a regime type. Obvious examples are declarations that the state is, for example, 'socialist'.[39] Should statements like these go into a constitution? We saw that for the two previous candidates for inclusion, broad agreement is important and desirable, but that it may not be absolutely necessary. Inclusion in the constitution may be a way of affirming a normative commitment to a shared framework or to human rights even if in fact we know that some parts of the population find these commitments difficult. Part of the reason for constitu-tionalisation is precisely the wish to give these arrangements a security that cannot be supported, in each particular case, by the political system. We may have a broad agreement on this need for stability and entrenchment even if we do not have agreement on the merits of the particular arrangements that we have adopted.[40] The same reasons for entrenchment and superiority do not obtain for inclusion in the constitution of a value commitment endorsed by the majority, but rejected and challenged by a significant minority. The elected majority can enact its preferences, but why should it impose them on everyone as a part of the shared constitution? The inclusion would make people who disagree with the ideal, or feel they cannot identify with it, not only political opponents of the majority, but also 'enemies' of, or at least strangers to, the constitution. It seems to follow that commitments like these should be included in a constitution only if they do reflect a general sen-timent.[41]

The same applies to self-definition of the state in terms of a particular religious or national character. A close-to-home example is the fact that Israel is defined in its 1992 Basic Laws concerning human rights as a 'Jewish and democratic' state. 'Democratic' is neutral and innocent, but the 'Jewish' in the formula has already raised a heated debate. Many constitutions contain an affirmation of a particular identity. But usually, the reference is ambiguous, and it can be interpreted as an affirmation of the nation whose state it is, and the nation can be credibly identified as the body of citizens of that state. In many other cases, states are defined as 'nation-states' in ethnic terms. This does create a problem, especially when in that country there is a sizeable minority of people not belonging to that ethnic group.

I have dealt elsewhere with the substantive problems arising from the definition of Israel as both Jewish and democratic.[42] Here, my concern is only with the question whether such descriptions should be included in a state's constitution. For the Founding Fathers of a state like Israel, writing a constitution, which will not include an affirmation of the fact that it is a Jewish state, would be almost unthinkable. Even the UN decision supporting the establishing of the state described it as a Jewish state. This description is emphatically affirmed in Israel's Declaration of the Founding of the State of 1948. However, declarations like this would make non-Jewish citizens of Israel feel less-than-full citizens of the state. This consideration was raised in the discussion of Israel's constitution in 1950. It fitted well with the decision adopted then – that Israel will not enact a constitution, and will instead seek to develop legislation of constitutional materials in a series of 'basic laws'.[43] In the same spirit, Israel has decided not to entrench its Law of Return, adopted the same year. Many see this law as the essence of the Jewishness of the state. Yet when it was proposed that this law would contain a provision making changes thereof impossible, Israel's first Prime Minister, *David Ben-Gurion*, declined. He conceded, of course, that no Israeli legislature will change the law, but preferred to leave the matter to political realities, without a formal entrenchment.

No constitution can change the realities of states. Israel is, in many senses, a Jewish state even if it does not define itself in this way in its constitution. However, because of the role constitutions play, incorporating such a declaration into Israel's constitution in an explicit way may not be an easy or a simple decision. I would suggest that such complications might well justify not including any commitments to general values in the constitution, so that if issues of this nature exist, it may well be to exclude the entire third cluster from the constitution.[44] At the very least, the part of the credos should indeed contain only commitments which are in fact widely shared. The story of Israel teaches us another lesson. At times it is wiser to decide not to include a contested commitment in a constitution or a basic law. It is much easier to agree not to mention a feature that is a part of social reality, then it is to remove an already existing affirmation.[45]

ENFORCEMENT MECHANISMS

Some constitutions explicitly specify ways in which their provisions may be enforced. Frequently, when this is the case, special constitutional courts are established to deal with questions of constitutionality.[46] Some constitutions explicitly specify that the constitutional provisions will be self-enforced by the political branches.[47] Yet other constitutions grant superiority and entrenchment to the constitution, and do not specify an enforcement mechanism. In two such cases – notably the US and Canada – the regular courts, and especially the Supreme Court, assumed the power of judicial review of the constitutionality of primary legislation.

This variety of constitutional schemes shows that the choices are contingent and do not follow from the very notion of supreme constitutions. Nonetheless, I believe that explicit constitutional regulation of the enforcement mechanism is preferable to the US model. First, explicit regulation enhances certainty in this important area, and thus increases the legitimacy of whatever enforcement mechanism has been chosen.[48] Secondly, it permits the reasoned decision to combine constitutional superiority and entrenchment without judicial review. Thirdly, and most important, it stresses the distinction between judicial review of legislation and judicial review of actions by the government and the administration. Fourthly, it allows thinking explicitly about the institution most suitable for judicial review in constitutional matters, and design it in a way that will reflect the special nature of reviewing laws passed by the majority of representatives. When judicial review is a judge-made declaration derived from the 'meaning' of the superiority of the constitution, as Marshall reasoned in *Marbury v. Madison*, it is inevitable that regular courts will deal with constitutional challenges. However, these courts may not be well suited to the constitutional task.

Let me elaborate a bit on this last point. Judicial independence is a primary feature of the rule of law. We expect judges to be removed from political pressures, and to have the structured autonomy and the professional integrity to apply the law to the facts of the case without prejudice or fear and without wishing to please the powers that be. One way of encouraging this independence is the emphasis on the professional integrity of judges, and a structural autonomy from political fiat. Most often, this is achieved by granting judges life tenure in their job. Another feature aiding judicial independence is the emphasis on the professional ethos of judges. Often, this professionalism is seen as incompatible with clear and explicit involvement in public life, especially in partisan politics. Clearly, sitting judges are expected to be non-partisan. Consequently, there is a structured attempt in adjudication to refrain from addressing questions of ideology and policy, and to derive the judicial conclusion from exclusive reliance on the law. However, all analytical theories of jurisprudence agree that the law cannot always dictate the bottom line of judicial decisions. The explicit attempt to ignore non-legal premises of judicial action only leads to confusion, and weakens the belief in judicial autonomy. Legal theory usually concedes that in adjudication there is a mixture of application of pre-existing law and of creative discretion, and that the legitimacy of adjudication is based on the fact that application of the law is central and paradigmatic, whereas creative discretion is parasitic and incidental.

All this is true for all judges. Interpretation of statutes often requires invocation of values and ideologies not explicitly reflected in the written law. The democratic 'corrective' to this aspect of adjudication is the ability of the legislature to amend the law, so as to indicate that the judicial interpretation did not reflect its judgement. Clearly, this corrective cannot work as easily when the court pronounces on the constitutionality of statutes. One of the main purposes of a constitution, as we saw, was precisely to remove certain topics from the simple discretion of regular legislatures. Many feel that this feature of judicial review of statutes requires a profile quite different from that of regular judges. First, it is thought that no person should have the power to review primary legislation for life.[49] Secondly, while explicit prior involvement with partisan politics may indeed be a problem for a regular judge, raising fears that he may be distrusted by people not sharing his political commitments, such involvement may in fact be an asset for a term on the Constitutional court. Finally, while judges for regular courts should be elected and promoted on the basis of their professional competence alone, judges for the constitutional court should be of the highest professional standards, but should also be sensitive to the public and political complexities of constitutional adjudication. This requirement may be met by a special mode of appointments, which will guarantee that the judges of the constitutional court will enjoy the respect and the trust of the public and of its representatives. All of these aspects of the constitutional court get lost if we treat the constitutional court as an extension of the regular courts of the system.[50]

The debate about judicial review and the organ most suitable to pass it goes far beyond my topic. In these days of global growth in the power of courts, based in part on our disillusionment with representative democracy and its institutions, it may seem completely out-of-tune to suggest caution when this question is raised. It may be proper to remind ourselves, therefore, that the debate is still raging.[51] As we saw, the main issue is not the entrenchment and superiority of Bills of Rights, but the question whether unelected judges should have the power to undermine the considered judgements of policy approved by a significant majority in the legislature.

The debate about the desirable scope of judicial review on such matters is connected to the fact that rights discourse may be expanded in many ways. Mostly, we do want our courts, Supreme or Constitutional, to help us save our society from moments of rage or indiscretion leading to gross violation of the human rights of minorities. In many cases, Bills of Rights and constitutional courts are established precisely to indicate a break from a past regime in which this protection was wanting. We hope these institutions will minimise the chance that our government may torture or execute people without trial, or discriminate against them for reasons of religion or race. Courts cannot always deliver on these hopes, but they can clearly help. The problem is that courts then move on to decide on the legality of laws prohibiting (or permitting) abortion; or on matters of social and economic policy; or on sensitive issues of the relationship between state and religion. On these issues, reflecting deep moral controversy within society, it is not at all clear that the courts have a relative advantage over the legislature, or that they enjoy the legitimacy required to make authoritative decisions for society at large.

For these reasons, the decision concerning the scope of judicial review over primary legislation, and the identity of the organ performing such review, should be discussed explicitly and decided on the merits.

SUMMING UP

I can now return to the question with which I started. In most cases, a new state will do the right thing if it seeks to express its credo and its political structure and major commitments in the form of a constitution. For one thing, it will be easier for it to join the family of nations, among which such constitutions are the rule.

Regime structure is something every country must have, and there are good reasons to include the principles of the regime structure in a constitution. However, strong entrenchment may be a danger in fluid situations. Situations of transitions may thus provide both reasons for a constitution (entrenchment of break with the past) and reasons against it (unclear what the political situation is, and what the desirable arrangements are).

Detailed Bills of Rights and credos may make the constitution more meaningful and powerful. But they can also make it divisive rather then the cohesive, unifying civic force it is supposed to be. The latter functions should be preferred to the former, because a divisive constitution is unlikely to be able to perform its political tasks. It will weaken, rather then strengthen, the legitimacy of government.

This is why it may be wise, under some circumstances, to defer the enactment of a constitution (or to limit its contents to widely shared commitments). Such deferment may permit processes such as round tables and thoughtful negotiations, which may make the resulting document more acceptable and suitable than the idealised draft suggested initially.

All these points are not directly related to the question what should be in a constitution. But they show that this question must be seen as a part of a broader analysis of the role and the functions the constitution is supposed to play in the society which is considering its adoption. In some countries, when we start looking at the question what should be in a constitution, and who should be the body designed to enforce it, we may well reach the conclusion that a good supreme, and entrenched constitution is impossible. If this is the case, supporters of a constitution should seek to change those background conditions, which are responsible for this situation. If they succeed – they have done their societies a double service.

NOTES

1   I thank the participants in the workshop in the Berlin Wissenschaftskolleg, June 29 - July 1, 2000 and especially the commentator on my piece, Professor Ulrich K. Preuß, for helpful comments. Special thanks go to Stefan Voigt for careful comments on the first draft.
2   See for example the provisions concerning amendment in section 79 of the *German Basic Law* (the Grundgesetz). Section 79(3) specifies that changes in the principle of federalism or in the Bill of Rights are 'inadmissible'.
3   A major difference is between systems, in which constitutional amendment requires the joint activity of some organs (say federal and state legislatures, or a certain number of state legislatures, or a referendum) and other systems, in which the regular legislature can amend the constitution by itself, and the entrenchment takes the form of a requirement of special majorities or a sequence of two votes.
4   This decision is required by the title, but its 'costs' should not be ignored. The distinction between 'constitutional' and 'legal' arrangements can be formal, in the sense described in the text, or material. When we choose to use the term 'constitution' to denote only formal

and entrenched arrangements, we lose the ability to discuss, for example, the 'constitution' of England. In fact, the ambiguity between formal and material constitutions is the essence of this paper. The candidates for inclusion in the formal constitution are those usually seen as parts of the material one.

5   See e.g. Article 2 of the 1958 French Constitution.

6   The idea of alleged inconsistency stems from the fact that formal constitutions limit the power of regular majorities to change political arrangements. This is often described as letting minorities have veto power over political decisions. For an interesting discussion of the tensions between the notions see: Jeremy Waldron, *Law and Disagreement* (Oxford, Clarendon Press, 1999).

7   An emphasis on democracy as a part of the credo is even more significant if the constitution seeks to stress a break with a non-democratic past.

8   A prime example of a constitution tailored and justified in terms of the particular society is the oldest constitution – that of the US. The Federalist Papers are a detailed analysis of the proposed constitution based on both universal considerations of human nature and society, and the special issues facing American society after independence. While the US constitution, and the literature supporting and opposing it, are a lesson well studied by countries intending to enact a constitution, the universal and the particular elements of the US constitution should be distinguished carefully.

9   I will return to some of these implications below, especially in the discussion of consti-tutional protection of human rights. Other universal aspects of thinking about constitutions are those related to assumptions about human nature, and the nature of power structures within social groups. One such assumption is that in situations of scarcity and conflict, people in power will tend to invoke public interest to justify and perpetuate their own privileges. Another is that having power tends to corrupt, and the more absolute the power is- the more serious the danger of absolute corruption. Stefan Voigt pointed out to me that a public choice analysis of constitution making will tend to be over-determined rather than under-determined, as I suggest: If politicians are well-informed and behave rationally, they would know what rationality requires be done in a constitution. I beg to differ. Politicians may indeed seek to promote only their own self-interest. However, we all know that constitutional discourse seeks to disguise this fact, by talking a lot about 'public interest'. Some suggest that talk of 'public interest' may be totally reduced to self-interest goals. Even if this is so, discourses and structures tend to have their own dynamics. Often, the result of a variety of self-interests, all couched in terms of 'public interest', does yield a system of arrangements that limits the power of politicians against their own best judgement of what is good for them. Public choice theory is extremely useful in directing our attention to the implications of agents' rationality. This reminder is very important since we often tend to fall victim to our own 'normative' talk and disregard interests. One of the main features of debates about constitutions and laws is that there are conflicts of interests involved. No single perspective of rationality (defined as maximising the self-interests of individuals or groups) will thus dictate the optimal constitutional arrangement.

10 I share the main approach taken to comparative constitutionalism by S.E. Finer. See his introduction to '*Five Constitutions*' (Harmondsworth, Penguin books, 1979). The updated work is S.E. Finer, Vernon Bogdanor, and Bernard Rudden, '*Comparing Constitutions*' (Oxford Clarendon Press, 1995).

11 Notable examples of developments of this sort are the new constitution of South Africa, as well as the constitutions of Poland and Bulgaria.

12 For an argument that the New Deal in the US was a development of the first sort see the writings of Bruce Ackerman: 'Neo Federalism?', in J. Elster and R. Slagstad (eds.), *Constitutionalism and Democracy* (Cambridge, 1988), p.153.; Bruce Ackerman, '*The*

Future of Liberal Revolutions' (New Haven, Yale University Press, 1992). For a seemingly minor constitutional amendment incorporating a major change see, e.g. the constitution of Hungary. It should be noted that Germany did not give an explicit constitutional expression to its dramatic re-unification. The Basic Law of West Germany was simply applied to the state as a whole!

13   Israel, for example, is still debating its electoral system. In 1992, the pure parliamentary system was replaced by a mixed system, in which the Prime minister is elected directly, but parliament can still vote the government out by a no confidence vote by an absolute majority of Members of Parliament. Many argue that the experiment failed miserably, and wish to return to an amended parliamentary system. The debate is about the *content* of the arrangement, not about its *status*. Nonetheless, since the arrangement is controversial, some are reluctant to incorporate this law and grant it more entrenchment than it has at present. Naturally, supporters of the new system want to entrench it even further against possible future change. See also note 19 below.

14   Canada was an interesting exception. Before 1982 it did not have a formal internal regulation of these issues, and in part the judiciary developed rules. But this was because of the fact that until 1982 the power to change the constitutional arrangements by legislation was, at least formally, vested in Westminster.

15   And in fact, there is quite a lot of unilateral determination of powers and structures which is done by interpretation of the constitution by the various powers, including the courts affiliated with states or federal government, which may result in a unilateral change. Nonetheless, an entrenched constitution makes such changes more difficult, and more vulnerable to a challenge if one is presented.

16   It should be noted that while the framework of states- national government relations will be included in the constitution, the details may be very dynamic and may change with time. A fascinating illustration is given by the results of the US presidential elections in 2000. The result of the federal election was decided by the results in one state – Florida. The deadlock attracted attention to the fact that the legislation of election laws for the federal government is in the province of the states, so that there are important and crucial differences between these laws among states. Americans will now have to face the question whether this power of the states to determine results of federal elections may offend against the principles of the Union.

17   The relationship between stability and legitimacy is a cornerstone of conservative thought. It is thus not surprising to find it in the works of Burke. But the importance of stability to legitimacy appears in the thought of Hume as well. Awareness to this connection explains the different attitudes of Madison and Jefferson to constitutional amendment. Jefferson thought democracy required that people would be able to amend their constitutions easily. Madison, on the other hand, believed that only an entrenched constitution could generate the awe and veneration that people should feel towards their basic laws. Madison won the battle.

18   A good example of a special entrenchment of this sort is the rule that each state in the US has two representatives in the Senate, irrespective of size or population.

19   Israel just experienced such a careless change, which would probably have been prevented had the structure of government been entrenched. Until 1992, Israel was a 'pure' parliamentary democracy, designed after the British model. It therefore did not need safeguards against irresponsible legislation by the Knesset, since the government had control over Parliament. A few years of political deadlock initiated the introduction of a hybrid: The Prime Minister is now elected directly by the public. The change did help prevent the power of small parties to decide who will form the government. However, since other aspects of the powers of central organs were not amended at the same time, the new

system lacks some basic mechanisms ensuring the ability to govern. One of them is the fact that parliament can pass legislation which requires huge public expenditure, and the government cannot prevent such legislation.

20   See, for example, the controversial decision by the Canadian Court re the power to pass constitutional amendments in the absence of unanimous support by the provinces: Re *Amendment of the Constitution of Canada* [1981] 1 S.C.R. 753 (The *Patriation Reference*).

21   CJ Moshe Landau, an adamant critic of judicial review of a Bill of Rights in Israel, was the one who initiated judicial review of an entrenched provision dealing with election laws: *Bergman v. Minister of Finance* (1969) 23(i) P.D. 693 [Hebrew]. The election laws are part of the basic laws, which intent to develop the constitutional materials in a series of 'basic laws'. Similarly, Justice Oliver Wendell Holmes, a great advocate of judicial deference in matters of values and social and political philosophy, supported judicial review on matters of federalism.

22   We all know there are countries in which judges are appointed in ways that deny them significant measures of independence, despite constitutional guarantees thereof. Clearly, this may apply with greater force to the appointment of Attorneys-General or directors of public prosecutions.

23   Complaints of this sort were made against Kenneth Star, the special prosecutor appointed to look into some of President Clinton's affairs. In Israel, some claim that the Attorney-General, a creature regulated only by government's decisions and some committee's reports adopted by them, has become too independent. Similar concerns are raised about the alleged excessive independence of the director of Israel's central bank, who maintains a monetary policy that is not related to the government's goals of inflation and employment. The Israel Bank Act, and legal conventions, permit the government to replace a director or an attorney-general with whom it cannot work, but despite serious controversies and debates between the government and these functionaries, no government in Israel until now dared do this. (There was one case in which an attorney general's term was cut short because of a major debate, but even then the government explicitly invoked the AG's prior declaration of his intention to quit once a replacement is found. The government appointed a replacement overnight...) By now, it is hard to imagine that the power to fire either of these officials is a real political power.

24   It may well be that in a well-formed constitution, it would have been impossible to change the constitution so that Basher el-Assad could be made a credible candidate for president. It is far from clear that a period of uncertainty with open-ended elections is what Syria needed after Hafez-el-Assad's death. It is hard to speculate on the political desirability of a power struggle in the wake of Hafez-El-Assad's death. It is clear that the bold change of the constitution, which was clearly an ad-hominem ad hoc amendment, of the kind discouraged by constitutions, prevented quite a lot of political turmoil.

25   A good example of such a development is the interpretation of the rule demanding Senate approval for international agreements made by the US president, US Constitution, Art. 2, para.2(2). The text of the constitution has not changed, but various agreements have been taken out of this framework by various creative distinctions.

26   Ackerman's model, *supra* note 12, of informal constitutional amendment, by either popular demand or by judicial interpretation, are good illustrations of situations in which social realities find ways to work around entrenchment mechanisms that are found to be too rigid. However, it may well be that the US constitutions could have been improved in many smaller ways had the formal amendment procedure been more flexible.

27   Israel again may provide an interesting example. In 1950, the Israeli Knesset decided not to enact a constitution. Instead, it decided to develop a constitution piecemeal, through a series of basic laws. At the same year, Israel's law of Return was passed, declaring the

right of every Jew to immigrate to Israel [the *Law of Return* (1950)]. Some people suggested that the law should be entrenched against all future changes. The motion was refused. Israel's First Prime minister, David Ben Gurion, explained that no one will ever think of changing the law, but that formal entrenchment was not advisable in view of the decision made re the constitution. In fact, the law is indeed very hard to change, but it was changed in a significant way in 1970.

28   I will not go into the fascinating question whether Bills of Rights should include social, economic and cultural rights in addition to the classical civil and political rights. Many constitutions do (see e.g. India and South Africa), but many new Bills of Rights do not (e.g. the *Canadian Charter of Rights and Freedoms*). Similarly, I will not discuss the question whether constitutions should protect the right to property.

29   An important difference between democracies and non-democracies may be in the actual content of the laws. The impact of a constitution on the actual protection of rights is a fascinating subject that goes much beyond my present paper. It may be related to the external and internal constraints on the independence and the integrity of the courts. See, for example, the argument that the US Supreme Court has not been an effective protector of minorities: Girardeau A. Spahn, *Race Against the Court: The Supreme Court and Minorities in Contemporary America* (1993). In Israel, it has been argued the Court has been very weak on protecting the rights of individuals in the occupied territories.

30   See Ordeshook [add cite] .

31   The tradition of human rights has a complex nature. I prefer to talk about 'moral theory' and not to invoke natural law or natural rights, so as to avoid possible controversy. The complex relations between the moral and the international law validity of human rights is another important subject which I cannot enter. In a nutshell I will say that morality provides rights, in one sense, a more secure basis that does international law, since morality does not depend for its force on man-made institutions. On the other hand, one part of the strength of rights is their preemptive force and their enforceability. International law may be weaker than municipal law, but it provides enforcement mechanism not available to 'mere' natural rights. The strength of human rights in our era is therefore a combination of their moral validity and their institutional support. See Ruth Gavison 'The Relationships between Civil and Political and Social and Economic Rights', forthcoming, UNU 2003.

32   For a more detailed argument see Ruth Gavison 'The Controversy over Israel's Bill of Rights', *Israel Yearbook on Human Rights,* vol. 15 (1985), p.113.

33   It is rare for a country without a constitution to consider enacting and entrenching just a Bill of Rights. But this is precisely what took place in England, culminating in the Human Rights Act of 1998. This approach might be fruitful especially in countries where it is hard, for a variety of reasons, to constitutionalise the regime part of the constitutional arrangements, but there is a felt need to strengthen the formal protection of rights.

34   A few examples from US history will suffice. *Dred Scott v. Sanford* 60 U.S. 393 (1856) was a judicial decision that did not make a contribution to accelerating the end of slavery. That issue had to be decided by a civil war. In the Lochner era, the US Supreme Court invalidated progressive labour legislation by invoking the constitutional provisions of freedom of contract. But in 1956 the Court declared that legal segregation in the schools was unconstitutional (*Brown v. Board of Education* 349 U.S. 294 [1954]), and in 1964 it declared that states could not punish and impose heavy fines on political speech (*New York Times v. Sullivan*). The courts tolerated segregation and silencing under the colour of laws for many years, but when they were ready – they had the tools to make progress.

35   New Zealand adopted a non-entrenched Bill of Rights without judicial review (New Zealand Bill of Rights 1990). England recently adopted, after a long debate, a semi-constitutional arrangement in its Bill of Rights Act. For a forceful argument against judicial

review see e.g. Jeremy Waldron, *supra* note 6. Waldron's position is of special interest because he comes from the liberal progressive part of the political spectrum, which usually endorses judicial review quite enthusiastically. He is also a forceful advocate of the centrality of rights. In Israel, one of the most liberal Judges on the Court, Moshe Landau, persistently argues against the adoption of a constitutional Bill of Rights.

36 Although Jeremy Bentham said that natural rights are nonsense upon stilts, it is not clear that he would have objected to a declaration of positive legal rights.

37 By 'divided' or 'rifted' democracies I mean societies characterised by structural conflicts of interests between groups. Deep rifts between groups pose serious threats to democracy, which is ideally built on a vision of equality among citizens. For a classical account see Arend Lijphart, *Democracy in Plural Societies: A Comparative Exploration* (Yale 1977).

38 Unless, of course, the commitment to a universal ideal seems as a threat to groups who would like to define their states in particularistic terms...

39 See, e.g. the Hungarian constitution declaring it to be a 'social' state.

40 We can see the distinction very dramatically in the Philadelphia constituent assembly. Delegates had bitter debates, and disagreed about most of the arrangements. However, most of them agreed that the package deal reached was superior to the present situation, and the best arrangement that could have been reached. They thus supported the package as such, without endorsing each and every detailed arrangement.

41 Some people argue that from this general approach it follows that all liberal states should include in their constitutions an affirmation of the secularity of states, and of a separation between state and religion, including a component of non-establishment. This is indeed the situation in the first amendment of the US constitution. However, it was not the case in many states in the US, and in fact most liberal countries have neither a declaration of secularity nor a regime of separation. The status of religion(s) in a state may be a subject dealt with in a constitution, but it does not have to be included, and the arrangement is not necessarily one of separation. In fact, some countries include in their constitutions that they are of a certain religion. There is a good reason for including this arrangement in a constitution when, for example, leaving this issue to regular political forces may generate instability. The US experience, as well as that in France and Turkey (three states in which there is an explicit constitutional commitment to secularity of the state as such) show that these declarations do not, and cannot, solve the issue once and for all, and that questions about the role of religion in public life persist. This is a general lesson about constitutions: while they may help in removing some subjects from the realm of regular politics in some contexts, their success in this goal is always temporary and fragile.

42 Ruth Gavison, *Israel as a Jewish and Democratic State: Tensions and Challenges* (Hebrew) (Tel Aviv, 1999); Ruth Gavison, ' Can Israel be Both Jewish and Democratic? A Rejoinder to the Ethnic Democracy Debate', 3 *Israel Studies* (1999).

43 Ruth Gavison, *supra* note 32. The decision not to enact a constitution in 1950 was not influenced by the wish not to offend Arab citizens of Israel. It had more to do with the intra-Jewish debate about the place of religion in the new state, and with the reluctance of the government to impose legal limits on its powers.

44 The fact that there was a controversy on whether the state should be socialist was one of the reasons explicitly mentioned to explain why Israel did not adopt a constitution when it was founded. When one MP mentioned the difficulty of the status of Arabs in the Jewish state, he was censured by all his colleagues. Now the issue cannot be avoided. Arabs have joined those who object to the continuation of legislation of basic laws, or of a constitution, that will entrench the definition of Israel as a Jewish state. So the lesson of Israel in this respect may in fact be even more complex: It was possible to include the affirmation of Israel as a Jewish state when it was founded, and the description would have been accepted

with no serious challenge. Dealing with the tensions and the complexities of this characterisation of the state would then be the task of political and judicial interpretation. In 1992, the inclusion of the characterisation was not so self-evident, but now its explicit removal may be impossible.

45   Until 1992, Israel was seen by most of its Jewish population and by most of the world as a Jewish state, despite the fact that this was never declared in its laws. Now that the definition was introduced into the law, removing it would be interpreted by many as a decision to stop seeing Israel as such. Under present political conditions, it is very unlikely that such a removal will be possible. In terms of the constitutional process in Israel, this is a reason for not entrenching the existing basic laws and making them into a formal constitution. Rather, a formal document based on existing arrangements (where they are deemed desirable) may make it possible to avoid declarations about the nature of the state altogether.

46   This is the model frequent in Europe. The judges of the constitutional court are usually appointed in a way different from 'regular' judges, and their term on the court is limited. The appointment is more 'political' than is the appointment of regular judges. Most European countries adopted this model, as well as South Africa. In some of these countries, the distinction between the regular court and the constitutional court was motivated, in part, by the fact that the regular legal system was a remnant of a past regime, and there was a wish to declare a break with the past. The distinction however was suggested by Hans Kelsen on pure jurisprudential grounds, based on the major difference that he saw between interpretation of the law and reviewing its constitutionality.

47   The Netherlands are an important example. In Switzerland, too, the constitution explicitly rules out judicial review of primary legislation.

48   The US is an interesting example, which supports this point only in part. The power of judicial review was first established in the early *Marbury v. Madison*, 5 U.S. 137 (1803), in which Marshall derived the power from the very supremacy of the constitution. Nonetheless, the persuasiveness of the move is still contested by many. Now, of course, no one doubts that the American courts do have the power of judicial review. Yet the uncertainty did have some serious costs. For a compelling historical analysis see: Robert Lowry Clinton, *Marbury v. Madison and Judicial Review,* (University Press of Kansas, 1989).

49   Indeed, the life tenure of Supreme Court Justices in the US is one of the main criticisms of the system there. See Eskridge William and Sandy Levinson (eds.), *Constitutional Stupidities, Constitutional Tragedies* (1998). In most constitutional courts, the term of judges on the court is indeed not renewable. Hungary has a different system, but the political system chose not to renew the terms of the judges when their first term elapsed. A former Justice in the Hungarian court, conceded that the decision of the government not to renew the appointments to the court once the original term elapsed should be adopted as a constitutional convention.

50   In the US this may be less obvious than in other countries, because the process of appointing judges is more political than it is in most other jurisdictions. See 'USC Symposium on Judicial Election, Selection and Accountability', 61 S. Cal. L.Rev. 1555 (1988). This is clearly the case in appointments of federal judges under Article III of the US constitution. In fact, many thought that one of the main stakes in the Gore-Bush presidential election fight of November 2000 was the fact that the president may have the power to appoint up to three of the Justices of the Supreme Court. While all federal judges are appointed in the same process, there is a much higher visibility and public debate when the appointment of a Supreme Court Justice is involved. Robert Bork had no trouble being appointed as a federal judge, but his appointment to the Supreme Court was undermined

because of his views on judicial activism, abortion, and the proper role for a court. The system of appointment to constitutional courts (or councils, as in France) guarantees that the people elected will indeed have a profile broader than that required of a regular judge, and that they will be more representative than regular courts. When the system of appointment cannot guarantee this (as is the case in Israel, for example) – this may create a crisis of legitimacy if the courts, especially the Supreme Court of the land, use broad powers of judicial review.

51   For a recent discussion suggesting the disadvantages and limitations of courts as sole or primary interpreters of the constitution see Tushnet Mark, *Taking the Constitution Away from the Courts*, 1999. The book contains a broad review of previous relevant literature.

2. Comment

Horst Hegmann

IT ALL DEPENDS!

At first sight, the answer to Ruth Gavison's question seems to be quite obvious. There are two approaches towards delimiting the possible contents of a constitution. On the one hand, a constitution should contain last resort rules on all those issues for which a generally accepted position is necessary in order to permit stable, peaceful human intercourse. On the other hand, one may neglect all issues which are so evident that citizens will not question them anyway. The evident aspects of reality constitute a topographical setting, so to speak, to which a formal constitution needs to be adapted like works of construction or civil engineering to a given landscape.

Because people in different cultures perceive different things to be evident, the appropriate sets of explicit rules will differ from one society to another. Each legal system is based on different tacit knowledge foundations and it is impossible to design a 'one size fits all' constitution to suit every different kind of society. The sum of the constitutionally relevant aspects of a country's political culture can be treated as its material constitution. Like Ruth Gavison, I will therefore concentrate in the following on the interplay between this material constitution and the formal written constitutional document (Gavison note 4).

The material constitution of a society is embodied in the latter's political culture. According to Berger and Luckmann (1967) a culture should not be treated as a simple accumulation of individual preferences and attitudes towards politics. Culture rather is a systemic complexity of knowledge consisting of interrelated roles and objects, the whole constituting reality for a given society's members (on the specific characteristics of political culture see Rohe 1987). This reality is common to all members and its specific form results from a shared history. Members of the same society do not only share common ideas about relevant facts, they also share goals and values and notions of how best to reconcile facts with aspirations. Newcomers do not simply pick up isolated pieces of information but internalise a reality in which others are already living; together they recreate and renew this reality over the course of the years and adapt it to new circumstances.

Insofar as their common worldview is not questioned, it becomes a matter of routine. The shared knowledge eventually seems to be so evident, that it is taken as the normal starting point for the activities of all citizens. If the particular society is growing, people will start to develop a variety of viewpoints about the shared evident aspects of their lives. In discussing these different perspectives, they will develop notions which make sense only in relation to the reality of their own group. Outsiders trying to understand what they are talking about will first have to explore the socially accepted form of life (Wittgenstein 1953) on which their communication is based. Within a socially differentiated society, there comes a stage at which perceptions have diverged so much that the conventions of language no longer suffice and further explicit agreements are required. At this point, legal concepts enter the picture. If citizens' disagreement on relevant aspects of reality is affecting their ability to co-ordinate activities, they may find it useful to define an 'official' point of view, to ensure continued co-operation (Hegmann 2001).

If all explicit knowledge results from the accepted interpretations of a common life pattern, one which is by no means identical in different cultures, different legal arrangements are required. The normative branch of constitutional economics (Buchanan 1991) provides useful tools with which to compare such arrangements and to determine appropriate contents for a constitution. It offers a theoretical framework in which the constitutional consequences of a given reality can be expressed and compared. Starting from a sound knowledge of the political culture in question, researchers can sketch out the situation in which citizens find themselves. They can learn how the citizens perceive the circumstances in which they act, their aims and scope for action. Only then are the researchers able to say something about the citizens' constitutional interests (Vanberg/Buchanan 1989) and the set of rules best suited to these interests.

There are two more reasons for proposing Buchanan's specific brand of normative constitutional economics in this context. First of all, Buchanan's normative starting point is to give equal weight to the demands of each individual citizen. This neatly matches Ruth Gavison's own normative intentions. The second reason is that Buchanan concentrates his efforts on legitimising a legal framework as a whole. He does not start from individual rights, but constructs the corresponding duties out of self-interest. This does not produce exactly the results he would like (Hegmann 1998), but his approach is much more compatible with constitutional law than approaches that take individual rights as their starting point (e.g. Nozick 1974).

How does this relate to Ruth Gavison's three candidates for inclusion in a constitutional document: 'basic governmental structures and the relations between the main powers and functions, basic values and commitments and human rights' (Gavison p. 1)? In general terms, normative constitutional economics states that a rule shall be adopted, if that improves the lot of at least one person and nobody else loses thereby (Pareto-optimality). Society should opt for constitutional change if the expected benefits in this sense exceed the expected costs. How such costs and benefits are determined, however, depends entirely on a society's particular reality. It is only on the basis of society's shared knowledge system that a set of legal rules can be judged to be appropriate or not.

Just as a certain life pattern gives meaning to certain specific linguistic constructions, such constructions, embedded in a common life pattern, give meaning to a specific set of legal rules. Especially in this respect Ruth Gavison is right to stress that 'always, the reality of societies is more important than the relationships and values declared in a constitution' (Gavison p. 3). The constitution adopted by Japan after World War II is a telling example: here a constitutional document exported from one culture to a very different culture acquired an entirely different meaning (Inoue 1991). Not by means of theoretical reflection, therefore, but by historical inquiry into the interplay between the evident aspects of a society's reality and its explicit rules can we learn how political institutions work in reality.

Constitutional change, therefore, can never be an entirely apolitical enterprise. There is no way to restrict an evaluation to purely legal or economic considerations. Even judicial review will always remain a political issue (Gavison p. 15). But Buchanan assumes certain external limits to the allowed contents of a constitution. The normative starting point of his approach restricts, for example, the possibility of denying some citizens all their rights. He believes such a rule could be legitimate only if the enslaved agreed to it and even then it would be open to question whether individuals should have the right to sell their autonomy for something else. Within the set limits, an observer may ask only whether a rule is appropriate with respect to society's legitimate aims. To judge whether a specific constitutional commitment is wrong or not he has to find out if it contradicts society's established values or, alternatively, if it conflicts with some superior good. In the latter case, however, he would be obliged to explain the basis for his value statement and demonstrate why it must overrule a specific society's particular choice.

In order to be considered legitimate by constitutional economists in this tradition, efforts directed towards constitutional change must abstain from furthering only particular ends. Of course, from an economist's point of view, individuals will always act in their own interest. But they will improve their lot by agreeing on rules which guarantee that their individual and public interests run as parallel as possible. But this, again, does not lead necessarily to a specific outcome. What individuals consider to be in their interest, what they perceive to be a social trap and how they hope to avoid such a trap, all that depends on their society's political culture (Hegmann 1997).

It is not only the perception of individual citizens which determines their constitutional interests and shows whether the latter are legitimate. The same holds true the other way round. Not only do the rules of a legal system embedded in a certain political culture determine an individual's scope of action, they also shape his perception of reality. If he has grown up in a society with formally stated sanctions for criminal offences, for example, he will not simply view these sanctions as price tags for socially undesirable behaviour but as signs that help him to distinguish between good and evil. Because nobody has specially privileged access to truth, such signs necessarily influence his evaluation of certain patterns of behaviour. Therefore, writing commitments into a constitution may, indeed, help to change reality in the long run.

This, however, should not lead us to assume that changing the law will suffice to change reality. Rules have to be socially accepted as appropriate for certain circumstances. They are not just negotiated in order to improve one's individual situation, but contain elements of true interaction. When citizens sense a mismatch between their tacit knowledge and a certain rule, a constitutional entrepreneur may well propose reforms (Vanberg/Buchanan 1991). However, neither the proposer nor his addressees will assess the beneficial effects of such change on their given situation alone. They will also check whether the new rule 'is better' in the sense that it suits their common reality better. In communitarian terms we can say that the citizens attempt to correct the explicit set of rules by reference to shared intuitions and these intuitions by reference to a generally accepted explicit model of reality. They move back and forth, thereby, between an intuitive and a reflective understanding of their condition (M. Walzer, 1987, 17 ff.), which in both cases is common to them all.

To conclude, I agree with Ruth Gavison that it is impossible to determine once and for all what belongs in a constitution. The perception of an individual's environment, his interests, and possibilities, depends on the culture to which he and the observer belong. Constitutional economics or similar theoretical devices may facilitate the comparison between different constitutions, but they cannot replace the sound knowledge of a society's culture and history in order to give advice for constitutional design. Whether a constitution should contain specifications on governmental structures, on values and commitments or on human rights, is not something that may be laid down once and for all. If, in the modern world, different lifestyles become more and more similar, we may see constitutions starting to converge. But whether that will really happen still remains an open question.

REFERENCES

Berger, Peter L. and Thomas Luckmann (1967), *The Social Construction of Reality,* London: The Penguin Press.

Buchanan, James M. (1991), *Constitutional Economics,* Oxford: Blackwell.

Hegmann, Horst (1997), 'Differing World Views and Collective Action: The Case of Research', *Constitutional Political Economy,* **8** (3), 189-204.

Hegmann, Horst (1998), 'Normativer Individualismus, konstitutioneller Fortschritt und die Rolle der Kultur', in Stephan Panther and Gerd Grözinger (eds), *Konstitutionelle Politische Ökonomie,* Marburg: Metropolis, pp. 251-278.

Hegmann, Horst (2001), *Die Verfassung der kulturell fragmentierten Gesellschaft. Zur wissenssoziologischen Grundlegung eines verfassungsökonomisch formulierten Sozialvertrags,* Marburg: Metropolis.

Inoue, Kyoko (1991), *Mac Arthur's Japanese Constitution. A Linguistic and Cultural Study of its Making,* Chicago: The University of Chicago Press.

Nozick, Robert (1974), *Anarchy, State, and Utopia,* New York: Basic Books.

Rohe, Karl (1987), 'Politische Kultur und der kulturelle Aspekt von politischer Wirklichkeit', in Dirk Berg-Schlosser and Jakob Schissler (eds), *Politische Kultur in Deutschland. Bilanz und Perspektiven der Forschung,* PVS Sonderheft 18/1987, Opladen: Westdeutscher Verlag, pp. 39-48.

Vanberg, Viktor and James M Buchanan (1991), 'Constitutional Choice, Rational Ignorance and the Limits of Reason', *Jahrbuch für Neue Politische Ökonomie,* **10,** 61-78.

Vanberg, Viktor and James M Buchanan (1989), 'Interests and Theories in Constitutional Choice', *Journal of Theoretical Politics,* **1** (1), 49-62.

Walzer, Michael (1987), *Interpretation and Social Criticism,* Cambridge (Mass.): Harvard University Press.

Wittgenstein, Ludwig (1953), *Philosophische Untersuchungen/Philosophical Investigations,* Oxford: Blackwell.

3. On the Relationship Between State and Economy in Transformation

Hans-Jürgen Wagener

INTRODUCTION

The main task of the state in the transition from plan to market is to do what, according to Marx, it should already have done under communism – to wither away. Such de-etatisation is widely held to have been the gospel of Western transformation consultants and their Eastern believers who, therefore, are lumped together under the heading of 'neo-liberals'. The so-called Washington consensus is considered the accepted dogma of the creed – and the source of all evils that befell the transformation countries after the turnaround.

Looking at the ten commandments of the consensus confirms by implication the view, ascribed to neo-liberals, that abolishing all state authority in oeconomicis will spontaneously create markets which by their very nature maximally promote development. These ten commandments are (see Williamson 1990 and Rodrik 1997, 419):

(1) Fiscal discipline
(2) Redirection of public expenditure priorities towards health, education and infrastructure
(3) Tax reform including broadening the tax base and cutting marginal tax rates
(4) Unified and competitive exchange rates
(5) Secure property rights
(6) Deregulation
(7) Trade liberalisation
(8) Privatization Elimination of barriers to direct foreign investment
(9) Financial liberalisation

The list is the result of the disappointment with active government development policies, especially in Latin America, and of neo-classical micro-theory and new classical macro-theory. It may be astonishing that monetary stabilisation is not mentioned explicitly among the commandments. However, active monetary policy has long been out of the question and the only danger for monetary stability rests with the state budget, hence the recommendation of fiscal discipline. It should be mentioned that the consensus was not considered a comprehensive reform programme, but rather that part of it which found general agreement among economists (in Washington). And secondly, it was not meant to be a blueprint for the transition from plan to market, but rather for the Latin-American problem of transition from a mixed to a full-fledged market economy. But in 1989-1990, when the communist economic and political system collapsed, the ten commandments were gladly taken up by Western consultants as well as by Eastern reformers as a guideline for their policy design clearly not implying that the state, or what was left over from it, should engineer its own disappearance.

The consensus has come under heavy attack targeted at two different points. First, those, like the Keynesians and Post-Keynesians, who do not subscribe to the underlying economic theory, in particular the macro-theory, criticise the prescriptions in themselves (see, e.g. Laski and Bhaduri 1997). And second, those who are basically in agreement with the economic theory have an easy target in the limited scope of the consensus with respect to the transformation task. Several arguments are found in the literature (e.g. Stiglitz 1999a, Stiglitz 1999b, Ahrens 1999):

- the consensus disregards the initial situation,
- it disregards the fact that the method by which the market is introduced influences its operation (path dependency),
- it ignores the embeddedness of the economic system or the interdependence of economy, polity, and culture,
- it has nothing to say about institutions, in particular legal regulations and their enforcement mechanisms,
- the underlying neo-classical micro-theory overestimates the role of the market and underestimates market failures,
- the consensus is silent about the social costs of its implementation.

Indeed, the consensus prescribes economic policies without saying a word about the institutional – let alone the cultural – infrastructure which is necessary to implement the policies and make them work as expected. It may be assumed that the reformers and their advisors were aware of, for instance, the importance of an independent central bank for monetary stabilisation. The statement about the neglect of institutions, however, says nothing in itself about the adequacy of the policy recommendations. They have been relativised by Rodrik (1997) in the context of the comparatively successful North-East Asian growth policy, or the Japanese development model, which complied with the first five commandments, while the second five were much more loosely followed. Development is among the ultimate objectives of transformation and competitive markets may be seen as only instrumental to that end. Yet if we follow Hayekian and other liberal thinking, competitive markets are an element of a free society and, as such, an end in themselves. Inasmuch as transformation aims at a transition from a totalitarian to a free society, policies have to be evaluated not only from a developmental point of view which prevails in the arguments pro and con the consensus.

Many of the incriminated 'neo-liberal' consultants, including Jeffrey Sachs, could claim that their transformation program embraced not only stabilisation, liberalisation, and privatisation, but also institution building. It is true, however, that they have not made sufficiently clear that appropriate institutions are the precondition for competitive markets to work properly and even less so that a powerful state is at the core of these institutions. It should not remain unmentioned that, for neo-liberal thinking in the Freiburg tradition of Eucken (1990), the institutional implications of competitive markets and the role of the state were self-evident and central to their transformation advice.

The chief witness against the Washington consensus has recently become Joseph Stiglitz (1999a, 1999b). This is not the place to evaluate his arguments in depth (which has convincingly been done by Dabrowski, Gomulka and Rostowski 2000). He has many good points about path-dependency, sequencing, and the mechanical implementation of stabilisation, liberalisation, and privatisation. But when he juxtaposes unsuccessful Russia and China as paragons of transformation success, he not only misses the successes of Central Eastern Europe, he also fails to take account of a free society as ultimate objective of transformation. This raises the interesting question whether China is a valid example of successful transition to a competitive market order in which the type of state governing the economic system does not matter as long as it conforms to the market order. Clearly, the rule of law belongs among these conformity conditions, but it is unclear whether there is a binding relation between the rule of law and political freedom (see, for instance, Przeworski and Limongi 1993) – which does not automatically imply that China already enjoys the rule of law. Alternatively, it could be held that what we see in China is not the establishment of a full-fledged market order, but the only successful attempt up to now to decentralise a socialist planned system yielding some kind of market socialism. Economic growth in China is undeniable, bringing the Lipset hypothesis (Barro 1997) to the fore: prosperity stimulates democracy. So we should be careful not to interpret the connection between state and economy as a one-way relationship.

Given the fact that the modern market order and the modern state co-evolved over the last four centuries, it looks rather strange to learn only recently from economists (e.g. Rodrik 1997, Stiglitz 1999a) that markets and governments are complements, not substitutes for each other. The explanation of this remarkable phenomenon lies in the history of economic theorising. When the problem of theory became the Smithonian metaphor of the invisible hand, i.e. of analysing the conditions of existence and stability of a competitive equilibrium, and these conditions turned out to include perfect information and perfect competition, there was no economic role left for the visible hand – if not, as the Freiburg school has stressed, to create and protect the institutional prerequisites for perfect information and perfect competition. This theoretical puzzle, together with perfect information and perfect competition, has little in common with historical economic systems (it never claimed it did, as a matter of fact). Historical and institutional approaches, on the other hand, always were interested in the economic role of the state. However, they lacked the ability to give a theoretical rationale for what they observed and described. By and large, this is still the state of the art (see the rather brief chapter on the new institutional economics of the state, on the one hand, and the recourse to G. Schmoller as ancestor of the new institutional economics, on the other, in Richter and Furubotn 1999).

So when we try to look a bit more closely at the relation of state and economy in the rest of the chapter, there will be a lot of ad hoc observation and ad hoc theorising, which is typical for the treatment of the economic role of the state. The following paragraphs first briefly treat the state and the rule of law, second some more and some less accepted economic roles ascribed to the state, third the age-old fact that the economy thrives only under a regime of good governance, and finally the question whether there is a specific role for the state in the process of transformation. The aim of the exercise is to find out whether or not any state would do for a well-functioning market order and whether transformation assigns the state specific tasks.

THE STATE, GOVERNMENT, AND THE RULE OF LAW

The friendly request for the state to wither away is targeted at a specific type of state, not at the state as such. For Marx, this was the class-state, to be substituted by rational public administration. For transformation, this was the totalitarian communist state which Marxist-Leninist theory saw as an instrument for rebuilding society according to the well-understood laws of history. As long as different interests prevailed in society, thus ran the argu-ment, the dictatorship of the proletariat was deemed necessary to promote the unity of state and society. As soon as there was harmony of interests, the state would express and carry out the collective will of all. In both cases, the ulti-mate decision-making power rests with the state, there is no separation of the private and the public spheres. Yet in theory there is no conflict between power and consent, i.e. between markets and hierarchies, because of the assumed harmony of interests: democratic centralism can be perfectly demo-cratic and perfectly centralistic. In practice, the ensuing state turned out to exercise universal petty tutelage and all-pervasive highly incompetent inter-vention, thus blocking individual freedom. In addition, it failed to live up to its promise, namely to provide an ever-increasing level of welfare. To abolish the communist state and to de-etatise the economy was the logical conse-quence of the anamnesis of the economic catastrophe to which it had led.

Abolishing the totalitarian communist state did not imply abolishing state activity altogether, nor did it imply introducing Western-type democratic states whose economic role is not clearly defined, anyway. Yet to cut a long argument and a long history short, we may assume that most transformation countries aimed at such Western-type democratic societies. From this it follows that the private sphere and the public sphere ought to be neatly separated and the former protected against arbitrary intervention from the latter. The separation of private and public spheres requires the introduction of private property rights. The protection of their free use requires the rule of law, which by its very nature is the antithesis of arbitrariness. Let us already mention here that predictability of law and of government policy is considered conducive to economic performance (and enumerated among the core institutional elements of a competitive order by Eucken 1990, 285).

Up to here, I have equated the state and the public sphere. Even if it is not in line with juridical definitions, it could be a workable definition. However, such a definition disregards the non-state domain of the public sphere, non government organisations or the organisations of the civil community (in contrast to firms that are meant to operate in the private sphere, NGOs are meant to operate in the public sphere). Since Putnam (1993), this part of the public sphere has attracted new attention, for he was able to show its importance for the functioning of the statist part of the public sphere. Already Marxist-Leninist doctrine was deeply convinced thereof, which made the Party monopolise practically all NGOs in communist society: the unity of state and society resulting in the fact that in the end the domain of non-government organisations was almost an empty set – the church being the most conspicuous exception in some countries that was regarded with highest suspicion by Party and State.

Among economists (for instance, Stiglitz 1989, 21, Richter and Furubotn 1999, 301) it is common to think that the state is all about authority and coercion, i.e. to define it, following Max Weber, as the part of the public sphere with the monopoly of legitimate power. Surely, the state is the only societal subject to use coercive power legitimately. But this does not imply that it can use compulsion at any time and on any occasion. However, we have to be very careful to differentiate positive from normative statements. For, looking back at totalitarian rule, the state can use compulsion deliberately there being no exit option for its citizens (just remember Trotzky's idea of the militarisation of labour, a feasible mode of regulation as many war economies show). When we distinguish with Hayek (1960; see also Kläver 2000) state action with and without coercive power, we do so in the normative context of the rule of law.

The state with coercive power legitimately uses power to enforce general laws. The constitution and the material definition of the rule of law – as distinguished from the formal definition of legality – delimits what is ultra vires of legislation and government, for instance in the relationship between the government, the market, and the individual citizen. Where the authorisation of state action does not have to be confirmed constitutionally, as is mandatory in the United States, it is at least bound to well-understood criteria such as legal security, prohibition of excessive action, and liability. To test for these criteria is the task of administrative jurisdiction, a branch of jurisdiction which, by the way, was introduced in Eastern Europe only in the very last days of communist rule. The state without coercive power takes care of certain tasks which, in principle, could be handled by other organisations, non-government organisations or commercial organisations with whom the state competes in this domain. A public school cannot use coercive power to enrol all pupils of a given district, whereas government, on the basis of an appropriate law, may control compulsory schooling.

In short, in the public sphere we find the state as 'state' and the state as ordinary institutional consumer and producer. The two activities are motivated and legitimised differently, the first by the guarantee of liberty and freedom from private coercion, the second by considerations of efficiency (which does not rule out that a public police may also be more efficient than a private one). Between the legal state – the English language places the rule of law above the state, whereas in German it is the Rechtsstaat (the legal state), both having similar material intentions – and the productive state (Leistungsstaat) we may place a third domain of state activity, the social state, which is motivated by considerations of equity. It is more controversial than the other two and some, such as Hayek and other liberals, even regard it with greatest suspicion. Its task can be normatively determined in very different ways ranging from the Zorro model (the state as defender of the poor) to the Caterpillar model (creating a level playing field of equal opportunity). The rule of law requires that the social state be based on general laws, and the state can use its coercive power to tax to finance it. This brings the social state into close proximity with the legal state.

The political economy of the state has been interpreted as a market, with politicians as entrepreneurs supplying government services and the public, or any given rent-seeking group of it, as consumers exercising demand. It can, as well, be viewed as a game over government policies between multiple principals, the people, and multiple agents, the politicians. The difference is hierarchy, but the concept of consumer sovereignty makes it clear that there is no essential difference – the consumers ideally being principals of the producers. This view underlines the proposition that the power of compulsion is a public good as much as any other demanded by the public. Although the state can, within given constitutional limits, exercise certain monopolies, there is competition in the market for politics, competition between governments – the internal exit option to vote a government out of power and the external exit option to leave the country. And there is the voice option with all its instruments of the public media to remind government of public demand, lest it be confronted with the exit options. It is typical of the totalitarian state, to be substituted by such a democratic state in transformation, that it reverted the roles of principal and agent. It prohibited the voice option by censorship and competition between governments by banning opposition parties and setting up the Iron Curtain. Not only the economic system, but also the political system of socialism was supply- and not demand-driven, which means for the consumer or the general public: take it, you can't leave it.

THE ECONOMIC ROLE OF THE STATE

The question about the economic role of the state can be now formulated in various ways:

* what has been the role of the state?
* what should be the role of the state? and
* what can be the role of the state?

'What has been the economic role of the state?' implies the empirical-historical aspect. Economic history and comparative economics show quite different national approaches even within the competitive capitalist paradigm (see, for instance, Crouch and Streek 1997). The cooperation of market and state is shaped according to divergent national traditions and cultures without necessarily resulting in significant differences in performance. Globalisation, that is intensified competition, will lead, it can be conjectured, to convergence in certain fields, in particular outcomes, but there is no compelling reason why it should destroy the plurality of organisational solutions that bring about the outcomes. As a measure of state influence, the relative size of the government budget is only one indicator, reflecting predominantly the weight of the social state. In this respect Japan, for instance, scores rather low while the Japanese government plays an important role in development and industrial policy. In industrial relations and wage policy the Japanese government, again, has very little influence (see Hayami 1998). Therefore, distinguishing a market-oriented (Anglo-American countries), a corporatist (Germany, Japan), a statist (France, Italy), and a social democrat (Sweden, Austria) model (Boyer 1997, 90) reflects certain tendencies, but cannot fully render the actual diversity of market – state relations. These relations are by no means stable over time within particular national economic systems. The failure of Keynesianism confronted with stagflation or the wave of liberalisation and privatisation in the wake of increased international competition and technical innovation has certainly changed, but not necessarily diminished, the role of the state in the economy.

'What should be the economic role of the state?' implies the normative-theoretical aspect. Here we can discern two extreme positions of political-economic theory and vision: the liberal, with the 'nightwatchman-state' as its caricature, and the Marxist-Leninist, with Lenin's idea of the whole society organised like a huge German post office as its caricature. Closer to reality is the liberal vision of the state's responsibility for law and order and the economy being driven by individual decision and coordinated by voluntary contract, and the socialist vision of the state's responsibility for modernisation and development and the economy guided and coordinated by state governance and planning. Between the two we may position the social-democratic vision ascribing to the state a responsibility for social fairness or equity as well as for law and order. Both extreme views share the conviction that the market and the state are substitutes for each other. This conviction is neither historically nor theoretically compelling.

Economic theory has for long maintained neutrality between the two extremes. The neo-classical model was able to show that both, the market and the plan, could attain the same equilibrium under similar conditions, in particular perfect competition or perfect planning, full information, and no transaction costs. Starting from here, Western economists developed a predilection for the market and postulated a kind of subsidiarity principle: the state should come into the picture only where the market fails. Since the subsidiarity principle derives from a holistic vision of society, market and state are no longer considered substitutes for each other, but complements with a primary responsibility for economic decision-making in the private sphere and an over-all responsibility for systemic stability (law and order is only part of it) in the public sphere. The holistic vision goes back to Althusius' (1995) Politica of 1603, which 'presented a theory of polity-building based on the polity as a compound political association established by its citizens through their primary associations on the basis of consent rather than a reified state imposed by a ruler or an elite' (Elazar 1995, xxxv). The gradual transition from the private to the public sphere and their organic, non-antagonistic relation are important in this context.

There can be consensus about this principle, its operationalisation is controversial: the instances of market failure, in particular when social justice is an argument. However, economic theory has found the trick to keep the state off the market in the latter case or, phrased more positively, to organise the cooperation of market and state. The second fundamental theorem of welfare economics – any desired market equilibrium can be attained by an appropriate distribution of initial endowments – leaves the state with the distributional task to implement fair initial endowments while the market can fulfill its allocational task (Stiglitz 1989, 37-40). Very concretely, this theorem can be applied to social security systems: pension funds and health insurance can be supplied by the private sphere, the public sphere need do only two things: ensure that everybody takes the necessary provisions (regulation) and put the indigent in a state to pay for it (redistribution which, of course, affects allocation in other parts of the economy). The provision of systemic stability is no less controversial. For it can be argued that markets stabilise automatically and that there is no need of a lender of last resort, prudent regulator, or competition guard. A long history of crises in the market economy, however, has proven these functions to be essential for the smooth working of the system.

When economic theory left its ideal world of perfect competition, full information, and no transaction costs, things became much more difficult. Once it is realised that neither the market nor the state operate without cost and that information, if available at all, is not costless either, the cooperation of market and state may become especially fruitful, but the assignment of tasks to one or the other is contingent upon the specific place and time. To return to the above example: the costs of running a public social security system may be much lower than the up-keep of markets for health insurance and old-age retirement pensions. No a priori statements are possible.

The non perfect world of costly and limited information, imperfect competition, and, eventually, bounded rationality made clear that allocational efficiency and distributional justice are heavily dependent upon the institutional infrastructure of the economic order. But in order to function properly even the most perfect market economy needs a number of institutions, in the sense of behaviour-constraining rules, and of organisations supporting them. Core elements of a well-functioning market system are secure private property rights, freedom of trade and freedom of contract, hard budget constraints or clear liability obligations, and stable money. In addition, the market system will be protected against degeneration by competition control, provision of consumer protection and of public goods, regulation of externalities, and a basic fairness. It is by no means clear to what extent all this has to be supplied and administered by the state. The fact, however, that contract enforcement, for instance, is quite often controlled by private arbitration, is no argument against state legislation and its judiciary. For the latter determine the opportunity costs of the former and thus limit their arbitrariness and cost. This becomes quite obvious in countries where the public legal system does not function well. On the other hand, the fact that the market is not well prepared to provide public goods does not automatically imply that the state has to produce them. The only thing government has to do in this case is to specify demand and to organise the financing. What societies consider public goods, by the way, is more often than not a matter of public preference, rather than of objective criteria (non-rivalry and non-exclusion) of the respective goods.

'What can be the role of the state?' implies a theoretical-practical aspect. The socialist ambition to govern the entire economic system by central administration has clearly turned out to be impossible. In similar fashion, the Keynesian ambition to fine-tune economic activity and to guarantee full employment could not be realised. The market is obviously better suited to the first task, but not to the second. Economic theory should be able to show why this is so. There are many more instances in which the market fails and in which the state does not fare better, because of imperfect information, equally high transaction costs, a lack of price signals, and moral hazard. The state is not run by a benevolent dictator nor by impartial Weberian bureaucrats, but rather by opportunistic administrators. This entails the dangers of state capture, rent seeking, and the diversion of public funds and assets. All these are arguments in favour of the aforementioned subsidiarity principle. Nevertheless, it cannot be denied that modern economic growth was accompanied by an increasing economic role of the state, that successful development models, like the East Asian, were characterised by close cooperation between the public and the private sphere, and that high levels of productivity correlate strongly with high levels of social infrastructure. It is only recently that economic theory has tried to identify the specific factors and relations which lie behind these facts. When we know them, the answer to the question 'What can be the role of the state?' will perhaps be more positive.

SOCIAL INFRASTRUCTURE AND GOOD GOVERNANCE

Not every state is a good state, and not every government does a good job in terms of economic development and provision of welfare. The more economists look into it, the more they find that here we may find answers to questions such as 'Why don't poor countries catch up?' (Keefer and Knack 1997) or 'Why do some countries produce so much more output per worker than others?' (Hall and Jones 1999). The puzzle 'Why growth rates differ?' (Denison 1967) is an old one. It was treated by growth accounting in the context of growth theory with capital, labour, and 'technical progress' as explanatory variables and with the result that the greater part of the variation was explained by exogenous factors or remained unexplained. The 'catching-up effect' was theoretically deduced from the assumption of diminishing returns to capital and empirically confirmed for Western Europe and Japan vis-à-vis the United States. It was not asked, however, what made the catching-up effect operative. New in present attempts is that convergence is put in the conditional mode and that explanations of actual growth performance are also sought in the institutional environment of private economic activity (Barro 1997). And here the state plays a predominant role.

The basic idea holds that social infrastructure lowers transaction costs and gets the prices right, to the effect that individuals capture the major share of social returns to their economic activity (production and investment) as private returns (Hall and Jones 1999, 84). In an unfriendly environment, a sizeable share of the returns will be diverted by people who do not contribute to the result. In the long run, this will induce the producers to cut back their efforts. Uncertainty is the major brake to investment in physical capital as well as in human capital. From this it follows that investment in social infrastructure is a sine qua non for economic development and welfare production. This idea is known as the Hobbes hypothesis: comparing the state of nature (unregulated competition) with the civic state, it is in the well-understood interest of each to consent to collective action (the implementation of which, then, may be preferable along the lines of Althusius rather than of Hobbes).

One of the most efficient instruments for the diversion of returns, it can hardly be denied, has been the state. Confiscatory taxation, expropriation, and government corruption are examples of direct public diversion. In an indirect way, government can yield to rent-seeking activities of the private sphere and install regulations which unduly benefit particular individuals or groups. In other words, the role of the state is ambivalent: it is responsible for the social infrastructure and it can exploit its position and power of compulsion for predatory purposes. Apparently, the visible hand can be a helping or a grabbing hand. Hence the importance of good governance. That good governance (buon governo) makes the economy thrive is already illustrated in Ambrogio Lorenzetti's famous 14th century frescoes in the city hall of Siena.

Governance can be understood as 'the traditions and institutions by which authority in a country is exercised. This includes (1) the process by which governments are selected, monitored and replaced, (2) the capacity of the government to effectively formulate and implement sound policies, and (3) the respect of citizens and the state for the institutions that govern economic and social interactions among them' (Kaufmann, Kraay and Zoido-Lobatón 1999, 1). So broadly speaking we may equate good governance and a high level of social infrastructure. The basic institutions that are needed derive from the aforementioned core elements of a market system: secure and stable property rights, freedom of trade and of contract, enforceability of contracts, clear liability rules, stable money, and well-defined and predictable administrative and judicial procedures as well as policy regimes. Secure property rights and a credible government inhibit diversion of income from production and investment, and they lower transaction costs through high transparency and reduce the risk of unexpected policy change. Thus, entrepreneurs face lower costs, inducing them to higher investments, and commercial success depends only upon static and dynamic efficiency. On the other hand, 'where institutions are inadequate, entrepreneurs succeed on the basis of political rather than economic criteria: inefficient entrepreneurs survive who happen to have the personal ties with state officials that are necessary to protect against expropriation' (Keefer and Knack 1997, 591). The Russian 'oligarch' Beresovsky is reported to have said: the best investment at present is in politics. The Russian growth statistics of investment in construction and equipment, negative for the last decade, seem to corroborate his view.

Good governance is not big government. Barro (1997, 26) has confirmed the old liberal hypothesis that 'big government is bad for growth' where he measures government size by government consumption, excluding expenses for education and defence as productive government spending. This, of course, is a typical example of ad hoc theorising. To determine the necessary institutions for good governance is one thing, to assess their existence and measure their functioning is a different one. It is important to note that there is a great diversity of established institutions in countries which are held to exhibit good governance. Just compare Europe and the US or Singapore and Sweden. So it is hard to imagine that there is an optimal set of institutions. It is rather the local mix adapted to the cultural traditions of the individual country and accepted by public officials and the people which makes for security and credibility of policy. Yet the fundamental aspects of governance, like the rule of law, bureaucratic quality, and corruption are of general importance. In their recent studies, Kaufmann, Kraay and Zuido-Lobatón (1999, 2000) have attempted to identify a set of governance indicators and to aggregate them into a data set fit for testing. These indicators, whose representation, probably unwittingly, follows Lorenzetti's model of confronting buon governo with mal governo, may serve here as an example (Kaufmann, Kraay, Zoido-Lobatón 1999, 8-10).

In a first cluster of indicators called 'voice and accountability', the political process is assessed, i.e. the selection and replacement of those in authority, public participation, and political rights, in particular the independence of media. The second cluster is, so to speak, the mirror image of the first, labelled 'political instability and violence'. The chance that a government may be overthrown by unconstitutional means contributes to insecurity and discontinuity. The third cluster 'government effectiveness' should cover the state's ability to formulate and implement sound policies and to have transparent administrative procedures. The credibility of the government's commitment to its declared policies is an important element in this context. The civil service will tend to act arbitrarily when exposed to political pressure if it has no clear institutional framework, if there is no effective judicial control, and, of course, if the quality of the administrative personnel is poor (see also Keefer and Knack 1997, 594). Again as a kind of mirror image, a cluster 'regulatory burden' is introduced. It measures excessive regulation and market-unfriendly policies. The final two sets of indicators should reflect the state – citizen relation, in particular the respect and acceptance – let it be clear by both sides – of constitutionally established institutions. The cluster 'rule of law' captures the predictability of the courts and the enforceability of contracts. Obviously, the rule of law is strengthened by sound political institutions, to which may be added a clear division of powers, in particular an independent judiciary. The mirror cluster 'graft' measures the perceived extent of corruption, defined as the abuse of public power for private gain. Corruption can take many different forms. In the state – economy relation, it is above all state-capture and public-procurement corruption which make for bad governance. State-capture can be defined 'as the capacity to influence the formation of the basic rules of the game (i.e. laws, rules, decrees and regulation) through private payments to public officials', and public-procurement corruption is 'the efforts to alter the implementation of government policy through high-level kickbacks' (Hellman, Jones, and Kaufmann 2000: 2). In both cases, the firms engaging in these activities seek to extract rents that they would be unable to obtain by ordinary market transactions.

It should be rather obvious that the variables of good governance are hard to measure. In many cases, it is only the subjective perception of foreign investors aggregated into country risk and business risk indicators which sheds some light. Nevertheless, it is astonishing that all mentioned studies are unanimous about the result: governance matters. Hall and Jones (1999) are quite sure the can explain much of the variation in economic performance by differences in social infrastructure, and they show that the countries most influenced by Europeans over the past centuries have social infrastructures that are conducive to high levels of output. Barro's (1997, 75) similar regression of economic growth on previous colonial status did not yield significant results. Social infrastructure triggers high capital intensity (investment in physical capital), high human capital, and high labour productivity. Keefer and Knack (1997) focus on the ability of backward countries to benefit from the advantage of the latecomer or catching-up effect. They find strong support for what may be called a generalised Gerschenkron hypothesis. According to Gerschenkron (1962), the state had a beneficial effect on the catching-up of backward countries. In Keefer and Knack, institutions in general or institutional quality, mostly through government action, produce this result. Kaufmann, Kraay and Zoido-Lobatón (1999) find that strong institutions and good governance have a very large payoff in economic development. There may be a problem of the chicken and the egg. Putnam (1993) has suggested that strong institutions are the result of very long periods of cultural history, so we may assume a virtuous circle of good governance and economic welfare. Barro (1997, 86) has confirmed the aforementioned Lipset hypothesis that there is a positive relation between democracy and prior measures of prosperity. The finding of Hall and Jones concerning European influence indicates that part of the tradition can be transplanted. If the result turns out to be robust, this sheds a new light on colonial history. However, the 'warning' of Barro (1997, 59) should be also mentioned: too much democracy is bad for growth. He has found an inverted U-shaped relationship between democracy and growth: the increase of liberalisation and the rule of law enhances investment and growth, but because of popular redistribution claims, full-fledged democracies reduce their growth potential. Right now, there seems to be a lot of measurement and a comparative lack of theory. But there can be little doubt that institutions matter.

All these studies work with large samples of countries all over the world. Hellman, Jones and Kaufmann (2000) concentrate on transformation countries. Here they get the result that state capture pays only in a favourable environment, i.e. where there is a market for it. In low capture environments, the efforts are a dead weight loss for firms that nevertheless try, in contrast to public-procurement corruption, which always pays in the short run, since it is a much more direct quid pro quo. Low-capture countries are typically those where transformation of the political and economic system has either not really started yet (like Uzbekistan and Belarus) or where it has already progressed very far (Estonia, Poland, Czech Republic, Hungary, Slovenia). These are also the countries which either have had no dramatic transformation crisis yet or which have already overcome it. This prompts the conclusion that good governance may sooner be found in the pure system types, rule-of-law democracies or rule-of-party autocracies, than in transitory mixed forms. High-capture countries are those which have started economic reforms (liberalisation and privatisation), but which did not succeed in implementing correspondingly far-reaching reforms in the political and judicial systems. These are also the countries which are still in a deep economic depression. Evidently, where a weak state and strong entrepreneurs come together, the risk of state capture must be greatest. This is the danger of partial reforms or gradualism. To design and implement reforms of the political and economic system as well as policy reforms is the genuine task of government, which brings us to our last point, the role of the state in transformation.

But before turning to it, we should mention the somewhat puzzling 'paradox of the successful state' stated by Rodrik (1997, 427-28). He summarises four rules of thumb for good governance, which certainly will meet with the broadest approval:

- apply simple and uniform rules, rather than selective and differentiated ones,
- endow bureaucrats with few discretionary powers,
- incorporate safeguards against frequent, unpredictable alteration of rules,
- keep firms at arms' length from policy formulation and implementation.

'[T]hese rules were almost perfectly negatively correlated with actual outcomes' (ibid. 428). The empirical test ground in this case was East Asia, where there has been economic development with an active state and close cooperation between industry and administration. The solution to the puzzle, in my eyes, lies not in discarding the rules as simplistic, but rather in their lack of cultural embeddedness. If there is a high culture of civil service, then discretionary bureaucratic power, differentiated rules and regulations, and close personal links between managers and government officials may not end up in excessive corruption or, at least, not in suffocating protection. For Russia, on the other hand, I would surmise that the four rules of thumb are highly advisable. Generalisations which start from the theoretical assumption of opportunistic behaviour may be valid, but not necessarily applicable in societies that have developed forceful institutional and cultural checks against myopic opportunism.

THE ROLE OF THE STATE IN ECONOMIC TRANSFORMATION

Transformation is a multi-faceted process. It aims at many different levels of the politico-economic architecture of society. As far as the transformation of the economic order from plan to market is concerned, stabilisation, liberalisation, and privatisation describe the most important steps to be taken. What our introductory paragraph called the 'Washington consensus' reflected these steps and did, in fact, enjoy an even broader consensus in the region. However, stabilisation, liberalisation, and privatisation do not occur by mere fiat, they are the result of purposeful and well-balanced government policies. And the newly established private firms, whether they came into existence de novo or are privatised formerly state-owned enterprises, together with their clients, the consumers, need a legal and institutional environment that allows for uncomplicated, stable and reliable private transactions. These structures and reform policies will not develop spontaneously from the bottom up, but are generated by a political authority that designs and implements them.

There can be little question about it: transformation is a fundamental challenge for any government; for a post-communist government it is a Herculean task. Such a government must transform not only the economic, the legal and the administrative system, but also the political system which supports the very government. The paradox of the state in transformation is that it is supposed to retreat from the dominant position it held under communist rule and at the same time be the prime actor in the transition. In this, government is helped by two circumstances, by what is called period of extraordinary politics (Balcerowicz 1995, 160), i.e. the public's expectation that radical, even painful, measures have to be taken, and by the organisational void left by the old system which means that not all potentially powerful interests are already organised and politically represented. Both circumstances, however, are ambivalent in their effect upon policy. For if politicians behave opportunistically, the period of extraordinary politics allows for extraordinary private gains and the organisational void leaves the field to those who happen to be organised or in power. We might also conclude that successful transformation, the reaching of a good institutional equilibrium, is a highly improbable event.

The transition from big government to a strong state lies at the core of transforming the economic system in former communist countries. Apart from a market-friendly and effective legal system, the good equilibrium, i.e. the strong state, has a government and administration with clearly defined and limited tasks. Government and administration together are autonomous and at the same time accountable, and work under conditions of executive authority. Even if the Washington consensus is accepted as a promising policy program, it needs leadership to be put on the rails and it needs good governance to be credibly implemented and carried through. Both requirements have a political and an administrative aspect. The formulation and launching of reforms is the task of the reform team, which ideally comprises the whole government, but mostly is only a subset of it. However, the strength of the reformers within government and the strength of government within the newly emerging political system are decisive for the coherence of the reform package, its comprehensiveness, and its timing. Risk aversion and short time horizons make for impatience, whereas system transformation is an operation with long-term effects. Commitment to reform has to be independent of changing government coalitions.

Bönker (2001) has analysed in Central Eastern Europe the political economy of fiscal reform, i.e. one central element of the ten Washington commandments, and found that these factors play an important role. Tightening the fiscal regime, beneficial for long-term stability as it may be, is well known to have embarrassing transitory social costs. In any political context, this constitutes a problem, but in the context of transformation the problem must be immense, given the transitory social costs of all other measures, like restructuring, for instance. Correspondingly strong and determined must be the position of the reform team and the government that wants to implement fiscal and monetary stabilisation. It might be thought that the social costs of transition will be satisfactorily taken care of by the remains of the socialist welfare state. Such a proposition would be utterly erroneous. Even if health reform and pension reform can be considered second-phase transformation tasks, there is an immediate need for state action (see Wagener 1999). The socialist welfare system was organised around the firm. People with no firm or other organisational affiliation were in a difficult or underprivileged position. If this system is not changed, that is to say made independent of the firm, resistance against necessary restructuring measures will be particularly strong.

Looking at transformation performance, it is pretty obvious that there are transformation successes like Poland and poor transformers like Russia. All European and post-Soviet transformation countries were initially hit hard by the transitional crisis. However, while Poland's GNP reached about 125 percent of its initial value at the end of the 1990s, Russian GNP is approaching the 50 percent level. Recovery is by no means automatic. Structural reform policies are a necessary precondition, i.e. liberalisation, privatisation, and the build-up of monetary and legal institutions. But the main driving force is the supply reaction: entrepreneurs engaging in production and investment. The immediate explanation of the difference between the Polish success and the Russian failure is to be found in reform policies and the supply reaction (see also Dabrowski, Gomulka and Rostowski 2000). Careful research on the conditions of recovery and self-sustained growth in transformation countries corroborates the importance of comprehensive and rapid reform measures (de Melo et al.1997 and Berg et al. 1999). Comparing the performance of the former Soviet Union, in particular Russia, with Central Eastern Europe, in particular Poland, the analysis boils down to the conclusion that the former had slightly worse initial conditions, making the initial decline more dramatic. But the lack of recovery is mainly due to a lack of consistent reform policy. Frye and Shleifer (1997 and Shleifer 1997) experienced this at the grassroots. They interviewed Moscow and Warsaw shopkeepers about how they were helped or hindered by government in their daily business. The result was that the Russian government is less effective than the Polish in serving the market. Moscow shopkeepers feel a more severe tax and regulatory burden, a greater legal vulnerability, and a greater burden of corruption. '[T]he Polish shop keepers have their rents extracted by competitors, while the Russian ones by the bureaucrats' (Shleifer 1997, 394).

There is no better way of saying that Poland has succeeded in establishing a market economy and Russia has not.

The failure of Russia is a policy failure, or, more correctly, a governance failure, in that the reform policies were not carried out consistently and decidedly, and a failure to give space to new men with new ideas. What is lacking is a strong state and entrepreneurial activity. The Russian state is weak: physical and social security is poor, the economy is demonetised and the rule of law is not credible. The universal quest for a krysha, a cover or protection, shows that the state and its law cannot fulfil this function. Where the vital institutions of a market economy are lacking, enterprise has neither incentive nor confidence and trust to produce and invest with a long-term perspective. The only behaviour to be expected is 'grab and run'.

Governance and the emergence of new entrepreneurs explain the divergent performance of Poland and Russia. The latter is secondary, in that it may be the consequence of the former: bad governance deters entrepreneurial activity. Good governance in the context of transformation – implicitly, we have seen this already – means among others:

- a clear vision of the intended new system and recognition of its constitutive elements,
- commitment to this vision even under changing parliamentary conditions,
- implementation of the necessary reforms as soon and as decidedly as possible, and
- introduction of a sober, impartial, and predictable administration, a Weberian instead of the Leninist or, even worse, a patrimonial bureaucracy.

But why was Russia not able to establish a regime of good governance, while Poland, starting from a similar communist regime, apparently was? Several explanations have been offered: a less radical change in government structure and government personnel, different degrees of identification with the Soviet model, the historical and the prospective distance from the European Union, the constitutional history of the country, different attitudes towards legality and bureaucracy, different traditions of civil community or social capital, and religious attitudes (Shleifer 1997, Wagener 2000). These explanations are not mutually exclusive. This is not the place to assess their validity. What is important in our context is the suggestion that the relation between the private and the public sphere differs largely among countries for geographical, cultural, and historical reasons. Certain elements of good governance may be created in the short run by vigorous leadership and sound administration, but credibility and trust in continuity, or the supporting social infrastructure in general, will emerge only over time – as it seems, very long periods of time. Bad governance is not an accident that may or may not happen, it is, once entrenched in habits, attitudes, and expectations, a kind of bad equilibrium that requires special long-term efforts to be overcome.

CONCLUSIONS

The public sphere exhibits a multiplicity of organisational forms, and it performs a multiplicity of different tasks across countries and times. In many instances, it cooperates successfully with a private sphere that is integrated by competitive markets. Are we to conclude from this fact that size, function, and organisation of the state do not matter for the good functioning of the market? This is obviously not the case. There are good states delivering good governance and there are bad states delivering bad governance, whatever activities that may imply in the concrete case, and the two seem to be the result of rather lengthy evolutionary processes. The properties of good governance with respect to a private sphere integrated by the market are more or less known. Foremost stands the rule of law, binding the state not to interfere with the private incentives that promote economic activity and guaranteeing private property rights and the fulfilment of contracts between economic subjects. The welfare benefit of the rule of law derives from uniformity, transparency, and predictability. Equally well known are the properties of bad governance, prominently featuring arbitrariness, intransparent and selective treatment, diversion of private gains, corruption, and state capture. The welfare loss of bad governance derives from uncertainty, high transaction costs, and social injustice. Next to bad governance, there is market-incongruous governance, like the all-pervasive political control of the communist party-state, disregarding the separation of the public and the private sphere. It is open to question whether constitutional provisions, rather than political practice, can secure good governance for the community.

This said, the implications for the organisation of the public sphere and for the delimitation of its tasks are entirely unclear. We have seen that the market and the state are not substitutes for each other, but rather complements: where one fails, the other may step in, with some tasks where apparently both fail. The market does not function in an institutional vacuum. On the contrary, each single market needs a tailored framework of regulations, and if it is a sensitive market, like the money market, of prudent regulations. But a glance at the different national banking systems shows that many roads lead to Rome. There is no optimal set of institutions, but rather a list of common problems which can be solved in different ways. Complementarity is enhanced by the widely accepted principle of subsidiarity, which envisages a continuum from the individual to the commonwealth, giving pride of place to private economic activity. But here the consensus ends. For it is not equally clear in every case which are market failures and which are state failures. This depends in addition upon the shared views about the objectives, which may differ particularly with respect to social justice or fairness. Redistributive measures, eventually deemed necessary for fairness considerations, conflict with non-interference with private incentives. The possible solution, a change of initial endowments, is only adopted in the context of human capital, the education state, but rarely in the context of physical capital, since it seems to be in conflict with the protection of property rights.

The separation of the public and the private sphere, one of the major tasks of transformation, implies only a relative autonomy of the private sphere, which, for the purpose of certainty and reliability, has to be legally well established. Apart from that, the market model of politics makes it clear that size, scope, organisation, and tasks of the public sphere depend, in fact, upon the demand from the citizens, the private sphere. This has several consequences for the economic system. One is the possibility of bundling interests and lobbying for special treatment. Another is imprudent consumption habits. Just as demand for drugs creates drug markets, demand for subsidies creates subsidy markets (rent seeking), which may be detrimental to efficiency. A third is beggar-my-neighbour policies. In other words, an uncontrolled market for policies may degenerate the market order. Although there is, of course, no demand for bad governance, good governance is in permanent danger of deteriorating. This idea haunted Eucken and the Freiburg liberals. Their solution, a class of educated politicians dedicated to the good order and good governance, looks rather Platonic. However, there is the problem of how constitution cum culture can protect the good institutional equilibrium, which seems to be much more delicate than the bad one.

Transformation, finally, does not ease the task of the state, on the contrary the state is burdened with a task much more difficult than in normal times. The emergence of a market economy, the intended aim of the operation, is by no means a spontaneous act after the removal of the planning state's restrictions. A comprehensive program of economic policies and institutional reforms has to be designed, politically decided, and consistently implemented to bring the change about. The reform of the political system need not stay at the beginning of the process which, after the collapse of the old regime, increased the burden of the state and most probably aggravated the transitional crisis in Eastern Europe. The example of China shows that any government dedicated to reform can get far in economic transformation. It remains to be seen whether it can avoid political reform. For, after all, China's type of governance is market-incongruous. The stability of Chinese government perhaps made possible a very gradual process of reform that started in 1978 and is still not accomplished. Under less stable conditions, partial reform steps create the danger of state capture and other features of bad governance. The two attractors good governance and bad governance are at work particularly under conditions of transformation, with bad governance having special power, since neither the rule of law nor stabilising political practice are firmly grounded. Those countries which succeeded in transforming their economic and political order at the same time must have operated, it seems, under particularly advantageous conditions.

REFERENCES

Ahrens, Joachim (1999), 'Toward a Post-Washington Consensus: The Importance of Governance Structures in Less Developed Countries and Economies in Transition', in Niels Hermes and Wiemer Salverda (eds), *State, Society and Development: Lessons for Africa?*, CDS Research Report 7, Groningen: University of Groningen, pp. 18-64.

Althusius, Johannes (1995), in F. S. Carney (ed), *Politica*, Indianapolis: Liberty Fund.

Balcerowicz, Leszek (1995), *Socialism, Capitalism, Transformation*, Budapest: Central European University Press.

Barro, Robert J. (1997), *Determinants of Economic Growth. A Cross-Country Empirical Study*, Cambridge Mass.: MIT Press.

Berg, Andrew et al. (1999), 'The Evolution of Output in Transition Economies: Explaining the Differences', *IMF Working Paper*, WP **99/73**, Washington: IMF.

Bönker, Frank (2001), *The Political Economy of Fiscal Reform in Eastern Europe: A Comparative Analysis of Hungary, Poland and the Czech Republic*, Cheltenham: Edward Elgar.

Boyer, Robert (1997), 'French Statism at the Crossroads', in Colin Crouch and Wolfgang Streek (eds) (1997), *Political Economy of Modern Capitalism. Mapping Convergence & Diversity*, London: Sage, pp. 71-101.

Crouch, Colin and Wolfgang Streek (eds) (1997), *Political Economy of Modern Capitalism. Mapping Convergence & Diversity*, London: Sage.

Dabrowski, Marek, Stanislaw Gomulka and Jacek Rostowski (2000), *Whence Reform? A Critique of the Stiglitz Perspective*, Warsaw: mimeo.

Denison, Edward (1967), *Why Growth Rates Differ: Postwar Experience in Nine Western Countries*, Washington D.C.: Brookings.

Elazar, Daniel J. (1995), 'Althusius' Grand Design for a Federal Commonwealth', in Johannes Althusius, *Politica*, Indianapolis: Liberty Fund, pp. xxxv-xlvi.

Eucken, Walter (1990), *Grundsätze der Wirtschaftspolitik*, 6th ed., Tübingen: Mohr.

Frye, T. and Andrei Shleifer (1997), 'The Invisible Hand and the Grabbing Hand, American Economic Review', *Papers and Proceedings*, **87,** 354-358.

Gerschenkron, Alexander (1962), *Economic Backwardness in Historical Perspective*, Cambridge, Mass.: Harvard University Press.

Hall, Robert E. and Charles I. Jones (1999), 'Why Do Some Countries Produce So Much More Output per Worker Than Others', *Quarterly Journal of Economics*, **114,** 83-116.

Hayami, Yujiro (1998), 'Toward an East Asian Model of Economic Development', in Yujiro Hayami and Masahiko Aoki (eds), *The Institutional Foundations of East Asian Economic Development*, Basingstoke: Macmillan, pp. 3-35.

Hayek, Friedrich A. von (1960), *The Constitution of Liberty*, London: Routledge.

Hellman, Joel S., Geraint Jones and Daniel Kaufmann (2000), 'Seize the State, Seize the Day: An Empirical Analysis of State Capture and Corruption in Transition', paper for the ABCDE Conference, Washington D.C.: The World Bank.

Kaufman, Daniel, Aart Kraay and Pablo Zoido-Lobatón (1999), 'Governance Matters', *Policy Research Working Paper*, **2195**, Washington D.C.: The World Bank.

Kaufman, Daniel, Aart Kraay and Pablo Zoido-Lobatón (2000), 'Aggregating Governance Indicators', *Policy Research Working Paper*, **2196**, Washington D.C.: The World Bank.

Keefer, Philip and Stephen Knack (1997), 'Why Don't Poor Countries Catch Up? A Cross-National Test of an Institutional Explanation', *Economic Inquiry*, **35**, 590-602.

Kläver, Michael (2000), *Die Verfassung des Marktes – F.A. v. Hayeks Lehre von Staat und Markt im Spiegel grundgesetzlicher Staats- und Verfassungsrechtslehre*, Stuttgart: Lucias & Lucius.

Laski, Kazimierz and Amit Bhaduri (1997), 'Lessons To Be Drawn from Main Mistakes in the Transition Strategy', in Salvatore Zecchini (ed), *Lessons from the Economic Transition. Central and Eastern Europe in the 1990s*, Dordrecht: Kluwer, pp. 103-121.

de Melo, Martha et al. (1997), 'Circumstances and Choice: The Role of Initial Conditions and Policies in Transition Economies', *Policy Research Working Paper*, **1866**, Washington D.C.: The World Bank.

Przeworski, Adam and Fernando Limongi (1993), 'Political Regimes and Economic Growth', *Journal of Economic Perspectives*, **7**, 51-69.

Putnam, Robert D. (1993), *Making Democracy Work. Civic Traditions in Modern Italy*, Princeton: Princeton University Press.

Richter, Rudolf and Eirik G. Furubotn (1999), *Neue Institutionenökonomik*, 2nd ed., Tübingen: Mohr Siebeck.

Rodrik, Dani (1997), 'The 'paradoxes' of the successful state', *European Economic Review*, **41**, 411-442.

Shleifer, Andrei (1997), 'Government in transition', *European Economic Review*, **41**, 385-410.

Stiglitz, Joseph (1999a), *Whither Reform?*, Washington D.C.: World Bank.

Stiglitz, Joseph (1999b), *Quis Custodiet Ipsos Custodes?*, Paris: World Bank.

Stiglitz, Joseph et al. (1989), Arnold Heertje (ed), *The Economic Role of the State*, Amsterdam: Bank Insinger de Beaufort.

Wagener, Hans-Jürgen (1999), 'Social Security – A Second Phase Transformation Phenomenon?', in Katharina Müller, Andreas Ryll and Hans-Jürgen Wagener (eds), *Transformation of Social Security: Pensions in Central-Eastern Europe*, Heidelberg: Physica, pp. 13-30.

Wagener, Hans-Jürgen (2000), *Why Has Russia Missed the Boat?*, Frankfurt (Oder), mimeo.

4. Comment

Mark Oelmann

In his article Wagener gives an interesting overview on various studies. These support his view that not every state is appropriate to install and maintain a properly functioning market order. In addition they prove that the state even faces a couple of more specific tasks in the transformation process. A number of these both theoretical and rather empirical aspects would be worth discussing by a commentator. Yet, I will adhere to the main line of reasoning neatly developed by Wagener.

In the first part of the comment, I will restate Wagener's line of argument ending in his statement that a successful transition would have been higly improbable and that the successful countries must probably have operated under particularly advantageous conditions. He ascribes the latter to a high level of social capital. This has to be analysed in order to obtain a more complete picture of a country. Whereas Wagener chooses an also convincing kind of ad hoc observing and theorising, I will present an approach used by Leipold. It is not an 'economic theory of social capital' approach but aids in structuring the empirical findings.

Wagener commences with the notion that the cooperation of the market and the state may be very fruitful in a world with transaction costs on the one hand. On the other hand the assignment of tasks to one or the other realm would depend on the specific situation determined by place and time. Put differently, markets and states are therefore complements rather than substitutes. Thus the specific relationship between the state and the economy cannot be defined absolutely even though we may have some theoretical insight into constructing both an economic and a political order.

Regarding the elements of an economic order, Wagener refers to Eucken, who was one of the founders of the German ORDO-school. Eucken differentiates between constituent and regulating principles. The former principles establish a functioning market system. They comprise e.g. private property rights, freedom of trade, freedom of contract, stable money, hard budget constraints and clear liability obligations. The latter principles, consisting e.g. of competition control, correction of external effects and redistribution of market income are meant to protect the already formed economic order against degeneration. Wagener formulates that even the most perfect market economy would need such elements or institutions as behaviour constraining rules and organisations. In raising the institutional aspect of the economic order, he correctly stresses that a misconception ensues from the history of economic theory. It is presented by assuming that markets can be created instantaneously.

As markets do not evolve spontaneously, they have to be actively installed by someone. Eucken has assigned the task of implementing these principles to the state. Due to the findings of the New Institutional Economics and, in particular, the Political Economy of the State, Wagener is correct in mentioning that a strong and benevolent state cannot be taken for granted anymore. In a political market, politicians act as entrepreneurs who for the most part mainly pursue self-interests. Even in an established western democracy it is a rather difficult undertaking to set and enforce formal institutions.

Whereas a quite functioning state exists at least in a western democracy, Wagener points out that the market and the state in transition countries co-evolved. He argues that not only the economic but also the political system was supply-driven. While the plan determined the provision of goods, the socialist government provided for its people without actually including them in the decision processes. As Wagener summarises, the totalitarian state prohibited the voice option by censorship, the vote option by banning opposition and the option to leave the country by closing the Iron Curtain. Therefore, transformation can in fact be regarded as an 'Herculean task' for a post-communist government.

In the parallel evolvement of both the modern market and the modern state, an organisational void becomes apparent. For Wagener this period of time, where neither the rule of law nor a stabilising political practice is firmly grounded, was determined by the 'paradox of the state in transformation'. On the one hand, the state is supposed to retreat from the dominant position held under communist rule. On the other hand, at the same time the state should be the main actor in transition. According to Wagener, a successful transformation process had to be highly improbable and must have operated under particularly advantageous conditions.

Nevertheless, some countries have been successful. To explain this success, it appears necessary to specify these particularly advantageous conditions. Since the entire workshop deals with the analysis of constitutions in the transition process to gain more positive knowledge as a prerequisite of each normative theory, Wagener defines these advantageous conditions in a broader sense. In my understanding, his main message seems to be that it isworth taking a closer look at specific constitutions but, in the same way, other institutions have to be looked at too. Using the expressions of the New Institutional Economics, the hypothesis is that the informal institutions have to be observed in the same way as the formal ones when the institutional setting of a society is analysed. Here culture defined as the whole institutional framework matters!

How do we actually approach these particularly advantageous conditions? Wagener emphasises that some type of ad hoc observation and ad hoc theorising may aid in gaining some deeper positive insights into the relation between the state and the economy in the transition process. He discovers a number of highly interesting aspects. For example, he discusses Rodrik's 'paradox of the successful state'. In criticising Rodrik, Wagener comes to the conclusion that the presented four rules for good governance are not simplisistic but merely lack cultural embeddedness. According to Wagener, 'social capital' best describes this embeddedness. To draw a full circle social capital defines the way how the market and the state complement each other.

For the most part, I completely agree with Wagener. Nevertheless, his view of 'social capital' seems to be comparable to the technological progress in old exogenous growth theories. Undoubtedly, it is very important but is not really tangible. Although Wagener's argumentation of ad hoc observing and ad hoc theorising is convincing and probably the only choice one has, a closer look at the research of economic institutionalism is instructive. I do not see a satisfying 'economic theory of social capital' yet, but Leipold's approach which I will present later, may originate some ideas of what in fact to look at when we speak of social capital.

Wagener already mentions the main idea which can also be found in Leipold's argument. He mentions that uncertainty is the major impediment for investment. On the one hand, uncertainty can be reduced by establishing and maintaining an effective economic order and by following a number of political rules. Wagener mentions the Rodrik rules. Eucken (1990, 334-337 or Chapter XIX) may help as well. On the other hand, uncertainty may also be diminished by trust. At this point, Wagener does not go into detail but states that investment in social capital would be a sine qua non for economic development (see also Fukuyama 1995, 416, 418). On the other hand, Leipold (2000) asks what actually generates trust and how it can be described.

Before turning to Leipold as a prerequisite I have to summarise some components of North's New Institutional Economics even though they may already be well-known. My argument mainly builds on North (1994, see also Hayek, 1969). The starting point is the idea mentioned earlier that a number of institutions, i.e. behaviour constraining rules and organisations, have to be installed for a successful transition .

The terms 'institution' and 'organisation' are essential for his considerations. For North, institutions are humanly devised constraints which structure human interaction. He distinguishes between formal and informal ones and their respective enforcement characteristics. Rules, laws, constitiution etc. are regarded as formal institutions, whereas norms and conventions are examples for informal ones. Together with technology, these institutions determine the transaction and transformation costs. It is their main purpose to facilitate exchange via the predictability of human beings and, hence, to solve Prisoner's Dilemma situations as far as possible. Formal rules set by polity are in accordance with informal ones, if they emerge from the system itself. In this case, both tend to reinforce each other (Pejovich 1998, 10). The opposite is true if formal institutions conflict with the informal ones. Such a disparity leads to high transaction costs in the form of individual uncertainty. This will be further discussed later.

Naturally, a potential conflict exists if formal institutions are externally imposed on a society. A transition from a centrally planned economy to a market economy per definition will change the formal institutions, the rules of the game. Then, the principal question is whether the informal institutions succeed in preventing the old rules of the game from changing or whether they will adjust so that they are again complements to the new formal rules. Even this short consideration reveals the misconception of neoclassical economists concerning a possible spontaneous reorganisation (see also Leipold 1997, 52, 65).

Having introduced institutions as the rules of the game, we may regard the organisations as the players. An 'organisation' is the second important term to clarify here. A group of individuals is characterised by some common purpose to achieve certain objectives. Organisations are e.g. political parties, enterprises, churches, schools, or trade unions. They reflect the opportunities provided by the set of institutions. Wagener quotes the Russian Beresovsky who is said to have the opinion that currently the best investment would be in politics. If we consider institutions as the incentive structure of a society an incentive for an organisation to seek rents surely is an impediment for economic growth.

With the definitions of both an institution and an organisation, it is obvious that the interaction between these two constantly shapes the evolution of an economy. Polity can at first only change the formal institutions. Naturally, we may consider some formal institutions as being helpful for a transition process and others not. As mentioned earlier, we know the main components of a targeted economic and a political order. Undoubtedly, these normative concepts should be the clear vision of the intended new system. Yet, that is all we can say!

The recent history has witnessed that we cannot expect organisations such as political parties, an administration, a jurisdiction, etc. as organisations to spontaneously emerge. Therefore, the predictability of the rule of law, i.e. the enforcement of formal institutions, also can not be guaranteed. Formal institutions understood as incentives for organisations to perform in the desired way can be developed to a certain degree. For example Shleifer (1997, 402) observes that local politicians in Russia have no incentives to support private businesses. Changes in the formal institutions, such as enforcing the politicians' liability for their tax base, may help to change their behaviour. Through e.g. financial grants from abroad or a promised full EU-membership (see Salzberger and Voigt in this volume), one may gain at least partial influence on promoting a 'political entrepreneur', i.e. someone who is able to communicate the consequent and unavoidable political action to the public.

We may conclude that certain elements, e.g. formal rules, could be installed, whereas credibility and trust have to exist already or alternatively have to emerge over longer periods of time. In order to discover the tasks for future research on positive economics scrutinising the term 'social capital' is useful. Here, social capital is defined as the informal norms that promote cooperation between individuals (Fukuyama 2000, 3). Cooperation in possible conflict situations will only emerge if the individuals restrain from pursuing their self-interest. We may regard an economy to possess social capital if the interest of other persons is taken into account by individuals during their decision-making-process and if the possibility to defect in a Prisoner's Dilemma situation (Leipold 2000, 14) is dropped. Therefore, social capital not only arises from iterated Prisoner's Dilemma situations but is also a byproduct of religion, tradition, shared historical experiences and other factors that lie outside the control of the state (Fukuyama 2000, 15).

Following Leipold (2000, 14), the problem of establishing credibility and trust as a prerequisite for economic change can, therefore, be reduced to a problem of morale. What are the factors leading to a moral-bound behaviour and how does someone incorporate this attitude, he asks?

In a first step, Leipold (2000, 15-21) argues that moral-bound informal institutions can be divided into three groups, namely emotionally-bound, religiously-bound and ideologically-bound informal institutions. Secondly, he identifies the sources for the first group as moral sentiments (and reason), for the second one as belief (and moral sentiments, reason) and for the third kind of moral-bound informal institutions as conviction (and moral sentiments, reason, belief). Finally, by analysing anthropological and psychological research results, he concludes that differing education, experience and learning processes form an individual conscience. These processes are the main variables for explaining the path dependency of institutional evolution.

As mentioned earlier, Leipold's approach is not a kind of 'economic theory of social capital'. Nevertheless, it may help to structure the different empirical, theoretical and historical findings. Leipold himself applies his scheme to differentiate between the German and the US culture. He draws highly interesting conclusions of e.g. how to organise the social security systems in the different countries. Due to the different path dependencies of Germany and the US he gathers that the policy implications have to be different too.

In the diagnosis of the relation between the state and the economy Leipold and Wagener therefore share the same view. Market and state are complements rather than substitutes. To define the specific relation, e.g. in a transition country, there is no doubt that it is important to analyse the formal institutions like constitutions and, especially, their development over time. Yet, we have to focus on the informal institutions too to attain a complete positive picture of the evolution of a society and why the formal rules of the game were shaped the way they were. How can 'constitution *cum* culture' protect – we may add generate – a good institutional equilibrium? as Wagener asks.

In approaching the informal institutions the main methodological question which has already been discussed over decades remains and surely cannot be solved here. So, I agree with Boettke (2000, 4) that a 'thick' description is only possible with the guidance of a 'thin' one. Put differently, a detailed observation can only be meaningful when it is integrated into a broader theoretical context.

REFERENCES

Boettke, Peter J. (2000), 'Why Culture Matters: Economics, Politics and the Imprint of History', *Peter J. Boettke (NYU) – Working Papers*, obtainable from: http://www.gmu.edu/departments/economics/pboettke/culture.htm or http://www.econ.nyu.edu/user/boettke/culture.htm.

Eucken, Walter (1990), *Grundsätze der Wirtschaftspolitik*, 6th ed., Tübingen: Mohr.

Fukuyama, Francis (1995), *Konfuzius und Marktwirtschaft – Der Konflikt der Kulturen*, München: Kindler.

Fukuyama, Francis (2000), 'Social Capital and Civil Society', *IMF Working Paper*, **WP/00/74**, Washington: IMF, also obtainable from: http://www.imf.org/ external/pubs/ft/wp/2000/wp0074.pdf.

Hayek, Friedrich August von (1969), 'Arten der Ordnung', in Friedrich August von Hayek, *Freiburger Studien – Gesammelte Aufsätze*, Tübingen: Mohr, pp. 32-46.

Leipold, Helmut (1997), 'Der Zusammenhang zwischen gewachsener und gesetzter Ordnung: Einige Lehren aus den postsozialistischen Reformerfahrungen', in Dieter Cassel (ed), *Institutionelle Probleme der Systemtransformation*, Berlin: Duncker & Humblot, pp. 43-68.

Leipold, Helmut (2000), 'Die kulturelle Einbettung der Wirtschaftsordnungen: Bürgergesellschaft versus Sozialstaatsgesellschaft', in Bettina Wentzel and Dirk Wentzel (eds), *Wirtschaftlicher Systemvergleich Deutschland/USA*, Stuttgart: Lucius und Lucius, pp. 1-52.

North, Douglass C. (1994), 'Economic Performance Through Time', *American Economic Review*, **84** (3), 359-368.

Pejovich, Svetozar (1998), 'Toward a Theory of the Effects of the Interaction of Formal and Informal Institutions on Social Stability and Economic Development', *Freiburg Discussion Papers on Constitutional Economics*, **98/2**, also obtainable from: http://www.vwl.uni-freiburg.de/fakultaet/ wipo/discpap/ 98_2bw.pdf.

Shleifer, Andrei (1997), 'Government in transition', *European Economic Review*, **41**, 385-410.

5. The Demand for Constitutional Law

Katharina Pistor[1]

INTRODUCTION

The transition economies of Central and Eastern Europe and the former Soviet Union have, over the past ten years, implemented far-reaching legal reforms. These reforms encompassed all major areas of the law from constitutional law over civil and commercial to administrative and criminal law, but encompassed also procedural rules as well as laws on the organisation of courts and the legal profession. Overall, constitutional and civil/commercial lawmaking has taken the lead over administrative and criminal law reform. This reflects what were perceived to be the fundamental issues of transition: the political transition from a one party system to a pluralistic rule of law based system on the one hand, and the economic transition from a centrally planned economy to a market based system on the other. In the world of policy makers, countries need three things: reasonable laws, adequate institutions, and market-oriented incentives (Gray and Hendely 1997). They got the first item mostly by way of legal transplants from the West. The task now is to work on items two and three, as lack of law enforcement in transition economies has become an endemic problem (Kaufmann and Kaliberda 1996). This paper suggests that the problem of lack of enforcement may run deeper than is commonly assumed. Weak enforcement is generally perceived to be a supply side problem, which could therefore be fixed by improving these institutions. Weak enforcement may, however, signal a lack of demand for legal rules and for the institutions that enforce them (Pistor 1996). Without a demand for law, law will not be effective, as the experience of two hundred years of legal transplantation from the West to other parts of the world documents (Berkowitz, Pistor and Richard 2002). The reason is that no state controls sufficient resources to ensure legal compliance by means of coercion only. Every formal legal system therefore relies heavily on voluntary compliance. The challenge of developing effective formal legal systems is to ensure that they respond to and foster demand. This paper develops an analytical framework for the demand for constitutional law. Its major point is that to be effective the constitution should establish a credible framework for solving the major cleavages in a given society. What constitutes a major cleavage differs from country to country. This calls for different legal solutions in different countries, but also requires that the key parties to a conflict participate in or at least support the lawmaking process. Absent legitimacy of the lawmaking process, the constitution will fail to solve the underlying cleavages. As a result problem solving will take place outside the constitution, undermining the respect for and effectiveness of the formal legal framework.

The paper proceeds as follows. Section 2 discusses the relation between formal law and social norms and its implication for the importance of a demand for law. Section 3 links this discussion to recent findings about the impact of the process of lawmaking on the effectiveness of legal institutions. Section 4 applies the lessons of these findings to the process of constitution making. It suggests that as in other areas, a critical level of identification with, or internalisation of, formal legal devices is necessary for them to matter in practice. Section 5 applies this framework to the Russian constitution of 1993. The paper argues that the process of lawmaking impaired the subsequent use of constitutional mechanisms to solve major cleavages in Russian politics. The major cleavages discussed are the allocation of control rights over the economic reform process between the president and the parliament on the one hand, and over the future of the federation between the center and the regions, on the other. As a result, the constitution plays only a marginal role for conflict resolution with respect to these issues. Section 6 makes suggestion for future research and concludes.

FORMAL LAW, SOCIAL NORMS AND THE DEMAND FOR LAW

The process of lawmaking as used in this paper refers to the process of developing legal rules that are enforced by the state in a particular jurisdiction. There is an extensive literature on the development of social norms and informal rules (Coleman 1990; Cooter 1996; Ellickson 1991) as well as a growing literature on the interaction between informal and formal rules (Knight 1998; Sunstein 1996).[2] Social norms develop among members that belong to the same social group. They are effective only as long as members of that group observe them. Lack of observance implies that the norm ceases to exist. Existing social norms are transmitted to new members through a process of internalisation, which is re-enforced by social sanctions. New norms develop in response to new challenges. To become part of the prevailing normative system, norms must be widely accepted. Changes in normative systems depend on the authority of the first movers, the affinity of the new to pre-existing norms, and the pressure the social group faces in adapting to a changing environment.

Formal lawmaking differs from the production of social norms in that the jurisdiction of formal rules is not determined by membership and common observance of norms, but by the reach of the state. Thus, formal law can transgress social groups and create norms irrespective of their affinity to existing normative systems. Formal rules can exist on the books without ever being enforced. Their enforcement is determined by the allocation of resources to coercive law enforcement. The primary resource of the state, however, is its citizenry. The ability of the state to tax its citizens depends on its ability to offer public goods for which there is a substantial demand. If the taxes charged exceed the benefits citizens expect from the state, they will opt out of the formal legal system. The more people opt out, the lower the state's ability to provide public goods, leading to a downward spiral. The result is a weak state and high social costs, because transactions that benefit from the provisioning of public goods will not be carried out or only at substantial transaction costs. The common view of the nature of public goods, of course, suggests that precisely because reliance on market forces alone will result in under-investment, the state steps in, and as a result, everybody is better off. This view assumes that the state commands the resources to force all dissenters to comply, i.e. that they will pay their taxes voluntarily. If this is not the case, the success of state intervention will depend on a general consensus that the production of public goods is legitimate and desirable, even though the individual may not be convinced that the specific purpose is a worthwhile cause. Demand for public goods thus refers to a general consensus about the legitimacy of state action, not necessarily to the production of a particular public good. Yet, constant failure to meet demand will undermine the legitimacy of state actions.

The question then is, how legitimacy is created. This paper proposes two crucial ingredients: General alignment of formal norms with underlying social norms; and legitimacy of the lawmaking process. If the formal law fails to provide solutions for actual conflicts, it will be ignored. An important implication is that there is not an optimal law independent of pre-existing norms and beliefs. The alignment of formal with social norms (Cooter 1996) does not imply the need for unanimous or even majority consent about the desirability of each formal rule. If the process of lawmaking is generally perceived to be legitimate, even rules that do not find widespread support may be observed. Only when the result of formal lawmaking consistently contradicts underlying beliefs, will the legitimacy of the lawmaking process be called into question. The following two stylised examples of lawmaking in a weak state and lawmaking in an all-powerful state illustrate this point.

The emergence of formal legal systems, i.e. a comprehensive body of law enforced by the state, is associated with the emergence of the modern state in Europe (Ertman 1997).[3] Rulers who were able to enforce peace within their own lands and collect resources form their subjects were at an advantage over others that failed to do so. Enforcing the peace of the land implied that state rules prevailed over the interests of social groups who used self-help and feuds to enforce their rights. The success of these new fragile institutions depended on the legitimacy of the transfer of law enforcement (and by implication lawmaking) to state institutions. At a time when the state did not command a police force and a well-developed criminal justice system, the major impact of state intervention was to disallow private enforcement and to induce parties to accept a court's ruling instead (Jacobi 1998). Parties opted into this system of formal law enforcement, because they expected a significant gain, namely the discontinuity of widespread feuds and anarchy. The sustainability of this system depended on the respect for court rulings. This was crucial, because private actors rather than the state enforced court verdicts, as the latter lacked the necessary resources. The major sanction for violating the peace of the land was for the delinquent to be placed outside the protection of the law: he was declared 'vogelfrei" (free as a bird) and as a result could not seek legal protection to enforce his own rights. The effectiveness of this sanction depended on actions taken by other private parties, i.e. they would terminate business relations and refuse to deal with this person in the future. If courts consistently contradicted what was widely perceived to be just, their rulings had little chance of being enforced. Still, conflicts between court rulings and social norms were unavoidable in a conflict situation in which both parties based their claims on conflicting social norms. The respect for court verdicts therefore hinged on a general consensus that being inside the law was superior to being outside it, i.e. that state intervention was overall legitimate.

While the alignment of formal law with social norms and legitimacy of the lawmaking process is crucial when the state is powerless, a powerful state should be able to do without much reliance on social norms, or legitimacy for that matter. Dictatorships and totalitarian regimes have demonstrated time and again that it is possible to rule against society for long periods of time. While these regimes in fact do not command unlimited resources, the threat of arbitrarily enforced and excessive punishment is a powerful means to disguise the state's actual weakness and keep the public at bay. In addition, such regimes typically invest heavily in propaganda and mass education, i.e., they seek to create top-down the social consensus that shall legitimise their regime. These strategies become vulnerable when the power of the ideology wears off, i.e. when the regime fails to deliver, and when an increasing part of the population senses its actual weakness. The toppling of the communist regimes in Central-Eastern Europe and the former Soviet Union and most recently the ousting of former President Milosevic of Yugoslavia provide ample evidence of the vulnerability of regimes that rely on a combination of ideology and perceived threat rather than on legitimacy and social consensus.

It is tempting to describe modern constitutional democracies as lying somewhere between these two extremes – the weak state that depends on private law enforcement on the one hand, and the totalitarian state that uses arbitrary and excessive enforcement to achieve high levels of voluntary compliance on the other. This would, however, miss an important characteristic of constitutional democracies, namely that in these regimes the state draws its legitimacy from the formal legal system. Constitutionalism rests on the premise that the state is at once subject and object of the law. State action is not unlimited, but confined by formal legal principles that establish the procedure for the transfer of power, allocation of rights and responsibility among different branches of the government, and the protection of fundamental rights. Constitutionalism imposes important limitations on the principle of democracy, or the responsiveness of the legal systems to changing demands of society (Holmes 1995). The principles enshrined in the constitution can typically be changed only with supermajority and some constitutions place the fundamental principles of the state order entirely beyond the reach of the legislature.[4]

The fundamental importance of the formal legal order in constitutional democracies shifts attention to the design of this order, to constitutional engineering, and away from the problem of social norms, and the demand for law. It is therefore not surprising that the transplantation of constitutions that have withstood the test of time in other countries has been seen as a viable strategy to build a similar order elsewhere (Sartori 1997). However, the crucial role the formal legal order plays in constitutional democracies does not mean that the link between the state and society can be dispensed with entirely. Only to the extent that the constitutional order is perceived to be legitimate does the state benefit from the presumption that its actions are also legitimate. Where a general consensus about the legitimacy of the formal legal order does not exist, voluntary compliance with the law will be low, which in turn undermines the respect for the formal legal order. The key question thus becomes what it takes to build a legitimate constitutional order.

LAWMAKING AND EFFECTIVE LEGAL INSTITUTIONS

The development of a constitutional order is one element in the increasing formalisation of legal relationships since the late eighteenth century. Before turning to the specific tasks of building a legitimate constitutional order, a brief discussion of the evolution of formal law therefore seems in order.

Virtually all countries around the world today have a well-developed formal legal system, consisting of a constitution and a set of formal rules governing commercial and civil relations as well as the right of the state to inflict punishment or to impose administrative regulations and sanctions. Countries can be divided into those that developed their formal legal order internally and those that copied it from other countries. The first group is called 'legal origins', the second 'legal transplants'' (Berkowitz, Pistor and Richard 2002).[5] The group of legal origins comprises primarily countries in Western Europe, especially England, France, and Germany. The legal systems of France and Germany, though to a lesser extent England, were strongly influenced by Roman law and they have also borrowed extensively from each other. Nevertheless, their classification as origin countries is justifiable on the grounds that despite their geographic proximity and common roots, these countries produced quite distinct legal orders, suggesting a strong influence of domestic actors on the lawmaking process. The rest of the world received their formal legal order from origin countries by way of colonisation, warfare, or through voluntary reception. The strong influence of origin countries on transplants is best documented in the area of civil law.

Countries around the world are commonly classified as countries that belong to the English common law family, the French or the German civil law families (Glendon, Gordon and Osakwe 1994; Merryman, Clark and Haley 1994; Zweigert and Kötz 1998). The dissemination of constitutional law does not follow the same pattern as that of civil law. For example, for civil law the Latin American countries belong to the French civil law family, while they borrowed their constitutional order to a large extent from the United States (Kolesar 1990). For the current discussion, this is less relevant than the fact that the constitutional order was also derived from foreign models.

The remarkable similarities in the law on the books of members of the same legal family raises the question, whether legal systems in these countries also perform similarly. We lack systematic data for the performance of the constitutional order. However, recent findings on the effect of transplanting civil and commercial codes in the nineteenth century and its impact on the development of effective legal institutions hold potentially important lessons for the functioning of constitutions. Berkowitz et al. (2002) coded 49 countries according to the origin of their formal legal systems, classifying them as either legal origins or legal transplants.[6] Regressing the source of formal legal systems (origins vs. transplants) against indicators for the effectiveness of legal institutions *today*, Berkowitz et al. find that legal institutions in origin countries are significantly more effective than in transplant countries.[7] The results hold even when controlling for GDP, refuting the suggestion that the wealth of countries alone determines the effectiveness of their institutions (La Porta, Lopez-de-Silanes, Shleifer, and Vishny 1998). From which legal families transplants received their formal legal order is largely irrelevant for these results. In other words, legal families have virtually no predictive value for the effectiveness of legal institutions.

The results appear to be rather discouraging for any attempt to transplant law from one country to another. Yet, the same study finds that in transplant countries where a demand for the transplanted formal legal order existed at the time of the transplant, the effectiveness of legal institutions is not statistically significantly different from origin countries. Demand is captured by two variables: an independent choice over and/or the adaptation of the transplanted legal order to the country's own needs; or the existence of a population in the law receiving country that was familiar with the fundamental principles of the formal legal order. Countries that exhibit either of these demand variables are called receptive transplants. Examples for countries that adapted foreign transplants include Japan, Chile and Argentina.

Examples of countries that were familiar with the transplanted legal order are neighbouring countries of Germany or France in Europe who shared the same legal traditions as well as the settler colonies of England, US, Canada, Australia, and New Zealand. The settlers 'brought the law with them', rather than the law being imposed on a society with a very different social order, as in occupied territories of Southeast Asia and Africa.[8] Countries that lack these features, i.e. on whom the formal legal order was imposed without adaptations and without any regard for the familiarity of the population with the transplanted law are called unreceptive transplants. Most former colonies are unreceptive transplants. They are saddled with significantly less effective legal institutions.

Analyses of legal development in transition economies support the importance of initial conditions in the law receiving countries for the development of effective legal institutions. Transition economies that had developed their own formal legal order prior to World War II exhibit significantly more effective legal institutions than countries that lacked similar preconditions (Pistor, Raiser and Gelfer 2000). By contrast, countries that either made no effort to reform the legal order they had earlier received as part of the Ottoman or the Austro-Hungarian empire after acquiring independence following World War I, or countries that had not developed a formal legal order before becoming part of the Soviet Union, have much weaker legal institutions today. Major efforts to improve the law on the books in these countries have not neutralised the negative effect the weak institutions have had for the development of financial systems in these countries.

To summarise, past experience with the development of a formal legal order around the world suggests that the transplantation of formal law alone is not sufficient for building an effective legal order. For the latter, the initial conditions, or the demand for the received order is crucial. The following section discusses the implications of these findings for the development of constitutionalism.

BUILDING A LEGITIMATE CONSTITUTIONAL ORDER

The adoption of a constitution usually signals the emergence of an independent nation that has acquired the right to determine its own affairs. Constitutions are typically not imposed, but are adopted by the people inhabiting the territory that comprises the state. Thus, the very act of adopting a constitution seems to place countries in the category of receptive transplants. After all, they are free to make an independent choice about which model to adopt or to design their own constitution.

Constitution making may, however, be captured by an interest group that uses its current dominance to impose a structure that benefits its interests rather than building a constitutional order for a broad constituency. Or it may be used to signal respect for rule of law, while power is allocated and enforced outside the constitutional order. Thus, the adoption of a constitution alone does not mean that there is a demand for the particular order that is adopted. The formal constitutional order is of relevance only, if the allocation of rights and responsibilities in the constitution has a significant impact on how rights and responsibilities are allocated and exercised in society. This does not imply that the constitutional order must be a true and complete reflection of the allocation of power in society or vice versa, that any evidence of power and influence that cannot be traced to the constitution implies irrelevance of the formal constitutional order. Rather, the relevance of the constitution is contingent on its ability to solve major cleavages of the society it governs. The more divided a society on ethnic, religious, ideological grounds, in the distribution of wealth and social power, the more complex the task (Chua 1998). A constitutional order that fails to meet these challenges, however, is unlikely to have much more than a book life.

Developing constitutional mechanisms to solve major cleavages in society requires that the parties who represent different fractions participate in the drafting and/or ratification process. Public support by representatives of organised social interests seems more important than a general support expressed by all the people in a referendum. Disorganised individuals may support a formal order simply for its own sake. The support of the organised elite is crucial in order to commit it to using constitutional rather than extra-constitutional mechanisms to solve future conflicts.

Assessing the relevance of the constitutional order requires the identification of major cleavages in a given country. Major cleavages are defined as key issues of potentially prolonged conflict in a society. Examples include ethnic and religious divides or conflicts between different regions that comprise a state, which frequently have their roots in ethnic and/or religious conflicts or in significant differences in their access to wealth and political control.

There are important historical and contemporary examples for the creation of a formal framework based on the cooperation of representatives from both sides of the religious or ethnic divide. For example, a major contribution to the (relative) success of the Peace of Westfalia (1648) was the inclusion of the different religious factions in the peacemaking process. The parties committed to respect their respective religions and that of their subjects. The formal device they used to buttress this commitment was unanimous rather than a majority vote for all matters concerning religious affairs (Wyduckel 1998).

Similarly, the South African transition from apartheid to the new 1994 constitutional order can be attributed to the participation of both parties in the design of the transitory legal order. The creation of specific institutional mechanisms for the incorporation of particular interests helped the old elite embrace this process despite the fact that it would almost certainly be deprived of direct political control in the new order (Klug 2000). An important element was the instigation of a constitutional court even prior to the adoption of the new constitution and the inclusion of previous as well as new judges. Moreover, the creation of a truth and reconciliation commission ensured that past atrocities were addressed, but the creation of a new constitutional order was not made conditional upon resolving them. Not all institutional devices were genuine new inventions, nor were all of them successful. The point is that borrowing took place in light of the specific conflicts that existed in South Africa and that their creation was supported by the opposing fractions.

Temporary political or economic circumstances may develop into major cleavages, because mechanisms to resolve conflicts are absent, or they aggravate rather than mitigate them. An example is the allocation of political control rights under the constitution of the Weimar Republic in Germany. The lost war, the political turmoil following the abdication of the monarch, and the deteriorating economic conditions created the potential for conflict in an otherwise relatively homogenous society. The conflicting interests were represented in parliament, but a combination of party fractionalisation, high turnover of governments, and the shift of control rights to the president who had extensive emergency powers increasingly deprived parliament of its political leverage. As a result, parliament lost its function to resolve conflicts to the street and to a president who sought to establish law and order top down. In what can be described as conscious institutional design to avoid these problems, the *Grundgesetz* (Basic Law) of 1949 forced parliament to resolve important conflicts by enhancing its responsibility. Parliament was refused the right to dissolve itself and its right to replace the government prior to the end of its term was made conditional upon its ability to elect a new government (constructive vote of no-confidence). Moreover, the strong president of the Weimar Republic was replaced with a figurehead. Political power was vested with the government, headed by a chancellor who was directly accountable to parliament. Party fractionalisation was contained by the five per cent clause. Whatever the merits of these formal solutions analysed in isolation, against the background of the political experience of the Weimar Republic and its aftermath they are perceived to add to the political stability that was achieved in the German Federal Republic. Attempts to dissolve the parliament have been rare, most likely because of the high threshold established by the law for dissolving the parliament. Only one constructive vote of no confidence and three votes of confidence were ever posed,[9] and the instrumentalization of the vote of confidence as a means to circumvent these high barriers have been severely critized.[10]

An important lesson from these experiences is that the process of norm transmission by way of internalisation is not confined to social norms. A shared consensus about the important role of institutions to resolve conflicts creates a commitment by parties to use these institutions in future conflicts. This raises the prospects for success, which in turn re-enforces the commitment to the institutional design.

CONSTITUTIONALISM IN TRANSITION ECONOMIES: THE CASE OF RUSSIA

This section applies the above framework to the development of constitutionalism in Russia. Russia is a particularly interesting case, because a constitution was adopted after the major cleavages of the transition process had become apparent. Moreover, unlike the countries of Central and Eastern Europe, who sought to re-establish their link with the Western legal tradition, Russia was committed to find its own way. Thus constitutional development in Russia exhibited greater potential for innovative solutions for genuine Russian problems. Finally, the size and diversity of the country facilitates the identification of major cleavages, which in smaller and more homogenous countries may be more subtle. Still, the framework developed in this paper is equally applicable to other transition economies.

The major cleavages that had become apparent by the summer of 1993 were the struggle between the president and the parliament over who should control the economic reform process, and the relation between the federal government and the regions on the other. Both issues were closely intertwined as parties to each conflict tried to benefit from and build coalitions with parties to the other conflict. Their particular significance resulted from the fact that whoever obtained control during the decisive first years after the end of the communist regime would have substantial leverage over the reallocation of economic and political control rights in the country. In the conflict between the federation and the region, control rights over natural resources and taxation were at the forefront. In the conflict between the president and the parliament it was the control over the budget and the privatisation process. For neither case did the existing constitutional order provide a framework for resolving the dispute.

The wave of declarations of independence by republics and other subjects of the Russian Federation following Russia's own independence called into question the viability of the existing formal order. It had rested on the presumption that the relationship between the federation and the 89 republics, autonomous republics and regions was a purely intra-statal relationship. The 'subjects' of the Russian Federation now called for a new relationship based on treatises between quasi-independent entities. In March 1992, a federal treaty was signed between the Russia and its 'subjects'.[11] The language as to the exact nature of the relationship remained ambiguous, but its adoption, evidences that neither side considered the previous formal legal order as binding.

The relation between the president and the parliament was more complicated. By accepting the emergency powers the parliament gave the president in the fall of 1991, the latter implicitly recognised the superiority of the parliament under the prevailing constitution over matters of economic reform. Once the emergency powers had elapsed, however, he refused to relinquish his prerogative over the economy. Formally, the constitution supported the position of the parliament, although ultimately it remained ambiguous. According to Article 104 of the constitution then in existence, the Congress of Peoples' Deputies was recognised as the supreme organ of state power. But this formulation dated from before the creation of the Russian presidency. The relation between these two organs of state power was never clarified.

President Yeltsin tried to resolve the conflict by calling a referendum in April 1993. But even though the people supported him, the referendum could not possibly accomplish a sustainable solution for the political stalemate. It supported the President on the issues that were included in the referendum, but did not establish the framework for resolving future conflicts and thus could not serve as a commitment device for the parties involved. Obviously, it would not be possible to hold a referendum on every issue. Attempts to pass a new constitution with the support of Russia's republics and regions were unsuccessful, but they testify how the president sought to play out the conflicting parties in both conflicts against each other. Ultimately the stalemate was resolved by gun power. The president used his temporary victory to push through a new constitution. It was ratified by referendum in December 1993.[12]

Neither of the opposing parties in the two conflicts – the parliament or the subjects of the federation – participated in drafting the constitution. A draft constitution that had been promulgated by the parliament was ignored in favour of a constitution that came out of the presidential administration. The constituent parts of the Russian Federation were equally ignored, as they were not called upon to ratify the constitution.

Not surprisingly, the new constitution biases conflict resolution in favour of the president. The decisive influence of the President over key decisions rests on his power to appoint and dismiss the government (Art. 111). Parliamentary approval is still required, but the threat to dissolve parliament after it refuses to support the President's candidate for three consecutive votes, degrades the approval to a hold up game. In effect, as long as the parliament disapproves of the President's position, it has little influence over the main political agenda. It therefore does not provide the function of a forum for seeking consensus and cooperation among diverging factions.

Similarly, the constitution establishes the priority of the federal constitution and of federal laws, albeit in somewhat disguised form. The key issues of conflicts are placed under the joint jurisdiction of the federation and the regions, including the use of land and natural resources. The issue of whether the constitutions and other legal acts of the federation's subjects are consistent with the federal constitution is under the joint jurisdiction of the federation and its subjects (Art. 72.1). Yet, in case of a conflict between federal and regional laws, the federal laws shall prevail (Art. 76). This outcome is not automatic, i.e. regional laws and regulations that violate the law are not null and void. The procedure foreseen by the constitution for such events is a petition to the Constitutional Court (Art. 125).

The fact that the constitution formally resolves conflict areas by shifting the ultimate control rights to one of the parties has not helped solve the underlying cleavages. For this to happen, the conflicting parties would have had to perceive the new allocation of rights to be legitimate, to be a necessary compromise to achieve the benefit of a functioning state. Instead, the formal devices are for the most part ignored, and persisting conflicts carried out outside the constitutional framework. The showdown between the President and the parliament in the spring of 1998 over the appointment of Sergei Kiriyenko as prime minister demonstrated to the parliament its ultimate powerlessness – and to the rest of the country that deputies valued their privileges as members of the Duma higher than principles.[13] The selection of the political outsider Vladimir Putin as prime (and subsequently as Yeltsin's successor) further underlined the fact that actual decision making in Russia takes place primarily within the President's entourage.

That the constitution did not provide a viable mechanism for resolving conflicts between the Russian Federation and its constituent parts is best evidenced by the two wars in Chechnya. Leaving aside this extreme case, evidence suggests that the constitutional structure has little impact on actual behaviour. Thirty-nine of the eighty-nine subjects of the Russian Federation have signed bilateral treaties with the federation in open defiance of the framework established by the constitution. Conflict between laws and regulations passed by the regions and federal legislation is widespread, but little is done about it. One may argue that this is in part a design-fault, and instead of referring conflict cases to the Constitutional Court, regional laws that violate federal laws or the constitution should be declared null and void. However, this alone would not be a guarantee that law enforcers in the regions would abstain from enforcing these regional laws and would uphold federal laws instead. Rather the conflict is so endemic as to defeat any simple formalistic solutions.[14]

After his election as President, Putin vowed to re-establish law and order and to stop the de facto decentralisation of power and decision making throughout the Russian Federation. He used his decree power to create seven federal districts, each of which will be administered by a presidential representative.[15] The question, whether this could be done without amending the constitution did not even arise. An additional element in his strategy has been the reshuffle of the upper house of the parliament, the Federation Council. Under the new rules, each Federation Council Member will be replaced by two representatives, one nominated by the executive branch, the other by the regional legislature.[16] While there has been resistance against the adoption of this law, the Federal Council surprisingly quickly accepted these changes.

The reason may well be that comparatively little was at stake and that the battle over the control of the subjects of the Russian Federation will be fought elsewhere.

In summary, formal law in general and constitutional law in particular plays only a minor role in Russia today – the flood of new legislation notwithstanding. The importance of law has certainly been enhanced since the collapse of the socialist system. Rulings by the constitutional court have more often than not been accepted by those in power. Yet, there is also evidence of open defiance, perhaps not surprisingly, particularly in cases surrounding the conflicts between regional and federal rules.[17] It is therefore questionable that law has been accepted as a primary means for resolving major cleavages in society. The continuing use of law as an instrument in the battle over power undermines the prospects for transforming law into a framework for solving conflicts.

CONCLUDING REMARKS

The above analysis draws from a growing literature about the relation between formal law and social norms and applies the major lessons of this literature to constitutional law. It argues that constitutional law does not differ from other areas of the law in the importance of an alignment of formal law with underlying social norms and a general perception that the formal law-making process is legitimate. Establishing a legitimate constitutional order is not primarily a design problem even though major flaws in the design can undermine the functioning of that order. Without an active engagement of parties that represent major social cleavages the formal law will remain a formality. To be sure, a constitution cannot possibly resolve all existing or anticipated conflicts. But it should allocate decision-making rights and establish procedural devices for solving conflicts revolving around the delineation of these rights. The credibility of the allocation of decision-making rights as well as of the procedural devices depends on the organised elite committing to using these procedures rather than other means now and in the future. A commitment device cannot be imposed, but must be engendered by demand. The implication is that the process of constitution-making is crucial for the future of constitutionalism.

The brief analysis of the recent Russian experience with constitutionalism lends support to this analysis. The fact that the conflict between the President and the parliament has lost much of its drama after the adoption of the new constitution is no proof for a workable framework. It simply reflects the realisation of the parliament's reduced role. Lack of law enforcement, wide spread corruption and a still growing informal sector are ample evidence that many have opted out of the formal legal system. So is the spread of regional legislation that is in open conflict with federal law.

Further analysis is warranted to buttress these claims and to test more broadly the demand theory for constitutional law. The primary focus of such an analysis would be the process of lawmaking and the operation of the constitution in practice. Constitutional engineering of the specific design features of a constitution, would be considered as the transmission belt between the process of constitution making and outcome, not the ultimate focus of analysis. With regard to the process of constitution making, the task would be to identify major points of conflicts and the interests behind them. In many cases, this may not be as straightforward as in the case of the Russian constitution in 1993. In fact, it would have been a more difficult task in Russia at the end of 1991, as the lines of conflict had not been so clearly drawn at that time. There is an obvious danger that conflicts that arise at a later point might influence the identification of cleavages at the time of constitution making. Yet, these obstacles do not seem to be insurmountable. As far as the actual operation of the constitution is concerned, the simplest solution would be to use existing data on the effectiveness of legal institutions. They typically include variables on the perceived effectiveness of the judiciary, rule of law defined as the priority of law over other devices for transferring power and solving conflicts, low levels of corruption, of government expropriation of private property and government contract repudiation.[18] In addition, more direct measures of the functioning of the constitutional order could be introduced, including the use of formal dispute settlement devices such as the constitutional court in critical areas and evidence of compliance or defiance of their rulings. The paper hopes to stimulate such research, but also to bridge the gap between the different legal disciplines by showing that the underlying problems for the development of effective legal orders are similar in commercial and constitutional law.

NOTES

1   Assistant Professor of Law, Columbia Law School.
2   See also the contributions to several recent symposia on social norms, including 'Social Norms, Social Meaning, and the Economic Analysis of Law', *Journal of Legal Studies* **27**, 553; 'Law, Economics, and Norms: Social Meaning and Social Norms', *University of Pennsylvania Law Review* **144**, 2181.
3   The Roman law, which was rediscovered during this period, has similar features. See Stein (1999).
4   Compare Art. 79 s. 3 of the German Basic Law: The principles of federalism, a social rule of law state, democracy and the respect for the dignity of human beings cannot be changed even by the supermajority required for amendments of the constitution.
5   Legal transplants have a long history. Indeed, many elements of the formal legal order in origin countries result from extensive borrowing. See Watson (1974).
6   For a detailed classification of countries as transplants and origins, compare Berkowitz et al. (2002).
7   Standard indicators for the effectiveness of legal institutions were used for this analysis, including rule of law, the effectiveness of the judiciary, the absence of corruption, low risk of contract repudiation and expropriation by the state. All of these indicators are perception data generated from surveys.
8   The indigenous population in these territories quickly became marginalised or extinct, wherefore their pre-existing social order had little influence on the receptivity of the country to the foreign law.
9   In September 1972 by the Willi Brandt government following the failed vote of no-confidence; by Helmut Schmidt in an attempt to safe his government in May 1982, and by Helmut Kohl after the successful vote of no confidence in October 1982.
10 The harshest critique has been raised against the Kohl government's use of the vote of confidence, which was seen as a strategic device to call early elections. See Epping in (Starck 2000) Art. 68, regs. 5, 6. On the constitutionality of this decision see BverfGE 62, 1.
11 The treaty was signed on 31 March 1992. Two republics, Tatarstan and Chechnya, refused to sign the treaty.
12 Constitution of the Russian Federation, adopted by referendum on 12 December 1993.
13 For a detailed account of this affair, see the report on Russia, in *East European Constitutional Review* 1998, 25-28.
14 State Prosecutor Yuri Skuratov noted at the end of 1998 that more than 2000 regional laws contradicting the Russian constitution had been revoked. He estimated that about one third of the 16,000 laws that had been issued since 1995, i.e. well after the enactment of the new constitution were in violation of federal legislation. See report on Russia in *East European Constitutional Review* 1998 (Winter), 30-34 at p.32.
15 Ukas of the President of 13 May 2000, *Sobranie Zakonodatel'stva* **20** (15 May 2000), Item 2112.
16 Law of the Russian Federation On the Procedure for Forming the Federal Council of the Federal Assembly of the Russian Federation, adopted on 26 July 2000; available at http://www.akdi.ru/sf/form.HTM.
17 See Katanian (1998) for a discussion on how the rulings of the Constitutional Court on residence permits has been ignored by the Moscow city government and other regions.
18 Some of these data were first introduced by Knack (1994) and Mauro (1995). They are used in many studies, including the above cited studies by La Porta et al. (1998) and Berkowitz (2002).

REFERENCES

Berkowitz, Daniel, Katharina Pistor and Jean-Francois Richard (2002), 'Economic Development, Legality, and the Transplant Effect', *European Economic Review* (forthcoming).

Chua, Amy L. (1998), 'Markets, Democracy and Ethnicity: Toward a New Paradigm for Law and Development', *Yale Law Journal,* **108** (1), 1-107.

Coleman, James S. (1990), *Foundations of Social Theory,* Cambridge, Mass: Harvard University Press.

Cooter, Robert D. (1996), 'The Theory of Market Modernization of Law', in M. Bruno and B. Pleskovic (eds), *Annual World Bank Conference on Development Economics,* Washington D.C.: The World Bank, pp. 191-217.

Ellickson, Robert C. (1991), *Order Without Law – How Neighbors Settle Disputes,* Cambridge, Mass.: Harvard University Press.

Ertman, Thomas (1997), *Birth of the Leviathan: Building States and Regimes in Medieval and Early Modern Europe,* Cambridge: Cambridge University Press.

Glendon, Mary Ann, Michael W. Gordon, and Christopher Osakwe (1994), *Comparative Legal Traditions: Text, Material and Cases on the Civil and Common Law Traditions, with Special References to French, German, and English,* St. Paul, Minn.: West.

Gray, Cheryl W. and Kathryn Hendely (1997), 'Developing Commercial Law in Transition Economies: Examples from Hungary and Russia', in J. D. Sachs and K. Pistor (eds), *The Rule of Law and Economic Reform in Russia,* Boulder, Co.: Westview Press. pp. 139-164.

Holmes, Stephen (1995), 'Constitutionalism', in S. M. Lipset (ed), *The Encyclopedia of Democracy,* London: Routledge, pp. 299-306.

Jacobi, Jessica (1998), *Besitzschutz vor dem Reichskammergericht,* Frankfurt a. M.: Peter Lang.

Katanian, Konstantin (1998), 'The Propiska and the Constitutional Court', *East European Constitutional Review,* **6** (Spring), 52-57.

Kaufmann, Daniel and Aleksander Kaliberda (1996), 'Integrating the Unofficial Economy into the Dynamics of Post-Socialist Economies – A Framework of Analysis and Evidence', in B. Kaminski (ed), *Economic Transition in Russia and the New States of Eurasia,* Armonk, New York: M.E. Sharpe.

Klug, Heinz (2002), 'State Reconstruction: Constitutional Transformations in a Globalized World', in T. Halliday, B. Garth and R. Nelson (eds), *Law's*

Disciplinary Encounter: New Frontiers in Law's Engagement with Social Sciences (forthcoming).

Knack, Stephen and Philip Keefer (1994), 'Institutions and Economic Performance: Cross-Country Tests Using Alternative Institutional Measures', *Economics and Politics*, **7**, 207-227.

Knight, Jack (1998), 'The Bases of Cooperation: Social Norms and the Rule of Law', *Journal of Institutional and Theoretical Economics*, **154** (4), 754-763.

Kolesar, Robert J. (1990), 'North American Constitutionalism and Spanish America: A Special Lock Ordered by Catalogue, Which Arrived With the Wrong Instructions and No Keys?', in G. Billias (ed), *American Constitutionalism Abroad*, New York, Westport, Connecticut, London: Greenwood Press.

La Porta, Rafael, Florencio Lopez-de-Silanes, Andrei Shleifer, and Robert W. Vishny (1998) 'Law and Finance', *Journal of Political Economy*, **106** (6), 1113-1155.

Mauro, Paolo (1995), 'Corruption and Growth', *The Quarterly Journal of Economics*, **CX** (3), 681-712.

Merryman, John Henry, David S. Clark, and John O. Haley (1994), *The Civil Law Tradition: Europe, Latin America, and East Asia*, Charlottesville, Virginia: The Michie Company, Law Publishers.

Pistor, Katharina (1996), 'Supply and Demand for Contract Enforcement in Russia: Courts, Arbitration, and Private Enforcement', *Review of Central and East European Law*, **22** (1), 55-87.

Pistor, Katharina, Martin Raiser, and Stanislav Gelfer (2000), 'Law and Finance in Transition Economies', *Economic of Transition*, **8** (2), 325-368.

Sartori, Giovanni (1997), *Comparative Constitutional Engineering: An Inquiry into Structures, Incentives and Outcomes*, New York, NY: New York University Press.

Starck, Christian (ed) (2000), *Das Bonner Grundgesetz: Kommentar*, München: Frans Fahlen.

Stein, Peter (1999), *Roman Law in European History*, Cambridge: Cambridge University Press.

Sunstein, Cass R. (1996), 'Social Norms and Social Roles', *Columbia Law Review*, **96**, 903-968.

Watson, Alan (1974), *Legal Transplants: An Approach to Comparative Law*, Edinburgh: Scottish Academic Press; London: distributed by Chatto and Windus.

Wyduckel, Dieter (1998), 'Rechts- und staatstheoretische Voraussetzungen und Folgen des Westfälischen Friedens', *Rechtstheorie*, **29** (2), 221-234.

Zweigert, Konrad and Hein Kötz (1998), *Introduction to Comparative Law*, 3 ed, Oxford: Clarendon Press.

6. Comment

Ivan Baron Adamovich

In a recent paper Katharina Pistor and her co-authors (Pistor, Raiser and Gelfer, 2000) have proficiently shown that getting commercial law on the books 'right' does not necessarily mean that it is effective. Assuming that this is also valid for constitutional law, in her stimulating new paper Pistor tries to find out under what conditions constitutions are effective. She argues that 'without a demand for law, law will not be effective'. In other words: the demand for constitutional law is (at least) a necessary condition for an effective constitution. Key groups in a given society have to participate in – or at least support – the constitution-making process in order to create a commitment to a constitutional framework which can solve major cleavages in the country.

As the paper claims to develop 'an analytical framework for the demand for constitutional law' I will concentrate on the theoretical issues raised. I very much agree with the ideas presented by Pistor and thus I will seek to further elaborate some of her main thoughts. First I will try to examine the relationship between legitimacy and effectiveness which remains rather blurred in the paper. Secondly I will take a closer look at demand which I believe to be a factor which is to be separated from variables like the familiarity with the new law system or the adaptation of transplanted laws to the social norms[1] of the country. Finally I will go beyond 'The Demand for Constitutional Law' and ask some questions about the supply of law.

LEGITIMACY AND EFFECTIVENESS

While in Part 2 ('Formal Law, Social Norms and the Demand for Law') Pistor focuses on the ingredients of the legitimacy of state action virtually without speaking about effectiveness, Part 3 ('Lawmaking and Effective Legal Institutions') deals with the effectiveness of law without touching the subject of legitimacy. In general, the paper leaves the relationship between legitimacy and effectiveness to the interpretation of the reader. Assuming that there is a relationship and ruling out the possibility that effectiveness is a precondition for legitimacy, there are two possible relationships between legitimacy and effectiveness:

(a)   legitimacy of state action is a precondition for effectiveness of the law; or

(b)   legitimacy of state action and effectiveness of the law are synonymous.

Before answering this question, it is necessary to clarify what Pistor actually means by legitimacy of state action. She proposes two crucial variables: first, general alignment of formal with informal institutions and, second, legitimacy of the lawmaking process.

As to the first variable there is considerable evidence that formal laws which reflect the underlying *informal institutions* are not only perceived to be legitimate, they are also – Pistor implicitly says it – effective. In fact, the alignment of formal with informal institutions is represented by the two variables elaborated by Pistor in Part 3: familiarity of the society with the fundamental principles of the new legal system and adaptation of the trans-planted system to the country's own needs. Countries that exhibit either of these variables are supposed to be receptive transplants with largely effective legal systems.

As to the second variable, legitimacy of state action builds on a process of lawmaking that 'is generally perceived to be legitimate.' In other words: legitimacy exists if there is a *consensus* about the fundamental rules (the con-stitution) for solving conflicts in society. If this is the case, even unpopular laws may be observed as long as they are constitutional. As a matter of fact, the consensus can be perceived as being identical with the commitment of all the key groups in a given society towards a constitutional order. This in turn is captured by the demand variable, which is defined as the active participa-tion of all key groups in a constitution-making process or at least their passive support for it.[2]

If the above interpretation is correct, Pistor explains legitimacy (in Part 2) and effectiveness (in part 3) basically with the same variables. Consequently it would be fair to say, that legitimacy and effectiveness are (largely) synonymous – at least according to the above standards. If this is so, effec-tiveness (legitimacy)[3] is influenced by at least three variables: demand, familiarity and adaptation. Demand captures the commitment of the key groups in society towards using constitutional rather than extra-constitutional mechanisms for future conflict solving. Familiarity and adaptation on the other hand capture the relationship between formal and informal institutions.

DEMAND, FAMILIARITY AND ADAPTATION

According to Pistor, the demand for constitutional law is captured by the two variables familiarity and adaptation. As I have already pointed out, I do not agree with this taxonomy. Instead, for several reasons, I propose to look at the three variables as equals. First of all, demand and familiarity are both initial conditions that can exist independently of each other. Demand cannot induce familiarity although on the other hand familiarity could, under certain circumstances, induce demand. Secondly, adaptation is not an initial condition but rather some kind of 'engineering-tool' for constitution-making. It is independent from familiarity, as there is no (or at least less) necessity to adapt laws if the society is historically familiar with the transplanted laws. Finally, adaptation can theoretically be independent from demand. For example, if a powerful group manages to introduce a new (adapted) constitution against other interests in society, according to our standards 'demand' has to be put in inverted commas because of the lack of consensus. Last but not least, it is also imaginable that a colony receives adapted laws from the colonial power without the key groups demanding it.

The following illustration shows effectiveness as a function of demand, familiarity and adaptation. It contains the assumption made by Pistor that demand is a necessary condition for an effective constitution. It also takes into account that countries that exhibit either familiarity or adaptation are so-called 'receptive transplants' expected to have an effective legal system. In a crude simplification the conditions are shown as either fulfilled ('yes') or not fulfilled ('no').

Table 1: Effectiveness as a function of demand, familiarity and adaptation

	Initial Conditions		Engineering	Consequence
	Demand	Familiarity	Adaptation	Expected Effectiveness
Case A	Yes	Yes	Not relevant	Yes
Case B	Yes	No	Yes	Yes
Case C	Yes	No	No	Yes (?)
Case D	No	Not relevant (?)	Not relevant (?)	No (?)

Looking at the four cases, examples already presented by Pistor come to mind: case A countries would for example be the settler colonies of England or neighbouring countries of Germany and France, a typical case B country would be Japan, case C countries would be the western origin countries for legal systems (England, France, Germany) and, finally, Russia would be a case D country. Nevertheless, looking at the illustration a couple of questions remain open:

- Is demand not only necessary but also *sufficient* for effectiveness (case C)? Or are there examples for countries with a demand for transplants without fulfilling familiarity and adaptation where constitutions were not effective? Probably yes: Bulgaria could be a case in point.

- Is demand really a *necessary* condition for effectiveness (case D)? Or are there examples for effective legal systems where familiarity and/ or adaptation were fulfilled and where a constitutional order was imposed on the society. Even that is conceivable – India could be an example.

Of course the analytical framework presented here is a very crude one. For empirical studies, the different variables would have to be considerably refined. For example, it is not entirely clear what is meant by adaptation. Does it mean that a foreign constitution is adapted to a country by consciously redesigning it in some kind of a master plan? Is that at all possible? Or does adaptation rather mean something like an evolutionary process, where the laws gradually change in the political process and thus adapt to the institutional environment of a country? Especially in the second case one would expect the adaptation to be a very long or even never-ending process.

Another question would be, if the level of effectiveness improves with more conditions considered to be fulfilled.

BEYOND 'THE DEMAND FOR CONSTITUTIONAL LAW'

Looking at the illustration in the preceding section, there is at least one obvious variable missing: supply. In her paper, Pistor deliberately neglects the supply factors because she wants to stress the importance of demand. I completely agree with her when she affirms, that 'no state controls sufficient resources to ensure legal compliance by means of coercion only.' Indeed, weak enforcement of the law seems to be to a large extent a demand problem. This of course has consequences for another supply factor: the legal advice by western specialists and governments. In this context it is puzzling that Pistor declares in her introduction that the transition economies in Central- and Eastern Europe received 'reasonable laws ... mostly by way of legal transplants from the West'. Are (as the author herself stresses) laws that obviously are not enforceable 'reasonable'? To what extent do we at all know what laws are 'reasonable' for a certain country?[4] If we agree that similar sets of rules have different consequences in different societies, this calls for diffe- rent legal solutions in different countries. And it calls for more caution by western advisors in their attitude towards constitutional engineering.

If demand and familiarity are variables capturing the initial conditions in a given society at a given point in time, supply and adaptation can be per- ceived as engineering variables. Concerning the latter, there seem to be two general positions in the literature. They differ in their expectations as to the chances of enforcing the 'right' laws against unfavourable informal institu- tions or even initial conditions in general. On the one hand there are authors who are *fundamentally optimistic* about the possibilities of constitutional engineering. They recommend a constitution which counteracts and/or cor- rects traditions or customs obstructing the development towards market economy and democracy (e.g. Sunstein, 1991, 385). Surprisingly, an idea by Hayek (1979, 108) also fits into this category. He proposes, that unwritten traditions, which have been inhibiting the abuse of power in the successful democracies of the west should be formulated and written down for the new democracies. On the other hand there are authors that are *fundamentally sceptical* about the chances of enforcing rules against unfavourable informal institutions. Three positions can be distinguished here:

- The first position advocates designing a constitution which is compatible with the informal institutions and reflects the institutional reality of the society as accurately as possible. It has a certain sympathy for constitutional engineering but (i) stresses that constitutional rules should not be too far away from institutional reality; and (ii) acknowledges the importance of the demand factor, insisting that there should be a consensus about rules 'correcting' the status quo (Voigt, 1999, 8 and 23).

- The second position proposes drawing up some kind of a minimal constitutional document expecting it to be the starting point of a dynamic process of interaction with the informal institutions. In this case the contents would not be as important as the fact that there is a constitution enacted at all (Ordeshook, 1998, 102).

- The third position is pessimistic about the possibility of achieving any changes through constitutional design, if the initial conditions are unfavourable. An example is Gray (1993, 28): 'it is neither feasible nor, in many cases, desirable that the institutions of Western democratic capitalism be transplanted to the post-Communist states, aside from a few of them that retain European cultural traditions.'

At least in the light of the perceived crucial role of initial conditions for the effectiveness of constitutional law, a fundamentally sceptical attitude towards the possibilities of constitutional engineering seems to be adequate. This is especially true if one takes into account that law on the books which is not effective, undermines the credibility of any written law.

In general, I think that whenever law is supplied, its expected effectiveness in the very specific conditions of a country must be taken into account. This is why the supply of laws should be included into the analytical framework proposed by Pistor. And this is true both for laws in general, and for constitutional law. This point is particularly relevant where Western advisors and governments exercise their influence on key actors in transition countries.

CONCLUDING REMARKS

In their impressive empirical study, Pistor, Raiser and Gelfer (2000) show that the commercial law on the books has dramatically changed during transition in Central and Eastern Europe. This, in fact, is also valid for constitutional law: every single transition country has adopted a new constitution during the last ten years. Moreover, constitutional law was extensively copied from different western constitutions.[5] Pistor, Raiser and Gelfer (2000) show that the effectiveness[6] of the law greatly varies between the different transition economies. In general, there seems to be a large difference between more effective laws in Central Europe and the Baltics and much less effective laws in other former members of the Soviet Union, while South-Eastern Europe is perceived to be a case in-between. In any case the 24 transition countries are a gigantic laboratory: while there are some common features (e.g. the fast introduction of new legal systems), there are considerable differences in the four variables defined above (demand, familiarity, adaptation and supply). Studying the influences of these variables on the effectiveness of legal systems could lead to a big step in explaining how institutions work. May be the solution to the mystery of building an effective constitutional order is hidden right at its birth: in the process of constitution-making.

NOTES

1   In the language of institutional economics these are the informal institutions of a country (i.e. sanctions, taboos, customs, traditions and codes of conduct) as opposed to formal institutions (constitutions, laws, property rights). See North (1991).

2   As Pistor rightly stresses, the adoption of a new constitution alone is not identical with demand in the sense of our definition, because mere adoption does not necessarily mean that there is a consensus in society.

3   From now on I will use the notion of effectiveness as in my view it reflects the problem better.

4   This of course is an extremely complex question. It is already not easy to define the 'reasonable' commercial laws. It gets even more difficult with constitutions, as constitutions are more complex and much more emotionally and politically loaded than commercial laws.

5   Hungary, as a matter of fact, is the only country where a constitution older than 1990 is formally still in place (the constitution of 1949). Of course, it was completely modified in the course of the transition process.

6   Effectiveness is measured by tree variables: the rule of law rating composed by the Central Economic Review (CEER); the effectiveness index of corporate and bancruptcy law taken from the EBRD transition reports; and the enforcement index published in the World

Business Environment and Enterprise survey (BEEPS). See Table 5 in Pistor, Raiser and Gelfer (2000, 343).

REFERENCES

Gray, John (1993), 'From Post-Communism to Civil Society – The Reemergence of History and the Decline of the Western Model', in Ellen Frankel Paul, Fred D Miller Jr. and Jeffrey Paul (eds), *Liberalism and the Economic Order*, Cambridge (et.al.): Cambridge University Press, pp. 26-50.

Hayek, Friedrich A. von (1979), *Law, Legislation and Liberty – Volume 3: The Political Order of a Free People*, Chicago: The University of Chicago Press.

North, Douglass C. (1991), 'Institutions', *Journal of Economic Perspectives*, **5**, (1), 97-112.

Ordeshook, Peter C. (1998), 'Lessons for Citizens of a New Democracy', in Charles K. Rowley (ed), *Classical Liberalism and Civil Society,* Cheltenham (et.al.): Edward Elgar.

Pistor, Katharina, Raiser, Martin, and Gelfer, Stanislaw (2000), 'Law and Finance in Transition Economies', *Economics of Transition*, **8** (2), 325-368.

Sunstein, Cass R. (1991), 'Constitutionalism, Prosperity, Democracy – Transition in Eastern Europe', *Constitutional Political Economy*, **2**, (3), 371-394.

Voigt, Stefan (1999), *Choosing How to Choose – The Narrow Path Between Effective Constitutions and Wishful Thinking in Constitutional Choice*, Jena: Max-Planck-Institut zur Erforschung von Wirtschaftssystemen.

7. Some Remarks on the Separation of Powers in the Polish Constitution

Hanna Suchocka

INTRODUCTORY REMARKS

The last decade of the 20th century was an exceptional period for constitutional law. It was a time in which a great number of European states found themselves in a dynamic process of creating new constitutions. The period was unique in that most of these states found themselves plunged into this process without any preparatory stage. In most cases, no profound theoretical debates on political models and solutions preceded the period in which new constitutions were drawn up. The rapid pace at which social and political changes took place in the early stages of the transformation required constitutional 'action', with intellectual discussion taking a secondary role effectively limited to a kind of commentary on the constitutional measures being taken and the solutions being chosen. Poland was probably the only exception, since theoretical work on the future constitution had been conducted prior to the changes that took place in 1989. But even there, the dynamics of events and political decisions preceded scholarly analysis during the Round Table talks. The profundity of the changes taking place after the elections of June 1989 required constitutional-law studies and analyses from a completely new and different perspective. They no longer involved a modified or improved form of socialism, but a different political system based on totally different premises. The challenge at hand was to determine what exactly those premises should be.[1] The new situation raised a number of questions. The taboos that limited discussion in the previous period had disappeared; every query was permitted and legitimate. There were no forbidden questions, just as there were no longer any ready, pre-planned 'solely correct answers'. There were only the generally outlined goals that individual states wanted to achieve as a result of constitutional changes. All these states wanted to break in various ways with the past of their authoritarian, centrally-ruled states, both in the political and in the social sphere.

Without a doubt, the demands and proposed solutions expressed at that time were formulated in an exceptionally general manner. They were often presented in the form of a slogan or battle cry meant to symbolise a certain democratic tendency. In a social atmosphere marked by the pursuit or, rather, expectation of something new, slogans were needed to rally public support and acceptance for what was being done. That acceptance, as time would show, was rather short-lived, probably because of the generality of the outlined goals. In the initial phase of transformation, however, it was sufficient.

The new situation, however, created not only opportunities but also the danger of errors. In the most general terms, the situation might be compared to the constitutional atmosphere that prevailed when the American constitution was being drawn up. As one American writer put it. 'Americans sometimes speak of there having been a 'constitutional moment' – the era that produced the federal Constitution and Bill of Rights. Reinforced by such metaphors as Catherine Drinker Bowen's 'Miracle at Philadelphia', this notion of the constitutional moment obscures the fact that the founding period of American constitutionalism was one of trial and error. The state constitutions drafted beginning in 1776 were often quite flawed documents, and the Articles of Confederation (1781) soon proved inadequate to the purposes of the emerging nation. By the same token, the countries of Central and Eastern Europe seem to have embarked on a process of trial and error in the making of new constitutions.'[2]

The new constitutions arose from the rubble of the shattered constitutional monolith of the previous period. The constitutions of the previous system had been created according to a similar pattern. Often even the breakdown was nearly identical. This situation resulted from the subordination of all constitutional law and constitutional structures to the model of a centralised state, based on the principle of the unity of power, which in reality meant the leading role of the party. The principle of the unity of power in its doctrinal and constitutional construction meant parliament's domination as the highest expression of the nation's will – in reality, domination by party structures. The principle of the unity of power was reduced to the concept of the overriding role of the Communist Party within the system of state organs. Constitutions drawn up on the basis of that principle were essentially divorced from the cultural roots and the political traditions of individual states. All of them were modelled on the Soviet constitution of 1936. Their characteristic feature was rifts between the form of the constitution, its articulation, its expression as written documents, and the tradition from which that constitution grew. It was not surprising then that one of the questions asked at the threshold of work on a new constitution was its connection with tradition.

One of the important elements seen as a part of tradition was the separation of powers. Returning to the principle of the separation of powers was intended as a return to democratic roots. At the start of the road toward the creation of new constitutions, a number of questions and problems of various kinds arose. They included more complex questions that continue to absorb constitutional lawyers to this day, as well as some issues that, 10 years later, may appear downright infantile. Back then they were justified because, as I have already pointed out, there were no ready prescriptions and no pre-planned answers.

Before 1989, Polish society strongly desired the establishment of the rule of law, democracy, and justice. However, at the beginning of the transformation there was no place for deeper discussion of those three values, even though European standards of human rights have been implemented in Polish law.

The rule of law, democracy, and justice were rather slogans with a very clear aim: to gather people around them. The fact that two of them, the rule of law and justice, could to some extent contradict each other was completely ignored. Law was seen as an instrument that could solve all political and social problems. This kind of thinking inevitably led to misunderstandings and tensions between different agencies.

The Polish transformation was launched in 1989. Its origin was the Round Table Agreement, which led to the April 1989 amendments to the Constitution of 1952. There was, however, relatively little discussion of the concrete model of the system of government to be adopted. Instead, discussion focused largely on specific institutions and structures of state powers that needed to be established pursuant to the April 1989 amendments. The scope of suggested reforms depended on the political interests of the two main participants in the round table talks: the democratic opposition, allied under the banner of Solidarity, on the one hand, and the Communist Party, on the other. In view of the intense political tensions at that time, there was no opportunity for a thorough analysis of the complex problems involved. However, there was a general consensus that the principle of the separation of powers should distinguish the new political system from that of the communist era. The opposition considered this principle a symbol of transition from a totalitarian regime to a liberal democracy. Such strong support for the principle of the separation of powers was a natural reaction to the communist concept of the unity of state power. In theory, the principle of the unity of power aimed to reflect the dominance of Parliament – the supreme body expressing the will of the nation. The 1952 Constitution officially recognised Parliament as the supreme organ of the state, but in reality Parliament was subservient to the Communist Party because that party always commanded the majority of votes.

In this situation, returning to the principle of the separation of powers, known in Poland prior to World War II, and incorporating this idea into the new system became the chief aim of the first stage of the 1989 transformation period. However, as I mentioned before, the principle was not clearly defined, and its meaning remained vague. Its main functions were to serve as a symbol of democracy and as a negation of the principle of the unity of state powers, which was seen as a symbol of the 'old system'.

As Letowska rightly stated: 'The theory of the separation of powers, and one rather rigorously interpreted at that, appears to us today as a soothing balm, an antidote to the Stalinist infringements of the democratic and legalistic order of the functioning of the State'.[3]

Pullo gave a similar opinion on the principle of the separation of power in the Polish political debate: 'The principle of separation of powers seems to discharge today the function of identification and legitimisation of a democratic structure of state organs. (...) The separation of powers in the system of government has become a dogma lacking any clear meaning, or a myth revived in new circumstances and solutions, or a stereotype of false generalisation which is accepted as obvious. Hence, the principle of the separation of powers in this sense can by no means serve as a measure of democracy or of the efficacy of a system of state government.'[4]

Sokolewicz also expressed a critical opinion on the role of the principle of the separation of powers: 'In spite of all accepted opinions, the principle of the separation of powers is not placed amongst generally recognised standards of a democratic constitutionalism.'[5] This point of view, however, has not been shared in Polish constitutional debate.

THE EVOLUTION OF THE IDEA OF THE SEPARATION OF POWERS SINCE 1989

In Spring 1989, when the amendments to the Constitution of 1952 were proposed, the communist government was not ready to retreat from the principle of the unity of power, especially because the Round Table Agreement recognised the leading role of the Party expressly guaranteed by the 1952 Constitution (as amended in 1976). The amendments of April 1989 did not explicitly recognise the principle of the separation of powers as the foundation of the system of government, even though they introduced institutions that were incompatible with the concept of the unity of power. Therefore, the amended constitution was full of inconsistencies, if not contradictions, particularly in terms of the separation of powers. For example, despite the introduction of a second chamber of Parliament (the Senate) and of the office of President of the Republic, both to be chosen in completely free elections, the previous constitutional wording defining Parliament as the supreme organ of state power was left untouched. From a normative point of view, the Sejm retained the role it played under the former constitutional regime. This role was clearly inconsistent with the other constitutional provisions and, in particular, with those concerning the role of the Senate and the President.

At that time, however, the goal of the two main political forces and main negotiators at the Round Table was to limit the power of their respective political adversary, rather that to search for mechanisms designing and implementing a very clear system of separation of powers[6]. The mechanisms adopted were thus designed to block opponents rather than to promote cooperation between the branches of government. For example, efforts were made to adopt constitutional provisions ensuring the continued political dominance of the Communist Party and the supremacy of the Sejm, where the majority of votes was guaranteed to the coalition of the Communist Party and two small satellite parties, while the Senate was elected by entirely free elections.

Another anomaly found in the April 1989 amendments and continued in the December 1989 amendments was the President's right to dissolve the Sejm. Thus, the President, a state office the Constitution did not consider supreme, was given the power to dissolve another body formally recognised as the supreme organ of state authority. The amendments included, *inter alia*, the right to dissolve the Sejm if it adopted a bill or resolution that prevented the President from exercising his constitutional powers[7]. There was no doubt that these provisions were aimed at guaranteeing the leading role of the Com-

munist Party and at preserving the country's international alliances mentioned in the Constitution. This arrangement did not reflect the idea of the
separation of powers in its classic form.[8]

The principle of the separation of powers was not expressly formulated
even in the December 1989 amendments to the Constitution. Nevertheless,
these amendments, among others, abolished the constitutional principle of the
leading role of the Communist Party. One would think that in such a situation
there would be no reason not to incorporate the principle of the separation of
powers directly in the Constitution.

The next step in our constitutional development was the Constitutional
Act on the Mutual Relations between the Legislative Executive Powers of the
Republic Poland and on Local Self-Government, the so-called 'Small Constitution' adopted in 1992.[9] At that time, a consensus emerged that the principle of the separation of powers should be expressly stated in the constitution. The regulation was modelled on the pre-war 1921 Polish Constitution.
Article 1 of the Small Constitution provided that 'legislative power shall be
vested in the Sejm and the Senate of the Republic of Poland and the Council
of Ministers, and the judicial power shall be vested in independent courts'.
This was a somewhat static approach. Its value consisted in the fact that the
principle of the separation of powers was expressly formulated, thereby
becoming a constitutional principle. However, no clear answer was given to
the consequences of the principle for the functioning of state organs or to the
meaning of the division as a distinct separation of powers and especially as
the powers' cooperation and balancing. On the contrary, the wording of
Article 1 created doubts about its assessment.

A more elaborate and precise step-by-step definition of the separation of
powers evolved later. This process was influenced by general constitutional
doctrine and by the experience of state organs operating under the Small
Constitution. These experiences were reflected during the debates of the first
Constitutional Committee, a body established in the early 1990s to draft a
new constitution. Moreover, at that time it was assumed that the principle of
the separation of powers should include the idea of mutual checks and balances between the branches to provide a framework and their 'harmonious
cooperation'. The constitution was seen as the foundation for such a system.
This created an opportunity for a more dynamic approach to the problem. But
on the other hand, the very general formula also led to a great deal of tension
between various state organs.

I would like to cite here one instance among many, the dispute over countersigning. In parliamentary states, countersigning is a way of distinguishing presidential decision-making functions requiring a minister's participation from the President's personal prerogatives. The Small Constitution of 1992 gave the President rather broad personal powers. This undoubtedly resulted from the popular election of the president. President Walesa, however, sought to expand the scope of these prerogatives. Conflicts emerged over the government's and the presidential chancellery's differing interpretations of the constitution.[10]

The President, who derived his powers from popular elections, argued for the need for stronger authority. He therefore interpreted a number of prerogatives contained in the Small Constitution according to the principles of a presidential rather than a parliamentary system. Under such circumstances, clashes between the written constitution and the real state of affairs were unavoidable. Through such moves, the president obviously wanted to bring pressure to bear on the constitutional committee and influence the state's future form of government. He interpreted every constitutional ambiguity in favour of broader presidential powers.

The political discussion ran parallel to the debate among experts working for the Constitutional Committee. Differing opinions were heard. There was difficulty in understanding one another, especially in matters connected with the system of government and relations between state organs. The definition and legal consequences of the principle of the separation of powers were very unclear. As A. Pułło writes: 'The term separation of powers may be counted among the phrases that are most often found in the constitutional debate but that are, at the same time, the most obscure.'[11]

Finally, after very long and controversial debate, the principle of the separation of powers was explicitly formulated in the 1997 Constitution in Chapter 1, which delineates the fundamental principles of the political system. Article 10 declares that 'The system of government of the Republic of Poland shall be based on the separation of and balancing between the legislative, executive and judicial powers.' The idea of 'balancing' emerged during the later stages of legislative debate. Its core concern was the development of mechanisms that balanced rather than blocked the powers. As K. Działocha stated: 'It is mostly understood that the organisation and functioning of the supreme authorities of the state are based on a kind of functional and organisational separation of powers as well as the mutual relations between them consisting of mutual control, checks, and restraint'.[12]

Article 10 was expanded during the final meetings of the Constitutional Committee to include Paragraph 2, which incorporates the substance of Article 1 of the Small Constitution, declaring that 'legislative power shall be vested in the Sejm and the Senate, executive power shall be vested in the President of the Republic of Poland and the Council of Ministers, and judicial power shall be vested in courts and tribunals'. The addition of Paragraph 2 clarified the nature of presidential power. In the Polish constitutional debate, some argued that the President should not be recognised as part of the executive branch, but should instead be placed outside the framework of the separation of powers to serve a coordinating role within the state organs. The clear constitutional provision expressing that the President is a part of executive power solved one of the discussed problems.

THE SEPARATION AND BALANCE OF POWERS IN THE LEGISLATIVE PROCESS

The concept of the separation of powers implies that various branches of government have limited powers. It also means that legislative power can be checked or limited by other branches. In my opinion, despite many shortcomings, the new Polish Constitution contains a set of checks and balances inspired by the principle of the separation of powers.

The aforementioned concept of the separation of powers includes the President's participation in the legislative process. Under the 1997 Constitution, the President has the following legislative powers: the right to propose legislation (Article 118); the right to refer a statute to the Constitutional Tribunal to decide its constitutionality (Article 122, Paragraph 13); and the right to veto a statute (Article 122, Paragraph 5). During the extensive debates about the scope of presidential powers, suggestions were made that the President should be deprived of this last right. These suggestions were made in reaction to former President Lech Walesa's frequent and, in the opinion of some politicians, improper use of this right.

These suggestions opened a wider discussion concerning the prerogatives of president. The right of the head of the state to veto legislation is a well-established prerogative of the office. For this reason, the new Constitution slightly curtailed presidential powers in this area, including the right to veto.

Under Article 18 of the Small Constitution, a legislative override of a presidential veto of a bill did not prevent him from referring the matter to the

Constitutional Tribunal before signing the bill. The new constitution does not allow this. Therefore, the President may now use only one power in respect to one bill, either the veto or constitutional challenge. Article 122, Paragraph 5 specifically provides that, in the event of the re-passage of a bill by the Sejm after the President has vetoed it, the president may not refer it to the Constitutional Tribunal. Furthermore, pursuant to Article 122, Paragraph 3, once the President has referred a statute to the Constitutional Tribunal in accordance with the procedure prescribed therein, the President may not exercise the right specified in Paragraph 5, that is, to refer the statute to the Sejm for reconsideration. Paragraph 3 expressly provides that 'the President of the Republic shall not refuse to sign a bill that has been adjudged by the Constitutional Tribunal as conforming to the Constitution'.

Many controversies, motivated largely by political considerations, appeared during the debate in the Constitutional Committee on the issue of the majority required for a legislative override of a bill vetoed by the President. The rule ultimately adopted in Article 122, Paragraph 5 requires a three-fifths majority vote in the presence of at least half of the statutory number of deputies. This was seen as a weakening of the presidential powers in the light of the constitutional provisions, as compared with the two-thirds majority required under the Small Constitution.[13]

Practice shows, however, that presidential power has not been weakened. Since the Constitution of 1997 went into effect, President Aleksander Kwaśniewski vetoed and returned a bill to the Sejm nine times. Only once did the Parliament manage to override a presidential veto, when some deputies representing the opposition voted the same way as the governing coalition. From a purely statistical point of view, the governing coalition parties did not have a sufficient majority of votes to override a presidential veto. When the AWS and the UW were in the governmental coalition, the opposition parties had four more seats than needed to sustain a veto. Since June 8, 2000, when the UW left the coalition, there has been a minority government, so the role of President in this area became stronger.

The new constitution further clarified the role of government in the legislative process. The right to initiate legislation is still guaranteed to the government. The new prerogatives include the right to classify a bill as urgent, which triggers a 'fast-track' legislative process, as well as the right to withdraw a bill during its consideration by Parliament. The latter prerogative is based on experience gathered during the years immediately preceding the new constitution. In 1991, President Lech Wałęsa submitted to the Parliament a draft of the Small Constitution, considerably extending presidential powers. The Parliament substantially modified the draft, contrary to the President's expectations, by limiting his powers. Consequently, the President decided to withdraw the bill from consideration. This provoked heated discussion whether such action is legal. Parliament expressed its opinion that the President is not empowered to withdraw the bill from the Parliament. The President decided not to support this bill and withdrew his representative from the parliamentary procedure. In this situation, the parliamentary committee took the legislative initiative and changed the presidential bill into a parliamentary one. The discussion resulted in the adoption of Article 15 (4) of the Small Constitution, which established the right of a body that introduced a bill to withdraw it at any time prior to the conclusion of the bill's first reading in Parliament. The 1997 Constitution has retained this right and has even extended its scope. Article 119 (4) permits an initiator to withdraw a bill from deliberations before the conclusion of its second reading in Parliament. This raises the question whether such a power is consistent with the principle of the separation and balance of powers. My opinion is that such a power is an important element of control over the legislative processing of bills that originate outside parliament, i.e. from the Office of the President or elsewhere in government. Moreover, such control can be exercised as late as the second reading. Thus, the more changes the Sejm makes to a bill, the greater the risk of its withdrawal. If the President is the initiator, then it may reasonably be assumed that he would either exercise the right to veto or withdraw the bill if he considers the proposed amendments unacceptable. This power of the President is thus an important check on legislative power.

One of the crucial elements in the system of the separation of powers is the role played by the Constitutional Tribunal. The primary significance of establishing the constitutional courts is the addition of a new dimension to the system of checks and balances.[14]

The Polish Constitutional Tribunal was formally introduced into the country's constitutional system in 1982. However, the appropriate parliamentary statute was not passed until 1985. It must be kept in mind that the Tribunal was established at a time when the principle of the unity of power was in effect, with all the aforementioned political ramifications and limitations. Consequently, the Tribunal was unable to fully perform the role that such institutions are designed to play in democratic systems.

The old constitutional provision – recognising the Sejm as a supreme organ of power – was seen as supporting the argument for not considering

Constitutional Tribunal judgements on the constitutionality of a statute final. This argument lost its validity in 1992 when the Small Constitution was adopted. Nevertheless, the finality of the Tribunal's judgements was still neither accepted nor established. The 1997 Constitution introduced a significant change in this matter. A general rule expressed in Article 190 (1) states that judgements of the Constitutional Tribunal are universally binding and final. The much-criticised rule under the previous system, whereby parliament could review and 'overrule' the Tribunal's judgement declaring a statute unconstitutional, has been rejected.

The old rule conflicted with the principle of the separation of powers and was clearly a relic of the concept of the unity of power and the dominant position of parliament. Returning to the idea of the separation of powers has led to the restoration of a proper balance between parliament and the Constitutional Tribunal. The aforementioned power of the Constitutional Tribunal indirectly delineates the scope of parliamentary and presidential powers. First, if the Tribunal finds a statute unconstitutional, the statute loses its binding force on the day of publication of the Tribunal's judgement or after a period (not exceeding 18 months) specified by the Tribunal. Parliament cannot overrule the Tribunal's decision; it may only pass a new statute that is not in conflict with the constitution. Therefore, the Tribunal's power must be seen as a substantial check on the legislature. Second, if the Constitutional Tribunal finds that a statute is in conformity with the constitution, the President cannot refuse to sign it. This is a further curtailment of the scope of presidential power.

THE SITUATION OF THE COURTS IN THE LIGHT OF THE PRINCIPLE OF THE SEPARATION OF POWERS

Until 1989, the functioning of courts was subject to the principle of the unity of power. In practice, this principle subordinated the judicial system to the principle of the leading role of the Communist Party. The first serious debate on the independent judiciary in Poland began in 1980-1981. The year 1989 was crucial for the new thinking on the judiciary. The discussion was strongly connected with the principle of the separation of powers and pointed out the urgent need to revert to the principle of the separation of powers, a principle that very laconically and concretely determines the position of the third power in the political system. The independence of the judiciary and judges is strictly tied to the position of judicial organs within the state's institutional system – a fact that had apparently gone unnoticed for decades.

In the past (before 1989), the criteria for appointments to the courts were political, and the independence of judges was a declaration, condoned as long as courts, in their adjudication, met the expectations of the actual power holders. An instrument for exerting influence on judges, which undermined the principle of independence, was the statutory duty to apply Supreme Court resolutions in adjudication in all courts, on equal footing with laws. They contained so-called guidelines for the administration of justice and the practice of the law. Likewise, binding the bench of the Supreme Court by the interpretation once adopted by the same Court in a resolution, equal to laws in its effect, was a way to limit judicial independence. It required that an interpretation made by another bench should be applied on the same footing as the law.

The problem of the third power was regarded as a key issue of Poland's political transformation.[15] The amendments introduced to the Polish constitution in April 1989 based on the elements of the principle of the separation of powers changed the position of the courts. This subsequently led to basic changes in the law on common courts as well as the law on the Supreme Court in December 1989.[16]

The Constitutional Tribunal has repeatedly taken a stand on the issue of judicial independence.[17] Of fundamental significance was the Constitutional Tribunal's ruling of November 9, 1993, which clearly stated that 'one of the elements of the principle of the separation of powers and of the foundations of the democratic construction of a law-abiding state is the principle of judicial independence. [...] The concept of judicial independence has an unambivalent and well-founded substance providing a basic guarantee of impartial decision-making. Independence must therefore mean a judge's independence both from the parties to a dispute as well as from state organs. The correlate of the principle of independence on the part of the judge is the duty of impartiality...'.[18]

As I mentioned above, the principle of the separation of powers was incorporated in the Constitution of 1997. Despite Article 10 of the Constitution, this principle was also repeated in Article 173, which reads: 'The courts and tribunals shall constitute a separate power and shall be independent of other branches of power.' An important move to emphasise the significance of the third power and to mark its distinctiveness was the establishment of the National Judiciary Council. Noteworthy is the right of the National Judiciary

Council to participate in electing new judges by submitting nominations for presidential appointment. The Minister of Justice was deprived the right to appoint and remove judges from the judiciary.

In accordance with the Constitution of 1997, the National Judiciary Council gained the right to give opinions on the laws pertaining to the judiciary and the right to apply to the Constitutional Tribunal with inquiries concerning its constitutionality of normative acts affecting the independence of courts and of judges.

Article 178 paragraph 1 rendered the principle of independence of judges normative by stating that 'judges, in the exercise of their office, shall be independent and subject only to the Constitution and statutes' (laws). A new and important definition of the position of judges is the clear constitutional indication of their subordination not only to statutes (which had often been interpreted as subordination to the whole of sub-statutory law), but also to the constitution. Consequently, the status of a judge is defined in a completely new manner and constitutes a new, important element of the concept of the separation of powers. Not only the Constitutional Tribunal, but also the courts are obliged to exert control over the legislative power by determining the constitutionality of statutes. These provisions were and still are widely discussed among constitutional law experts. In this respect, two significant questions may be raised: What is the exact meaning of the above provisions, and what rights and obligations result from these provisions for an individual judge? Clearly, this new situation requires that a judge should consider the constitutional context of the Act on which he bases his adjudication. Professional commentators have emphasised that this indicates the subordination of the third power to the law as a system, crowned by the Constitution, rather than reducing that obedience to a concrete regulation. This is a kind of appeal to a judge's creativity in interpreting the law, which also has a positive bearing on the issue of judicial independence. As Letowska writes: 'While the judges' subservience to the Constitution has never been questioned, the explicit characterisation of the Constitution as the foundation of the judge's everyday work and, at the same time, as the limit of his subservience is a laudable principle. This formulation may make judges more aware that what matters is not only the most specific provision to be relied upon as a direct basis for resolution of a particular dispute, but also that the Constitution is the structural and axiological basis of the entire legal system'.[19]

The controversial question is whether, in the light of this constitutional provision, a common court might decide not to apply a statute that the court considers inconsistent with the Constitution, or whether it should refer a 'legal question' to the Constitutional Tribunal. Arguably, a hypothetical common court decision not to apply a given statute certainly does not directly result in the repeal of the statute the court considers inconsistent with the Constitution. Nevertheless, this is also a one of the important elements in the concept of the separation of powers.[20]

To bolster the independence of the judiciary, the constitution explicitly states that a judge cannot be affiliated with any political party or trade union and that he or she cannot engage in any public activity that would be irreconcilable with the principles of the independence of courts and of judges. The constitution ultimately prohibited combining judicial functions and any other state functions, including holding the mandate of a parliamentary deputy or senator.

From a legal standpoint, judicial authority is acknowledged as an equal partner vis-à-vis the legislative and executive branches. But certain difficulties have been encountered when attempting to precisely define that equality in practice. Discussion has begun on budget autonomy, which is perceived as an important factor guaranteeing that equality. Two drafts are now in parliament: one pertaining to the organisational structure of common courts, the other dealing with the National Judiciary Council. Both propose budget autonomy. This means that the National Judiciary Council would draw up its own budget, to be included in the governmental draft budget without granting the government any possibility to change it. The proposal has sparked intense discussion. The main argument on the side of the judiciary is based on the principle of the separation of powers, but argumentation has been demagogic.

This problem is closely connected with the question how, within the framework of the separation of powers, to define or better to re-define the role of the Minister of Justice. The Minister of Justice belongs to the executive branch, but at the same time he supervises the administrative activities of common courts and is politically accountable to the parliament for the functioning of justice. This question has not been clearly answered and involves tensions between the Ministry of Justice and the judiciary.

CLOSING REMARKS

In evaluating the new constitution, one must also be aware that, under the principle of the separation of powers, the written constitution is not the only thing defining relations between particular bodies, which are also influenced by the existing political system, constitutional customs, and the decisions of the Constitutional Court. Frequently, individual institutions were based on selected generally known models of government that the constitution's creators, as well as politicians, regarded as democratic. In this way, solutions taken from different systems – semi-presidential, chancellarian, parliamentary – were combined, often with little regard for the cohesion of the overall model of government that would emerge from such an eclectic combination. This inevitably evoked tensions between individual organs of power. This eclecticism must be gradually eliminated as a result of interpretations reflecting the experiences of a concrete state and its own traditions. But that takes time. An important but often forgotten feature of countries undergoing transformation was their lack of constitutional customs. Writing a constitution is not only a legal act. A constitution means established forms of conduct that take shape against the background and within the framework of binding constitutional regulations. Not everything can be written down in the constitution. All attempts to do so are doomed to failure. In such cases, a constitution becomes too detailed a document and turns into self-commentary. These are not simply theoretical remarks divorced from reality. Such dangers exist and to some extent has emerged in some provisions of the Polish constitution. The long period required to prepare the Constitution gave rise to a tendency to include in it provisions responding to instances of improper practice. Such behaviour was partially justified, but not in all cases. The history of all countries possessing established constitutional traditions teaches us that precedents and constitutional customs play an extremely important role. However, for such customs to take shape, a constitution must be in force over an extended period of time. Amid constantly changing laws or even, worse, changing models of government, it is difficult for clear customs to take shape; they require decades to crystallise and belong to a concrete political tradition. The role of the Constitutional Tribunal should also be seen in that light.

NOTES

1   It was crucial at that time to consider the axiological bases of the future constitution, compare: P. Winczorek, 'Aksjologiczne podstawy nowej konstytucji', *Państwo i Prawo* 1988/12; Z. Ziembiński, '*Wartości konstytucyjne, Wydawnictwo Sejmowe*', Warsaw 1993.

2   Howard, Dick A.E. (1993), 'Constitutional Reform', Richard F. Staar (ed), *Transition to Democracy in Poland*, New York, p. 107.
3   Letowska E., Letowski J. (1996), *Towards the Rule of Law*, Scholar, Warsaw, p.102.
4   Pullo A. (1999), 'The Principle of Balancing Powers in the Constitution of the Republic of Poland', in M. Wyrzykowski (ed), *Constitutional Essays*, Institute of Public Affairs, Warsaw, p.110.
5   Sokolewicz W. (1995), 'Podział władz – idea polityczna czy zasada prawna?, Z dylematów współczesnego ustrojodawcy', *in Prawo w okresie przemian ustrojowych w Polsce*, Warsaw, p. 17; ('Separation of Powers – A Political Concept or Legal Principle? A Contemporary Legislator's Dilemma', in *The Law During the Changes of Political System*).
6   Ciemniewski, J. (1993), 'Podzial wladz w Malej Konstytucji' ['The Separation of Powers in the Small Constitution'], in M. Kruk (ed), *Mała Konstytucja w procesie przemian ustrojowych w Polsce (The Small Constitution during the Systemic Changes in Poland)*, Warsaw, p.20.
7   Article 32, para. 2 of the Constitution imposed upon the President the duty to ensure observance of the Constitution, safeguard the sovereignty and the security of the state, protect the inviolability and integrity of its territory, and uphold political and military treaties.
8   Suchocka H., 'Checks and Balances under the New Constitution of Poland', *Constitutional Essays*, pp.131-135.
9   The Constitutional Act of 17 October 1992, The Sejm Publishing Office, Warsaw 1993.
10   One such conflict involved the appointment of members to the National Broadcasting Council. To ensure the Council's independence, it was decided that the Sejm, Senate, and President should each appoint three members. In the light of the Small Constitution, the presidential decision needed to be countersigned. The President, however, did not submit his decision to the Prime Minister. Nonetheless, the decision remained in force.
11   Pullo A. *op. cit.*
12   *Biuletyn Komisji Konstytucyjnej Zgromadzenia Narodowego*, Warsaw 1994, VIII, 53.
13   See also: H. Suchocka, *op. cit.*
14   As J. Zakrzewska stated several years ago, 'the application of Montesquieu's doctrine has been enriched by the constitutional practice of several European countries where many new constitutional courts were established, in particular after World War II.' J. Zakrzewska: *Spór o konstytucję [Disputes Concerning the Constitution]*, Warsaw, 1993, p. 96.
15   Extensively discussed in 'Changes in the Constitutional Regulation of the Judiciary and Prosecution Effected in 1989' by H. Suchocka and L. Kański, *Państwo i Prawo (State and Law)*, 1991 **1**, 21-23.
16   The changes in the law effected in 1989 concerned all the key problems relating to judges' independence. Particularly noteworthy are the following changes: 1. Restriction of the role of the administration in the appointment and promotion of judges; 2. Adoption of the principle of judges' irremovability; 3. Depriving the Supreme Court of the right to establish so-called guidelines for the administration of justice and the practice of the law; 4. Depriving so-called legal principles of binding force in relation to adjudicative Supreme Court panels.
     Also removed from the law on common courts were regulations permeated with ideological phraseology, e.g. Articles 3 and 4, which dealt with the tasks of courts, and Article 67, dealing with the aforementioned duties of judges, including the duty of fidelity to the Polish People's Republic.
17   Compare the ruling of the Constitutional Tribunal of 9 November 1993 [OTK 1993/2/37]: the ruling of the Constitutional Tribunal of 8 November 1994 [concerning the suspension

of the valorization of judges' salaries]; the ruling of the Constitutional Tribunal of 11 September 1995 [in reply to a query by the Supreme Court regarding the principles governing judges' salaries]; the verdict of 24 June 1998; and the ruling of the Constitutional Tribunal of 22 March 2000 [regarding determination of the amount of judges' salaries within the context of Article 178 of the Constitution of the Republic of Poland].

18   Ruling of the Constitutional Tribunal 1993/2/106.

19   Letowska E, 'Courts and Tribunals under the Constitution of Poland', *Constitutional Essays, op. cit.*

20   Polish courts have a very good position in the system of separation of powers. However, as E. Letowska has stated: 'This is not only the result of growing awareness of their role in the system of checks and balances, as the power that controls and restrains the legislature and the executive, but also a consequence of the weakness of legislation, of public fatigue with the politicking within the other powers.' See: E. Letowska, J. Letowski: *op. cit.*, 123.

8. Invisible Contexts, Invisible Constraints. The Limits of the Normative Explanation of Constitutional Change

Ivan Krastev and Ralitsa Peeva

A piece of paper called a constitution can be many things: an empty ideological gesture, a narrowly legalistic document, or a profound act of self-definition (Ackerman, 1992). It can be a puzzle for historians and the Bible for constitutional lawyers.

Building a normative theory of constitution-making is certainly a tempting and noble intellectual enterprise. Prior knowledge about the difficulties in each stage of the process would provide future constitution makers with the advantages of political learning and experience. Such a theory would inform the debates in polities undergoing historic constitutional changes about the course to follow and the procedures to apply, about the mechanisms to discuss and the answers to seek. If societies possessed a manual for successful constitution-making, there would be less misunderstandings and false attempts, hence fewer political risks in potentially volatile situations. The promise of normative constitutional theory is the promise of liberal democracy.

Creating a general theory that explains particular constitution-making choices is also a tempting and noble intellectual enterprise. But is this theory the same? Can normative constitutional theory be used to explain various decisions and failures resulting from the process of creating the basic law of a polity and to disentangle the complicated procedure of negotiations and compromises, of resolutions and political bargaining that inevitably affect the work of constituent assemblies? Can the normative explanation serve as a historical explanation of constitutional change?

All these questions re-emerge ten years after the creation of the Center for the Study of Constitutionalism in Eastern Europe at the University of Chicago Law School.[1] The Center has embodied the ambition to create a normative constitutional theory that will also serve as an explanatory framework for the constitutional changes in Eastern Europe.[2] After 1989, twenty-seven countries from the region had to choose the new democratic rules of the game and create their new constitutions. To the scholars of constitution-making the situation resembled the old dream of a constitutional laboratory: 'The constitution-making processes in Eastern Europe amount to a gigantic natural experiment.'[3] The number of countries was sufficient to render valid comparisons, the process allowed for direct observation, and the participants could be interviewed and advised. The ambition of the enterprise was to formulate the principles of a normative constitutional theory, and today it seems that this task of the project has been successfully completed indeed (Elster, 1997).

The other goal of the project, however, was to explain the process of constitution-making in each of these countries. By keeping an accurate historical record, the Center aimed to decipher the origins of every institutional choice and the particularities of constitution-making in each parliament. The Center was quite successful in this direction as well. Some of the most insightful analyses of the constitution-making process in Poland or Russia were published in the *East European Constitutional Review* and written by participants in the project. But what is the relation between normative constitutional theory and the ambition to create a general theory explaining constitutional change? Is normative explanation really possible? And does it remain sensitive to the numerous invisible contexts and constraints that always accompany the process of creating constitutional provisions?

The aim of this article is to address the paradox of normative explanation. We argue that the design of an optimal structure for constitution-making and the formulation of normative principles inevitably require a common context for the different constitutional choices. And yet, it is this presupposed context that may confront the theoretical 'why' with the historical 'how' in explaining the logic of constitutional change. The successful formulation of a normative constitution-making theory depends significantly on the readiness not only to analyse closely the formal elements of the constitution-making process, but also to reconstruct the context of the actual constitution-making. The analysis of the invisible constraints motivating the constitution framers is instrumental in understanding the mechanism of negotiation and the origins of certain institutional agreements. It is precisely the focus on particular discussions that will help to disentangle the strategic vision of the political players and to render the context comprehensible. An abstract normative viewpoint risks overlooking a number of key variables motivating the actors and resulting in misleading conclusions.

We will try to identify the problems facing normative constitutional theory in its ambition to explain constitutional changes by reconstructing the historical context of certain constitutional decisions in Bulgaria. The Bulgarian constitution-making process is a promising test case for evaluating the potentials and limits of the normative framework in explaining constitutional change. Bulgaria was too impatient to adopt a new constitution to wait for the establishment of the Chicago Center. As a result of this impatience, the details of the constitution-making process remained hidden to foreign observers. The insiders' perspective was lost, and the Bulgarian case, due to its marginality, was treated more 'abstractly' than the Polish or Russian cases. The explanation of the Bulgarian constitutional choices is a classical example of the promises and failures of the normative explanation of a constitution-making process.

Our approach in testing the limits of normative explanation is to restate five questions already answered in the normative-explanatory paradigm:

- Why was Bulgaria the first in Eastern Europe to adopt a new constitution?
- Why was an article banning parties based on ethnic or religious principle introduced in the Bulgarian Constitution?
- Why did the Bulgarian Constitution adopt the institution of the vice-president?
- Why was the Bulgarian Constituent Assembly composed of 400 founding fathers?
- Why did the Bulgarian Constitution impose three conditions for eligibility on the presidential candidates: to be older than 40, to be born in Bulgaria, and to have lived in the country for the last 5 years?

The normative-explanatory framework has offered its answer to each question. According to the normative explanation, the early adoption of the new constitution reflected the strategic interests and organisational capacity of the old Communist elites. The ban on parties based on ethnic or religious principles resulted from the nationalistic bias of the former elites and their strong resources to impose it. And while the Chicago project has never addressed the issue of the number of deputies, the logic of the normative-explanatory framework interprets the institution of the vice-president and the limits imposed on presidential candidates as direct borrowings from other constitutions, i.e. as externally imposed elements rather than contemplated political choices by the constitution framers. Alternatively, recreating the invisible constraints, contexts, and particular negotiations in the Bulgarian constituent assembly, we will reconstruct the questions as historical and search the limits of normative explanation. History is the best friend of theory, but it is also its worst enemy.

How did Bulgaria become the first post-Communist country to adopt a new constitution?

The particular timing of the new Bulgarian Constitution was first noticed in the analyses of Jon Elster, Stephen Holmes, and Cass Sunstein: 'Why should the least liberal leadership in the region have been the first to create a liberal constitutional framework?' [4] The authors conclude that the old regime elites in Bulgaria and Romania had not only greater power than other post-Communist elites to impose their vision in the constitutional document, but also greater incentives to implement new liberal constitutions. The urge to write constitutions was motivated by their wish to gain legitimacy when presenting themselves as the initiators of the new liberal order and by their willingness to secure immunity for crimes committed under the previous system. In addition, the argument continues, the Communist elites had a strong organisational motive because they could easily discipline the Communist-dominated parliaments. The normative explanation is a convincing one. Ultimately, the hypothesis suggests that the Bulgarian Round Table's decision to hold elections for a Constituent Assembly was a strategic choice by the old regime leaders. The historical evidence from the Bulgarian case, however, presents a radically different account.

The type of the future parliament, hence its mission, was among the first contested issues in the round table talks. Despite common perceptions among political analysts, the idea for a Constituent Assembly belonged to the opposition and for awhile was vehemently opposed by the ruling elite. Therefore the proper question is not why the old regime elites had an interest in adopting a new constitution early, but why the post-Communist elites came up with this proposal. The rhetoric of the Union of Democratic Forces (UDF) involved three arguments. Its leaders insisted, first, that in contrast to an ordinary Parliament, the constituent assembly, the Grand National Assembly (GNA), would represent a genuine break with the Communist past. Second, with its larger number of MPs, the GNA would endow Parliament with greater democratic legitimacy at a crucial time of regime change when it had to create the new constitution of the polity.[5] Finally, the opposition considered the GNA a symbolic return to the political traditions of the Bulgarian state before the establishment of the Communist regime in 1944.

The arguments of the opposition were more the arguments of justification than the arguments of motivation. Two other strategic considerations motivated the position of the UDF. According to its leaders, the gist of this debate was actually about the mandate of the first freely-elected parliament. Since the main task of the GNA would be the creation of the new constitution, its mandate would be significantly shorter than the mandate of an ordinary assembly. Therefore, the decision to have a GNA instead of a regular parliament also implied that a second round of general elections would be held relatively soon. Recognising its organisational weaknesses and fearing a possible loss in the coming first free elections, the Bulgarian opposition tried to keep open the opportunity for a 'second chance.' A member of the UDF delegation claimed in his memoirs, 'The main argument, open or tacit, to accept the idea of a Grand National Assembly was that if we lost the elections, soon there would be new ones and we would be able to retaliate.'[6] The UDF's resolution to insist on the most preferable option was reflected in the words of its leader, Zhelyu Zhelev:

> 'We should agree first on the type of the new Parliament a Grand National Assembly. This is our firm position and we will fight for it. We will not retreat – we state this clearly.'[7]

The arguments of some Communist leaders that the short mandate would bring a 'temporary government with tied hands' and would delay urgent legislative initiatives were ineffective.[8] The final agreement declared that the elections would be for a GNA.[9]

Our conclusion is that in the strategic vision of the Bulgarian opposition, the discussions on the type of parliament were primarily negotiations for the date of the second post-Communist elections. It was this understanding of the debate that pushed the UDF to insist on a constituent assembly and the adoption of a new constitution. There is little doubt that such strategic calculation was entirely acceptable to the old elite when it calculated its own benefits in the opposition's proposal. Nevertheless, the subtle internal context of the debate about the constitution suggests an alternative answer to why Bulgaria was the first Eastern European country to adopt a new liberal basic law. It was not the old elite's search for legitimacy but the post-Communist elite's insecurity about the outcomes of the founding elections that made Bulgaria the first Eastern European country to adopt a new constitution.

How did the Constitution ban the existence of parties on ethnic, religious, or racist basis?

Article 11, Section 4 of the Bulgarian Constitution states: 'There shall be no political parties on ethnic, racial, or religious lines, nor parties that seek the violent usurpation of state power.' This article is among the most debated elements of the new constitution. It also had an enormous political impact when, in 1992, with the weight of just one vote, the Bulgarian Constitutional Court confirmed the constitutionality of the Movement for Rights and Freedoms (MRF), a political movement of the Bulgarian Turks, founded in January 1990. The inclusion of the article in the basic law is most often interpreted as evidence of unwavering control by the old Communist elites, whose nationalistic convictions and lasting resources for political influence imposed an obvious transgression of basic human rights principles.

The events that followed, however, revealed significant inconsistency in the presented logic. Explaining the apparent paradox of the MRF, we argue that, first, the unfortunate nationalistic bias was not exclusively confined to the Communist elite but also marked the activity of some constitutional framers from the opposition as well, and, second, that if the nationalistic attitudes of the old elites were the immediate source of the ban, then the MRF would not exist at all. The political and legal fate of the Movement reveals that the Communist and post-Communist elites were motivated more by strategic calculations in the given political context than by internalised xenophobic convictions. We claim, therefore, that the ban was not designed to forbid just any party based on ethnic principle, but was a disguised attempt to control the activity of such party.

The first important detail undermining the existing explanations is the fact that the article was drafted initially not in the Constituent Assembly but in the Bulgarian Round Table, where both sides assertively pushed to impose the ban. The minutes from this single closed session of the forum reveal that the opposition leaders were just as active in supporting the decision as the Communist party figures.[10] Evidently, the appearance of the MRF provoked a faltering reaction in the opposition circles. On the one hand, the Movement posed a serious political challenge to the UDF's reputation as the sole representative of the Turkish minority interests. The emergence of the MRF would undoubtedly split support for the opposition in the regions with mixed population. On the other hand, the opposition feared that the nationalistic cause was already too popular and any further attempt to rally the case of the ethnic minorities would undermine its chances for electoral victory. Gripped by these concerns, in stark contrast to its pre-1989 legacy, the opposition was making careful attempts to dissociate itself from minority issues. The electoral logic overran the human rights sentiments of the opposition. Thus the opposition was just as involved in strategic calculations regarding the ethnic minority issue as the Communist party.

A further challenge to the existing logic is the fact that, a few weeks after the closed session of the Round Table, it was Prime Minister Andrei Lukanov who helped the MRF with its court registration. Indeed, the existence of a Turkish minority party this early in the process of political transition could not be an option without the tacit approval of the top party leadership. Still having a firm grip upon the judicial system, the BCP could affect the fate of the Movement upon the whim of the power holders.[11] It is true that the existence of nationalistic fervor influenced the decisions of the authorities, but in a much more subtle way than the normative theory explains. Rather than abruptly eliminating the channel of political participation for the Turkish minority, the governmental actors tried to take advantage of the MRF's presence. Facilitating its registration instead of fighting it, the party activists gained a strategic lead in the attempt to control ethnic minority issues. In addition, the existence of a Turkish minority party would certainly take away a significant number of votes from the UDF in the coming elections.

Undoubtedly, Article 11 breaches the norms of ethnic tolerance and democratic liberalism and is a shameful article in the Bulgarian Constitution. Its inclusion in the new constitution, however, did not result directly from the nationalistic fervor of the Communist elites. Rather, it seems plausible to argue that the logic of banning ethnic parties and at the same time legalising the MRF is the logic of the 'governable exception'. The MRF has become the only channel for political representation of ethnic Turks. As we see once again, the variety of invisible constraints and a particular context had a major impact upon the constitutional decisions of the Bulgarian Constitution framers.

How did the new constitution adopt the institution of the vice-president and how was it related to the presidency?

Our third question proposes an alternative argument why a theory explaining constitutional choices should remain sensitive to the fact that constitutions are often driven by invisible constraints. If this factor is ignored, we would never understand why the Bulgarian Constitution created the office of the vice-president. Following the logic of normative explanation, the vice-presidential post is yet another example of constitutional borrowing, due especially to the irresistible charm of the American model. Two issues, however, question the presented logic. First, of all the basic laws of the new democracies, the Bulgarian Constitution was the only one that created this office. Second, a comparative look would show that the vice-presidential institution is not popular among presidents in parliamentary regimes such as the Bulgarian one. In short, reading the Bulgarian Constitution, the institution of the vice-president seems strange and useless. Its presence can be explained by origin and not by function.

The Bulgarian vice-president is among the least powerful political figures in the republic. Only three constitutional clauses refer to him, the most empowering of which is his role upon the death (or permanent disability) of the president, i.e. the clause that defines the vice-president as 'the widow' of the president.[12] The only prerogatives that the president can devolve to the vice-president are to appoint and dismiss from legally-established office other state officials; to grant, restore, relieve from and withdraw Bulgarian citizenship; to grant asylum; and to exercise the right to grant pardon. Analysed outside of the particular context of its creation, the office of the vice-president does not contribute anything to the functioning of the democratic system. Instead, it imposes an unnecessary burden on the taxpayers. What, then, explains the paradoxical emergence of the Bulgarian vice-presidency?

Once again, the first indication about this peculiar institutional choice appeared during the round table talks. The vice-presidential post was mentioned initially in the heated debates over the establishment of the presidential office. There was an emerging consensus between both sides that some form of acceptable interim solution should replace the discredited institution of the State Council, a creation of the former regime that openly clashed with the principle of separation of powers. The two sides, however, seriously disagreed over the type of election, the mandate, and the powers of the future president. While the BCP argued for a strong president elected directly for a five or six-year mandate, the UDF was willing to restrict the presidential powers and to avoid a direct election, which would endow the most likely winner, the reformist party leader Petar Mladenov, with strong democratic legitimacy.[13] Instead, the UDF was willing to strike a compromise, agreeing that Mr. Mladenov could be the first president, but only if elected by the old Communist parliament. The final resolution sealed the compromise:

> 'The delegates agree to a constitutional amendment in chapter five of the existing constitution. This amendment will dissolve the State Council and establish the institution of the president who will be elected by the current National Assembly. The participants agree that the acting head of the State Council [Petar Mladenov] will be elected as a head of state.'[14]

The agreements on the presidency understandably captured the attention of political observers. Most analyses, however, overlooked a key aspect concerning the function of the future vice-president. Summarising the limits of a possible compromise, the UDF leader, Dimitar Ludzhev, stated:

> We are dropping the text about the vice-president for now. We agree in principle that such an institution can exist, but it should be discussed after the election. The text is the following: 'The vice-president should be elected after the parliamentary elections in June 1990, when the results of the elections will be taken in consideration.'[15]

Evidently from its very initiation, the vice-presidential post was designed to serve as an institution of political compromise. It was designed as the hidden emergency exit for the political process. This hypothesis is also confirmed by the fact that the old parliament, while duly passing a constitutional amendment that created the presidential post, declared: 'The vice-president shall be elected by the National Assembly upon the proposal of the president. The vice-president shall assist the activity of the president.'[16] Another piece of evidence that the vice-presidency was established to serve as the institution of political compromise came when, a few days later, Mr. Mladenov, elected by the old parliament to be the first president of the country, never raised the issue of nominating a vice-president. Apparently the position was reserved for political crises and compromises 'when the results of the elections would be taken in consideration.'

The peculiar fate of the Bulgarian vice-presidency was inevitably associated with the fate of the compromised presidency. The round table consensus about the presidential institution suffered an unexpected shift only three months after it was reached. Recorded to say, 'Let the tanks come,' during a UDF demonstration in December 1989, President Mladenov was forced to resign soon after the parliamentary elections in June 1990. His resignation immediately generated political strife in the Constituent Assembly, which, only two weeks after the convening ceremony, faced the difficult task of electing a president with a qualified majority. The already routine search for a compromise was unavoidable, because the electoral victory of the BSP undermined the initially intended institution-sharing formula based on the Polish model 'our president – your prime minister.' [17] The reformist party leaders realised that the electoral results forced them to accept a different power-sharing structure. With the UDF holding one-third of the seats in the Assembly, BSP conceded that the opposition should also hold one of the three key positions in the country – President, Prime Minister, or Speaker of Parliament.[18] The question was how to design an acceptable compromise, and evidently the vice-presidential post would play the key role in this.

The following days of mounting political tension, risky bargaining, and five unsuccessful rounds of voting threatened a constitutional crisis. If the newly elected Grand National Assembly failed to meet its self-imposed deadline to elect a president, it would have to dissolve and organise new elections under the interim rules enforced by the round table. It was in this tense political situation that, on 1 August 1990, the Constituent Assembly (dominated by socialists) elected the UDF leader, Zhelyu Zhelev, as president. Zhelev's election involved serious political bargaining between the BSP and the UDF. Although the BSP leadership was eager to take the risk and support his candidacy, it had to persuade its own constituency why, despite its overwhelming victory on the elections, a compromise on the presidency was inevitable. The vice-presidential institution was the logical key bargaining provision. During the crucial meeting between the leadership of the two parties, when trade-offs were discussed, the BSP posed several conditions to Zhelev, among which was: 'The vice-president will be from the BSP.'[19] The negotiations were completed. Only minutes after his election and in compliance with the constitutional amendment and the negotiated compromise, Zhelev nominated a BSP leader and army general, Atanas Semerdzhiev, as vice-president. The socialists sold the presidency, saving their face at the same time.

This rather detailed review of the vice-presidential post supports the argument about the deeply negotiated nature of the constitution-making process, in which everyday, interest-based motivations and context-related rationalisation had a major impact upon the constitutional choices. The vice-presidency was a clear compromise between the two main political forces in their attempt to answer the concerns of their respective opponent, to meet the demands of their constituencies, and to alleviate the rising public tension. It was introduced, not as an institutionally efficient structure, but as a safety valve against an imminent constitutional crisis. Analysed in this perspective, it is hardly surprising that the Bulgarian vice-president has only emergency functions.

Why did the vice-presidential office survive when the context it served was changed? Normative constitutional theory suggests the most convincing explanation of this survival. The Bulgarian vice-presidency is a clear confirmation of the hypothesis that once an institution has been established, it is most likely bound to stay. Moreover, the major players in the next parliaments continued to be the two political forces who authored the compromise in 1990-1991. So the normative constitutional theory has no difficulties explaining why the 'strange' institution of the vice-president has found a place in the new constitution. But it is unlikely that the normative constitutional theory can guess why the vice-presidency appeared during the round table talks.

How was the Bulgarian Constituent Assembly composed of 400 deputies?

The decision on the number of the constitutional framers, although never discussed in the analyses of the Bulgarian Constituent Assembly, is an additional example revealing the importance of invisible constraints and their subtle influence on strategic calculations.

The last Communist constitution did not foresee the existence of a Grand National Assembly as a special forum charged with creating a new constitution. Rather, the 1971 Constitution provided for 400 members of parliament who also had the authority to ratify and amend the constitutional document.[20] Had the two sides at the round table followed the regime's paper constitution precisely, the new constituent assembly would have been an ordinary parliament mixing constitutional and ordinary politics in a constitutionally undefined mandate. Such an option was obviously unacceptable to the opposition. Its opinion was that a Grand National Assembly had to create the new constitution. According to the first Bulgarian Constitution of 1879, such a forum would comprise twice as many deputies as an ordinary parliament, thus allowing for expansion of democratic participation when decisions on key issues were involved.[21]

The round table discussions about the number of deputies in the first democratically elected assembly, however, did not refer to either constitutional document. While the UDF delegation argued persistently that a larger number of deputies would endow the new parliament with greater democratic legitimacy and urged having 500 MPs in the Constituent Assembly, the government side doubted the efficiency of a large forum and proposed 300 people. Soon the Communist party delegation reduced the number to 250 and then to 200.[22]

Following a few days of heated debates, the two sides surprisingly relented. An agreement reached in the contact group declared that there would be 400 delegates, and the plenary sessions witnessed no more discussions on the issue. What unexpectedly changed the delegates' position was a simple comment on logistics. In the midst of the tense arguments, a member of the contact group from the BSP quota, Ginyo Ganev, observed that the hall of the Bulgarian Parliament could accommodate a maximum of 400 deputies. This little detail played a major role in resolving one of the difficult discussions at the round table. The event shows that sometimes particular constraints force the constitution makers to cooperate, not according to the best strategic option, but in a rather trivial accommodation to realities. The decision on the number of deputies in the GNA is a powerful illustration of the type of invisible constraints that are involved in any constitution-making process. It is these unimaginable constraints that predetermine the complexity of the historical re-construction and are missing in the normative explanatory framework.

How was the Bulgarian presidency limited by three conditions of eligibility: age over 40, born in Bulgaria, and having lived in the country for the last five years?

This last question is more evidence that historical explanation should consider the often underestimated contextuality of the constitutional debate of a new democracy. Analysed outside of the political context, the clauses defining the limits of the Bulgarian presidency are not unusual. A number of constitutions impose such conditions on future presidential candidates. Likewise, in the justification strategy of the normative explanation, the Bulgarian constitutional clauses limiting presidential candidates could be interpreted as an obvious instance of constitutional borrowing, rather than as a result of internal bargaining and elite negotiations.

However, the political compromise that led to the current format of the Bulgarian presidency was much more influenced by the existing political context and the fears of the constitution framers than by the constitutional choices of other polities. Actually, the article defining the eligibility of future

Bulgarian presidents is among the most obvious examples of a constitutional compromise corresponding to a specific situation. While a number of clauses were designed to avoid or enforce a rather abstract course of events or political processes, the eligibility constraints for the presidential office had to do with specific political figures prominent at the time of constitution-making. The age limit, admittedly a frequent clause in constitutional documents, was an institutional device preventing the young and radical leader of the first independent trade union 'Podkrepa,' Konstantin Trenchev, from entering the presidential race in the elections of 1992. The requirement to be born in Bulgaria was devised to prevent the nomination of the most popular reformist leader of the BSP, Andrei Lukanov.[23] Finally, the condition of five consecutive years of residency was a subtle way to guarantee that the Bulgarian monarch in exile, Simeon, would not be allowed to enter the race.

The limits on the Bulgarian presidential candidates were among the most conspicuous examples of how particular interests and favourable arrangements can affect institutional choices. What, seen from Chicago, looks like ordinary constitutional 'borrowing' turns out to be a complex political bargain, when read in the historical context of Bulgarian constitution-making.

CONCLUSION

Making a constitution is a rare activity. And 'forgetting' the contextuality of the process is what transforms the constitution from a puzzle for the historians into a Bible for constitutional lawyers. What is lost in the process of forgetting is the multiplicity of contexts in which the constitution-making took place.

The normative constitutional approach failed to explain the logic of major constitutional choices in the process of constitution-making in Bulgaria. It remained uninterested in the multiplicity of contexts. The answers to the historical question 'How did it happen?' did not coincide with the answers to the theoretical question 'Why did it happen?' Trying to resurrect the motivations of the framers, the normative approach failed on several occasions to distinguish motivations from justifications and to identify the context in which the players rationalised their strategies. The question is: Why was the Chicago laboratory tempted to use the normative perspective as an explanatory one?

The answer, in our view, goes to the very heart of the Chicago project. Building the normative constitutional theory was not simply an academic exercise, it was an attempt to create a practical instrument to be used by the would-be founding fathers in Eastern Europe. The Chicago star team believed that constitutions matter and that what post-communist societies needed were constitutions that matter.

The universalisation of the American constitutional experience and the belief in the Eastern European 'constitutional moment' made the Chicago laboratory believe that what we see in Eastern Europe is a revolution that is going to be constitutionalised. Normative theorists were convinced that, in order to grasp what was happening in Eastern Europe, it was necessary to read Lech Walensa in terms of George Washington (Ackerman, 1992). But this romantic normativism has its limits.

Normative constitutional theory can serve as a historical explanation of the constitution-making process only if we assume that Ackerman's distinction between constitutional politics and normal politics, between a higher lawmaking track and a lower lawmaking track, is an absolute one (Ackerman, 1988). It is this romantic stress on the unique character of constitutional politics that hid from the Chicago scholars the fact that, in the case of Bulgaria, on many occasions normal politics were conducted dressed in a constitutional toga. They thought the context in which the constitution-making process could be explained was the level of constitutional politics. In Bulgaria, however, as this article demonstrates, constitutional bargaining took place much more on the basis of normal politics than on the basis of high principles.

The various invisible contexts revealed in our article are far from challenging the conclusions of normative constitutional theory. The discussion only argues for modesty about the explanatory power of normative theory. Borrowing the language of the transitologists, we simply want to stress that, in the process of constitution-making, constitutional politics is not the only game in town. Ironically, Bulgarian public opinion seemed to be always aware of this, as shown by the fact that it never endowed the Bulgarian constitution-makers with the respected title 'founding fathers'.

NOTES

1   Stephen Holmes (1992), 'Introducing the Center,' *EECR* **1** (1).
2   Jon Elster, 'Constitutionalism in Eastern Europe: An Introduction,' in *University of Chicago Law Review* **58**, 449.
3   Jon Elster and Stephen Holmes (1992), 'Special Reports,' *EECR* **1** (1), and Stephen Holmes and Cass Sunstein, 'The Politics of Constitutional Revision in Eastern Europe' in Sanford Levinson, (ed) (1995), *Responding to Imperfection: The Theory and Practice of Constitutional Amendment,* Princeton: Princeton University Press.
4   Zhelyu Zhelev, March 27, 1990, see Kruglata masa: stenografski protokoli [The Round Table: Minutes from the Negotiations], Sofia, 1999, p. 499.
5   See Petko Simeonov, *Goliamata promiana: 10.XI.1989-10.VI.1990 [The Big Change: 10.XI.1989 – 10.VI.1990]*, Sofia, 1996, p. 388. Also interviews of the authors with Dimitar Ludzhev, the leader of the UDF delegation in the contact group of the Round Table where most of the key decisions were made.
6   See note 4, *op. cit*, p. 444
7   Such remarks were made by the leader of the BCP delegation, Aleksander Lilov and by the chairman of the Legislative Committee in the old Communist parliament, Vasil Mrachkov, who often took part in the talks on the side of the party elite. See *ibid.*, pp. 406-07, 523.
8   *Ibid.*, pp. 677-78.
9   *Ibid.*, pp. 431-498.
10 See Petko Simeonov, *op.cit.*, p. 391.
11 Petar Stamatov argues that the fact that the MRF 'was allowed to function prior to, and during the first free elections in 1990, depended ultimately on the 'good will' of the ex-communist government' and Roumyana Kolarova explains that 'because the judicial procedure created by the new bill [on political parties] was highly centralized and thereby easily controlled by the Communist party/state authorities, the top party officials essentially had the power to decide whether and how the MRF would be registered.' See Petar Stamatov, 'Ethnicity and the Structuration of the Political Field in Bulgarian Transition', MA thesis, Department of Political Science, CEU Budapest, June 1996, p. 28 and Roumyana Kolarova, 'Tacit Agreements in the Bulgarian Transition to Democracy: Minority Rights and Constitutionalism,' *University of Chicago Law School Round Table*, 1993, p. 34.
12 Article 92, section 2 states that the President shall be assisted in his actions by a Vice President. According to Article 97, section 1, the President's or Vice President's authority shall expire before the expiry of his term of office upon any of the following occurrences: 1) resignation submitted before the Constitutional Court; 2) lasting incapacitation caused by a grave illness; 3) following Article 103 (providing for impeachment for high treason, or a violation of the Constitution); 4) death. According to section 3 in instance 1, the Vice President shall assume the duties of the President until the expiry of the term of office.
13 The position was presented first by the chairman of the parliamentary Legislative Committee, Vasil Mrachkov, March 19, 1990. See *Kruglata masa: stenografski protokoli [The Round Table: Minutes from the Negotiations]*, Sofia, 1999, pp. 402-3. The BSP position was subsequently clarified by the party leaders, Alexander Lilov and Georgi Pirinski, March 19, 26, and 27, 1990. See *ibid.*, pp. 407, 447, 493, 503. The UDF's position was summarised by Dimitar Ludzhev and Zhelyu Zhelev, March 26 and 29, 1990. *Ibid.*, pp. 449 and 566.
14 Final agreements signed March 30, 1990. See *Kruglata masa: stenografski protokoli [The Round Table: Minutes from the Negotiations]*, Sofia, 1999, p. 677.
15 *Ibid.*, p. 552.

16   *Stenografski dnevnitsi, Deveto Narodno Subrannie* [*Minutes from the Sessions of the Ninth National Assembly*], Sofia, 1991, Session 16, March 30 and April 3, 1990, p. 391.
17   Adam Michnik.
18   Interview of the authors with participants at the round table and advisors to the BSP delegation, May 1999, Sofia. See also Evgeni Dainov and Dimitar Varzonovtsev, Eds., *Elitat i promianata v Bulgaria* [*The Elite and the Change in Bulgaria*], Sofia, 1998, p. 196-97.
19   Zhelyu Zhelev, selections from *Moiata politicheska biografia* [*My Political Biography*] (forthcoming), published in the daily *Trud*, No. 199-203, July 2000.
20   Article 78 from the Constitution of People's Republic of Bulgaria (1971). Vesselin Metodiev and Luchezar Stoyanov (eds) (1990), *Bulgarski konstitutsii i konstitutsionni proekti* [*Bulgarian Constitutions and Constitutional Projects*], Sofia, p. 69.
21   Chapter XX from the Turnovo Bulgarian Constitution (1879) in Vesselin Metodiev and Luchezar Stoyanov, *op.cit.*, p. 33.
22   The proposal for 300 delegates was made by the chairman of the Legislative Committee in the old Parliament, Mr. Mrachkov, on January 29, 1990; the one for 250 delegates was made on March 15, 1990; the BSP proposal for 200 MPs was made on March 27, 1990. See *Kruglata masa: stenografski protokoli* [*The Round Table: Minutes from the Negotiations*], Sofia, 1999, p. 206, p. 402-03, and p. 500.

REFERENCES

Ackerman, Bruce (1988), 'Neo-federalism', in Jon Elster and Rune Slagstad (eds), *Constitutionalism and Democracy*, Cambridge University Press, pp. 153-193.

Ackerman, Bruce (1992), *The Future of Liberal Revolution,* Yale University Press.

Elster, Jon. (1997), 'Ways of Constitution-making', in Axel Hadenius (ed), *Democracy's Victory and Crisis*, Cambridge University Press.

Holmes, Stephen and Cass Sunstein (1995), 'The Politics of Constitutional Revision in Eastern Europe', in Sanford Levinson (ed), *Responding to Imperfection: The Theory and Practice of Constitutional Amendment*, Princeton University Press, pp. 275-307.

9. Market-making as State-making. Constitutions and Economic Development in Post-communist Eastern Europe[1]

Laszlo Bruszt

In 1989, the year of the 'final victory of free markets', states in advanced capitalist societies displayed a robust capacity to preserve market order, enforce competition, and regulate relations among economic actors. More specifically, these states had a well-developed capacity to uphold economic rights, enforce obligations, maintain predictable policy environments for economic actors, and prevent these actors from misusing asymmetries in economic and informational power. Added to these capacities were mechanisms to reduce the dangers of arbitrary policies and the risks that powerful economic groups would capture general regulative power. Most of the Central and Eastern European nations did not have such states at the start of economic transformation,[2] and according to some surveys, many of these states are still weak in this area and have not fully developed the capabilities typically present in advanced capitalist societies.

To date, there are three elements of state functions that remain in short supply in the region. The first is the state's capacity to uphold the general rights of economic actors and to create a predictable policy environment for them. According to a World Bank survey, such state capacities are the weakest in the world in the countries of the former Soviet Union – weaker even than in the countries of Sub-Saharan Africa or Latin America (Brunetti 1998). In the Central European countries, the capacity of states to uphold rights and maintain a predictable policy environment is somewhat stronger, but still weaker than in most advanced capitalist societies (Brunetti 1998). The second type of state capacity in short supply is the capacity to prevent powerful private groups from using state institutions to redistribute wealth and opportunities to themselves. According to a recently published survey, in many Eastern European countries, economic actors can reasonably expect that competitors can literally purchase policies and regulations in the different branches and levels of government (Hellman 2000). Perception of such capture of the state by private groups is low only in a smaller group of post-Communist countries (Hellman 2000). Finally, the third capacity is that of regulating relations among economic actors in a balanced way and of preventing the misuse of asymmetries in economic and informational power within the market. Again, according to recent surveys, most of the states of the region have not been able to introduce extensive and effective regulations enforcing competition and/or market orientation, even in such decisive areas as financial markets.[3]

These are exactly the state characteristics that shape the overall capacity of states to constitute and preserve market order and to enforce competition and market orientation. In several of the countries of the region, the absence of these capacities made economic actors hesitant to invest in the formal sector of the economy and more likely to prefer to enter into only very elementary forms of economic transactions, such as barter. In several of these countries, predatory groups dominate 'markets', and states are captured by these very same groups (Gaddy 1998; Hellman 1998; Polishchuk 1997; Stiglitz 1999; Woodruff 1999; Bruszt 2000). Problems of social and economic development in these countries are different than in those post-Communist countries that have more or less functioning market economies. While the question the latter countries face is how to correct the economic and social problems of otherwise functioning market orders, in the former countries economic and social problems are related to the nonexistence of functioning markets or, more precisely, to the corruption of states and markets by self-seeking groups. In these countries, economic stagnation after the loss of 40-60 per cent of the GDP and the mounting social problems associated with growing poverty and social inequalities are related only partly to the weak incentives of economic actors to enter into productive activities. At least as importantly in these countries, powerful economic actors have strong incentives and corresponding opportunities to profit primarily by redistributing wealth and opportunities to themselves, both in the public and the private spheres.

In this paper I argue that the characteristics of constitution-making played an important role in allowing the corruption of states and markets by self-seeking groups in several of the countries in the region. There are several different constitutional orders, and only a few of them increase the likelihood of generating a state with the capacity to preserve markets, resist corruption, and regulate the relations of economic actors in a balanced way.[4] Constitutions shape such state characteristics primarily by establishing a specific structure of representing the diversity of social interests within the state. It is through the structuring of representation that, to paraphrase Vincent Ostrom's formulation, constitutions might establish associations facilitating mutually productive relationships and constrain mutually destructive ones (Ostrom 1987). In the worse case, through a specific structure representing diversity, constitutions might contribute to the emergence of states with diametrically opposing effects.

The quality of market economies is largely a function of the characteristics of the state. Even a minimalist definition of a functioning market order might suffice to make this point.[5] From such a minimalist perspective, one can speak of a well-functioning market order only if economic actors can have stable expectations that (a) they can safely profit from rational enterprise and that (b) profit can be realised only from rational enterprise. The first expectation can probably be stable if a state can wield enough power to maintain the rule of law and uphold the rights to private property and if this power includes the ability to honour these rights within its own actions. A state with these qualities has the capacity to guarantee that economic actors can safely transact without fear of being deprived of their property either by economic predators or by arbitrary state intervention.

The second expectation, profit only from rational enterprise, is likely to be stable if there are robust mechanisms in place to prevent powerful economic actors from using the state to encroach upon the rights of other private actors and to redistribute wealth and opportunities to themselves. The stability of this second expectation, on the other hand, is also a function of the state's capacity to regulate relations among economic actors and prevent their misuse of economic power for the redistribution of wealth and opportunities within the private sphere of the market. To put it simply, the first expectation has largely to do with the guarantees of *freedoms from the state*. The second expectation can be said to be stable if the *freedom of the state* from capture is guaranteed and the state is strong enough to uphold the *freedom of the market* from the corruption by powerful economic actors. In this minimalist sense, one can speak of a functioning market order if economic actors can safely transact and none of them can corrupt either side of the equation: the state or the market.

States that can guarantee these conditions can be said to function as mechanisms of economic governance. Constitutions that increase the likelihood of the emergence of such a state will structure representation within the state in an associative way. They create a *heterarchy*, a specific type of democracy that represents diverse associations of heterogeneous interests within the state, prevents any of them from dominating, and bases the making of binding decisions on the orderly conflicts and compromises among institutions representing diverse ideas about the public good.[6] As discussed below, this specific organisation of representation makes a state a *heterarchy*, enabling it to uphold the freedoms of citizens, preserve its own freedom from capture, and regulate relations among economic actors so as to maintain competition and facilitate mutually beneficial cooperation. In this regard, I present preliminary evidence below that suggests that several of the post-socialist democracies of Central and Eastern Europe hardly qualify as heterarchies.

The paper is organised around the discussion of two interrelated questions. The largest part of the paper is devoted to the discussion of the specifics of the constitutional order that structure representation so as to strengthen the aforementioned state characteristics. The second question, addressed only preliminarily in this paper, concerns the creation of such constitutions. I stress the importance of one factor, namely that of the structure of the agenda of constitutional change, understood as understandings shared (among the bargaining participants in the constitutional change) about the problems to be addressed and the general principles/norms of solving them.[7] I will argue that, at the time when they were remaking their constitutions, most of the Eastern European countries could not focus on the conditions of constituting a functioning market economy. The agenda of constitutional change in most of these countries was shaped instead by positional struggles to create legitimate political power.

Constitutions that can provide the probability of creating the aforementioned state characteristics can come about two ways: first, as the outcome of successful bargaining and the constitution-makers' deliberate and successful efforts to address the constitutional lessons of previous interrelated economic and political failures, as in the case of the American and German constitutions.[8] In this paper, I will discuss the American case, arguing that in the United States, first in 1787 and then at the time of the New Deal, the remaking of the state was explicitly linked to a shared desire to create/ improve the aforementioned state characteristics.

The second way in which such state characteristics can come about is simply that *bona fortuna* smiles on the constitution-makers. The pursuit of goals not related to market-making might result in a constitutional order that, as an unintended side effect, contributes to the emergence of a state with the characteristics and capacities for economic governance I have described above. As it happened, in most of the Central and East European countries, fears and hopes related to the remaking of the *political field* dominated in the constitutional debates, and concerns related to market formation played only a marginal role, if any. The agenda of constitutional change was structured mainly by questions related to political legitimacy, sometimes including issues related to redrawing the boundaries of the nation. In several of these countries, the resulting constitutions did not increase and in some cases even directly weakened the probability of the emergence of states with a capacity to constitute and preserve markets (Bruszt 2000). As briefly discussed in the second half of the paper, this is the case in most of the former Soviet republics and in several of the Southeastern European countries. While the constitutional provision of rights in these countries correspond *grosso modo* to the requirements of constituting market order, in several cases their institutional/ structural provisions allow unchecked actors and institutions to usurp the representation of the public good within the state. Also, the constitutions in many of the countries led to states with virtually no or only weak defences against powerful economic groups or arbitrary politicians. Corrupted by the latter, these states could not evenhandedly enforce universal economic rights, regulate balanced relations among economic actors, or prevent the corruption of fledgling market institutions.

The questions discussed in this paper are linked to the broader debate on the role of constitutions in market-making in the post-Communist countries. This debate was structured by the question of what features of a constitution actually matter for market-making. In the first half of the 1990s, the debate was mainly about the conditions of *introducing* market reforms that impose hardships on large social groups. Conversely, the second half of the decade shifted the debate to questions concerning the conditions of creating functioning markets. The dominant view of the early 1990s stressed the importance of the hierarchical elements of the state, like the concentration of executive power or the insulation of economic policy-making as the precondition for introducing reforms (for references and a critical overview of this literature, see Stark and Bruszt, 1998). This approach was challenged in the second half of the decade by a colourful group of authors, including property-rights economists, representatives of the new institutional economics, political scientists and sociologists,[9] who stressed the importance of the extended accountability of executives, the separation of powers, federalism as the conditions for successful coordination among economic actors, or the establishment of a credible commitment by the state to preserve markets.[10] This paper aims to contribute to the debate by discussing the role of the specifics of the structure of representation, based on the analysis of constitutional change in the United States in the two distinct historical periods when market-making was directly linked to the remaking of the state. I argue that the problems many post-Communist countries face are similar to the problems addressed by the parties negotiating constitutional change in the United States at the end of the 18th century and in the period leading to constitutional changes during the New Deal era.

My use of the American case is not intended to suggest that any of the institutional solutions of the American state-makers should or can be copied by the newly democratising countries. Rather, I argue that the problems the Americans faced first at the end of the 18th century and then in the period from the end of the 19th century until the New Deal era are similar to the problems the new democracies face. Thus, the questions the American state-makers asked and the principles they used to answer them might have relevance for the new democracies facing the problems of market-making. Briefly, the major question of market-making at the end of the 18th century was how to create a national market order by constituting a state that was strong enough to uphold economic freedoms and empowered enough against self-seeking politicians or strong private groups.[11] Barry Weingast has dealt with this issue in several of his papers (see e.g. Weingast 1993; Weingast 1995). Based upon his analytical framework focusing on what he called 'market-preserving federalism', he described the emergence of a mix of institutions and complementary informal norms that allowed the creation of the American national market economy underpinning rapid economic development. I depart from his analysis in one important way: In his studies, Weingast portrays the prohibitions against the national government's exercise of economic regulation as the major factor that reduced government's political responsiveness to interest groups.[12] If that was the case, the emergence of the American regulative state in the New Deal era would have meant the end of the state's general capacity to resist capture by private redistributive coalitions. By focusing on the structure of representation, instead of the specific institutions of the division of powers, as Weingast did in his analyses, I will try to show that this was not the case. I argue that it was not the limitations on the economic interventions of the federal state, nor federalism *per se*, but rather the structure of representation that was the major safeguard against state-capture. During the New Deal era, issues related to the creation of a state with the capacity to regulate relations among economic actors in a balanced way dominated the constitutional agenda. In this period of constitutional change, the structure of representation created in 1787 remained intact, while the relations of power among the various levels and branches of the government underwent dramatic changes. It was the rearrangement of the power relations within the state that allowed the emergence of the federal regulative state. On the other hand, I argue that it was the continuity in the structure of representation that perpetuated the capacity of the state to resist capture and enabled it to regulate relations of power among economic actors.

More generally, I argue that, in terms of the characteristics of the state, what really mattered was not the specific institutional arrangements or the actual distribution of powers among the specific institutions, but the general principles shaping the structure of representation. While the previous two underwent important changes several times in the last two centuries, the latter has remained intact. From this viewpoint, the creation of market order at the end of the 18th century was about the parallel constitution of a specific structure of rights and of a state with a specific structure of representation allowing the endurance of these rights and their defence against tyranny or corruption. The structure of representation was built upon an innovative accommodation of liberal, democratic, and republican principles. The *liberal* aspect of the state, its capacity to defend rights, was strengthened by the use of the association of diverse interests to counteract the association of groups with the same interests.[13] Far from being solely counter-majoritarian, the associative representation of diversity within the state was a specific system of organising and maintaining social and economic diversity by preventing any group with the same passions and interests to associate and become dominant. People's *democratic* participatory rights in this system took the form of the right to delegate. Delegation was organised so as to represent the same passions and interests as parts of several different representations of the public good competing with each other. Preferences in this system were not merely represented at the different levels and branches of government; instead they formed a part of differing, competing accounts of the public good consisting of different associations of diverse interests. The validity of each representation of the public good was limited, and decision-making

within the state was structured in a way preventing any of them from dominating the others. Representation was organised in a way allowing the
greatest diversity of various formulations of the public good to appear within
the state, as represented by the various branches and levels of the state and
the actors occupying them. The *republican* aspect of the state, the capacity to
represent in state decisions something that can be called the public good, was
strengthened by forcing decision-makers to take into account these diverse
representations of the public good and to find orderly accommodations for
them, through either deliberations or compromises. The 'public good' represented in binding decisions was a specific association of several diverse
accounts on the public good, itself with limited validity and exposed to
questioning in the next round of political struggles. A diversified system of
representation within the state, the separation and division of powers, combined with the system of checks and balances, was the institutional foundation of the new state empowered to constitute and preserve market order.
This was an order in which economic actors could have a stable expectation
that they could safely profit from rational enterprise and, as a rule, only from
rational enterprise.

The relevance of late 18th century American constitution-making for the
present problems faced by several of the post-Communist countries may be
better understood in terms of the contrast between the agenda of constitutional change in the America of 1787 and that of England at the time of the
Glorious Revolution. In the later case, fears and hopes related to *freedoms
from the state* dominated the constitutional agenda. The otherwise united new
bourgeoisie fought for a state guaranteeing economic freedoms.[14] Roughly
one hundred years later, the agenda of constitutional change in America consisted not solely of issues related to freedoms from the state, but also of fears
related to the *freedom of the state* from being used by groups representing
particularistic passions and interests to encroach upon the rights of others.
The American constitution-makers rejected the English constitutional solution largely on the grounds that, by allowing the domination of a single representation of the public good through 'legislative usurpation', it did not
provide enough safeguards against such 'wicked projects'. The formal rules
of decision-making in the United Kingdom still do not provide sufficient
safeguards against arbitrary policies and capture. It is the working of a set of
cumbersome informal rules of legislative decision-making, within party
consensus-forming and policy implementation, that provides informal checks

and balances – functional equivalents of the American solution of 1787[15] (Levy and Spiller 1994).

Constitutional development in the United States after 1787 was incremental and the outcome of political struggles within the society, among the different levels and branches of government, and – not independently of the previous two factors – the result of courts decisions.[16] Perhaps the most important changes happened in the period of the emergence and consolidation of corporate capitalism, between the late 19th century and the late New Deal era. In this period, when in the uneven distribution of economic power increased dramatically, the question of the functions of the federal state and of the corresponding sources of state capacity to fulfil these functions became a central political issue again (Sklar, 1992). By this time, the evenhanded upholding of universal rights and the capacity of the state to prevent particularistic groups from misusing the *public sphere* to redistribute wealth and opportunities to themselves no longer seemed sufficient to preserve market order. In the new era of corporate capitalism, with the emergence of dramatic inequalities in economic power, one of the emerging central political issues was how to prevent economic actors from misusing their economic power to redistribute wealth and opportunities to themselves within the *private sphere* of the market.[17] Political actors saw this redistribution not only as unjust, but also as self-destructive, as a major factor undermining fair competition and the possibilities of balanced social and economic development. This was a period in the economic history of the United States when the remaking of the market order was again strongly and directly linked to the remaking of the of the state. Basically until the New Deal era, the courts largely prevented the politicisation of economic rights and the distribution of economic thereby minimising the possibility of state intervention in these matters.[18] The decisions of the Supreme Court in this period reflected the view that the existing structure of rights and the distribution of power was natural and required protection from politicisation and state intrusion. A minority that became dominant by the New Deal era saw the market, as a specific structure of rights, as the outcome of the political process. More specifically, the market was 'state-made' and nothing could justify preventing the state from structuring or regulating these rights in the interests of the public good. The New Deal era dramatically altered the role of the federal state in market-making. It created a state that, in addition to upholding general rights, was empowered to restructure rights and monitor and regulate continuously the relations among economic actors in order to prevent the misuse of asymmetries in economic power. The re-balancing of relations of power among economic actors was partially about the restructuring of their rights: increasing the rights of weaker groups like consumers, small business, labour, and minority shareholders and decreasing the right of others. On the other hand, specific institutions were created with the task of monitoring the use of economic power in the specific segments of the market; they were empowered to reestablish balance if this was necessary for the functioning of the market and/or to further the public good. The remaking of the market order and the state's newly-gained capacity to monitor and regulate relations among economic actors was made possible by the remade relations of power among the various levels and branches of the state. This meant a dramatic increase in the powers of the federal level vis-à-vis the state level and an increase in the powers, initially, of the federal executive branch and, later, that of the legislature vis-à-vis the courts. It is important to stress that the re-balancing of the powers within the state, both during and after the New Deal era, was not the outcome of explicit constitutional change, but of an orderly political process. Once the (potentially) negative effects of too many powers of one branch or level were politicised, re-balancing was left to the outcome of political struggles and compromises within the unchanged structure of representation.[19] These changes during and after the New Deal era did not alter the basic organising principle of the state, which remained based on the representation of the diversity of the conceptions about the public good within the state and on the orderly accommodation of these diverse conceptions via conflict and deliberation, mediated through the representative institutions of the state. The state built upon these principles had the capacity to make and remake the market order, uphold general rights, create predictable policies, and to prevent arbitrary decisions, the general capturing of the state by particularistic interests, and the corruption of the market by powerful economic groups.[20]

THE 'SCHEME OF REPRESENTATION'

While in Europe the making of centralised states was largely the unintended side effect of war-making, in the United States, state-making was intimately and deliberately linked to market-making.[21] For the founders of the federal state, the creation of market order was primarily about constituting a state with the capacity to evenhandedly uphold a specific structure of rights and with the capacity to accommodate the greatest diversity of interests. The founders wanted to constitute a state in which undertaking the second task did not endanger the first. The problems they faced were similar in many ways to the problems of the parallel extension of property rights and citizenship rights that the post-Communist countries faced at the end of the second millennium.[22] As now in Central and Eastern Europe, the problem at the end of the 18th century was not solely about the potential conflicts between the propertied and non-propertied classes. According to such a simplifying interpretation, the problem then and now was about preventing the non-propertied classes from occupying the state and using it to unmake or prevent the creation of private property, and with it, of the market order. To be sure, class was among the concerns of the American constitution-framers, but they were at least as concerned about the potential dangers of chaos caused by the struggles of different factions within the propertied classes and by conflicts of interests among the states (Morone 1990). The various regions, states with potentially divergent economic interests, the several different categories of owners, farmers, manufacturers, plantation owners, and 'moneyed interests' alike were seen as having potentially conflicting interests, with the capacity to encroach upon the rights of others through the corruption of the state.[23]

The outcome of the constitutional bargaining reflected these fears. The solution was based on the accommodation of the greatest diversity of interests through the associative structuring of representation in two stages: from the citizens to the state and, within the state, from the institutions of representation to the making of binding state decisions. The primary function of this two-stage system of representation was to prevent arbitrary decisions by state officials and the dominance of any particularistic group. The other expected function of this system of representation was to increase the likelihood that state decisions represented the orderly and balanced accommodation of the greatest diversity of interests – called the public good. The whole edifice was based on an innovative use of the traditional republican belief in the (as)sociability of diverse interests under some commonly acceptable notion of the public good. Contrary to traditional republicanism, however, the system was not based on the assumption of virtuous behaviour, but, as a liberal safeguard, on the deliberate use of self-interested behaviour to further the public good. On the one hand, the founders and most prominently the authors of the Federalist Papers rejected and painted a terrifying picture of the traditional republican ideal of direct democracy, in which virtuous people depart from their self-interests and associate their interests via deliberation. On the other hand, they believed in the possibility of associating diverse interests through mechanisms of representation that allowed potentially conflicting interests to find a common framework of understanding and defining interests. However, unlike the followers of traditional republicanism, this renewed republicanism built virtuous behaviour not solely and, as I will argue, not primarily, on the assumption of the existence of virtuous other-regarding characters seeking the public good, but primarily on the pursuit of self-interests.

This system of representation, in both of its stages, was built on the rejection of representation as a mere aggregation of given fixed preferences. Passions and interests of citizens were not factors exogenous to representation; they formed part of a process of representation whose major goal was to 'refine and enlarge the public views' (Hamilton 1961).[24] The goal was to create mechanisms that would increase the likelihood that diverse interests would be represented in a balanced and associated way, forming part of various encompassing conceptions about the public good.[25] In the first stage of representation, from the citizens to the state, the founders created a 'scheme of representation' based largely on the assumption of self-interested behaviour and inducing representatives to produce a diversity of 'virtuous representations'. Contrary to the mere representation of preferences, 'virtuous representation', as discussed below, was about producing common frameworks of understanding and (re)defining the preferences of the citizens. These representations were orderly associations of diverse interests with the double goal of the *refinement* of the content of the preferences of the citizens and of the temporal *enlargement* of these preferences.[26] The 'scheme of representation', as Madison called it, or the 'field of representation' or 'political field', as, following the work of Pierre Bourdieu, political sociologist now call it, was based on a variety of human motives.[27] 'The cords by which they will be bound to fidelity and sympathy with the great mass of people' were motives like 'duty, gratitude' or 'motives of a more selfish nature' like 'pride and vanity' (Hamilton 1961, p.352-53). Whichever motive was behind the representatives' ambition to be chosen, the pressure of the logic of political competition forced them to produce virtuous representations, to accommodate in their programs the greatest number of diverse interests in a balanced way. What emerged was a self-reinforcing system in which the very logic of representation within a competitive 'field of representations' forced ambitious players to produce a multiplicity of representations of the public good based on the balanced association of diverse preferences.[28]

The most important mechanism responsible for 'virtuous representation' has to do with accountability.[29] Actors competing in the political field open accounts and make accounts. They appeal to the electorate: 'Put your credit on my account, credit me, authorise me to act on your account, give me the power to represent your interests.' To get credited, to get support to be chosen, they produce programs, specific forms of narration or accounting. To maximise their credit, they try to take into account the greatest number of diverse interests. But they cannot represent these divergent interests as they are given. If they did only that, if they represented solely specific interests in their narratives, taking into account conflicting preferences as they are given, with potentially conflicting policy implications, they would be discredited. To improve their balances, they must find ways to link diverse interests in a balanced way, find innovative ways of linking them by forging new types of associations within the myriad of social forces and cognitive categories through which society is represented. They do not simply represent, simply give presence to fixed positions and existing divisions in the political field. While competing with each other to induce people to identify with their representation of what kind of association of interests best serves the public good, they also change the framework in which people define their interests; they reshape identities. Political programs are therefore doubly associative: In making claims to represent and to speak on behalf of named social groups (e.g. 'I (we) represent labour AND small business'), they attempt to create alliances; in making the case for a particular course of action, they attempt to modify the chain of association representing how society functions and how it can be transformed (e.g. 'I (we) represent the big developmental alliance: moderate wage demands accepted by labour can raise profitability, thereby increasing the level of investment and securing government revenues, to be used for upgrading infrastructure and investment in human capital, leading to stabilisation of employment and increases in wages in the framework of stable economic growth.') (Stark and Bruszt 1998).

Successful programs/representations are thus based on the *deliberate association* of previously separate interests and identities; and they break the boundaries of previously fixed social groups. Such alliance-building and transformative policy programs are functional equivalents of the idealised version of participatory democracy: a deliberative process in which actors with diverse interests and identities are ready to give up their fixed positions and ally their identities through the *deliberative association* of their interests[30] (Stark and Bruszt 1998; Sunstein 1985).

The balanced consideration of the largest array of interests is not the sole condition for winning the trust and support of citizens for political actors. While attracting commitments and resources through programmatic appeals, politicians have to position themselves in relation to competing politicians and their programmatic projects.[31] If they want people to identify with their program, they have to have an identity. They cannot represent just anything. If they do not want to lose their support and resources, they have to represent divergent interests in an identifiable way; that is, they have to position themselves by distinction. This also allows them to discredit those who do not even have an identifiable position or those who change their positions in an opportunistic way. Taking an identifiable position on changing or conserving the social order means that, in a competitive political field, competing representatives produce a structured diversity of the representations of the public good, i.e. diverging associations of social categories and functions. To stay in the field, politicians must offer a distinctive conception of the public good superseding a mere aggregation of the most encompassing and diverse common denominator of public interests.

The second goal of the framers with the new 'scheme of representation' was to attain the greatest diversity of virtuous representations called the public good within the state. The various groups of representatives at the various levels and branches of the state were elected and selected by various methods of elections and appointment. Based on different sizes of constituencies, this yielded representations of the public good with dramatically diverse content and complexity. The creation of a bicameral body of representation with representatives for the two houses (s)elected by the various methods and by the different and diverse constituencies was based on the desire to produce a balanced and diversified system of virtuous representations. The desire to form a balanced system of representations was not the outcome of theoretical debates alone; rather it reflected diverging interest configurations' concrete fears of the myriad of threats posed by diverse economic groups and the states. The framers saw this diversity of representations as the most elementary safeguard against the usurpation of the representation of the public good by any single group or actor. The founders here used a mechanism that investment fund managers would call the aversion of risk through the diversification of options.

To sum up, in the first stage of the new 'scheme', accountability was there to prevent representatives from merely representing particularistic interests, by forcing them to 'refine and enlarge public views' by taking into account diverse interests in an orderly way. On the other hand, instituting diverse modes of representations limited the capacity of any particular representative to further solely a particularistic representation of the public good, to speak alone in the name of the 'People'.

In the second stage of the 'scheme of representation', from the representative institutions to state decisions, the goal was to create mechanisms that would allow state laws and policies to represent the orderly association of the largest diversity of interests. Through mechanisms that prevented any branch or level of government from usurping the representation of the public good, the 'scheme of representation' within the state defended rights from arbitrary encroachment. It gave powers to actors in the various state institutions of representation to force decision-makers at each level and in each branch to *take into account* alternative representations of the public good. While, in the first stage of the scheme, the mechanism of accountability forced representatives to accommodate/associate diverse interests, the second stage was about *extended accountability* that served to ensure that state decisions were based on the accommodation of diverse conceptions of the public good.[32] The American system gave rights a multifaceted defence system that included a constitutional guarantee of the strength of basic rights and freedoms while making the amendment process an arduous task. Conversely, the 'scheme of representation' defended rights by the use of what Ordeshook called a 'natural competition among the state branches so that a balance of power that protects liberty prevails in equilibrium' (Ordeshook 1992).

Extended accountability, like the first stage of representation, was built less on the assumption of the existence of virtuous representatives than upon the self-interests of actors within the state. To be sure, the American constitution had strong Burkean elements: It created the conditions of discovering the public good through cool deliberative association of diverse conceptions about the public good insulated from direct public pressures (Sunstein 1988). On the other hand, extended accountability meant a dramatic departure from the Burkean scheme, which took virtuous representation largely for granted, with the next elections serving as the sole means of forcing representatives to *give* accounts. The basic difference between the Burkean scheme and the new 'scheme of representation' was the extension of the accountability of representatives to the whole period between two elections. The scheme allows for virtue, but it builds deliberately upon the conception of the self-interested representative who must constantly forced to be 'virtuous' and to continuously take into account other conceptions of the public good and who must be constantly checked by other institutions of representation. As Hamilton put it, the 'aim of every political constitution is, or ought to be, first to obtain for rulers men who possess most wisdom to discern, and most virtue to pursue the common good of the society; and in the next place to *take the most effectual precautions for keeping them virtuous whilst they continue to hold their public trust*' (Hamilton 1961, italics Bruszt L.). While virtuous representation in the first stage of the 'scheme of representation' was largely based on ambition, the goal in the second stage was to use 'ambition to counteract ambition' (Hamilton 1961, 51, 322). The founders created what we would call today an 'endogenous system of limitation of power' (Manin 1994). In this system, 'all the branches of government (were) connected by a network of reciprocal means of influence', empowered by what Madison called the 'necessary constitutional means and personal motives to resist encroachments of the others' (Hamilton 1961, 321; Manin 1994).

The new 'scheme of representation' was a major departure from the concept of a 'mixed constitution' based on the representation of distinct *social forces* in separate branches of government. It was not the founding fathers' goal to institutionalise within the state the *separation of homogeneous interests*. On the contrary, the entire scheme was based on the (as)sociability of previously static positions and the desire to constitute order by the orderly *association of diverse interests*, thereby preventing groups with the same particularistic passion and/or interests to associate and corrupt the state. Instead of representing distinct social forces, the various levels and branches of government represent different conceptions of the public good, different types of associations of diverse interests, with extended accountability serving the goal of making the state pursue balanced policies.

It is not the stability of relationships among the different representative institutions that enables the state to produce balanced policies and thus to preserve diversity within the economy – the major condition for the dynamic adaptability of the whole system. The 'scheme' was not built upon a static equilibrium; rather, it was based on a system of checks and balances built upon the institutionalisation of continuous struggle and negotiation among the various representative institutions. It was this continuous rivalry among representative institutions that allowed the periodic re-balancing of relationships among disparate conceptions of the public good and the creation of a new basis for making balanced policies. The (potentially) negative effects of too many powers of one branch or level and, with it, the overrepresentation of specific notions of the public good can be politicised through any branch or level. Re-balancing the state is then the outcome of struggles and compromises among the constitutive elements within the unchanged system of representation.

The 'scheme' displays two of the central features of highly adaptive organisations.[33] First, by preventing any notion of the public good from dominating and by maintaining a multiplicity of representations of the public good within the state, the scheme is based on the principle of *distributed intelligence*. It keeps social complexity present and alternatives open within the state. Second, through the system of checks and balances and extended accountability, the 'scheme' is based on the principle of *distributed authority*. Constrained by other political actors and representative institutions, actors within the state are forced to search continuously for compatibility among alternatives. In a complex, changing, and uncertain environment, these 'non-hierarchical elements of the hierarchy' allow the state to learn *ex ante* about the manifold potential consequences of its planned decisions and enable the state to adjust *ex post* after learning about the actual consequences of earlier decisions.

The emergence and continuous development of the *regulative state* in the United States, with its capacity to produce balanced regulations of relationships among economic actors, was the outcome of such political processes. The remaking of the state was not the outcome of explicit constitutional change based on conscious design. Rather, it was incremental. It lasted several decades and was the outcome of political struggles within the society, represented but not re-presented by struggles among the different levels and branches of government and made explicit by court decisions. The remaking of the state and the emergence of the regulative state started in the second half of the 19th century. In the new era of corporate capitalism, one of the central political issues became how to prevent powerful economic actors from misusing their economic power to redistribute wealth and opportunities to themselves within the *private sphere* of the market. The politicisation of this issue engendered a process of political struggles lasting several decades and resulting in the complete reconceptualization of the role of the state in the economy and in the remaking of the state through rearranging relations of power among the various levels and branches of government. [34]

The New Deal era dramatically altered the balance among the various levels and branches of government. A remade equilibrium among institutions allowed the emergence of a state that, in addition to upholding general rights, was empowered to restructure rights and continuously monitor and regulate relations among economic actors to prevent the misuse of asymmetries in economic power. A state emerged that had the capacity to balance relationships among economic actors. Balancing relationships was primarily about finding a balance between the need to maintain competition in domestic markets and the requirement for competitiveness in world markets; between the interests of the small-scale producers and the interests of the large corporations; between the rights of employers and the rights of employees; between the interests of the consumers and the interests of the producers; and ultimately, between liberty and the misuse of liberty.

The New Deal era and the emergence of the balancing/regulative state did not create a new static equilibrium among the various branches and levels of government, and thus it did not fix the nature of the state. As before, the 'scheme' allowed for the politicisation of the characteristics of state intervention, the excesses and failures of regulation. By re-balancing relationships among the various elements of the system of representation, it made it possible to increase or decrease the scope of regulation, to change the composition of interests given priority through regulation, or to extend the accountability of regulative agencies (Sunstein 1990).

POLIARCHIES AND HETERARCHIES IN POST-COMMUNIST EASTERN EUROPE

I have argued above that market-making was about creating a state with the capacity to uphold an economic environment in which economic actors could have a stable expectation about the stability of their rights, without having to fear *arbitrary* state interventions induced either by self-seeking state officials or powerful economic groups. I have argued that the constitutional sources of the emergence of such a state have to do with a specific structuring of representation, both from the citizens to the state AND within the state, from the institutions of representation to the making of state decisions. It directly follows from this analysis that democratisation of the *political regime* alone does not create such state capacities. If the structure of representation *within the state* is not built on the 'most effectual precautions' for holding representatives accountable within a political cycle and forcing them to accommodate diverse representations of the public good in their decisions, nothing prevents decision-makers from advocating the wildest particularistic interests.

Democratisation of the political regime is about restructuring the first stage of representation. It creates a *poliarchy*, a term first introduced by Robert Dahl, which is a system of representation from the citizens to the state based on free and fair elections (Dahl 1971). While most of the countries in post-Communist Eastern Europe are poliarchies in Dahl's sense, they differ dramatically in the ways representation is structured *within* their states. In many new democracies, after elections that *delegate* public authority to politicians, state institutions fail to articulate a diversity of modes of advancing the public good. Informal mechanisms of checks and balances, like the ones developed in the United Kingdom, are absent, and attempts to create them have failed. In these democracies, which O'Donnell labels *delegative democracies*, only a single platform of the public good dominates the functioning of the executive in the political cycle (O'Donnell 1994). There are no mechanisms to force incumbents to re-balance consistently the representation of the public good or even to stick to the original program to any great extent; the delegated representative has free rein without serious impunity. Under such circumstances, representation is arbitrary and precarious, resulting from weak accountability and a feeble credibility of the executive. Because of an inherent weakness or lack of extended accountability, there are no guarantees that elected politicians will refrain from abusing power or that pressure groups will be unable to effect a misuse of power to their benefit. In a state of this nature, there are only shallow guarantees of the upholding of rights or of some promise of state interventions intended to serve the public good (O'Donnell 1994; Schedler 1999). The developmental consequences on the economy in such a state may be deleterious: The enforcement of rights and the policies of the executive are both unpredictable. Since there is nothing to elevate the state over particularistic interests, the state is easy prey for powerful economic groups (Bruszt 2000). Once caught by them, these states might represent only a single voice: the loudest and strongest. Thus, instead of re-balancing the economy and constituting a functioning market order, the working of these states might exacerbate developmental traps inherited from past regimes (Bruszt 2000).

Many of the new poliarchies of the region lack the institutions and behavioural patterns that would extend the accountability of executives between two elections and thus force them to make balanced representations of the public good in their programs. In a smaller number of new democracies, policies and laws are based on an orderly accommodation of heterogeneous rationalities, interests, and considerations. Incumbents in such states are embedded in a network of interdependent and autonomous institutions that display diverse representations of the public good; and executives who form their representation of the public good are forced to make balanced representations, taking into account heterogeneous representations of the public good. In an earlier paper, I gave the name *heterarchy* to a specific type of democracy (a) in which representation is structured in a way that preserves the diversity of representations of the public good within the state between two elections and (b) that forces political actors to take into account heterogeneous representations of the public good while forming policy (Bruszt 2000). Seen thus, the type of state created by the Constitution of the United States was the first heterarchy. Since her creation, several other forms of heterarchies have emerged that build on the principles of the American founding fathers, but that differ in the ways diversity within the state is institutionalised and upheld. These heterarchies might differ in their methods of translating votes into seats, in the ways diversity of representations is maintained within the state, or in the ways relationships are structured among the diverse institutions of representation within the state. Also, they might differ in the ways the autonomous organisations of civil society can extend the accountability of incumbents.

One can call a state a heterarchy if two of the 'most effectual precautions' for keeping representatives virtuous are present at the same time. First, a state is a heterarchy when the *delegative powers* of the people are organised in such a way that people's preferences within the state are represented in the form of a multiplicity of diverse notions of the public good. To put it differently, the structure of representation within such a state is built upon the principle of *distributed intelligence*. From this viewpoint, simple majoritarian parliamentary regimes or strong presidential regimes are inferior to mixed political regimes. Mixed political regimes 'diversify the portfolio' of the representations of the public good. In such regimes, people have the right to delegate a multiplicity of representatives with diverse representations of the public good. In *bicameral parliaments* with electoral rules that permit the representation of both the plurality and the majority of 'passions and interests' and with non-simultaneous elections for the different houses, a balanced representation can be instituted within the state. Properly designed *mixed electoral systems* with proportional balances might be a basis for fusing balanced representation into the executive in the form of *coalition governments*. The various branches and levels of the state also have diverse representations of the public good. The *separation of powers* and the possibility for each branch and level to defend its autonomy and prevent other levels and branches from misusing their autonomy further contribute to upholding diversified representation of the public good within the state.

Second, a state is a heterarchy when the extended accountability of executives decreases the chance of the re-presentation in state policies of solely the interests of particularistic groups and when the making of binding decisions is based on an orderly rivalry among diverse notions about the public good. In such a state, executives forming policy have to take into account diverse representations of the public good, represented by coalition partners, parties in the different houses of the legislature, various levels and branches of the government, autonomous state agencies, and the organisations of civil society and the economy. In such a state, executives' horizontal accountability to other autonomous state agencies reduces the risk of misusing state power and of the encroachment upon the rights of non-state actors (O'Donnell 1999; Schedler 1999). Independent judiciaries with the powers of judicial supervision, along with rules that make changing basic rights an arduous task, prevent executives from arbitrary decisions and force them to honour and make non-state actors honour the laws. The existence of autonomous state agencies that can force incumbents to honour specific rules on using public resources and the existence of state agencies that represent specific rights or the rights of specific minority groups further extend the accountability of executives. Through the institution of distributed authority, the constant pressure on executives to take diverse representations of the public good into account enables the state to rise above the actual distribution of powers and interests within the economy.

It was not the goal of this paper to offer a case-by-case analysis of the various constitutions of the new democracies in the region. One can get a preliminary picture of divergence in the formal characteristics of the structure of representation of post-Communist states by applying several standard measures widely used in comparative politics. These include the measure of formal executive powers and various measures of the extent to which executives can govern alone, without being disturbed by competitive party systems and without being checked to various degrees by the parliament and/or parties in coalitions.[35] These approximate indicators already reveal great differences among the states in the region. In most of the former Soviet republics, executives can go on with their policies undisturbed by other representations of the public good within the state; their structure of representation qualifies these states as delegative democracies. According to the same measures, Central European states would qualify as more or less heterarchic, while several of the Southeastern European countries lie somewhere between delegative democracies and heterarchies. According to recent surveys, states that are more heterarchic made greater progress in market reforms, while states in which executives have greater freedom to monopolise the representation of the public good have introduced partial reforms at best – the latter condition being a strong indicator for state-capturing (EBRD 2000; Hellman 1998).[36]

Table 2 offers measures of the regional averages of the credibility indicator and its components. They measure private firms' perception of the extent of credible state commitment to preserving market order.[37] Based on this survey, one can speak about progress in market-making if states are in place that have the capacity to strengthen economic actors' stable expectation that their property rights are safe, that they can count on the state to enforce their contracts in case of disputes, and that they don't have to fear losing their gains because unpredictable or corrupt governments have made sudden changes in policies.

These expectations are weakest in the countries of the former Soviet Union. These are states typically ruled by elected presidents who usurp representation between two elections; these states lack any of the 'precautions' that would tie the hands of executives and force them to pursue in their policies something that can be associated with the public good. The expectations of private economic actors about state capacity to enforce contracts or to produce predictable policies without being corrupted are lower in these countries than even in the Sub-Saharan African countries or in Latin America. The subjective evaluation of state capacities to preserve market order are significantly higher in the Central and Eastern European countries that have a more diversified structure of representation in their states.

Table 2: Regional averages of the credibility indicator and its components

			Components of the credibility indicator			
Region	**Credibility indicator**	**Predic- tability**	**Political stability**	**Violance**	**Reliability of judiciary**	**Lack of corrup- tion**
All countries	3.23	3.21	3.25	2.80	3.04	3.86
High-income industrial countries	4.14	3.85	4.27	3.64	3.98	5.04
South and Southeast Asia	3.69	3.55	3.56	3.28	3.94	4.12
Middle East and North Africa	3.28	3.36	2.86	3.57	2.61	4.01
Central and Eastern Europe	3.22	2.93	3.51	2.72	3.14	3.82
Latin Ame- rica and the Caribbean	3.12	3.17	3.60	2.43	2.63	3.79
Sub-Sahara Africa	2.91	3.06	2.57	2.59	2.76	3.55
Common- wealth of Independent States	2.69	2.87	2.91	2.16	2.35	3.16

Source: Aymo Brunetti, Gregory Kisunko, and Beatrice Weder: *Credibility of Rules and Economic Growth: Evidence from a Worldwide Survey of the Private Sector* (The World Bank Economic Review, 1998 Vol. 12, No. 3: 353-84)

Finally, there is a third group of surveys, not presented here, that measures various degrees of state-capturing by private actors (EBRD 2000; Hellman 1998; Hellman 2000). While all of them demonstrate the association between the concentration of state power and state-capturing, the most interesting is the survey that clearly demonstrates the link between unchecked concentration of power and partial reforms (Hellman 1998). In the countries with 'partial reforms', privatisation and liberalisation have resulted in private actors usurping a large part of the state power over microeconomic decisions. However, in these countries private actors have the power to prevent states from introducing the legal and regulatory frameworks necessary for a market order (Hellman 1998). To put it differently, in countries with a high concentration of state power, the probability is higher that powerful economic actors can use the state to redistribute wealth and opportunities to themselves, within both the state and the 'market'.

CONCLUSIONS

After nearly a decade of experimenting with economic reforms, signs of the consolidation of market order and of competition are emerging in only a few of the countries in the region. In many of the post-communist countries that have undertaken the rapid liberalisation of prices and trade and the privatisation of property, one can find anything but the signs of the emergence of a functioning market order. Economic actors in these countries have little inclination to invest in the formal sectors of the economy. In several of these countries, powerful economic groups regulate access to various market opportunities and siphon away resources from weaker segments of the economy. Productive markets in many of these countries function only very poorly, because powerful economic groups control them. Capital markets in these countries have weak creditworthiness, because investors cannot credit banks and financial institutions and the later cannot credit the firms. Social problems in these countries have mounted, not because 'marketization' has been too fast, but because predatory groups have the capacity to prevent the emergence of balanced economic development. After nearly a decade of struggle to *liberate* economic activity *from the state*, many of these countries now face the question of how to *liberate the state* from capture by economic groups. If they want to create a functioning market order, they will need a state that is capable of regulating the highly uneven distribution of economic power in a balanced way. But to re-balance their economies, first they need states liberated from the hold of powerful economic groups. In many of the countries of the region, states still must be (re)made to give them the capacity to constitute and preserve market order.

NOTES

1 I would like to thank Nenad Dimitrievic, Claus Offe, David Stark, Stefan Voigt, and the participants in the seminar at the Department of Political Sciences at the Central European University for insightful comments on the first draft of this paper.

2 On the region's legacies of having states, see Stark and Bruszt (1998), pp. 112-17.

3 For an extensive survey of the divergence in the levels of effectiveness and in the extent of state regulations of financial markets in the region, see the EBRD Transition Report (EBRD 1999).

4 Apart from constitutions, factors like the quality of the state bureaucracy and the civil society shape these characteristics of the state. Cohesive 'Weberian' bureaucracies might increase state autonomy, and with it, the state's regulative capacity. As Peter Evans has demonstrated, a cohesive 'Weberian' bureaucracy is behind the market-making success of such authoritarian developing states as the pre-1990s South Korean state. Well-organized civil societies might constitute stable informal rules encouraging productive relationships, thereby unburdening states. The major problem of post-Communist countries with weak states is that it is precisely the capture of the state by powerful economic groups that prevents the emergence of such bureaucracies and that erodes the development of civil societies.

5 For a discussion of the link between the emergence of the modern state and the emergence of the market economy, see the works of Max Weber (Weber 1978). The minimalist definition of functioning market order used here draws upon the works of institutional economist and property-rights economists. Note, however, that these works focus mainly on guarantees of freedoms from the state, only a few of them dealing with the guarantees against state capture, and basically none with guarantees against the misuse of asymmetries in economic power. My 'minimalist' definition also includes the regulative functions of the state, i.e., its capacity to regulate relations among economic actors and prevent their misuse of asymmetries in economic power. (Commons 1924; North 1990; North 1989; Samuels 1992; Sklar 1992; Weimer 1997; Weingast 1993; Weingast 1995; Williamson 1994).

6 On the concept of heterarchy, see Bruszt 2000.

7 For an encompassing discussion of constitutional change, see the work of Stefan Voigt (Voigt 1999).

8 On the German case, see the comprehensive discussion of the issue by Donald Kommers (Kommers 1989).

9 See for example the works of Weimer, Hellman, Sachs and Pistor, Stiglitz, Weingast, Stark and Bruszt (Hellman 1997; Hellman 1998; Sachs 1997; Stark 1998; Stiglitz 1999; Weimer 1997; Weingast 1995).

10 For empirical evidence, see the works of Joel Hellman (Hellman 1997; Hellman 1998).

11 For various conceptualisations of the constitution-making process, see (Beard 1998; Manin 1994; Morone 1990; Sunstein 1985; Sunstein 1988).

12 See for example (Weingast 1995) p. 25.

13 For discussion of the liberal, republican, and democratic aspects of states, see the work of O'Donnell (O'Donnell 1999).

14 On the creation of a market-preserving state in England, see the work of North and Weingast (North 1989).

15 For the problems of countries adapting the Westminster model without having the aforementioned informal mechanisms, see the enlightening work of Levy and Spiller (Levy 1994).

16 On implicit constitutional change, see the enlightening paper of Stefan Voigt (1999).

17   On this period, see the works of Sklar and Sunstein (Sklar 1992; Sunstein 1987; Sunstein 1990).

18   (Sklar 1992; Sunstein 1987; Sunstein 1990).

19   While, for example, in the New Deal era the powers of the federal executive and of the federal monitoring agencies were radically increased, in the post-World War II era, Congress has increased its controlling powers (Sunstein 1990).

20   I use the adjective 'general' to modify the noun 'capturing' deliberately. It would be extremely hard to see the US system of government as free of group interests. Quite to the contrary, factions are everywhere, wherever the eye can see. Having said that, it would be a great mistake not to see the state's robust capacity to resist any long-term or general capturing by these interests, partly through orderly interest group politics whereby one faction might neutralize the ambitions of the other, and through the re-politicization of specific policy issues within the formal structure of representation.

21   On state-making in Europe, see Charles Tilly's work (Tilly 1985)

22   For a discussion of the problem in the American context, see the work of Morone; for a discussion of the same problem in the post-Communist setting, see Stark and Bruszt (Morone 1990; Stark and Bruszt 1998).

23   Of course the fears of the founding fathers were related not only to divergent economic interests, but also included the divergent 'passions', like religious sects. These two types of fears are addressed in one of the most frequently quoted part of the Federalist Papers, N.10. written by Madison (Hamilton 1961). Note that Madison names the 'various and unequal distribution of property' as the 'most common and most durable source of factions'. Both adjectives, 'various' and 'unequal', mattered to Madison. While the latter referred to the potential conflict of interests between 'those who hold and those who are without property', the first was a reference to different categories of owners, like creditors and debtors, 'landed interest, a manufacturing interest, a mercantile interest, with many lesser interests'.

24   On this, see the insightful analyses of Cass Sunstein (Sunstein 1985; Sunstein 1988).

25   As Madison put it, the goal was to 'adjust these clashing interests and render them all subservient to the public good' (Hamilton 1961, p. 80.).

26   The function of the 'scheme of representation', as Madison put it, was to produce representations by representatives who 'discern the true interests of their country' and 'prevent temporary or partial considerations to prevail' (Hamilton 1961, p. 82).

27   On the concept of political field, see the work of Pierre Bourdieu (Bourdieu 1981).

28   On the political field, see the work of Pierre Bourdieu; on the link between competition and characteristics of representation, see also Claus Offe's work; on the application of the concept of the political field to the study of post-Communist states, see Stark and Bruszt (Bourdieu 1981; Offe 1984; Stark and Bruszt 1998).

29   On the concept of accountability ,see more in Stark and Bruszt, 1998.

30   Proud of the proposal of the Federalists, Madison goes so far as to state: 'Under such a regulation it may well happen that the public voice, pronounced by the representatives of the people, will be more consonant to the public good than if pronounced by the people themselves, convened for the purpose.' (Hamilton 1961, p. 82).

31   On the structure of the political field and the positional 'games' of actors within this field, see the work of Bourdieu (Bourdieu 1981).

32   On the concept of extended accountability, see Stark and Bruszt (Stark and Bruszt 1998).

33   On this topic, see the work of David Stark (Stark 2000).

34   On this period, see the works of Sklar and Sunstein, (Sklar 1992; Sunstein 1987; Sunstein 1990).

35   For empirical materials on this issues, see the recent surveys of the European Bank for Reconstruction and Development (EBRD) (EBRD 2000).

36 'Progress in economic reforms' measures the introduction of policies and regulations seen as necessary for the emergence of market order (EBRD 2000). According to the same surveys, states in which representatives are more often exposed to electoral accountability are more likely to make progress in market-making then states in which incumbents can go on undisturbed by voters.

37 They measure the different elements of the capacity of states to credibly commit themselves to the preservation of market order. For more on this and on credible commitment, see Brunetti 1998; North 1989; Weingast 1995.

REFERENCES

Beard, C. (1998), *An Economic Interpretation of the Constitution of the United States*, originally published in 1913 by The Macmillan Company Edition, New Brunswick and London: Transaction Publishers.

Bourdieu, P. (1981) 'La representation politique. Elements pour une theorie du champ politique', *Actes de la recherche en sciences sociales*, **37**, 3-24.

Brunetti, A., G. Kisunko, and B. Weder (1998) 'Credibility of Rules and Economic Growth: Evidence from a Worldwide Survey of the Private Sector', *The World Bank Economic Review*, **12** (3), 353-84.

Bruszt, L. (2000), 'Heterarchies and Developmental Traps', in K. K. Hinrichs and H. Wiesenthal (eds), *Kontingenz und Krise, Institutionenpolitik in kapitalistischen und postsozialistischen Gesellschaften*, Frankfurt, New York: Campus Verlag, pp. 119-141.

Dahl, R. (1971), *Poliarchy: Participation and Opposition*, New Haven: Yale University Press.

EBRD (1999), *Transition Report 1998*, London: European Bank for Reconstruction and Development.

EBRD (2000), *Transition Report 1999*, London: European Bank for Reconstruction and Development.

Gaddy, C. and B. Weingast (1998), 'Russia's Virtual Economy', *Foreign Affairs*, **77** (5). http//www.foreignaffair.org/issues/9809/gaddy/html.

Greskovits, B. and H. Shamis (1999), 'Democratic Capitalism and the State in Eastern Europe and Latin America', *Annual Meeting of the American Political Science Association*, Atlanta, GA.

Hamilton, A., J. Madison, and J. Jay (1961), *The Federalist Papers*: The New American Library.

Hellman, J. (1998), 'Winners Take All: The Politics of Partial Reforms in Postcommunist Transitions', *World Politics*, **50**, 203-234.

Hellman, J. J. and D. Kaufmann (2000), 'How Profitable is Buying State Officials in Transition Economies', *Transition*, **11** (2), 8-11.

Manin, B. (1994), 'Checks, balances and boundaries: the separation of powers in the constitutional debate of 1787', in B. Fontana (ed), *The Invention of the Modern Republic*: Cambridge University Press, pp. 27- 62.

Morone, J. (1990), *The Democratic Wish – Popular Participation and the Limits of American Government*: Basic Books, Inc.

North, D. and B. Weingast (1989), 'Constitutions and Credible Commitments: The Evolution of the Institutions of Public Choice', in Alston (ed), *Empirical Studies in Institutional Change*, London: Cambridge University Press, pp. 129-165.

O'Donnell, G. (1994), 'Delegative Democracy', *Journal of Democracy*, **5** (1), 55-69.

O'Donnell, G. (1999), 'Horizontal Accountability in New Democracies', in Schedler et al. (ed), *The Self-Restraining State*, Lynne Rienner Publishers, pp. 29-51.

Offe, C. (1984), 'Competitive Party Democracy and the Keynesian Welfare State', in C. Offe (ed), *Contradictions of the Welfare State*: Hutchinson, pp. 179-206.

Polishchuk, L. (1997), 'Missed Markets: Implications for Economic Behaviour and Institutional Change', in J. Nelson, C. Tilly and L. Walker (eds), *Transforming Post-Communist Political Economies*, Washington, D.C.: National Academy Press, pp. 80-101.

Schedler, A., L. Diamond, and M. Plattner (ed) (1999), *The Self-Restraining State: Power and Accountability in New Democracies*, London: Lynne Riener Publishers.

Sklar, M. (1992), *The Corporate Reconstruction of American Capitalism, 1890-1916*, New York, New Rochelle, Melbourne, Sydney: Cambridge University Press.

Stark, D. and L. Bruszt (1998), *Post-Socialist Pathways: Transforming Politics and Property in Eastern Europe*, New York: Cambridge University Press.

Stiglitz, J. E. (1999), 'Whither Reform?', *World Bank Annual Bank Conference on Development Economics*, Washington, D.C.

Sunstein, C. (1985), 'Interest Groups in American Public Law', *Stanford Law Review*, **38** (29), 66-87.

Sunstein, C. (1987), 'Lochner's legacy', *Columbia Law Review, **87**,* 873-919.

Sunstein, C. (1988), 'Constitutions and democracies: an epilogue', in J. Elster et al. (eds), *Constitutionalism and Democracy*: Cambridge University Press, pp. 327-353.

Sunstein, C. (1990), *After The Rights Revolution*, Cambridge, Massachusetts: Harvard University Press.

Voigt, S. (1999), 'Implicit Constitutional Change – Changing the Meaning of the Constitution Without Changing the Text of the Document', *European Journal of Law and Economics*, **7**, (3), 197-224.

Weingast, B. (1995), 'The Economic Role of Political Institutions: Market Preserving Federalism and Economic Development', *The Journal of Law, Economics and Organisation*, **11** (1), 1-31.

Weisman, A. (1995), 'Notes and Comment: Separation of Powers in Post Communist Government: A Constitutional Case Study of the Russian Federation', *The American University Journal of International Law and Policy* (Summer 1995).

Woodruff, D. (1999), *Money Unmade / Barter and the Fate of Russian Capitalism*, Ithaca-London: Cornell University Press.

World, Bank (1996), *From Plan to Market*: Oxford University Press.

World, Bank (1997), *World Development Report*.

10. Comment

Claus Offe

LEARNING FROM HISTORY OR 'CONSTITUTIONAL LUCK'?

In his fine piece of what I would classify as comparative constitutional sociology, the author argues about the following. Markets are, most importantly, political creatures, or state-sponsored arrangements. They are 'made' through political decisions which, first of all, amount to the dismantling of pre-market monopolies and economic privileges. The demolition of this economic status order gives way to equal access to commercial interaction and state-protected property rights, specifying in universalistic terms the ways in which property can be acquired and used, as well as the way and in which the returns resulting from the use of property are to be appropriated, and by whom. Once brought to life, political decision making is also needed to provide the requisite framework for the continued functioning of markets – at the very minimum a monetary framework specifying the standard means of exchange and a civil law framework specifying the terms of contractual interaction and the (judicial) means by which contracts can be enforced. At the same time, the political system must be built in such a way as to commit itself to self-restraint so as to preclude arbitrary intervention into markets and property rights. Thirdly, political decisions and a market-appropriate institutional framework does not only set markets into motion and provide them with a predictable regulatory frame. Policies are also necessary in order to stem the tendency of markets to be subverted, be it by some market participant who acquires monopolistic power and/or by the state's appropriation of economic assets. Finally, one might add, markets are viable arrangements only if policies are put in place which are capable of limiting and correcting markets. That is to say, if most valued things are to be for sale, *some* valued things (such as, for instance, court decisions or professional certificates) must *not* be for sale; and some market outcomes ('excessive' exploitation of natural and human resources) must be either banned or mandatorily compensated for.

Once we have fully understood the 'non-natural', or 'state-mediated', nature of markets, Bruszt's argument leads us to consider the kind of polity and constitutional order that is needed in order to accomplish the introduction and preservation of a market economy. His answer is that it must be a polity that is sufficiently independent from economic interests to perform its market-making and market-sustaining mission. We thus get a model of reciprocal immunity. If markets are to be freed from discretionary political intervention, a state must be presupposed that is itself free from the risk of being captured by powerful economic actors. Not only are markets state-made, but also states made and shaped by society and the economic power relations prevailing in it. In order to have free markets, we need a free state – meaning a state that is responsive to *all* segments and interests within a market society, rather than dominated by any one of them. Thus we arrive at the core question of the paper: What constitutional arrangement allows the state to be free to allow markets to be free? As an answer, the author proposes the term 'heterarchy', perhaps not the most fortunate designation of what he has in mind, which is: In order for the state to succeed in market-making, powerful economic actors (nor, for that matter, autocratic elites) must not be allowed to succeed in state-making and policy-making.

The backdrop which makes this question such an urgent one is the realities of post-Communism. Here, states are weak, meaning: dependent upon and easily captured by powerful economic actors and consequently unable to institute anything that resembles the reality of a free market, as opposed to the clientelistic and opportunistic allocation of favours and privileges. What can, in these societies, 'increase the probability of the emergence of states with robust capacity to constitute and preserve markets'? According to the author, one answer to this question that comes easily to mind, namely 'liberal democracy', is clearly not good enough. If, in order for a market society to emerge, the state must leave the sphere of economic transaction to itself, the society, including powerful holders of economic resources, must leave the state to itself; for that, liberal democracy is a necessary, but not a sufficient condition. The government may well be elected, yet still, in the absence of countervailing social forces as well as checks and balances built into the system of governance, find itself at the mercy of either autocratic political leaders or/and powerful economic groups.

It is thus not the *fact* of representative government (defined by equal political rights of citizens and general elections), but a particular '*structure* of representation' for which the constitutional order must provide. The decisive condition here is not 'popular sovereignty', but 'diversity of representation', with the diverse representatives and their particular visions of the public good relating to each other in the mode of 'deliberation and compromise'. The emphasis is on the well-balanced heterogeneity, both among the societal interests and passions represented and the institutional centres and powers within the state (such as the executive branch, legislature, states, the judiciary, etc.). The former precludes the chance of any one group of powerful social actors to capture the state, and the latter reduces the danger of the state actually *being* captured, as no branch or level of government could possibly succeed in 'usurping the representation of the public good'. This Madisonian picture of the virtues of balanced factionalism and intended fragmentation as an antidote to state capture is supposedly to be implemented by a well-designed constitution. The charm of the argument is, of course, that it seems to allow for a republican order without a strong prerequisite of virtuous republican *citoyens*. Even though representatives, are motivated by passion and self-interest, republican reason will result as the by-product of the efforts of constituency-building and compromise-seeking representatives who act in a competitive political field. The constitution forces politicians to differ from each other in their respective way of reconciling differences within their constituencies. Such is supposedly the accomplishment of a well-designed constitution, or 'scheme of representation', that safeguards the state from being taken over by any socioeconomic 'faction' or autocratic elite elements.

At this point, I wish to raise a doubt, while at the same time radicalising the point of view of 'constitutional sociology'. Suppose an individual or corporate actor is charged with the task of drafting a constitution for a post-Communist society. Also suppose that he is fully aware of the story told so far, as well as deeply committed to the objective of creating, according to the model so eloquently recounted by Bruszt, a robust free state that would in turn be able to safeguard a free market society. Would this knowledge and intention, taken together, be sufficient to perform the job? My hunch is that the answer is: no, he wouldn't. Without drawing upon the evidence that might in fact support this sceptical assessment, let me dwell on how we can explain this (hypothetically) disappointing outcome, thereby putting into question the implicit rationalism of Bruszt's account. I am going to do so in three steps.

First, in order for the 'scheme of representation' to yield the intended results, the nature of the interests and passions that are to be represented and integrated must be 'pluralistic' in the first place, which means that they should neither be 'homogeneous' nor 'antagonistic'. In case that either of these latter attributes apply, the building blocks are simply not in place by which the ideal 'scheme of representation' could be erected. It is beyond the capacity of even the most intelligently designed constitutional scheme of representation to generate and shape the social 'substance' to which it is to be applied as a constitutional form. If this substance is overly 'homogeneous', e. g. the prevailing conception of who 'we, the people' are is framed in terms of ethnic nationalism or, for that matter, some popular unity forged and mobilised by some charismatic leader, the habits of differentiated associability, compromise, learning, and deliberation will be hardly inculcated by constitutional means alone. There must be, to cut a long story short, some sort of an educated and secular urban middle class with whose values the scheme resonates and forms an elective affinity. Similarly, a strongly antagonistic relationship – between nationalities, between centre and periphery, or between the losers and winners of economic privatisation – will stand in the way of a 'heterarchic' scheme of representation. While Bruszt is certainly not in need of being reminded that post-Communist societies, at least some of them, suffer from 'developmental traps inherited from the past regime' (as he himself puts it), the net result of these considerations is a circular one: You need a market society that generates the configuration of social forces which are suitable for forming a 'heterarchic' regime which is in turn sufficiently free to install and supervise a market society.

Second, and in a dynamic perspective, we might suggest that polyarchy precludes heterarchy, rather than giving rise to it or being gradually complemented by it. The trap is this: Post-Communist elites need to put a strong emphasis on 'unity' (*vs.* difference and complexity) in order to assemble the bare minimum of governing capacity which tends to be based on populist mobilisation. In their typical view, pluralist representation would be just a prescription for granting obstructive veto power to non-cooperative groups and interests who could thus hinder the work of economic reconstruction and prosperity the (typically presidentialist) government promises to perform. Also, the very idea of 'checks and balances' built into the regime structure tends to be anathema to these elites, who therefore try to neutralise, as much as they can, the role of the media, the constitutional court, the parliament, oppositional parties, and sub-territorial governments. Also, post-Communist non-elites having inherited the cognitive frame of 'democratic centralism', are all too willing to believe that heterogeneity (be it at the level of representation or at the level of the conduct of government) will spell nothing but friction, conflict, and obstruction. Although it may well be true that, 'objectively' speaking and in the long run, sharing power with others through negotiation and compromise is a way to *increase* (rather than to undermine) power, this truth cannot be pragmatically appreciated, as the type of action following from this insight is deemed unaffordable and risky. This obsession with 'unity' rather than pluralism increases the probability than the state will never become 'free' in the sense specified by Bruszt, but instead become easy prey to either (if not both) autocratic rulers or powerful economic groups who, after all, control the means on which such governments depend in order to assure their control over resources and their prospect for re-election. Thus, in still another pathology of circularity, democracy remains trapped in the 'delegative' mode without ever being able to escape to the 'heterarchic' mode.

Finally, the unaccountable symbiosis of corruptible governments and economic forces that manage, with the help of these governments, to escape the discipline and contractual obligations of the market can hardly be overcome by even the most ingenious constitutional design. To believe otherwise amounts to a fallacy of hyper-rationality. Even the most compelling account of what needs to be learned from constitutional history does not guarantee that the agents are in place who are willing to learn the lesson and comply with its prescriptions. Sure enough, some post-Communist regimes have done so, while others have failed. So the puzzle remains: Was it sheer 'constitutional luck' that some have embraced at least elements of the 'heterarchic' regime form (providing for social pluralism within their scheme of representation plus pluralism of governance through checks and balances)? Or has a more radical version of constitutional sociology explanations to offer as to why outcomes have been fortunate in some cases, yet highly unfortunate in so many others?

11. Are 'Western' Constitutions Relevant to Anything Other than the Countries They Serve?

Peter C. Ordeshook

INTRODUCTION

In the most recent period of democratisation we have once again come to appreciate the paucity of our knowledge about what we generally assume is essential to the process of erecting a modern democratic state – designing national constitutions. Anyone who has participated, however obliquely, in the recent spate of constitutional design enterprises in Central and Eastern Europe, or who has observed the revolving-door nature of those documents in Latin America, must appreciate the vast array of questions for which there are no universally accepted answers. To what extent can and should a democratic constitution accommodate a society's history, culture, and apparent peculiarities? Indeed, what features of history, culture and current circumstance are relevant to constitutional design and how precisely, in specific wording and provision, can we accommodate these things? Are there essential components of a democratic constitution that need to be present in any document, regardless of how that document tries to accommodate local tastes and circumstances; and if so, what are those components? Did the USSR's experience with communism yield a constellation of countries that require constitutional documents that differ fundamentally from their Western counterparts – in fact, has this history and the general history of the region rendered the West's experience with constitutionalism irrelevant to those who seek to implant democracy there? Can the same be said about Latin America, Africa, or Asia? Should constitutions be drafted as far removed as possible from the day-to-day pressures of political forces and interests; or are they more likely to be stable if there is broad and open public participation in their design? Are the documents we deem successes in historical perspective, successes because of the quality of their design or because of a fortuitous combination of circumstances that is unlikely to be repeated elsewhere? And finally: Can constitutions encourage political stability or are they mere 'parchment barriers' whose provisions are sustained for reasons wholly exogenous to their design?

Arriving at universally accepted answers to such questions is difficult not because politicians, lawyers, pundits and political scientists fail to address them. Rather, definitive answers elude us because rarely if ever does anyone approach these questions with anything more in mind than a vague or wholly ad hoc *theory of constitutional design*. We may have models and experience, hypotheses and conjectures, ideas and prejudices, but as with any intellectual undertaking, fundamental questions necessarily remain unanswered absent an encompassing paradigm that helps define our concepts and an associated theory that links these things to logically consistent propositions.

The absence of that paradigm and theory is no better illustrated by the fact that even today we continue to debate so basic an issue as the mechanisms of a constitution's enforcement. If a constitution is a contract – a 'social contract' – then who enforces its terms? And if it is something else, then what is that 'something else'? We are advised that a constitution ought to be brief and unencumbered by lengthy provisions and substantive policies. But where is the theoretical structure that allows us to define and measure flexibility, and where are the theoretically grounded principles that allow us to infer brevity as a worthwhile quality? We have arguments to be sure – arguments that tell us to exclude unsustainable social welfare guarantees, to leave the internal organisation of parliaments and legislatures to parliamentarians and legislators, or to keep a constitution silent on those things best treated by more flexible statutory provisions. But we typically label our utterances 'arguments' precisely because there are opposite opinions and no compelling theoretical tools for choosing among them.

The question that forms this essay's title is no different than any other we can ask. First, it requires a defensible answer, because much of the advice we might offer those trying to build a democracy is predicated on the presumption that the answer is 'Yes'. Second, like the questions posed earlier, the pursuit of that answer will, hopefully, encourage us to find its theoretical justification. Of course, we are not so bold as to assume that we can fill the gaps in our understanding in the space of a single essay. But we pose our question because we believe it can be answered in such a way as to direct us toward the requisite theory. Specifically, we sketch here the rudiments of that theory – or, more precisely, a conceptualisation of democratic constitutions – that allows us to infer some general principles of design with which any successful document must be consistent. On this basis we conclude that Western constitutions and the Western constitutional experience have universal relevance simply because *all* successful democratic constitutions, regardless of culture, history and circumstance, must accomplish the same generalised purpose and satisfy those same principles in a enquivalent theoretically prescribed way. To deny this is to assert that 'Western physics' is something different than 'Eastern physics'; that chemicals mixed in Asia produce different compounds than when mixed elsewhere; and that Galileo's conclusions depended on the fact that he conducted his gravitational experiments in Pisa rather than somewhere else. Thus, although the study of Western constitutions may not directly reveal the principles or design we need, our experience with those constitutions – with both their successes and failures – illustrate the operation of universal principles. It remains to discern precisely what it is that is being illustrated.

This essay, then, is organised thus: In section 2 we offer a conceptualisation of a constitution, first introduced by Hardin (1989) and elaborated subsequently by others (e.g. Ordeshook, 1992, 1995 and Voigt 1999), that differs markedly from the traditional view of constitutions as social contracts. We argue that this conceptualisation, which views constitutions in game-theoretic terms as equilibrium selection or, equivalently, coordination devices, is not merely more consistent with commonly accepted guidelines for good design than is the view of constitutions as contracts, but that it also provides the theoretical underpinning necessary to guide a general understanding of their operation and durability in specific contexts. Next, because this conceptualisation is inferred from some of the qualitative lessons of contemporary game theory, in Section 3 we explore the things that theory can teach us about design. Here we argue that although preambles, rights provisions, amendment procedures, definitions of the branches of government, the allocation of powers among branches, and a specification of the ways in which public officials are appointed or elected are essential elements of a constitution, these things need to be conceptualised in common theoretical terms before we can weave them together, accommodate contemporary circumstances, and form a sustainable document. More fundamental are the ideas of self-interest, incentive compatibility, expectation, belief, strategy, social norm, and equilibrium. In Section 4 and in the specific context of the Soviet Union's experience with constitutions, we then confront directly the argument that various societies are somehow immune to the restrictions a constitution, democratic or otherwise, seeks to establish on the state. In Section 5 we offer an over-arching First Principles of Democratic Constitutional Design, which subsumes all other principles and which is implied directly by the conceptualisation of constitutions this essay offers. Finally, in Section 6 we return to the question that forms the title of this essay.

CONSTITUTIONS AS COORDINATION DEVICES

Riker vs. Dahl

It is useful to begin our inquiry by comparing Dahl's (1956) *Preface to Democratic Theory* and Riker's (1982) *Liberalism Against Populism*, since they posit diametrically opposite preconditions for a stable political system and reach different conclusions about a constitution's role in facilitating stability. Riker's analysis relies heavily on social choice theory and two facts that theory reveals. The first fact is that coherence in majority-governed processes, in the form of a well-defined social preference order, requires a nearly-impossible-to-achieve balance of citizen preferences on all salient issues or a uniformity of tastes such that all public preferences map onto a single 'ideological' dimension. The second fact is that in the absence of such coherence, political outcomes, along with the identities of winners and losers, depend critically on procedural details and the comparative skills of political elites at manipulating those details to their own advantage. Riker uses these results to argue that populist institutions, which are defined as those that allow citizens direct access to and control of policy, exacerbate democracy's inherent instabilities, and rather than encourage democracy, they facilitate the rise of demagogues. Thus, constitutions should not themselves or through the institutions they erect allow the direct translation of individual preferences to social policy. Instead, their fundamental if not unique purpose is the avoidance of tyranny, which they can meet only by giving political elites countervailing motives, by guaranteeing citizens the right to replace one set of leaders with another, and by recognising that the relationship between individual preferences and public policy will ultimately be mediated by institutional detail and political skill. In Riker's analysis, then, constitutions play a critical role in facilitating or impairing democratic political stability.

Insofar as the question this essay poses is concerned, Riker clearly believes that his argument is wholly general and applies to any society – if only because the theory upon which his arguments are based are scientifically general. It is also evident that he believes that the philosophy of design of the United States Constitution especially holds important lessons for other countries: 'the fundamental method to preserve liberty is to preserve ardently our traditional constitutional restraints (p. 252).'

In contrast to Riker, however, pluralists such as Dahl evaluate differently the preferences that occasion political instability, the role constitutions play in encouraging stability, and, ultimately, the relevance (or irrelevance) of the Western constitutional experience to other countries and societies. In their view, stability, defined in terms of the avoidance of tyranny, requires the instability that social choice theory describes, since it is this instability that insures against the possibility of permanent winners and permanent losers. Here, then, the fundamental source of instability that social choice theory identifies – a complex nexus of individual preferences that do not admit of wholly determinate outcomes – is a necessary and perhaps even sufficient condition for democratic stability. Thus, while Riker seeks to control this instability, pluralists prefer to give it 'free play' and perhaps even encourage it.

The disagreement between Riker and the pluralists is anything but tangential to our purposes. In searching for the sources of stability and the role democratic constitutions serve, pluralists focus on the ability of citizens to participate in politics via a variety of extra-constitutional institutions (parties, trade unions, industrial associations, clubs) that are autonomous of the state (Dahl 1982) but impact its actions. The emphasis here, then, is on the notion of a *Civic Culture* and its associated constructs. Constitutional provisions may influence the form of that *Culture*, but that influence is not critical to the political system's ultimate survival. Thus, in sharp contrast to Riker, Dahl asserts that 'constitutional rules are not crucial, independent factors in maintaining democracy ... Constitutional rules are mainly significant because they help to determine what particular groups are to be given advantages or handicaps in the political struggle' (Dahl 1956, 134). Put boldly, 'to assume that this country remained democratic because of its Constitution seems to me an obvious reversal of the relation; it is much more plausible to suppose that the Constitution has remained because our society is essentially democratic (Dahl 1956, 143).'

Unfortunately, although both Riker and Dahl offer different but nevertheless compelling arguments as answers to the question that forms this essay's title, our problem in choosing between them is that neither scholar presents a complete argument. Riker advocates constitutional limits on direct citizen control of policy – a multi-cameral legislature, a separation of powers, federalism, and an independent judiciary. But he fails to address satisfactorily the core issue of the ultimate source of stability of constitutionally mandated institutions – the mechanisms for ensuring that these institutions do not merely inherit the instability that adheres to the policies those institutions imply. Pluralists, on the other hand, appear to give too little attention to the role of constitutional structure in encouraging a civic culture. Although stability may require that there not be any permanent losers, denying any critical role for constitutions denies the fact that the political strategies people choose in pursuing their policy preferences – as well as the definition of winners and losers – depend on the institutional structures constitutions establish.

Constitutions as Contracts

Any satisfactory resolution of this disagreement requires that we move beyond the confines of this debate to a definition of a constitution, and to a theoretically satisfactory specification of its purposes and the ways it achieves those purposes. And here we begin by noting that at least in their idealistic view, constitutions are often conceptualised as contracts – a social contract – whereby people establish authorities to resolve those social inefficiencies occasioned by externalities and public goods and to render coherent the processes whereby society reallocates wealth (e.g. Brennan and Buchanan 1985). Here, then, there is little disagreement as to what constitutions ought to accomplish. For Hamilton in *The Federalist* it was 'to obtain for rulers men who possess most wisdom to discern, and most virtue to pursue the common good of society; and in the next place to take the most effectual precaution for keeping them virtuous whilst they continue to hold their public trust.' More recent specifications suggest that constitutions should remove 'certain topics from public scrutiny and review (Sunstein 1988, 338)', 'insulate private property from self-interested government officials and from factional tyranny (Sunstein 1988, 342)' or simply 'tie the community's hands' (Holmes 1988, 196). However, in light of these objectives we can immediately see difficulties with this view of a constitution as a contract.

The most evident and important difficulty is that a contractual conceptualisation cannot specify how the terms and provisions of such documents are enforced – how it accomplishes its stated objectives. In the usual economic context, contracts do two things: (1) they specify the actions the various parties to the agreement are required to undertake under varied circumstances and (2) they specify appropriate sanctions in the event that one party or another defects from the terms of the contract. Enforcement, however, typically lies elsewhere, at least for the usual contracts we associate with economic exchanges – most notably, in the courts. What, however, is the exogenous authority that enforces constitutions as contracts?

If, as Madison says, 'a mere demarcation on parchment ... is not a sufficient guard against those encroachments which lead to a tyrannical concentration of all the powers of government in the same hands' (*The Federalist* No.48, 254) then it cannot be words themselves that offer the mechanism of enforcement. But if it is not the words that enforce, then we are led to a logical conundrum. First, if the mechanism of enforcement lies outside the constitution – if it lies in an oligarchy removed from constitutional constraint – then either we are no longer speaking of a democracy or we have only pushed the problem back a step, and must then ask: What constrains the actions of this oligarchy and how are *those* constraints enforced? If, on the other hand, we argue, as some do, that enforcement lies in the institutions a constitution establishes – for instance, a national court and the associated judicial structure – then where are the things that enforce the provisions which define and limit the judiciary's authority? If those things are entities that the constitution itself establishes and constrains, such as the legislature or the executive, then we have merely provided circular reasoning: the constitution is enforced by institutions that are constrained by other entities that are constrained by the constitution – in which case we must then identify the thing that enforces this entire edifice.

We can, nevertheless, begin to see our way out of this conundrum by considering the two-person Prisoners' Dilemma, which provides the simplest illustration of the state's essential role. Briefly, we know that owing to the dominance of strategies, this dilemma, played once, can be resolved and an efficient outcome achieved only if both persons contract to allow defections to be sanctioned – presumably by the creation of some new entity, the state. Thus, the essence of a constitution-as-contract must be the creation of a force empowered to coerce – a force that can render cooperation a new equilibrium to the game between the two original players. However, the creation of this new entity engenders two new problems. First, the two original players must design the incentives of their creation to ensure that it does not act in its own self-interest and against theirs – that they do not inadvertently create a game in which the unique equilibrium yields a worse outcome than before. This, presumably, they can accomplish with the common constitutional provisions of a separation of powers, regularly scheduled elections, and so on. But there is a second problem. Because the incentives of the two contracting players remain essentially unchanged absent coercion, how can any contract between them ensure that one player cannot collude with or otherwise co-opt their creation to the detriment of the other player? A complete 'solution', then, would seem to require an abdication of sovereignty by the original contracting players, since this is the only mechanism that gives their creation a 'life of its own' and, presumably, an ability and incentive to resist co-optation. However, abrogating sovereignty is at odds with the democratic requirement that sovereignty reside in the citizenry: 'In all governments, whatever their form, however they may be construed, there must be a power established from which there is no appeal, and which is therefore called absolute, supreme, and uncontrollable ... [and a democratic state, that supreme power] resides with the people .... they have not parted with it; they have only dispensed such portions of power as were conceived necessary for the public welfare' (James Wilson, as quoted in Wood 1969, 530). Thus, 'the view that the government can be bound by specific provisions is naive. Something must enforce those provisions, and whatever enforces them is itself unbounded... This problem of the self-enforcing constitution has so far evaded solution' (Tullock 1987, 317-18).

Before we wholly reject the view of constitutions as contracts, however, we should consider the contemporary theory of the firm and the role of contracts there (see especially Williamson 1979 and Gifford 1991). Briefly, this literature leads us to distinguish between two classes of contracts. The first, exchange contracts, are the agreements we normally associate with simple, short-term economic arrangements and which commonly are enforced by a pre-existing legal system. It is precisely contracts of this type that we argue cannot be used as models of constitutional arrangements. But there is a second type of contract that pertains to ongoing or repeated relationships (and which contemporary economic theory use to model the firm). We appreciate that even these contracts rely on pre-existing legal systems for their enforcement, but because they concern repeated interactions, there are additional mechanisms of endogenously enforcing agreement – of rendering cooperation an equilibrium to the extended game. Among these things is the desire of participants to maintain reputations for fairness and honesty, and by the corresponding desire to avoid being sanctioned in the future by others who are direct parties to the contract (Kreps 1990).

Reputation models and the implications of game theory about the sustainability of equilibria in repeated games is, as we elaborate shortly, important to our analysis. But there remain some problems with arguing for the equivalence of even these contractual types and constitutions. First, constitutions are designed not only to regulate the political affairs of some pre-existing society and the ongoing relations within it, but also the affairs of new members as they are added either through birth or immigration. Second, reputations – at least a reputation for being 'democratic' – may be of little value when compared to that of being a tyrant, in which case we must still ask how any constitution conceptualised as a contract or otherwise, can modify such values. Third, if repetition allows for democratic equilibria enforced by the threat of future sanctions, how are we to make certain that the threats are credible – that they will in fact be applied in the event of a defection? Indeed, one can argue that a constitution is of such a fundamental nature that its abrogation can negate the very opportunity to sanction.

The difficulty here is especially evident if we consider constitutional secession clauses. The general view of such clauses is that a constitutional right to secede 'would increase the risks of ethnic and factional struggle; reduce the prospects for compromise and deliberation in government; raise dramatically the stakes of day-to-day political decisions; introduce irrelevant and illegitimate considerations into these decisions; create dangers of blackmail, strategic behaviour, and exploitation; and, most generally, endanger the prospects for long-terms self-governance' (Sunstein 1991, 634). And if, as Sunstein argues further, a constitutional provision prohibiting secession is best interpreted as a contractual agreement whereby federal units pre-commit to strategies that preclude secession, what is the mechanism that in fact sets that precommitment in concrete. Defending such arguments, in fact, takes us to the core of a theory of constitutions, since it requires an answer to such questions as: If a political subunit of a federation chooses whether or not to secede strictly on the basis of self-interest, how can a constitutional clause influence that interest? If, as much of the theory of federalism suggests, people choose to form, maintain or dissolve a federation on the basis of its ability to resolve the economic efficiencies occasioned by Prisoners' Dilemmas among otherwise sovereign states, then why would mere words influence those economic calculations? And if a decision about secession is itself a response to beliefs about the responses of others who also act out of self-interest – a belief about the likelihood that secession will be punished or ignored – then why would a constitutional secession clause influence their self-interest and the likelihood that they will act in accordance with its terms (Chen and Ordeshook 1994)?

If we try to answer these questions with the argument that the ongoing nature of the 'game' played by federal subjects renders threats credible and agreements enforceable, we still cannot say that setting any agreement to paper without an exogenous agent of enforcement influences much of anything. If such an agreement corresponds to the situation's equilibrium, then presumably that outcome would be realised regardless of the words a constitution contains. A constitution conceptualised as contract may reduce the likelihood of misperception and error, but we still cannot reject the view that a federation survives or fails merely as a product of a nexus of exogenously determined self-interests and that, as Dahl might assert, the constitution is window dressing.

The Universal Necessity for Coordination

Despite these problems, this second interpretation of contracts does draw our attention to a feature of government that our initial discussion of the Prisoners' Dilemma ignores. Specifically, by focusing on a single play of that game we take too narrow a view of the substantive problems with which constitutions must deal. The Framers of the United States Constitution, for instance, did not envision solving a defence dilemma or an interstate commerce dilemma that would exist only for a few years. They saw these things as problems of potentially indefinite duration – as dilemmas that must be continually 'resolved'. Thus, the ideas of 'repetition', 'long term', and 'repeated' are central to the discussion of constitutional design and it is here that game theory offers a critical insight.

Suppose again that the Prisoners' Dilemma is played an indefinite number of times. The game that now confronts the players is changed in a fundamental way. The single-play Prisoners' Dilemma offers each participant only two strategies (e.g. 'cooperate' and 'defect'), one of which ('defect') is dominant. But if played an indefinite number of times, each player is confronted with an infinity of alternative strategies (plans of action), such as 'cooperate as long as the other person cooperates, but never cooperate again once the other player defects,' none of which is dominant. In addition, however, to expanding the set of strategies, game theory tells us in a wholly general context, without reference to any specific scenario such as the Prisoners' Dilemma, that this expansion also expands the set of outcomes that can be enforced without exogenous enforcement – the set of outcomes (or, equivalently, strategy *n*-tuples) that are noncooperative equilibria. In the infinitely repeated Prisoners' Dilemma, for example, if both players give the future sufficient weight in their calculations, then endless cooperation is an equilibrium that is supported by strategies in which each player is prepared to sanction the other for any defection. Indeed, the results that support these conclusions – referred to as the folk theorems of game theory – tell us, roughly, that in any ongoing complex social process there is the opposite of a paucity of alternative equilibria. There is, in fact, an abundance of them, from inefficient to efficient ones, and from 'unfair' to 'fair' ones.

It would appear, then, that the mere fact that all social processes are ongoing resolves 'automatically' the problem of endogenous enforcement, since nearly any agreement can correspond to an equilibrium. However, it is important to understand that even in a specific scenario such as the repeated Prisoners' Dilemma, although there are equilibrium strategy pairs that yield cooperation at every stage and give no advantage to one player or the other, there are other equilibria that give asymmetric rewards. Different players, then, will prefer and pursue different equilibria. This fact occasions a new complication. In the single-play Prisoners' Dilemma there is a unique equilibrium and little doubt that it will be realised. But if a game possesses multiple equilibria, there no longer is any guarantee that any equilibrium will be realised. For example, if *(a,b)* is an equilibrium strategy pair in some 2-person repeated game, where both *a* and *b* describe in full detail all contingent actions a player might take as the game is played, and if *(c,d)* is another such equilibrium strategy pair, the problem is that there is no guarantee that either *(a,d)* or *(c,b)* corresponds to an equilibrium. Thus, even if both players choose a strategy that is a part of some equilibrium *n*-tuple, there is no guarantee that the strategies they choose collectively will constitute an equilibrium. Hence, rather than being concerned solely with enforcing an agreement – with ensuring that their agreement corresponds to an equilibrium so that neither of them has an incentive to defect – the players must be concerned also about *coordinating* their actions so as to ensure that they can achieve an equilibrium that is acceptable to each of them.

Simply because players are trying to achieve an equilibrium they prefer to what is likely to prevail if they fail to coordinate does not mean, however, that coordination is simple or straightforward. Again, we emphasise that in most 'interesting' social processes, people will prefer different equilibria. In a constitutional context, for instance, those who see themselves as a chief executive will prefer a presidential system; legislators will prefer a parliamentary one; regional leaders will prefer a decentralised federal system, those who will be part of the national government will prefer a unitary state, and still others may prefer no democracy at all. Each of these governmental forms, moreover, can constitute a different institutional equilibrium. Agreeing to a specific equilibrium, then, poses problems of its own.

Suppose, nevertheless, that a consensus is reached as to which equilibrium ought to be chosen. Unfortunately, there is yet one more difficulty that must be overcome. Specifically, if there is no shared belief beforehand that coordination will be effective – if people continue to believe that most everyone else will act as before – then the presumption of failure will be a self-fulfilling prophesy. For example, suppose, as appears to be the case in most post-Soviet states, that the primary sources of domestic capital invest only on the basis of a high discount rate for future profits and prefer to reap gains immediately because of the supposition that the state is unstable and the future especially risky. Suppose these same investors meet and, recognising the social and individual advantages of investing with a longer-term perspective, agree to act accordingly. This decision, however, need not change anything. If the current situation is an equilibrium – if it is unprofitable to invest for the long term when everyone else does the opposite – then even if the alternative is an equilibrium as well, it may be difficult to alter a critical mass of actions simultaneously.

Successful coordination requires a change in beliefs – a change in people's expectations about what others believe and how they will act. Hence, society can be trapped in a coordination dilemma in which a change in expectations requires concrete evidence of action, but the requisite action will be forthcoming only after expectations themselves change. In game-theoretic terms, coordination to a specific equilibrium requires that everyone's intent to choose appropriately must be *common knowledge*: Everyone must know that everyone else will choose an appropriate strategy; everyone must know that everyone knows this; everyone must know that everyone knows that everyone knows this, ad infinitum. Knowing that others will choose strategies appropriate to a specific equilibrium dissuades you from defecting; knowing that they know that you know what they will do, dissuades them from defecting and thereby reenforces your initial belief, and so on.

Constitutions as Coordination Devices

The preceding discussion of coordination and beliefs is wholly general and does not require that society be concerned with resolving any specific game such as the Prisoners' Dilemmas. Our discussion applies to nearly any repeated game, and thereby illustrates the following general facts: (1) any ongoing social process is characterised by countless alternative equilibria; (2) nearly any pattern of outcomes can prevail regardless of the efficiency or fairness of this pattern; (3) different players will prefer different equilibria; (4) some form of pre-play coordination is required if participants seek a guarantee that one equilibrium or another will be realised; and (5) effective coordination requires a common knowledge belief about strategies.

The dilemma of coordination, then, is a problem common to any society, but it requires special notice in democratising countries because in this instance an explicit attempt is being made to establish and choose a different equilibrium. And the problem is that even if everyone prefers to live in a democracy; unless the common knowledge requirement is satisfied and everyone believes that everyone else will act accordingly – that everyone, especially political elites, will let themselves be constrained by constitutional provisions and the rule of law – no one will in fact let themselves be constrained thus. If everyone begins with the assumption that their society is unprepared for democracy or their culture inconsistent with it, that assumption is a self-fulfilling prophesy sustained by the actions everyone observes.

Game theory, any assessment of the concept of constitutions as a contract, and the imperatives of establishing a democracy, then, compel us to the view, first offered we believe by Hardin (1989), that 'a constitution does not depend for its enforcement on external sanctions ... Establishing a constitution is a massive act of coordination that creates a convention that depends for its maintenance on its self-generating incentives and expectations.' Indeed, we can make an even stronger assertion: Since all political processes are ongoing, since the realisation of efficient, coherent, and even 'fair' outcomes is achieved only through coordination, and since the agency of the state is necessarily a part of any of society's coordinative mechanisms, then a 'well-crafted' constitution is (in contrast to Dahl's view but in support of Riker's) essential for democratic stability. What remains, then, is to use this idea of constitutions as coordination mechanisms to specify what we mean by 'well-crafted'.

However, before we explore the meaning of 'well-crafted', there is one last point that needs to be made about the implications of the preceding discussion and constitutional design. Specifically, we need also to understand that coordination is fruitless if we are trying to coordinate to something other than an equilibrium. This, in fact, is something the framers of the US Constitution knew well. Anyone familiar with the process whereby that constitution was drafted and ratified is familiar with *The Federalist Papers* and such phrases as 'ambition must be made to counter ambition'. Perhaps less well known, however, is Benjamin Franklin's more substantive illustration of this idea. Briefly, Franklin offered the following commentary at the Federal Convention in Philadelphia with respect to the manner in which judges ought to be chosen (as reported by James Madison in his notes on the Convention):

> Doctor Franklin observed, that the two modes of choosing Judges had been mentioned, to wit, by the Legislature and by the Executive. He wished such other modes to be suggested as might occur to other gentlemen; it being a point of great moment. He would mention one which he had understood was practised in Scotland. He then, in a brief and entertaining manner, related a Scotch mode, in which the nomination proceeded from the lawyers, who always selected the ablest of the profession, in order to get rid of him, and share his practice among themselves. It was here, he said, the interest of the electors to make the best choice, which would always be made the case if possible.

We can restate Franklin's observation in terms of the jargon of microeconomics and, again, game theory. After identifying the primary component of individual self-interest (i.e., the expansion of their practices), Franklin suggests an incentive-compatible mechanism – a mechanism that (1) is itself an equilibrium in the sense that it is in the self-interest of the relevant decisions makers to maintain it, and (2) if maintained, yields incentives such that the desired social outcome is a Nash equilibrium to the game it engenders.

It is important to appreciate that Franklin nowhere suggests that the mode he offers for selecting judges is *the* uniquely incentive compatible one. Instead, Franklin was, in his usual style, reminding the Convention in a substantively way about the theoretical task that it confronted – choosing (designing and coordinating to) a governmental system that, given people's preferences and definitions of self-interest, could be sustained as an equilibrium to produce a socially desired outcome. Franklin's genius, of course, was in understanding this problem in a sufficiently general and theoretical way that allowed him to call upon his experience and find an instance that illustrated the principle he sought to impress upon the Convention's delegates.

Conceptualising a constitution, then, as an equilibrium selection device that, hopefully, selects an 'appropriate' incentive-compatible institutional equilibrium is little more than a 21st century restatement of Franklin's idea. It remains, nevertheless, a universal idea and one that needs to be applied to the design of *any* national democratic constitution. The specifics may differ, and, as with Franklin's example, there need not be any uniquely best design for a specific society, nor is there anything in the view which suggests that a design that works in one society will work in any other. However, regardless of specifics, every *successful* democratic constitution must satisfy the same theoretical objective Franklin's example illustrates. Thus, returning to the question that forms this essay's title, our answer is 'Yes, Western constitutions are relevant to other countries and societies,' if only because they illustrate both the successful and unsuccessful application of this idea.

SOME PRACTICAL AND UNIVERSAL IMPLICATIONS

It is one thing to assert that the Western experience with constitutional democracy is universally relevant because the theory that allows us to interpret that experience is general; it is another thing to identify the specific substantive lessons for other countries and societies that experience teaches us. Constitutions, after all, consist of specific provisions and institutional choices and the issue to which we must now turn is identifying the generalisable specifics implied by a conceptualisation of these documents as coordination devices.

We can begin with the fact that every *society*, virtually by definition, possess a great many things that facilitate social coordination in the same way we argue constitutions operate – things we identify as norms, customs, and social convention that also must be self-enforcing (Lewis 1969, Coleman 1987, Hardin 1989, Calvert 1995). Thus, a political constitution can at best be only one element of society's fabric, and to make its provisions an effective part of that fabric, a constitution should parallel the 'design' of those other self-enforcing mechanisms. The first thing to appreciate, then, is that social norms and customs are effective if and only if they are simple and readily understood by nearly everyone. Complex rules cannot coordinate. A rule or social norm such as 'give an old woman your seat on the bus if you are young and agile' may leave room for interpretation, but it is far easier to teach and implement than one which states 'if you are younger than 45 and in reasonably good health as determined by a licensed physician on the basis of an exam administered no more than fourteen months earlier, and if a woman stands before you, no more than 1 metre distant from your seat, relinquish your seat if she gives evidence of being older than 55, walks with difficulty, or is carrying more than 15 kilograms in groceries; otherwise, relinquish your seat only if requested to do so, and then only if her request is in the form of ...' It may be true that the actual application of a simply stated norm or convention will require complex individual choices and contingent decisions that parallel this legalistic contractual version. But simplicity is required if the general intent of the norm is to be effectively communicated and universally accepted. The ambiguity that accompanies simplicity can be accommodated on a case by case basis – by common sense and, if necessary, the development of additional conventions – in much the same was as a constitution is interpreted and reinterpreted over time by the courts, the other branches of government and by people directly. This view of constitutional provisions, then, suggests the following universal rule of constitutional design:

Rule 1: Constitutional provisions ought to be simple and concise, unencumbered by legalistic complexity.

Also, since a constitution, at least in its ideal form, ought to be a part of a social consensus that consists of all the norms and conventions that describe a society, and since, in fact, the demand for a written constitution may be a product of these other norms and conventions (Voigt 1999).

Rule 2: If a society has a democratic tradition – even one that lies in the distant past – then any constitution ought to make as few changes in those traditions as possible and link itself to that past as much as possible.

The US Constitution illustrates the application of this second rule, which requires that constitutions accommodate a society's political traditions and those amorphous things we place under the rubric of political culture. For example, readers of that document will search in vain for any reference to 'majority rule' or 'majority vote'. The only references to voting rules we find there pertain to special cases – amendment, impeachment, and the definition of a legislative quorum. The explanation for this 'omission' is straightforward: It was unnecessary for the Framers to say otherwise since, once the set of eligible voters is identified, there already existed a socio-political norm that, *unless otherwise stated*, presumed majority rule. Aside from the supposition that an extraordinary action such as impeachment requires a 'special' vote, there was no consensus on how special that vote ought to be. It is only here, then, that the constitution becomes specific, requiring a vote of two thirds in the Senate for conviction (Art. 1, s. 3.7). This requirement stands in sharp contrast to Article 1, Section 2.5, which states simply that 'The House of Representatives ... shall have the sole power of impeachment.' The implication here is that power of impeachment can be exercised by a simple majority, subject to the requirement that a quorum (a majority of members, as specified in Art. 1, s. 5.1) exists to consider the matter.

It is also worth noting in this context that the United States would be little changed if the Senate requirement had been set at three fifths, or four fifths, or even some less-obvious fraction like seven tenths. The specific number chosen is of less consequence than is ensuring that everyone is coordinated to the *same* number. Because everyone prefers to avoid ambiguity in so important a matter as conviction of impeachment, because there is a consensus that some number greater than one half is necessary, and because, behind their 'veil of ignorance', people are more concerned with agreeing to some number beforehand than to not agreeing or to arguing what that number ought to be in the heat of political passion, the specification of any number greater than a majority will be an equilibrium. Here, then, the constitution quite explicitly functions as an equilibrium selection device.

The argument for Rule 2 – that a stable constitution is a part of society's structure of norms and conventions – holds another universal implication. Briefly, we can infer that a constitution should not try to rewrite those preexisting norms and conventions insofar as they are consistent with democratic practice, since doing so jeopardises a constitution's legitimacy and ability to coordinate. Absent a reason for believing otherwise, it is far safer to assume that social norms and customs have more permanency than any newly imposed political document, at least in the domain of custom and everyday social convention. A constitution may choose to restate some of those customs and conventions, but there is always the danger that specific words open the door to a misinterpretation of things and to government meddling in matters best left to less precise social processes. In any event, our argument here is merely a restatement of the idea that a constitution should be molded to the culture it serves. But rather than try to draft a document that *explicitly* satisfies this objective, a far easier approach to implement is the minimisation of the document's domain. Here, then, is the rationalisation for a rule that is consistent with most of the constitutions we label 'Western':

Rule 3:   Constitutions should focus on the design of those minimal institutions and rights necessary to ensure society's ability to coordinate for the realisation of policy goals as expressed through such agencies as democratic elections.

The preceding three rules stand in sharp contrast to how we might draft a constitution based on a contractual conceptualisation. Like our legalistic norm, our instinct would then be to try to 'nail down' every detail, to defend against every tyranny, and to make plans for every contingency. But this approach merely pushes the problem back a step. The words we add can only open the door to additional ambiguities and the need for additional definitions and contingent choices so that the only 'solution' is to add further administrative, judicial, and legislative directives. The end result is a document that confuses but cannot coordinate. Indeed, because contracts can only be enforced by a higher authority, this view tempts us to begin a futile search for the philosopher-king, to the dangerous creation of the dictator, or to the construction of a governmental structure so mired in countervailing forces that stalemate prevails. Thus:

Rule 4:   The institutional design a constitution offers should be based on the presumption that any need for greater specificity and the resolution of ambiguity will be attended to by the legislative and judicial institutions it establishes and by the evolutionary development of subsidiary social norms and conventions.

Rule 4 is not an argument for wholesale ambiguity. Great skill and foresight may be required when trying to assess those things that require explicit provision and those things that can be left to evolutionary development. The most evident failure of the US Constitution, for instance, occurred with respect to an issue about which it was largely silent and for which there was no social or political-economic norm that could serve as a substitute – the right of secession. A great many things can be cited as 'causes' of the American Civil War, but certainly an important contributing factor was the fact that the Constitution neither explicitly allowed nor disallowed secession. The Confederacy, then, was free to argue that South Carolina had the right to secede while Lincoln and the Union had the right to see South Carolina as a state in rebellion. The states of the Confederacy might have chosen a different path had the constitution explicitly disallowed secession; and Lincoln might have been unable to rally the Union to war had it allowed it. We cannot, of course, test any hypotheses here, but it is evident that Constitutional ambiguity in this instance, absent a consensus on the legitimacy of one action or another as supplied by some other coordinating mechanism, left the Constitution and the country open to disruption.

One advantage of our interpretation of a constitution now is that it helps identify an *effective constitution* – which is a document that establishes stable and self-generating expectations about peoples' political choices. For instance, asserting that the strategy of tit-for-tat will solve a specific instance of the repeated Prisoners' Dilemma requires more than the supposition that both players intend initially to choose this strategy; it also requires that both players believe that the other will do the same. Moreover, as we note earlier, this expectation must be common knowledge – each player must expect the other to choose that particular strategy, each must believe that the other holds a similar expectation, each must believe that the other believes that this is so, and so on. Little is known, unfortunately, about expectations, their genesis and their evolution. But 'it is clear that communication is critical to the ability to settle on a coordinated outcome when interests conflict' (Calvert 1995, 252) if only because the condition of common knowledge is not likely to be satisfied otherwise. Thus, a conceptualisation of constitutions as a coordination device suggests the following with respect to how they ought to be written and ratified:

Rule 5: The writing and ratification process of a constitution should be separate enterprises. The preparation of the document should occur outside of public view, while its subsequent ratification should involve as broad a segment of society as possible.

This rule, of course, merely reiterates the history of the US Constitution. But this rule's logic is wholly general. First, widespread participation in the drafting process need not coordinate society to anything. Indeed, since not everyone is likely to share the view of constitutions as coordination devices as opposed to social contracts, broad participation in drafting is more likely to reveal society's political-economic conflicts in ways that compel drafters to try to incorporate political compromises within it even if those compromises are best left to subsequent legislation or to the gradual evolution of other social conventions. However, once the document is prepared, a way must be found whereby expectations are coordinated and the realisation of that coordination rendered common knowledge. And again, the American experience – which entailed widespread discussion, debate within state legislatures and specially organised assemblies, and the writing of the *Federalist Papers*, as well as those editorials and letters of the 'anti-federalists' – is a model for other states to follow.

We will not attempt to assess how that model can be mapped onto 21st century technology, but the principle – the necessity for generating common beliefs and expectations – remains valid today and for society generally. This argument, moreover, is especially relevant with respect to individual constitutional rights. Unlike those provisions that divide power between executive and legislative branches, specify the size of a legislature, the method of selecting judges, or mechanisms of impeachment, little in a constitution is as likely to impact citizens as directly as is the meaning and enforcement of rights. But here we have a profound difficulty: The remaining parts of a constitution define the rules under which political elites operate (as well as specify the rules under which they become 'elites'), and their conflicts there are likely to be with each other over the allocation of power. Rights, however, constrain the state generally and, thereby, all of those elites in the same way. Political elites, then, have a common interest in circumventing rights and, more often than not, will refrain from doing so only when it is part of a strategy of securing power against each other. We are reminded here of the movie *Armistad* in which John Quincy Adams argues before the US Supreme Court for the freedom of Africans following their revolt on a Spanish vessel. Despite the Court's ostensible pro-slavery sentiments, Adam ultimately sways the justices to his position with the argument that to vote against the Africans and to side with the Van Buren administration threatens to leave the Court subservient to the executive in much the same way as the Spanish court was subservient to the crown. The Court, then, certifies the rights of the Africans, but only to defend its authority against another branch of government.

This example, of course, appears to illustrate the traditional mechanism whereby rights are presumed to be enforced – a specific instance of Madison's 'ambition countering ambition.' And if this were the sole mechanism of enforcement – the balance of powers a constitution seeks to establish – then a contractual conceptualisation of constitutions might provide sufficient guidance for their design. However, even in this instance we should ask: Why would the executive branch be bound by the Court's ruling?

Why didn't the Van Buren administration simply ignore the Court's decision by using its authority over police and military to seize the Africans and, justifying its actions by the imperatives of foreign policy, return them to Spain? On the basis of the conceptualisation of constitutions we offer here, the answer to our question is a societal consensus not merely with respect to the rights a constitution offers, but also about the legitimate exercise of power and who has the authority to interpret those rights in specific substantive instances. Van Buren might have acted to thwart the Court's directive, but if he believed that everyone else outside of his immediate administration was coordinated to sanction such action or ignore his edict on the matter, then it was simply in his self-interest to abide by the Court's ruling. In this way the Court's decision was enforced by a common knowledge belief that the political equilibrium that prevailed would yield sanctions in the event of any defection.

Although we would not argue that widespread public debate, as part of a constitution's ratification process, is sufficient to generate such consensus of beliefs – in the American case, that authority was secured by the Court only over time and in an evolutionary way – we do suggest that such a debate can contribute importantly to it, especially in societies with little experience with a separation of powers and formally expressed rights that constrain the state.

It is at this point that we can address another issue – one that concerns the content of rights. Even when political elites are wholly disingenuous and allow the inclusion of rights they have little intent to enforce or abide by, there is a consensus that certain rights ought to be part of any ostensibly democratic constitution – the right to vote, to trial by jury, to free speech, to peaceful assembly, to protection from unwarranted searches and seizures, to private property, and so on. Debate, though, continues over the advisability of including two additional categories of 'rights' – 'rights' in the form of restrictions on individual citizens when the exercise of one right negatively impacts others, and rights in the form of substantive policy objectives for the state.

The first category of 'rights' – actually obligations – is the easiest to treat. Here we have in mind provisions such as the one found in early drafts of the Russian Federation constitution that 'children who have come of age and who are fit for work are required to take care of their parents'. Although we might agree that this clause expresses a worthwhile sentiment, it is unlikely that many Western specialists in constitutional design would be sympathetic to its inclusion in any constitutional document. Lawyers would decry its imprecision, economists its feasibility, and political scientists (at least the less liberal of the type) its invitation to unwarranted incursions into private affairs. But what of a clause that prohibits the burning of a national flag (as continues to be debated in the United States), that limits a person's ability to publish pornography, or that prohibits promulgation of Nazi ideas (as in Germany)? Here things seem murkier. However, recall our earlier argument that a constitution is only one of the many things that coordinates people to be a society – a governable polity. We find it easy to reject provisions that require children to care for their aged parents because there already are social norms (and associated statutory legislation) that regulate such things, just as there are norms but no constitutional provisions requiring the young to give up their seats on a bus to the elderly. Moving a constitution into this domain, then, is unnecessary. It is also potentially dangerous, because we are then more likely to succumb to the temptation of trying to use that document to establish and regulate all of society's norms and conventions. Perhaps someday, when we know all that there is to know about political-economic and social processes, we can write an all encompassing document. But that day exists only in the most fanciful science fiction. Hence,

Rule 6: Constitutions are necessarily limited documents, and to use them as a tool of social (as opposed to political) engineering can threaten their role as coordinating devices.

It may be true than in extraordinary circumstances, such as the one Germany found itself in following World War II, when people feared a gap in its social normative structure allowed for the rise of a Nazi dictatorship, that an extraordinary provision limiting the ability of people to pursue certain political acts seemed reasonable (although we suspect that West Germany then and Germany today would function as any other democracy without such provisions, given the institutions the other parts of the constitution establishes). It will remain true, however, that the political elites of some states, as well as the citizens within them, will be unwilling to authorise rights in any pure form. Rule 6, nevertheless, can still be adhered to without violating the idea that constitutional rights can legitimately limit only the state with some deft draftmanship. For example, a clause such as 'No law shall deny or abridge any Constitutional right. Laws that govern the manner and circumstances in which Constitutional rights are exercised must be essential to the realisation of those rights or to the fulfilment of some Constitutional responsibilities of the state that cannot be fulfilled by less restrictive laws, and even then they must leave all persons with some ready and effective means of exercising all their Constitutional rights. If challenged in court, the state shall bear the burden of proving that these conditions have been met' (Ordeshook and Schwartz 1993).

Despite the prejudice of political elites to tie their hands with bold statements of individual rights, it is, however, the second category of extended rights that is the more difficult one with which to contend. Examples of this second category in an extreme form are offered again by an early draft of the Russian federation constitution, which among other things provided that (1) 'Each employee is entitled to recreation. Wage workers are guaranteed the working hours, weekly days off, holidays, paid annual leave, and a shorter working day for a number of occupations and industries established by law'; (2) 'Everyone is entitled to qualified medical assistance in state or local systems of health care from the resources of social insurance'; and (3) 'Everyone is entitled to a dwelling place. No one may be arbitrarily deprived of a dwelling place. The state encourages housing construction and creates the conditions for the realisation of the right to a dwelling place. Housing is made available to needy citizens free of charge or on preferential terms from the housing of the RF, the republics, the lands, and local housing'.

The argument against the inclusion of such things is the supposition that by promising more than the state can reasonably be expected to deliver ultimately undermines a constitution's authority (Sunstein 1991). Our objection, for instance, to a balanced budget amendment to the US Constitution is not that the federal government should not have the authority to determine whether spending and taxes are in balance, or that institutional mechanisms should not be found to discourage wasteful spending. Rather, it is that such an amendment sets a specific policy goal which may or may not be feasiblely met. Despite this fact, however, the problem opponents of such provisions confront is that, following 40, 50 or 70 years of communist rule, large segments of the relevant populations believe that such 'rights' belong in a constitution and that legitimacy is lost if they are not somehow incorporated into it. This is a serious concern, since if constitutions are coordination devices, the concept of legitimacy – however imperfectly and imprecisely defined by academics – in critically important to political stability. Indeed, we can even define legitimacy as the extent to which a constitution establishes a common knowledge basis of beliefs and expectations, and performs is coordinating function. Our objection to the preceding clauses, then, is not that they are in a constitution, but simply that they are badly stated. Again, creative draftmanship can solve the problem of imbuing the document with legitimacy (e.g. rather than oblige the state to meet specific policy objectives, when authorising the state to act in specific policy domains, list things like 'adequate income for all,' 'adequate nutrition for all,' 'medical care for all' and so forth, followed by the provision that 'the state shall not act but in pursuit of these objects.')

LESSONS FROM RUSSIA

In questioning the universal relevance of Western constitutions, reference is often made to Russia – to the era of communist rule and also to today when a small cadre of elites, called 'The Family' appear to govern without meaningful constitutional restraint. The USSR's Constitution, both it's 1936 Stalinist and 1977 Brezhnevian versions, offered a full menu of constitutional rights. Chapter X of the 1936 document, for instance, 'guaranteed' the right to free speech, a free press, free assembly, equal protection, freedom of religion and thought, equal rights for women, the inviolability of the person and due process, and, conflating negative with 'positive' rights, the right to work, rest, material security, and education. The USSR's failure to meet these obligations – in combination with what can best be described as a shaky constitutional foundation today for Russia – is taken by some to indicate a failure either of Western-style constitutionalism in general or of its inapplicability to Russia in particular. Is it possible, in other words, that a coordinating constitution, regardless of how well-crafted, cannot overcome Russia's history, culture, and 'the Russian soul'?

Here, though, we argue that the fault of those documents – old and current – is not that they failed, but rather that they worked precisely as designed. Those who believe they failed owing to the gap between promise and reality are correct to assert that merely setting words to paper about rights and social welfare entitlements did not and, in general, cannot accomplish much. Society may be coordinated initially to accept certain rights and limits on the state as legitimate, but a state also requires appropriately designed institutions that lead to common knowledge acceptance of those rights and limits. Elites in particular must believe that other elites will act in accordance with the rules set down in a constitution, they must believe that others think they will act in this way, and so forth – and the institutions a constitution establishes must encourage everyone to signal their commitment to the new equilibrium.

Looking first at Russia's communist era, though, the presumption of failure is based on a preoccupation with the question: Did the constitution lead to the realisation of stated goals? The answer, clearly, is NO, at least insofar as rights and welfare guarantees is concerned. But before we draw any conclusions from this fact, we should consider two additional questions. First, did Soviet constitutions legitimise or contribute to the stability of the political institutions they prescribed. And second, were those institutions appropriate for the realisation of the rights and guarantees it identified as goals? Only if our answers to these questions are NO and YES can we say the constitution failed to operate in its theoretically prescribed way – as a coordinating agent for society. In fact, our answers are exactly the opposite.

First, even if Russia's Soviet-era constitutions failed to guarantee the realisation of lofty principles of human rights and civil liberties, those constitutions did succeed in their purpose to the extent that the system and institutions they sanctioned functioned as described for seven decades (Ordeshook 1997). Specifically, both the 1936 and 1977 versions legitimised the dictatorship of the Communist Party, and thereby rendered its provisions with respect to rights mere window dressing. This is not to say that either constitution coordinated anyone to those political structures: those structures existed before either document was written. At best, the 1977 document codified many of the post-Stalinist changes in Soviet law and, by institutionalising the role of the communist party more forthrightly (para. 6), signalled the transition from Stalin's personal dictatorship to that of the party. Because both documents merely sanctioned what already existed and because they were not designed to be operating law (Blankenagle 1992), we cannot judge whether they played any role in strengthening those institutions.

With respect to the adequacy of that structure for realising stated goals, we can debate whether the USSR's dissolution was inevitable. However, we can attribute the gap between constitutional promise and reality not to any breakdown of constitutional authority – the USSR's economy failed long before the 1991 coup and even before the series of amendments intended to facilitate Gorbachev's policies. Rather, that gap arose because the Soviet system, along with its constitution, were premised on a flawed social theory that failed to anticipate fully the inevitable consequences of unchecked power: inefficiency and corruption. This, nevertheless, was the structure those constitutions legitimised, and this was the one that prevailed. We cannot conclude, then, that Soviet-era constitutions failed to deliver on their promises because constitutionalism is somehow alien to the 'Russian soul', culture or history. If there is a lesson to be learned here it is either that the Soviet experience is an irrelevant experiment or that even bad constitutions can, for a time, be stable.

A more relevant example for purposes of assessing the coordinative powers of a constitution and the law in Russia comes from a different Soviet experience. Recall that although both the 1936 and 1977 versions allowed for secession in principle (paras. 17 and 72, respectively), both documents precluded such action by their failure to offer any procedure for separation. It was evident to every political elite, then, that the true state of affairs was a prohibition on secession. In 1990, though, believing that he could buy time for his reforms, Gorbachev acceded partially to Baltic demands and allowed the passage of implementing legislation that specified a clear, though tortuous, path to secession. The effect was other than what Gorbachev intended. By playing the coordinating role that is the ultimate basis of the enforcement of its provisions, the USSR's Constitution (along with its implementing legislation) coordinated expectations so that what was deemed illegal under one set of words became a legitimated and actively pursued policy by Baltic leaders under a different set (Sharlet 1992).

The flawed Soviet constitution also played a role in its own demise in a different context. Upon the dissolution of the USSR, Russia was left with a constitution that was largely a reprint of the 1977 Soviet text. And although it was amended to establish a president, to empower a constitutional court, and to proclaim the principle of a separation of powers, little attention was paid to logical consistency. Thus, Article 104, consonant with the revolutionary slogan 'all power to the Soviets,' remained and gave the Congress of People's Deputies the authority to legislate and govern in all important matters, despite the addition of competing centers of power. As long as there was a communist party to rule and negate all inconsistencies, such inconsistencies mattered little. But once that party ceased to exist in its original form, the document's logical flaws found full play in the conflict between Yeltsin and the Congress, resulting in a mini-civil war that was resolved only by military force. If anything, then, this progeny of a Soviet-era constitution proved that a logically flawed document can impact events as well as a properly written one.

At this point it is tempting to try to assess the coordinative prospects of Russia's current constitution. There are those, of course, who continue to believe that constitutionalism – at least a democratic form in which a document constrains the state and protects individual rights – is somehow alien to Russia. And as evidence the most cynical among them can point to the growing number of constitutional violations promulgated by a regime that appears to adhere to the law only when it is in its interest to do so. This evidence, however, can be given a different interpretation. Specifically, if the rules we set forth in the preceding section fail to guide a constitution's design, then there is no reason to suppose that a constitution can be an effective coordination mechanism. If, in fact, people begin their democratic constitutional experience with the expectation that their document will not coordinate, and if its design is so fundamentally flawed that it cannot establish a new basis of common knowledge, then that expectation will be realised.

And indeed, the current Russian constitution – both in the method of its creation and in its design – is flawed. First, wholly contrary to Rule 5, its creation involved a confusing mix of drafting by a small inner circle of Yeltsin advisors in combination with a presidentially appointed 400-odd member 'committee' whose ultimate impact on the final document remains unclear. Ratification, in contrast, was swift, entailed little if any public debate, and was performed in the context of a parliamentary election replete with allegations of fraud (Myagkov and Sobyanin 1995). Although many of those who participated in the two-to-three year tug-of-war over alternative drafts before Yeltsin chose to dictate the final outcome were familiar with Western practice, the different sides to these disputes were rarely motivated by principled notions of constitutional democracy (Cohen 1993). Residents of the Kremlin sought a strong presidency; conservatives in the People's Congress argued for a parliamentary system; leaders of the republics argued for a loose federalism because they wished to maximise their autonomy and control of the resources on their territories; politicians in Moscow preferred a unitary state because they sought to maintain control of governmental revenues and because they knew no other governmental form; the original Constitutional Reform Commission argued for an elaborate document since that was the style of their ill-prepared draft and to argue otherwise was to hand the constitutional agenda to competitors; competitors argued the opposite in the attempt to seize the label 'the James Madison of Russia'; and those who argued for extensive welfare entitlements did so because doing otherwise was to reject their heritage of democratic centralism. And again, little of this maneuvering occurred in a context whereby individual citizens or even regional assemblies could contribute much to the debate.

These disputes colored nearly every article of the various draft constitutions, and their final resolution is a document that contradicts many of its
loftily stated principles. Despite proclaiming Russia a federation (para. 5),
federal subjects are precluded from establishing their own independent judiciaries (para. 118) or from controlling the method whereby deputies to either
national legislative branch are elected (para. 96); regional governments
possess few if any exclusive policy jurisdictions paras. 71 and 72) and have
no authority over local governments (paras. 132 and 133); the president is
empowered to overturn those regional executive acts he deems unconstitutional (§ 85); regional governments possess no independent taxing authority
(§ 72); there is no guarantee of the obligation of contracts and no comity
clause. And, in perhaps the clearest reincarnation of Lenin's idea of democratic centralism, the constitution provides that 'federal executive bodies and
the bodies of executive authority of the members of the Russian Federation
shall form a single system of executive authority' (para. 77). Despite proclaiming the people as the ultimate sovereign (para. 3) and rights as inalienable
(para. 17), citizens have no standing before the Constitutional Court (para.
125), constitutional rights are confused with citizen duties (paras. 57-59), and
the law can limit rights in order to uphold 'the foundations of the constitutional system, morality, or the health, rights and lawful interests of other
persons or for ensuring the defence of the country and state security' (para.
55). Despite proclaiming a governmental form based on a separation of
powers (para. 10), in addition to the duties and powers normally associated
with that office and in addition to being anointed 'guarantor of the
constitution' (para. 80), the President is empowered to dissolve parliament
(para. 84), to appoint ministers without legislative oversight (para. 83), and,
as a way of giving the President the power to set the legislative agenda, to
issue decrees insofar as the law is silent (para. 90).

A FIRST PRINCIPLE OF DESIGN

Russia's current constitution, then, violates many of the ideas we might hold
about a balanced institutional design. However, if we review the rules set
forth in Section 3, it is possible to conclude that those violations are not so
serious as to preclude the possibility of their ultimate resolution through
amendment, judicial interpretation, and evolving tradition. The document is
not overly long, it makes few policy promises that a reasonably prosperous

society cannot keep, and it refrains from trying to be society's all-encompassing moral authority. Nevertheless, our assessment of Russia's prospects remain pessimistic. First, there is still the problem of people's expectations – the maintained belief that the document is little more than a meaningless 'parchment barrier', designed to serve a ruling elite. When corruption appears to permeate every branch and level of government, when murder as is sometimes a substitute for electoral defeat, and when a small self-perpetuating inner circle of elites control the important levers of state power, ordinary citizens are unlikely to believe that a new constitution has coordinated them to some new and better equilibrium.

The more serious problem, however, is that a poorly drafted document is unlikely to change expectations and beliefs, because of the opportunities they present for manipulation and circumvention of constitutional provisions will otherwise prove irresistible to political elites. The flaws in Russia's constitutional design go deeper than a few ill-chosen or badly worded provisions, since here we recall once again the homey lesson Franklin offered the drafters of the US Constitution about the necessity for an incentive compatible design. Specifically, if a constitution is to be a successful mechanism of coordination, then the nexus of institutions to which it seeks to coordinate must itself be an incentive-compatible equilibrium. That is;

Rule 7: in assessing a constitution's we need to examine whether any 'player' will have the power and incentive to circumvent unilaterally any of the constitution's provisions.

Rule 7, of course, is little more than the requirement that a constitution be balanced, but the application of this rule requires another – one that not only in the Russian case is too often forgotten or ignored. Indeed, so important is this last rule, which derives from the requirement that the constitution as a whole be an equilibrium, we label it the 'The First Principle of Design':

Rule 8 (The First Principle of Design): all parts of the constitution are interconnected . We cannot assess the consequences of one part without appreciating the meaning of all other parts – if one part fails, then the ability of the other parts of the constitution to coordinate to an incentive compatible equilibrium is necessarily undermined.

This is not the place to review the various features of the Russian constitution that illustrate the violation of Rule 8. It is sufficient to note that, with authors poorly schooled in democratic practice and motivated largely by the need to draft something that satisfied Yeltsin's taste for an especially strong presidency, the document is largely a cobbled-together version of the US, French and German constitutions, prepared as if each section – rights, the legislature, federalism, the presidency and the courts – could be treated separately from the others. More important, perhaps, is the fact that Russia is neither the first nor the last aspiring democracy to fail to satisfy or take full cognisance of Rule 8. The great difficulty here lies in the fact that democratic theory is itself too underdeveloped to inform us unambiguously about how to satisfy this rule. Even basic questions are difficult to answer with confidence. How, for instance, does a president's power with respect to the national legislature impact the authority of the courts? What constitutional mechanisms preclude an incoherent sovereignty of federal subjects that negates an effective national government but which at the same time keeps that government from overwhelming federal subjects? If it is true that 'political parties created democracy and modern democracy is unthinkable save in terms of political parties' (Schattschneider 1942, 1), what parts of the constitution most directly impact a state's party system, and how do different systems mediate legislative, judicial and executive powers? If the constitution establishes a supreme or constitutional court, are individual rights more likely to be protected if ordinary citizens are given standing before that court?

Unfortunately, questions of this type form a virtually endless list. Elsewhere we argue, for example, that the structure of the political party system is a critical component of a federation's design, operation, and stability (Ordeshook and Shvetsova 1995, 1997). Nevertheless, the role of parties and the necessity, when designing a federal state, for concerning oneself with the parts of a constitution that impact party systems (e.g. the power of the president or prime minister and his corresponding incentive to cultivate parties, the structure of legislative or parliamentary representation, the structure of regional constitutions, the timing of elections) are things the literature on federalism largely ignores (Ordeshook 1997). Our argument here, however, is that conceptualising constitutions as a social coordination mechanism will not only give us a better theoretical handle on devising the answers we require, but it also increases our incentive to do so. We suspect, in fact, that the absence of a requisite theory of constitutional design and the corresponding absence of a full appreciation of Rule 8 owes much to the earlier incorrect conceptualisation of constitutions as contracts. When viewed as contracts with the issue of exogenous enforcement unanswered, rather than as conventions or norms, there are two possible responses to the imbalances occasioned by the failure to write a wholly integrated document. The first is to suppose that those imbalances are not of great consequence, provided only that we avoid logical inconsistencies. Contracts can be amended and renegotiated, with details, including bridging gaps between provisions, supplied later. If defects are found, then the same forces that occasioned the document's implementation in the first place will operate to encourage the necessary revisions. A second and closely related response is to see a constitution as little more than a codification of what already exists and, as with Dahl, inessential to the stability and general operation of the state.

In contrast, if a constitution is a self-enforcing mechanism that must move beliefs and expectations to an incentive compatible equilibrium – an equilibrium that must, by definition, include a balance of interests and power among political elites – then such a balance should exist at the outset. We suspect, in fact, that given the complexity of human beliefs and expectations, as well as the information requirements of common knowledge, sociopolitical coordination is a delicate and difficult enterprise with little margin for error. Rule 8, then, is less a deduction from any theory than it is a commonsense advisory.

CONCLUSION

This essay began with a question to which some scholars, but not all, confidently offer an unqualified answer of YES. We concur with this answer, but believe it must be qualified in a particular way. The theory of constitutional design we seek is still too underdeveloped to allow us to say that if some nexus of provisions works in one country, it will work in any another, or if some set of 'successful' constitutions all contain provisions of a certain substantive type, those provisions belong in all constitutions. A secular society, for example, may be able to substitute religious law for a bill or rights or a clergy for a supreme judiciary. If norms, social conventions and constitutional rules are all manifestations of the same theoretical thing, then such possibilities cannot be excluded *a priori*. At the same time, our answer of Yes needs to be qualified also by the fact that our understanding of beliefs and expectations is too underdeveloped to give us full confidence in any prescription for how to best integrate a constitution in a new democracy.

Despite these cautions, the West's constitutional experience does have universal relevance, although the basis of our answer here is not much different than why an economist might assert the general relevance of, say, American economic history. There are those, of course, who might look at that history for solutions to specific problems and try to export what they learn directly to other countries. The United States still, after all, offers the world the largest example of privatisation in history – the 19th century privatisation of nearly one half of the land mass of a continent. Unfortunately, history never precisely repeats itself, and any attempt at adapting a policy or institutional arrangement that is successful in one context is no guarantee that it will be a success in any other. The same is true with constitutions – a constitutional provision that functions well for the United States, Germany, or Sweden may only discourage democratic stability elsewhere.

Nevertheless, the economic principles illustrated by any country's history of, say, land use, investment, social insurance, or technological innovation *are* general. There is, as with physics and chemistry, no Eastern or Western economic theory – there is simply *economic theory*. Parameter values may vary from one society or culture to another, just as the organisation of an economy, the structure of firms, and domains of private property vary across states. But economic laws are universal, and what we learn about their operation in China or Indonesia apply in Iowa, Bonn, and Lima. The same is true of constitutions and the West's experience with them. The difference here is that our theory of politics and democracy is far less developed than is that of economics. Indeed, it is only in the last ten or fifteen years that economics and game theorists have come to appreciate fully the importance of the ideas of coordination, belief, and expectation. In this essay, however, we try to offer a conceptualisation of constitutions that is grounded in the same theoretical primitives as contemporary economics – game theory – with the hope that by doing so we can establish a base upon which to construct a fully integrated and general theory of democratic design. Unfortunately, that task still lies before us, and the rules we offer here necessarily remain tentative implications. Our belief, though, is that this conceptualisation can yield principles of design that are sufficiently compelling so as to lead to the drafting of constitutions that place democracy on a firmer footing everywhere.

REFERENCES

Blankenagle, A. (1992), 'Toward Constitutionalism in Russia', *East European Constitutional Review*, **1** (2), 25-27.

Calvert, Randall L. (1995), 'The Rational Choice Theory of Social Institutions: Cooperation, Coordination and Communication', in Jeffrey S. Banks and Eric A. Hanushek (eds), *Modern Political Economy*, Cambridge: Cambridge University Press.

Chen, Yan and Peter C. Ordeshook (1994), 'Constitutional Secession Clauses', *Constitutional Political Economy*, **5** (1), 45-60.

Cohen, Ariel (1993), 'Comparing Russia's Constitutional Drafts', *Eurasian Reports: What Is Russia*, Center for American-Eurasian Studies, **3** (2).

Coleman, James (1986), 'Norms as Social Capital', in Gerard Radnitzky and Peter Bernholz (eds), *Economic Imperialism*, New York: Paragon House.

Gifford, A., Jr. (1991), 'A Constitutional Interpretation of the Firm', *Public Choice*, **68**, 91-106.

Hardin, Russell (1989), 'Why a Constitution' in Bernard Grofman and Donald Wittman (eds), *The Federalist Papers and the New Institutionalism*, New York: Agathon Press.

Holmes, Stephen (1988), 'Precommitment and the Paradox of Democracy' in Jon Elster and Rune Slagstad (eds), *Constitutionalism and Democracy*, Cambridge: Cambridge University Press.

Kreps, David M. (1990), 'Corporate Culture and Economic Theory', in James Alt and Kenneth Shepsle (eds), *Perspectives on Positive Political Theory*, Cambridge: Cambridge University Press.

Myagkov, Mikhail and Alexander Sobyanin (1995), 'Irregularities in the 1993 Russian Elections', working paper, California Institute of Technology, Humanities and Social Science.

Ordeshook, Peter C. (1992), 'Constitutional Stability', *Constitutional Political Economy*, **3** (2), 137-75.

Ordeshook, Peter C. (1993), 'Some Rules of Constitutional Design', in Ellen F. Paul, Fred D. Miller, and Jeffrey Paul (eds), *Liberalism and the Economic Order*, Cambridge: Cambridge University Press, pp. 198-232.

Ordeshook, Peter C. (1995), 'Institutions and Incentives', *Journal of Democracy*, **6** (2), 46-60.

Ordeshook, Peter C. (1997), 'Constitutions for New Democracies: Reflections of Turmoil or Agents of Stability', *Public Choice*, **90**, 55-72.

Ordeshook, Peter C. and Thomas Schwartz (1993), 'A Constitution for the Russian Federation', *Business World* (Moscow), March 20, 16.

Ordeshook, Peter C. and Olga Shvetsova (1995), 'If Hamilton and Madison were Merely Lucky, What Hope is There for Russian Federalism', *Constitutional Political Economy*, **6**, 107-126.

Ordeshook, Peter C. and Olga Shvetsova (1997), 'Designing Federalisms: The Critical Issue of Election Systems', *Journal of Democracy*, **8** (1), 27-42.

Riker, William H. (1964), *Federalism: Origin, Operation, Significance*, Boston: Little Brown.

Schattschneider, E. E. (1942), *Party Government*, New York: Holt, Reinhart and Winston.

Sharlet, Robert (1992), *Soviet Constitutional Crisis*, Armonk, New York: M.E. Sharpe, Inc.

Sunstein, Cass (1988), 'Constitutions and Democracies: An Epilogue', in Jon Elster and Rune Slagstad (eds), *Constitutionalism and Democracy*, Cambridge: Cambridge University Press, pp. 327-57.

Sunstein, Cass (1991), 'Constitutionalism and Secession', *University of Chicago Law Review*, **58**, 633-70.

Tullock, Gordon (1987), 'The Calculus: Postscript after 25 Years', *Cato Journal*, **7** (2), 313-21.

Voigt, Stephan (1999), 'Breaking with the Notion of Social Contract: Constitutions as Based on Spontaneously Arisen Institutions', *Constitutional Political Economy*, **10** (3), 283-300.

Williamson, Oliver E. (1979), 'Transaction-cost Economies: The Governance of Contractual Relations', *Journal of Law and Economics*, **22**, 233-61.

Wood, Gordon S. (1969), *The Creation of the American Republic: 1776-1789*, Chapel Hill: University of North Carolina Press.

12. Comment

Stephan Panther

Peter Ordeshook's contribution deserves praise for at least three reasons. Firstly, it is built on a theoretical base which, to my knowledge is both sound and relatively innovative in the field we are concerned with. Second, and this is the part I perhaps valued most highly, he has the courage to try to draw the lessons from his approach and develops a set of basic rules for constitution builders. Third, on the base of this he can give a reasoned judgement of the effect of the Russian constitution on Russian politics in the transition phase. This is thus a wide ranging and original effort in bridge building between theory, normative guidelines and present day politics.

My task as a commentator is to be critical, and I will start this task by pointing out that, in my opinion, the bridge between theory and normative guidelines is not as firmly built as it seems. Ordeshook's eight rules draw on greater wisdom than is contained in the game theoretical base. More precisely they are built on an anthropology which goes beyond the economic man of the theory. I will continue to argue that the concept of 'culture', central to the question the paper sets out to discuss, remains strangely opaque, since it is dealt with in an implicit and not in a systematic way. The rest of this comment then tries to sketch some implications of a systematic inquiry.

Let me start my critical task. The theory of repeated games Ordeshook builds upon is based on fully rational actors. While it is consistent with differential information between players, it does not assume any cognitive or data processing limitations of the actors. Rule 1 is simply not relevant for these actors. They do not care whether a rule is complicated or not as long as it is consistent. By way of contrast, Rule 1 is reasonable in a world where cognition is limited and reasoning costs time and effort. In such a world the idea, that constitutions are 'incomplete' in the sense of the theory of incomplete contracts, which is implicit in Rule 4 also is much more natural than in a world of rational superminds. We are unable to incorporate every possible future contingency into a constitution because reasoning is costly and fallible.

Fully rational game theory furthermore assumes that actors share a common view of the relevant portions of the world: the rational actors of game theory cannot agree to disagree, as is assumed in the justification of Rule 5. Their preferences are fixed and only the strategic aspects of the situation influence behaviour. Memories of a distant past not containing any strategic information for the present do not affect their behaviour, by contrast to what seems to be assumed in Rule 2.[1]

However, I find these rules reasonable (with the possible exception of Rule 5) despite their 'lack of foundation'. And I believe many readers will do so too. I am convinced that this is so, because these rules implicitly draw upon a more comprehensive anthropology than they pretend. However, since they do so only implicitly, the chance is missed to relate 'constitutions' to 'culture' in a systematic and integrated manner. Instead the concept is left largely in the dark, despite the reference to informal norms and conventions, which *are* a central part of culture, but are characteristically not related to the concept in Ordeshook's paper.

Let me briefly sketch such an anthropology here, which I have developed more fully elsewhere.[2] Optimising man/woman is replaced by 'habitual' man/woman, where the term habit has a very broad meaning including habits of perceiving, understanding, acting, thinking, problem-solving. One could categorise these as primary habits (habits to do something), secondary habits (habits to decide on an action), tertiary habits (habits of selecting a mode of action), and possibly extending this further.

Habitual man becomes 'cultural man/woman' if one realises that most of our habits are to a high degree collectively shared and learned by either observing them directly from others or by communication with them mainly through language and usually by a combination of the two.

Let me first emphasise that this anthropology does not preclude the use of the tools of game theory, nor the idea of an equilibrium, nor the idea of a constitution as an equilibrium selection device.

As to the first issue, this anthropology would however require a shift from fully rational game theory to evolutionary game theory. Especially the so called 'indirect evolutionary approach' proposed by Güth and Kliemt[3] is close to a habitual/cultural perspective in so far as their actors are not blindly programmed to act in a certain way, but retain their ability to choose, there preferences. However these, and more recently also their informational behaviour, are selected for in an evolutionary process.

The notion of equilibrium does survive this change. While in fully rational theory, equilibrium may be characterised as a state of the world, where no actor has an incentive to change his plan of action or his beliefs, it now becomes a state of the world where no actor has an incentive to change his habits (including: world views, problem-solving routines, internalised norms and values guiding behaviour, etc.).

Constitutions may also in this world be part of an equilibrium, and drafting a constitution may still be an exercise in equilibrium selection. However, it should be clear that in this perspective, the constitution is much more closely linked to non-constitutional norms, values, common understandings etc. as is apparent when looking at them using the more traditional perspective. At the same time, using this view the constitution in turn can help to stabilise an equilibrium because it focuses attention on certain values and principles, thus shaping values and norms itself, a process enhanced by the rituals of a 'civil religion' built around it, as for example in the United States.

Turning back to Peter Ordeshook's paper from this perspective, it becomes essential to note right away, that the notion of a 'democratic constitution' is itself heavily culturally impregnated. 'Constitution' implies minimally the idea of a separate political sphere, and, the rule of law without double-talk. These are by no means creations of the West, but they are not part of all cultural traditions of this world. 'Democratic' implies something like the idea of government of the people by and for the people. Phrased in economic jargon, it implies the idea of producing a collective good by joint action, where each actor takes part in the formulation of the plan of action to at least a minimal degree. Or phrased yet again differently referring to Tocqueville: It implies at least some acquaintance with the art of association. Again these ideas may or may not be available in a certain cultural frame.

From this perspective Ordeshook's eight rules are first of all given a firmer foundation. Besides the cases I have taken as my point of departure, this shows up for example in the reasoning about Rule 5. Widespread discussion of a constitution will serve not so much to provide the base for common knowledge, but in the sense of a deliberative process it may change peoples preferences, their norms and values, it may reinforce their identification with the constitution and create greater legitimacy for it. From this perspective it is however not self-evident, that participation should be limited to the stage of ratification only.

However, the change of perspective does not simply provide foundations and add a few minor changes. Two major critical points arise. First, Rule 8 is formulated too narrowly. As already alluded to above, constitutions may only select an equilibrium, which however is an equilibrium only when all relevant other cognitive routines, common understandings, worldviews, values, norms etc. have been taken account of. While Ordeshook seems to acknowledge this on page 166, he looses sight of it when formulating Rule 8. We cannot assess the consequences of a constitution without taking into account the habits of the mind and heart it builds upon and interlinks with.

This leads up to the second fundamental point. When comparing the draft and the drafting process of a real constitution like the Russian one with the ideals spelled out in the normative rules, one has to take account of the fact that the drafting process itself does not take place in a cultural void but is subject to cultural constraints. Drafting a constitution is a culturally endogenous process. If one forgets this, one commits a fallacy similar to the one criticised by public choice theorists with respect to welfare economics. Welfare economists propose reform disregarding the constraints put on policy by the political process, constitutional political economists seem to propose rules for constitution making not taking into account the cultural constraints inherent in the process of constitution making.

Does all this mean that constitutions don't matter or cannot change anything? I do not think so. Constitutions, and especially, well-crafted ones, may help to coordinate society into a new equilibrium path, when the old one is no longer firmly entrenched. This is typically so after severe crises, often violent ones like prolonged war, civil war or revolutionary periods, especially if those social interests which are powerful have suffered the crises themselves and thus are in a situation where any newly coordinated equilibrium path will improve upon the present status quo. However, even then, having an external guarantor of the process helps, like in the case of Germany or Japan after World War II, or to a lesser extent the EU in the present transition process in Eastern Europe.

For the constitution to be part of the establishment of a new equilibrium path three fundamental conditions have to be met. The relevant interests have to agree that new rules of the game are indeed written by writing of the constitution. Constitution writing is not an exercise in window dressing. This presupposes an expectation and therefore frequently the tradition of an effective enforcement apparatus, able to implement decisions in a coherent fashion. Which in turn presupposes that those acting in this apparatus have the appropriate incentives which includes a loyalty to the 'constitutional entity' overriding factional loyalties to family, lineage, clan, tribe, region etc. whenever necessary.

NOTES

1   The idea, that a constitution is helped by being 'legitimate' which, following Max Weber, I understand as being judged 'justifiable according to a set of internalised norms, is not strictly beyond a rational actor model. It does however build on preferences which are not usually assumed in repeated games and for the creation of which economics lacks a theory.
2   See Panther, Stephan (2000), 'Kulturelle Faktoren in der Ökonomik und die Webersche Protestantismusthese', in Priddat, Birger P. (ed), *Kapitalismus, Krisen, Kultur*, Marburg: Metropolis, pp. 165-188.
3   The seminal paper is Güth, Werner and Kliemt, Hartmut (1994), 'Competition or Cooperation. On the Evolutionary Economics of Trust, Exploitation and Moral Attitudes', *Metroeconomica*, **45**, 155-187.

13. On Implicit Constitutional Change

Imre Vörös

1.   INTRODUCTION

The Hungarian Constitutional Court began its work on 1 January 1990. Parliament passed the Constitution that provided the framework for this on 23 October 1989, before the first democratic elections of May 1990, and thus before the fall of communism. The new Constitution was formally promulgated as a modification of the old one, but only one sentence corresponds to the old Constitution, namely that the capital of the Republic of Hungary, independent of the political system, is Budapest. As is well known, the Hungarian Constitution harmonises with the constitutions of modern democracies and human rights conventions. Applied by the Constitutional Court, it has been one of the most important legal means for developing Hungary's democracy and market economy.

The text of the new Constitution was negotiated in the course of the so-called round table negotiations between the representatives of the then-ruling communist party and the interim government of 1988-99, on the one hand, and of the bourgeois opposition on the other. The parliament then enacted the negotiated text as the new Constitution. On the same day, the People's Republic of Hungary was renamed the Republic of Hungary.

The text of the Constitution places little weight on the economic Constitution or on economic constitutional law. The reason for this was that the then-opposition's primary goal at the round table negotiations was to lay the legal foundations for the public law and politological framework of the turn away from communism, especially the multi-party system and elections. Two other factors also played a role. On the one hand, some important elements of the market economy were already present in Hungary (a degree of independence for state companies in the legally secured form of so-called self-regulation; private initiative in the cooperatives; and in smaller so-called work coope-ratives that resembled German BGB companies). Also, two cornerstone laws of the market economy had already been passed: in 1986, corporate law; and in 1984, the law on competition. On the other hand, hardly any economists took part in the round table negotiations. The Constitution's provisions for the economy are correspondingly vague and in part contradictory.

The text was worked out under time pressure, within a few months, which also explains certain unclarities. All this means that Hungary's economic Constitution as a whole is covered by seven articles, of which two (those on state companies and cooperatives) have no practical significance.

I will also attempt to present some examples of the 'improvement' practice of the Hungarian Constitutional Court in 'six plus one' from the viewpoint of Hungarian economic constitutional law: the market economy as a goal of the state (Preamble, Article 9, paragraph 1), juristic persons as subjects of fundamental rights (e.g. the ban on discrimination, Article 70/A), the rule of law (Art. 2, para. 1), the guarantee for property rights (Art. 13, para. 1), free enterprise (Art. 9, para. 2), and finally the ban on discrimination. I will digress on the right to social security (Art. 70/E) in the context of various economic policies.

2.   THE MARKET ECONOMY AS A GOAL OF THE STATE

The Constitution mentions the term 'market economy' in the Preamble and in Article 9, paragraph 1. The preamble speaks of a Constitution intended to promote the transition to a multi-party democracy and to a social market economy. Articel 9, paragraph 1, however, defines Hungary's national economy simply as a market economy. In the example of *Lochner* v. *New York* and the investment aid judgement, the Constitutional Court's decision side-stepped, but did not dissolve the contradiction as neutral in terms of economic policy and categorised the market economy as a goal of the state. This does not explain the contradiction, but it solves the problem of categorising the declaration within the system of the Constitution.

Earlier, the Constitutional Court spoke of the legislature's intention of expanding the market economy as a constitutional basis for limiting fundamental rights. The court revised this position in the so-called taxi driver case (in which a municipal ordinance limiting of the number of taxi drivers was declared unconstitutional) when it underscored that Article 9, paragraph 1 of the Constitution did not establish a 'right to' and certainly no 'fundamental right to' the market economy, but a goal of the state whose realisation and the ensuring of whose preconditions was the task of the state.

The question of 'social' or 'simple' market economy was not directly answered. But – after its earlier rejecting stance – the Constitutional Court applies the right to social security anchored in Article 70/E of the Constitution as a fundamental right and, step by step, is interpreting its content in part as a guarantee of a minimum level of subsistence. We can conclude from this that the Constitutional Court's response to the contradiction has been to silently decide in favour of the Preamble. This removal of an internal contradiction can be seen as an 'improvement' of the Constitution.

Similarly, Article 9, paragraph 2, on the recognition and promotion of the freedom of economic competition, has also been 'improved', since the suits brought before the Constitutional Court have repeatedly cited it as a fundamental right. The Constitutional Court has qualified this declaration as a principle of the Constitution, one representing a precondition for the market economy, but not an independent constitutional criterion or content itself. Instead, it is to be protected by means of other fundamental rights, such as the guarantee for property rights and the principle of equality.

3. JURISTIC PERSONS AS SUBJECTS OF FUNDAMENTAL RIGHTS

The Constitution does not explicitly name juristic persons as subjects of fundamental rights. This already created difficulties in judging the ban on discrimination in the first year of the Constitutional Court's activity. Asked in the fall of 1990 whether Article 70/A also applies to juristic persons, the Constitutional Court answered that it did, and at the same time that this was also true for all fundamental rights whose terms could apply to juristic persons. The formulation of Article 70/A is limiting in that it regulates and exemplifies the content of the ban on discrimination from the viewpoint of human rights. The Constitutional Court generalised the wording, which refers to 'persons', determining that 'persons' is to be understood as including both natural and juristic persons. The exemplification of the kinds of discrimination against juristic persons had to be worked out step by step in practice.

4.   THE RULE OF LAW

Article 3, paragraph 1, which stipulates that the Republic of Hungary is subject to the rule of law, implies a demand for legal certainty, though this is not explicitly mentioned. In the context of legal certainty (and of the later-mentioned right to social security), the Constitution's failure to stipulate the economic constitution and especially economic policy led to a need for the Constitutional Court to work out a clarifying interpretation. The changes in the regulation of tax advantages for companies precipitated such an inter-pretation.

The Constitutional Court had to decide the degree to which and to what effect the legislative branch may alter the regulation and still maintain legal security. It underscored that tax advantages are an instrument of economic policy and not a right; thus, the state has a great degree of freedom to restruc-ture tax advantages occasionally. So tax advantages in themselves are not a constitutional problem. But the way such modification is introduced can have constitutional relevance: it must not be ex post facto and it should allow appropriate preparation time. In the given case, however, the new regulation revoked tax advantages already claimed by companies – current tax advan-tages.

The Constitutional Court felt forced to interpret and specify what the rule of law and legal security mean for tax law situations, and thus to improve the Constitution practically. The Court's decision elaborates the concept of relative legal security in the area of tax law, with the following content: when a company claims a tax advantage, it is 'accepting' the state's offer, thus con-cretising and individualising the abstract legal situation of the tax advantage in terms of the individual company. This creates an individual legal relatio-nship under public law between the state and the company, one that the state (one of the parties to the relationship) cannot alter at will (through legisla-tion), for this would violate Article 2, paragraph 1 of the Constitution.

But the constitutional demand for legal security does not mean the legal system can never be changed. It merely requires relative predictability, a relative foreseeability of tax advantages. This is shaped by how long the tax advantage lasts: the longer a tax advantage lasts, the more the demand for le-gal security is relativized, i.e. the more freedom of movement the legislative branch has to modify the regulation, since with a longer tax advantage, the state's maintenance of the tax advantage cannot be expected. The longer the tax advantage is intended, the more the demand for legal security is relativized; the shorter it is intended, the more strictly legal security is required. In the given case, the legislative branch reduced tax advantages promised and claimed for five years; so the Constitutional Court ruled that the regulation of the tax advantage (categorised as short-term) was unconstitutional and declared it null and void.

5.   GUARANTEE FOR PROPERTY RIGHTS

The Hungarian Constitution guarantees property rights as a fundamental right, but as 'the most limitable' fundamental right. It can even be limited for reasons of public interest, provided that this limitation is not arbitrary.

Article 13, paragraph 1 of the Constitution provides the guarantee for property rights, and is joined by two special laws: according to Article 9, paragraph 1, private and common property are equal and enjoy the same protection; and according to Article 12, paragraph 1, the state recognises the independence of cooperatives. In a misleading way, both rules seem to affect the guarantee for property rights, so the Constitutional Court had to clarify their relationship to Article 13, paragraph 1.

The Constitutional Court determined that Article 9, paragraph 1 has no bearing on Article 13, paragraph 1, but is a concretisation of the ban on discrimination (Art. 70/A) for every form of property. On the other hand, Article 12, paragraph 1 implies the following: The lawmaker cannot revoke the guarantee for private property from the (especially agricultural) cooperatives ('kolchoses') simply for the reason that they were founded before 1990. The Constitutional Court declared the unconditional revocation of cooperative property to be unconstitutional, agreeing only to a one-time partial claim for purposes of compensation, and this only if the cooperatives are converted to conform with the market economy: after conversion, they are fully and unconditionally entitled to the guarantee for property rights like all other actors (companies) in the market economy. At the same time, the Court underscored that Article 12, paragraph 1 does not, however, constitute in any way a special protection for cooperatives.

The roots of the two rules are in the provisional arrangement of the round table negotiations: those in power in 1989 wanted to save the agricultural production cooperatives from mandatory dissolution (Art. 12, para. 1); the bourgeois opposition of the time feared that state (common) property would be privileged at the expense of private property (compare Art. 9, para. 1).

Both regulations had to be assigned their proper 'levels of importance' so that they did not infringe on the general validity of the guarantee for property of Article 13, paragraph 1.

The content of the guarantee for property was interpreted on the model of the civil law concept of property.

After a short time, however, the Constitutional Court was confronted with the question of the constitutionality of the early 1980s ban on natural persons and small companies (comparable with German OHGs and KGs) purchasing copying machines as property. The Court pointed out the infringement of the guarantee of property and thus placed the acquisition of property under the protection of Article 13, paragraph 1, as an element of its content (the simultaneous mention of the ban on discrimination changes nothing about this). But later the Constitutional Court ruled that the ban on juristic persons acquiring real property was constitutional on the grounds that the guarantee for property can be claimed only to protect property already acquired.

The Constitutional Court did not initially recognise the unclear relationship between Article 13, paragraphs 1 and 2. So, as already mentioned, it restricted itself to interpreting the content elements of the guarantee for property on the model of civil law property (possession, use, access). But after only a few years, in the course of interpreting this fundamental right as the one most limitable, it determined that the essential content of this fundamental right is the guarantee of value, not of substance. The guarantee for property does not entail protection against being deprived of the substance of a thing, but that the value of the thing must be assured as compensation to the owner for the expropriation. Thus, Article 13, paragraph 1 was considered in the context of paragraph 2 (on the criteria of constitutionally permitted expropriation): expropriation is presented as the most extreme case of limitation of the guarantee for property, the latter being the most limitable fundamental right. In my view, in this case, the Constitutional Court has practically modified, but not improved the Constitution: the 'boundless' expansion of the content elements of the guarantee for property onto expropriation mixes the two institutions of the constitutions in a way that makes it impossible to know when a case is the limitation of a fundamental right (whose essence, according to Article 8, paragraph 2, may not be touched even by a law) and when a case of expropriation renders that right meaningless.

This path, unspectacular in terms of content, backfired later when the Constitutional Court was confronted with the extension of the protection afforded by the guarantee for property to include claims under public and social law, based on the application of Article 70/E (the right to social security). In 1995, when, in the course of restoring the national economy, the rigorous austerity package substantially reduced the social program benefits inherited from the socialist planned economy and society, the Constitutional Court extended the protection of the guarantee for property to include social program benefits, regardless of whether these were financial payments or non-financial benefits. In practical terms, this stance changed the content of the constitution's guarantee for property: the state's obligation to provide social benefits became practically unlimited, because the Constitution had made the protection of the 'socialist' status quo in the area of social benefits a criterion of the constitutionality of legal arrangements. This is closely connected with the right to social security, so later I will turn the question around from the standpoint of the connection between the constitution and economic policy. Noteworthy is that the Constitutional Court's rigorous stance could be maintained for about one year, after which this standpoint was quietly revised and the content of the guarantee for property was limited to financial social benefits.

6.   FREE ENTERPRISE SYSTEM

The regulation of the free enterprise system (Art. 9, para. 2) required clarification in connection with the right to work and the right to free choice of profession or trade (Art. 70/B, para. 1), since the interrelationship between the three categories was not defined by the regulation.

For example, in connection with the community traffic ordinance's limiting the number of taxi drivers in Budapest, petitions protested this as an infringement of this fundamental right. The Constitutional Court, pointing to its earlier practice, underscored that the free enterprise system is a specific case (lex specialis) in connection with the right to free choice of profession or trade (as a lex generalis) and formulated it as an aspect of the latter. The free enterprise system concretises the right to free choice of profession or trade in the sense that it gives everyone the right to practice entrepreneurial activity and to become an entrepreneur; the state and the lawmaker may not hinder this. But this does not mean that someone has the right to act as an entrepreneur in any particular profession, merely that the state may not prevent anyone from becoming an entrepreneur in some form or other. The Constitutional Court thus limited the fundamental right to the theoretical possibility of carrying out the activity and negated the derivation of a subjective right to a specific profession or enterprise.

Accordingly, the Constitutional Court also viewed the right to work from the institutional side and defined it as the state's resulting general duty to act to create jobs, i.e. to conduct employment policy. Thus, no one has a right to a specific job: Article 70/B, paragraph 1 does not guarantee that the state must secure someone any specific work opportunity.

The Constitutional Court's 'improvements' in interpreting the constitution thus eliminated actually existing misunderstandings based in the earlier 'socialistic' idea of full employment ('rescued' as reminiscences from the then-current government into the new Constitution in the 1989 round table negotiations). Due to the lack of clarity and the lack of regulation of the relationships among the three institutions doubtless appearing justified in the eyes of the petitioners, these misunderstandings doubtless seemed justified in the eyes of the petitioners.

7.   THE PRINCIPLE OF EQUALITY (THE BAN ON DISCRIMINATION)

The principle of equality (Art. 70/A), as mentioned in section 3, was the occasion requiring the Constitutional Court to grapple with the problem of applying fundamental rights to juristic persons. The regulation formulated for human rights considerations gave no concrete basis for criteria in regard to the ban on discrimination in the case of juristic persons (since, as mentioned above, the recognition and expansion of the area of applicability of fundamental rights in any form requires the improving/modifying intervention of the Constitutional Court). Thus, the Constitutional Court had to work out such criteria in 1991, when examining the constitutionality of privileges that corporate law granted the state and state organs. It thereby established several important principles of the Hungarian economic Constitution.

Corporate law granted privileges in subscribing stock, for example: when founding, founders could refuse oversubscription; but they did not have this right in the case of a financial institute owned by the state. By the same token, in cases of capital increase, such organs were privileged in subscribing stock. They also had the privilege that they could enjoy voting rights disproportionate to their share in capital, even if their share was not in preferred stock, thus making it possible for them to have, practically, a 51% vote while possessing only 1/3 of the stock. The background of this regulation stemming from 1986 was the wish to brake the already beginning wave of privatisation (in the form of the massive transformation of state enterprises into private companies) and to keep it more or less under the control of the Communist Party. To the Constitutional Court fell the task of revising this regulation through an improving/creating interpretation of the Constitution's ban on discrimination in relation to juristic persons.

As a thesis of principle, the Constitutional Court determined that the market economy is a pluralistically structured economy that functions on the basis of the equality of the various owners, competitive freedom, and the free enterprise system. It has cardinal significance that the functions and quality of the state as bearer of sovereign power are strictly separated from those of the owner-entrepreneur. In other words, the sovereign/state sphere and the entrepreneurial (the so-called competitive) sphere must be strictly separated from each other. Equality of opportunity can be secured only on the basis of corporate law's neutrality toward owners. Consequently, the privileged position of the state must be abolished, since these privileges violate the constitution's principle of equality. This is also the only way to secure the state goal of the market economy (see section 2 above) and the principle of competitive freedom. Accordingly, the Constitutional Court declared these norms unconstitutional and nullified them. (It is characteristic of the euphemistic stance of the lawmakers in 1986 that these privileges could not be claimed against foreign investors.).

With this improving intervention, the Constitutional Court thus did not simply establish the application of the ban on discrimination to juristic persons, but also worked out the content of the criteria defining the discrimination of juristic persons by the state as entrepreneur. Since this became the constant practice of the Constitutional Court, we can say that, remaining in the framework of creating interpretation, the Constitutional Court practically improved and 'supplemented' the constitution (Art. 70/A).

8.   DIGRESSION ON THE RIGHT TO SOCIAL SECURITY

To protect the country from the acute threat of insolvency, Parliament resolved an austerity package in 1995. This drastically reduced the budget's outlays, including the social benefits inherited from the 'socialistic'/ egalitarian times (e.g. birth assistance, completely government-run health insurance, etc.). The changes led to vehement debates in society and politics and also had their effects on the Constitutional Court. Numerous petitions challenged the regulations with the argumentation that they violated the rights to social security (Art. 70/E) and legal certainty (Art. 2, para. 1) and were therefore unconstitutional. The Constitutional Court tried to clarify the unclear relationship between the right to social security (whose character as a fundamental right it had already recognised), the guarantee for property (Art. 13, para. 1), and legal certainty/the rule of law. In my opinion, the Court failed.

The Constitutional Court declared a great number of changes to be unconstitutional, citing one institution of the Constitution or the other. The starting point for the justifications of the many decisions was always the following basic principle: according to Article 70/E, the right to social security, the lawmaker is obligated only to organise and ensure the functioning of the system of health and pension insurance on the one hand, and the system of social allowances on the other hand. More concrete kinds and amounts of services cannot be deduced from the Constitution, and the lawmaker enjoys great freedom in determining these.

In contrast, in regard to the modification of already granted services, the Constitutional Court took a position based on the guarantee for property and on legal certainty. It underscored that the changes were implemented without preparation time (true enough) and thus violated the principle of legal certainty (derived from the institution of the rule of law, Art. 2, para. 1) and that many parts of the overall regulation were thus unconstitutional. Acquired rights (droit acquis), rights that were acquired before 1990, were mentioned without naming the source of law, i.e. the constitution. Here, the Court associated undifferentiated, non-financial or insurance-based financial social benefits (health and pension insurance), which would otherwise have resulted from the right to social security, with the extension of the determined content of the guarantee for property to claims for state social benefits based in public law.

The decisions of the Constitutional Court triggered intense discussions centred on the following issue: Since the decisions directly affected the outlay side of the budget, the degree to which the Constitutional Court has the right to charge the state with the duty to pay allowances based on the right to social security is questionable. The maintenance of the kind and volume of the social services 'acquired' in the decades of the planned economy and one-party dictatorship has indeed little to do with the right to social security or with the guarantee for property (acquired rights). (In the old system, even wages were not paid on the market-economy basis of individual achievement, but were practically interwoven with the system of state social benefits as alms.) With this, by referring to the guarantee for property, the Constitutional Court blocked the begun transformation of the system of social benefits and required the lawmaker to maintain the old system as a precondition for constitutionality. Since many changes had precisely reduced the benefits while creating the institutional framework for individual provision against risk (private pensions, etc.), the Constitutional Court regarded all this as a violation of Article 2, paragraph 1 and Article 13, paragraph 1.

In my opinion, the Constitutional Court's attempt to apply in a complex manner the three institutions (legal certainty, guarantee for property, right to social security) failed because its decisions ignored the systematic character of the Constitution.

First, the court failed to recognise that the right to social security touches upon the guarantee for property only to the degree that it applies to financial payments from the state. In this area, one can operate with the extension of the determined content of the guarantee for property, since this is a question of limiting a (most-limitable) fundamental right, that of the guarantee for property. Here, too, public interest and the lack of arbitrariness (in an economic emergency) speak for constitutionality.

Second, Article 70/A does not stipulate the amount of the payments, but merely the creation of the institutional framework conditions for (financially provided) health and pension insurance on the one hand and the (non-financially provided) social allowances on the other hand. It adds to the latter that the latter must secure the subsistence minimum in sum (otherwise it would be senseless). This is contradicted by the subsequent change of argumentation for the decisions on the guarantee for property and on legal certainty, because they 'freeze' the legal system as de lege lata, as the status quo in this given area. Based on these criteria of judgement, the budget must provide what was earlier provided, regardless of actual possibilities. On the one hand, of course, this is senseless, and on the other hand it is a direct intervention in day-to-day economic policy. This contradicts the Constitutional Court's own view, previously mentioned, that the constitution is neutral in regard to economic policy.

Third, claims to non-financial services and to a certain degree also to financial services cannot be unconditionally placed under the protection of the guarantee for property. The reduction of non-financial services cannot be judged on the basis of the conventional dogmatics of fundamental rights, since in this area the state is not obligated to avoid interfering in the private sphere. The state's dare obligation is to positive action: it must perform services, i.e. it must 'invade' the individual's private sphere. The reduction of this obligation cannot be judged on the basis of the guarantee for property (since the examination in accordance with the necessity and proportionality test of the traditional limitation of fundamental rights is senseless), but as an aspect of the right to social security. Here, and especially in the area of non-financial services, the Constitution makes no statements about the kind and amount of services, nor about changes or reductions in them (except regarding the subsistence minimum). In other words, nothing conceptual can be said about this dare obligation.

Fourth, the Constitutional Court's attempt to show itself socially 'sensitive' also failed because it did not recognise the relationship between the guarantee for property as lex generalis and the (concrete) right to social security as lex specialis. For this interrelationship has two consequences. First, since lex specialis derogat legi generali, the guarantee for property may be applied only subsidiarily, i.e. when (after) no lex specialis is applicable. The cases analysed concern the facts of the right to social security, so there was no scope to apply the guarantee for property. Second, the 'boundless' application of the guarantee for property, including for non-financial social services, leads to the protection of the inherited status quo. But this is not the task of constitutional jurisdiction. As the protector of the Constitution, its task in the area of continually developing legislation is rather simply to apply the Constitution as a regulation good (enough) to apply or else to improve.

14. Comment

Frank Bönker

THE HUNGARIAN CONSTITUTIONAL COURT IN TRANSITION

The Hungarian Constitutional Court is widely regarded as one of the most powerful courts in Central and Eastern Europe, if not the whole world (Schwartz 1998, 105 f.). Its high profile has stemmed from the combination of a broad formal authority and an expansive jurisprudence. The Hungarian Constitutional Court has enjoyed vast powers to review legislation before and after promulgation. Part of these powers have resulted from the fact that the Court's implementing legislation permits anyone, even foreigners, to challenge the constitutionality of a valid law even if s/he is not directly affected by its implementation. Under László Sólyom, its first president from 1990 to 1998, the Court made heavy use of its competencies. The Court's assertive stance manifested itself in a number of controversial rulings. In the early 1990s, the Court voided about one out of three challenged laws (Scheppele 1999, 81). The Court's decisions hit both the conservative Antall government and its socialist-liberal successor. As for the former, the Court inter alia struck down the government's original plans to compensate the victims of Communist-era land collectivisations and nullified attempts to suspend or to extend the statute of limitations for the prosecution of politically motivated crimes under Communism (Klingsberg 1993; Sólyom 1995). In 1995, the Court voided about 23 provisions of the Horn government's ambitious fiscal austerity programme, the famous 'Bokros Package,' and forced the government to refrain from or to delay various cuts in social benefits (Sajó 1996; Dethier and Shapiro 1998; Sólyom 1997).

Imre Vörös, himself a judge of the Hungarian Constitutional Court from 1990 to 1999, provides an informative overview of the Court's rulings in the field of the economic constitution. Vörös reconstructs the Court's attempt to formulate a consistent interpretation of the seven articles in the Hungarian constitution that deal with economic issues; he traces the evolution of the

Court's dicta and identifies a number of shifts in jurisprudence; finally, he takes issue with part of the Court's controversial decisions on the 'Bokros Package'. Vörös's critique of these decisions echoes his dissenting votes as a member of the Court.

One theme in the Vörös chapter is the vague and contradictory nature of the Hungarian constitution, 'an internally inconsistent and indeed contradictory patchwork of a constitution' (Schwartz 1998, 112). Adopted by the incumbent Communist parliament as an amendment to the old Communist Constitution, the new Hungarian Constitution has born the imprints of a hasty preparation, pervasive political compromises and the relative neglect of economic issues. The inconsistency of the Hungarian Constitution has posed a strong challenge to the Court. As Vörös's analysis of the Court's 'improvement practice' underscores, the Court has struggled hard to formulate a clear and consistent interpretation of an unclear and inconsistent constitution.

The Court's interpretation has not been the only way of streamlining the Hungarian Constitution. Alternative options have included parliamentary amendments of particular constitutional provisions and the drafting of a new constitution. Both ways were tried in Hungary. Parliament changed the constitution several times. In the mid-1990s, it even prepared a completely new constitution. Due to last-minute defections by deputies of the post-Communist Hungarian Socialist Party, however, the new constitution was not passed (Arato 1996). One interesting question for further research, then, is how these different activities have been related and to what extent the Court's decisions have substituted for, triggered or complemented constitutional amendments.

A second interesting theme in the Vörös chapter is the observation that the jurisprudence of the Court has undergone substantial change over a relatively short period of time. As Vörös notes, this particularly applies to the Court's interpretation of property rights which changed substantially from 1990 to 1995. The decisions of the Court thus represent a clear case of implicit constitutional change, i.e. a change in the interpretation rather than in the text of the constitution (Voigt 1999, Chap. 7; Böckenförde 1993). The shifting jurisprudence of the Court, which is somehow at odds with the self-fashioned image of the Sólyom Court as a supreme guardian of legal consistency, highlights that a strong constitutional court is no guarantee for legal certainty. In recent years, constitutional economics has started to pay more attention to the dynamics of implicit constitutional change (cf. Voigt 1999, Chap. 7). It strongly seems as if the Hungarian Constitutional Court would provide a most interesting case study.

REFERENCES

Arato, Andrew (1996), 'The Constitution-Making Endgame in Hungary', *East European Constitutional Review,* **5** (4), 31-39.

Böckenförde, Ernst-Wolfgang (1993), 'Anmerkungen zum Begriff Verfassungswandel', in Peter Badura and Rupert Scholz (eds), *Wege und Verfahren des Verfassungslebens: Festschrift für Peter Lerche zum 65. Geburtstag,* München: Beck, pp. 3-14.

Dethier, Jean-Jacques and Tamar Shapiro (1998), 'Constitutional Rights and the Reform of Social Entitlements', in Lajos Bokros and Jean-Jacques Dethier (eds), *Public Finance Reform during the Transition: The Experience of Hungary,* Washington, D.C.: World Bank, pp. 447-475.

Klingsberg, Ethan (1993), 'Safeguarding the Transition', *East European Constitutional Review,* **2** (2), 44-48.

Sajó, András (1996), 'How the Rule of Law Killed Hungarian Welfare Reform', *East European Constitutional Review,* **5** (1), 31-41.

Scheppele, Kim Lane (1999), 'The New Hungarian Constitutional Court', *East European Constitutional Review,* **8** (4), 81-87.

Schwartz, Herman (1998), 'Eastern Europe's Constitutional Courts', *Journal of Democracy,* **9** (4), 100-114.

Sólyom, László (1995), 'The Hungarian Constitutional Court and Social Change', *Yale Journal of International Law,* **19** (1), 223-237.

Sólyom, László (1997), 'Interview with András Mink', *East European Constitutional Review,* **6** (1), 71-78.

Voigt, Stefan (1999), *Explaining Constitutional Change: A Positive Economics Approach,* Cheltenham, UK and Northampton, MA: Edward Elgar.

15. On the Delegation of Powers – with Special Emphasis on Central and Eastern Europe

Eli M. Salzberger and Stefan Voigt

INTRODUCTION

During the late 1980s and early 1990s, after half a century of Communist rule, the countries of Central and Eastern Europe went through a peaceful transition to democracy. All of these countries adopted a new (or significantly amended an existing) written constitution. The vast majority of them based their new system of government on the continental model, two of whose main features are parliamentary democracy and a special Constitutional Court. However, there are significant differences in the specific details of their governmental structures. In this paper, we try to determine the possible sources for the institutional differences in these regimes, which emerged in the same period of time and against a similar historical background. This is a very broad task, and obviously we will be able to address neither every possible feature that might be a viable explanatory factor for these institutional differences, nor every possible effect of such differences. The same limitation applies to the range of institutional components that will be scrutinised here. We will focus our analysis on the structure of the separation of powers and especially on the delegation of powers to domestic organisations, such as independent judiciaries and central banks, and to international bodies, such as international organisations.

This paper is part of a more general project on the delegation of powers, in which we attempt to explain why politicians delegate powers and their choice between international and domestic delegation, as well as an analysis of constitutional versus post-constitutional delegation (Voigt and Salzberger, 2000). In this sense, our project belongs to constitutional economics, in which the choice of (constitutional) constraints is endogenized.

Interest in explaining the delegation of powers by politicians and in distinguishing between domestic and international delegation means interest in nomological hypotheses, i.e. hypotheses that purport to be applicable everywhere and always. Thus, a paper with a particular focus on a group of countries with particular characteristics might seem awkward. Yet, there are a few reasons why such a specific focus can be important.

First, it has often been observed that, shortly after radical regime changes, everything is up for grabs. David Hume (1777/1987, 474), for example, wrote:

> '...and were one to choose a period of time, when the people's consent was the least regarded in public transactions, it would be precisely on the establishment of a new government. In a settled constitution, their inclinations are often consulted; but during the fury of revolutions, conquests, and public convulsions, military force or political craft usually decides the controversy.'

To analyse constitutional and post-constitutional choices, we draw on rational choice, broadly interpreted. We thus claim that this general framework should do. In times of radical constitutional changes, however, the identification of the constraints that the relevant actors are subject to might not be as clear-cut as in 'normal' times. In this paper we will try to address some of these constraints.

Second, the rapid changes in the scrutinised countries, not only in regard to constitutional and legal norms, but also in regard to economic and political performance, invite an examination of the interrelations between the institutional structures and de facto performance. Such a comprehensive examination is beyond the scope of this paper, but it sets an agenda for further research that might be relevant to the general theoretical questions we ask: why politicians delegate powers and to whom. If links are found between certain features of constitutional design (such as an independent judiciary) and end results (i.e. the degree of economic success), such links can add to the analysis of why politicians are interested in delegating their powers.

Third, delegation of powers can usually be viewed as 'post-constitutional constitutional choice' – choice made on the basis of an existing constitution. In the case of the countries of Central and Eastern Europe, this sequential choice might have turned into a simultaneous one, in which decisions to delegate are made at the same time as more basic decisions concerning who is to have the general competence to delegate power. It can be conjectured that this simultaneity will lead to different outcomes than sequential choices, because the post-constitutional choices will become part of more general package deals. This means that the analysis of decisions to delegate power will become more difficult, because it will be more complicated to detect the relevant restrictions under which the actors operate.

Candidates for relevant constraints include historical constitutions, which are often a symbol of national pride or unity. The Polish Constitution of 1791 is surely the most obvious example. In this sense, historical constitutions might serve as a focal point and as a source of constraining force.

The preceding Communist constitutions could be another constraint. They were often not taken very seriously under communism, but still, they had the potential to constrain the transition process. The round table talks were institutional innovations to overcome the difficulties Communist regimes had in entering into negotiations with interest groups that were not part of 'democratic centralism'.

If there is a broad consensus among the participants in a constitutional convention about the need to apply for membership in specific international organisations (IOs), the statutes regulating these IOs could also constrain the framing of the constitution. This would be an unusual trait, because in our thinking about IOs we usually assume a number of nation states with their respective constitutions as given, and that these form the basis for negotiating the founding of an IO. Here, the IO is already given and the constitution-makers can choose to comply with its rules in anticipation of subsequent membership. The procedural rules that a constitutional convention agrees upon (agenda-setting power, veto powers, voting rules, etc.) will, of course, also influence the content of the constitution.

Central and Eastern Europe might also be 'special' because of the pace of development of independent agencies. Independent agencies evolved very slowly in Western constitutional systems. In principle, the experiences that have been gained with various institutional arrangements in the West could be taken into account when deciding how to delegate powers in the newly-passed constitutions.

We cover eight countries in this study: four countries that the Freedom House Project found to be consolidated democracies and consolidated market economies (the Czech Republic, Estonia, Hungary, and Poland) and four countries assessed to be in transitional polities and transitional economies (Bulgaria, Romania, Russia, and Slovakia) (Karatnycky, Motyl, and Shor 1998, 4).[1] Eight countries are too many for serious case studies, but we wanted to provide the reader with varied information, including from countries which have been neglected so far and which bring interesting insights into the analysis. Eight countries are too few for doing regression analyses, so our conclusions ought to be understood as tentative.

The paper is organised as follows: In the next section, some theoretical conjectures concerning the delegation of powers will be presented after the key concepts have been defined. Section three deals with the constraints that the drafters of the new constitutions were subject to. Section four offers an overview of the newly created institutional arrangements in regard to delegation, both domestic and international. The paper concludes with an outlook that makes some open questions explicit.

SOME THEORETICAL CONJECTURES

Delineating Domestic and International Delegation

Our general question is whether it is possible to explain the variance in the structure of agencies and their independence across our sample of scrutinised countries by analysing the constitutional (and post-constitutional) competences and restrictions given to those organs that have the power to delegate power. The creation of an independent agency and the transfer of competence to that agency is thus to be explained, and it is our hypothesis that the modes of delegation chosen and the extent of powers transferred can be explained by constitutional structures, as well as by political considerations. In regard to Central and Eastern Europe, this approach might be too short-sighted, though, since the choice of constitution and the choice of post-constitutional delegation often occurred (quasi-)simultaneously. Therefore, we will try to carry our analysis one step backward. In that first step of our analysis, the currently valid de jure constitutions will not be assumed to be exogenously given any more, but will themselves be analysed as subject to deliberate choice.

Before spelling out some conjectures concerning these two levels of choices, we offer a definition of what we mean when we speak of 'delegation of powers'. Post-constitutional delegation of powers occurs 'whenever rule-making powers that are not constitutionally assigned to a body other than the legislature are in fact being exercised by such a body' (Salzberger 1993, 359). Similarly, constitutional delegation of powers occurs when the body that is drafting the constitution assigns powers to other bodies. If it is the legislature that drafts the constitution, constitutional delegation and post-constitutional delegation are very similar in scope, and the difference between them relates only to the normative status of the delegation. The delegatee (in both stages) can be the executive, the judiciary, a committee of the legislature, a local authority, a public corporation, a special administrative body, or various international organisations.

Special emphasis will be given to the distinction between domestic and international delegation. Domestic delegation occurs when the rule-making powers are exercised by a body created by the domestic legislature and is under the governance of the constitution. International delegation is a situation in which the rule-making powers are exercised by a body that is not entirely under the control of domestic constitutional organs. A government might participate in the creation of an international organisation to which legislative power is delegated, but it will not be the only actor having a 'say' in the modification and interpretation of its statutes. To qualify as 'international delegation', it is sufficient that the rule-making powers are not exercised by a body completely under the control of domestic constitutional organs. The involvement of an international body is, therefore, not necessary. This means that we would also speak of international delegation if rule-making powers are conferred to a constitutional organ of another state. To be analysable within a unified framework, domestic and international delegations have to be substitutes for each other. That means that international organisations that deal primarily with border-crossing externalities will not be taken into account here. The focus is, rather, on solutions that could, at least in principle, also be achieved domestically.

The most straightforward method of delegation of powers is when the legislature, by a statute, directs other bodies to create rules in a specific area, instead of creating them itself. Defined in such a way, delegation of power occurs on a different level from the separation of powers as envisioned by Montesquieu. The latter is usually interpreted as being confined to the separation of legislature, executive, and judiciary, each being assigned a different governmental function.[2] But since here we are interested in both the choice of constitutional rules and the choice of (post-constitutional) decisions to delegate, separation of powers can be perceived as a form of delegation of powers.

We assume that the relevant actors maximise their expected utility. We thus follow the public choice approach here and do away with competing approaches that assume that politicians will maximise some kind of social welfare. Rational legislators will only be ready to transfer competence if the benefits connected with delegation outweigh the corresponding costs. Put simply: among the three alternatives of (1) deciding themselves, (2) delegating competence to a domestic agency, or (3) delegating competence to an international organisation, rational legislators will always choose the alternative that promises the highest expected net gains. Note, however, that our concept of benefits and costs is not restricted to monetary or power components. It is thus one of our tasks to identify costs and benefits connected with the relevant alternatives. In Voigt and Salzberger (2000), we identify a number of benefits accruing from delegation. They include the following: legislators can secure influence beyond the end of the election cycle; delegation can be used as a tool to credibly commit, as a tool to reduce uncertainty, but also to reduce one's workload; it can be used to expand the public sector and to remain in power or maintain legitimacy. These possible benefits have to be weighed against possible costs, such as delegatee-drift, monitoring costs, reversal costs, coordination costs, and even legitimacy drift.

In Voigt and Salzberger (2000), we conjecture that the type and extent of the observed delegation of powers can be explained by the constitutional structure underlying the delegation decision. As already pointed out, Central and Eastern Europe is 'special' in the sense that here constitutional and post-constitutional choices have often occurred almost simultaneously. That is why we first deal with possible explanations for constitutional choice.

The First Step: Explaining Constitutional Choice

The economic approach analyses choices under conditions of scarcity. Actors are assumed to maximise their individual utility, subject to certain constraints. The choice of a constitution can also be analysed within this framework. Passing a new constitution is usually not an individual but a collective choice. The specifics of collective or public choice will therefore have to be taken explicitly into account. In analysing collective choices, it is still assumed that the actors try to maximise their individual utility, but an important constraint in so doing might be other relevant actors who do likewise, but whose interests might be partially conflicting. To explain constitutional choices, it will thus be important to identify the interests or preferences of the relevant actors and to identify the constraints that they are subject to in their choice.

The first step thus consists in identifying the relevant actors. Who is to propose and draft a new constitution and who will be responsible for ratifying it? What are their interests or preferences? If the group of people who are to propose a new constitution is called the constitutional convention, then one must ask: Who has the power to set the agenda within that group and what are the procedural rules that they use in their deliberations? Of special interest, of course, are the voting rules used. If the members of the constitutional convention know from the beginning of their deliberations who will have the power to accept or to reject their proposals, this would constitute a powerful constraint on the content of their proposals.

Thus far, we have identified two components that will determine the content of the constitutional rules, namely (a) the interests of the relevant players involved and (b) the procedural rules used to aggregate their preferences. A third factor playing a crucial role is the relative bargaining power of the various individuals or rather groups present at the constitutional convention. The bargaining power of a group is determined by its ability and willingness to inflict costs on others and thereby reduce the net social product. One crucial factor determining the bargaining power of a group is its fallback position, i.e. the level of utility it can secure if no agreement is reached (more on the relevance of bargaining power for explaining constitutional choice and change in Voigt 1999, Chap. 6).

Jon Elster's research agenda concerning constitutional economics strongly emphasises the analysis of the procedures used. He discusses the consequences of time limits for constitutional conventions, how constitutional conventions that simultaneously serve as legislatures allocate their time between the two functions, the effects of regularly informing the public about the progress of the constitutional negotiations,[3] and how certain super-majorities and election rules can determine the outcome of conventions (Elster 1991, 30; more on this aspect of constitutional choice in Voigt 1999, Chap. 4).

McGuire and Ohsfeldt (1986, 1989a, 1989b) have tried to explain the voting behaviour of the Philadelphia Convention delegates as well as that of the delegates to the 13 state ratifying conventions by looking at their individual interests. Similar analyses would, of course, be highly interesting in regard to Central and Eastern Europe, but cannot be carried out here. Instead, we merely offer some crude indicators concerning the possible relevance of the three factors just presented. Whereas McGuire and Ohsfeldt examine the individual interests of those present at the Philadelphia Convention (e.g., whether they were debtors to or creditors of the government, slaveowners, western landowners, potential exporters, etc.), we will confine ourselves to examining organisational or party interest. It is conjectured that constitutional conventions made up of members of a parliament still stemming from socialist regimes would have different preferences than those made up of newly-elected parliamentarians. Similarly, it is conjectured that members of ruling parties would have interests different from newly emerging parties.

In addition, the viscosity of the veil of ignorance (Rawls 1971) or the degree of uncertainty (Buchanan and Tullock 1962) can serve as an explanatory factor in the outcomes of the convention. In some of the scrutinised countries, this factor has been very thin, i.e. members of the constitutional convention had clear expectations about who could be in power after the next elections, etc. This means, for example, that we can expect members of a strong party who have a highly popular leader to opt in favour of a presidential rather than a parliamentary system. Parties that expect to be very popular will be in favour of first-past-the-post; parties that expect to get just three or four per cent of the vote will strongly oppose a high threshold, etc.

If interests do not coincide perfectly in a constitutional convention, or if the degree of uncertainty is low, consensus will be scarce. Since time is also scarce, members of the constitutional convention will look for any focal points (Schelling 1960) on which they can agree with relative ease. These might be procedural rules (how they want to organise their proceedings) or substantial ones. Since constitutions often reflect the aspirations of a society, we conjecture that constitutional conventions will examine their countries' former constitutions, especially those that were expressions of autonomy, sovereignty, etc. The Communist constitutions might also acquire a certain relevance, since the conventions have to start their deliberations on the basis of some set of rules. In this sense, the Communist constitutions have the advantage of being the status quo. Turning more clearly to constraints faced by the constitution-makers, the agreements of round table talks could be interpreted as such, because they reflect the first agreements between representatives of the old regime and the new groups of an emerging civil society. As was already alluded to above, if a majority of the constitution-makers want their country to become a member of an international organisation, they might care to pass a constitution in conformity with the statutes of the relevant international organisations.

If this conjecture proved to be correct, it would be a clear instance of path dependence: Although the constitutional conventions may intend to get away from the Communist legacy, that legacy might still loom large in that it forms the basis for the first post-Communist constitution. 'Constitutional culture' or a history of liberal constitutions might also play a role if there are focal points that make consensus easier.

The organisation of the constitutional convention will also have a great influence on the document it proposes. Jon Elster (1996) argues that the content of the constitution mirrors the structure of the constitutional convention. In particular, he argues that constitutional conventions that simultaneously serve as legislatures will give greater weight to the legislature than to the executive and judiciary. They will further assign an important role to the legislature in the amending process at the expense of extra-parliamentary ratification possibilities, such as referenda. Third, they will mirror the current structure of parliament, i.e. unicameral conventions will create unicameral systems and bicameral conventions will create bicameral parliaments.

The Second Step: Explaining the Choice to Delegate

The general logic of choosing not to choose was spelled out above. We will confine ourselves here to the presentation of several conjectures and hypotheses related to this decision. The first one is that the costs of abolishing an independent agency or reneging on its decisions are higher if the existence and independence of this agency are regulated on the constitutional level and not by ordinary legislation. Thus, delegation of competence on the constitutional level may be an indicator of the 'seriousness' of the delegation or of the high level of benefits expected from it.

It has often been pointed out that it can be a disadvantage to be too strong (Weingast 1993). A state that is strong enough to protect private property rights and to enforce private contracts is also strong enough to expropriate private wealth. Rational subjects know this and will therefore invest less than they would if they could be sure that the state will not misuse its strength. States that have not had the chance to build up a reputation as being solely an impartial arbiter will be especially affected. In such cases – and we conjecture that the states of Central and Eastern Europe belong to this group – the creation of post-constitutional domestic independent agencies will often not be a credible commitment because such agencies can be abolished with relative ease. It might therefore be rational for these countries to delegate relatively more powers in the constitutional stage and/or to delegate relatively more competence to international agencies. In both options, the resulting independent body cannot be easily influenced by the respective governments.

But this is only one part of the story: Many of these countries are independent for the first time ever. The popularity of the government in those countries might be (negatively) affected if competence that the society had long hoped to achieve is freely delegated internationally. Domestic constitutional delegation might therefore be preferred.

Taking the possible effects of international delegation into account, we hypothesise that the higher the prestige an international organisation enjoys among the electorate, the more likely it is that delegation to that organisation will occur. This hypothesis is based on the assumption that membership in an international organisation that enjoys prestige domestically will translate into votes, i.e. increased re-election probability. Making this hypothesis a little more elaborate, one could argue that the prestige of membership is not absolute, but relative, i.e. one wants to be in before the neighbours get in. In this case, we should observe a veritable race for membership.[4]

Furthermore, the amount of international delegation chosen by a specific government could also be a function of its ideological position. If we assume that right-wing governments are more in favour of markets than left-wing governments and, further, that international organisations are by and large in favour of markets, then we should expect right-wing governments to be more active in delegating to international bodies. To ensure that the road toward a market economy will be pursued even after its own demise, a right-wing government might be more keen to delegate internationally. Closely connected to this is the conjecture that, at the beginning of the transition, old (Communist) governments that expect to be outvoted soon might try to secure their influence beyond election date by quickly creating agencies and staffing them with ideological friends. Such governments are therefore more likely to delegate domestically rather than internationally.

On the other hand, if right-wing governments are less keen on human rights, especially social rights, then we can expect left-wing governments to be more keen than right-wing governments to delegate internationally to certain organisations. One can even argue that since right-wing governments are per se more credible in regard to market reforms, it is left-wing governments who will have to delegate more internationally to gain credibility.

We further expect the constitutions of those countries that early on expressed interest in membership in international organisations – especially in the EU – to anticipate in their constitutions some of the rules that they would have to conform to later on. The statutes of a central bank could, for example, already be in conformity with the requirements of European

Monetary Union. Antitrust rules could be in conformity with EU competition policies, etc.

CONSTRAINTS ON CONSTITUTIONAL CHOICE

As indicated in the introduction, the main task of our project is to explain constitutional and post-constitutional delegation decisions within the broad framework of rational choice. The variance between such decisions among the eight countries scrutinised here, on which we will elaborate in the next section, against their similar historical backgrounds of transition from Communist rule calls for a more careful look at the differences in the constraints that politicians faced in each of the countries. Some of these different constraints will be highlighted in this section. The connections between these constraints and the various institutional choices will be shown later.

Many scholars will point to historical experience as a significant factor explaining current choices. Specification of this general insight relevant to our study will result in a hypothesis that a liberal constitutional legacy is likely to constrain current constitutional choices. Although one of our major arguments is that delegation of powers is likely to be carried out as the result of politicians' self-interests, it does not mean that such delegation does not improve the well-being of the public at large and the protection of its rights and interests. An independent judiciary, for example, can strengthen the position of individuals vis-à-vis government, and an independent central bank can reduce inflation and thus make everybody better off in the long run.

Of the eight countries studied here, six have a liberal constitutional legacy of sorts: Poland, Romania, Czechoslovakia, Bulgaria, and Estonia. The same cannot be said about Russia and Hungary. The latter two had constitutions, but they cannot be regarded as liberal democratic ones. The most impressive constitutional legacy is that of Poland. It goes back to the onstitution of 1791, which was the first written constitution in Europe. This constitution was fairly modern and liberal. For example, it referred to the doctrine of separation of powers as the most fundamental principle of good government. The Polish post-World War I Constitution of 1921 re-enacted major parts of the 1791 Constitution.

Romania had its first constitution following the Crimean war, in 1866, and it was modelled after the Belgian (1831) Constitution, a fairly liberal one. Bulgaria had its first constitution in 1879. It was praised as one of the most democratic in Europe, but due to numerous Balkan conflicts, it did not hold for long. Estonia adopted a democratic constitution in 1918, following its recognition as a sovereign state, but it was replaced in 1934 by an authoritarian constitution. Czechoslovakia enacted a progressive constitution in 1920, modelled on the 1875 French Constitution of the Third Republic.

It is doubtful whether, on the basis of what was written above, the hypothesis regarding the effect of constitutional legacies on current constitutional and post-constitutional choice can be corroborated, at least in regard to the de jure state (in distinction from the de facto situation). The constitutions of the two countries lacking a real liberal legacy cannot be distinguished from the other six countries in terms of their liberal character and their degree of delegation of powers.[5] As for the de facto situation, Russia's case might support the hypothesis that lack of a liberal constitutional tradition has an effect on the current liberal status, but Hungary, which managed without such a legacy to establish itself in the forefront of the emerging democracies, cannot lend such support.

Many expected that Poland, Hungary. and Czechoslovakia would be the first to adopt a new constitution. But it was Bulgaria, followed by Romania, that, in 1991, enacted the first new constitutions (Hungary and Poland, however, introduced amendments to existing constitutions earlier). In 1992, it was the turn of the Czechs, Slovaks, and Estonians. Russia followed suit in 1993. Poland waited until 1997, and Hungary continued with amendments to its existing constitution, which culminated in 1997 with the replacement of about 95 percent of its 1949 constitution, without the enactment of a new one. Be that as it may, the sequence of formal constitutional constructions does not reveal their degree of liberal progressiveness; on the contrary, the earlier constitutions can be viewed as less liberal than the latter ones. We believe that the constraints (or lack of constraints) of the round table talks and the process of constitutional construction can be important explanatory factors for the sequence of constitutional enactment and for the end constitutional results.

In Bulgaria, the old Communist National Assembly voted to end the Communist party's monopoly on political power as early as 1989, following demands from the newly-formed Union of Democratic Forces. But in the early elections that followed in 1990, the Communist (re-named Bulgarian Socialist) Party won the majority of seats. This was a unique phenomenon among all the transitions in Eastern and Central Europe. Exploiting this window of opportunity from the point of view of the old guard, the parliament rushed to adopt a new constitution. It came into force without a referendum because the drafters feared that this constitution would not be approved by the people. All these components can explain why Bulgaria was the first country in the region to have a new constitution, enacted in July 1991. Moreover, they can explain the relatively strong form of the separation of powers (and presidency) prescribed by the constitution, which can be attributed to the communists' political calculations that they would not be able to dominate the parliament for long.

The Romanian case, which had similar results in terms of the pace of constitution-making and the degree of separation or delegation of powers, is almost the opposite of the Bulgarian case. Here, the lack of round table talks was the result of the reformers' seizure of power. A few days before Ceaucescu's execution in the last days of 1989, a newly-formed body called the Council of the National Salvation Front, comprised of some communists, dissidents, and intellectuals, seized power. The National Salvation Front won the May 1990 elections for both houses of parliament as well as for the presidency, all with a huge majority. The clear majority of the NSF in all political branches of government enabled it to go through a rapid process of constitution-making. Unlike the Bulgarian case, however, this power of the NSF allowed it to convene a special constituent assembly to draft the constitution and even to put the constitution to referendum, which was approved in November 1991.

The end results, however, have similarities with Bulgaria's. The Constitution prescribes a unique feature of bicameralism, with no real difference between the two chambers' structure of representation, and a strong president, to be elected by the people. The weakest branch is the judiciary, especially the Constitutional Court. The system has similarities with the French model. But unlike in France, the constitution permits the reversal of the Constitutional Court's decision by a two-thirds majority in parliament. It can be hypothesised that the overwhelming majority of the NSF in all political institutions, in contrast to the case in Bulgaria, led it to delegate powers generously, driven by the expectation that this majority in all branches would not hold for long. The only branch whose powers were relatively limited was the Constitutional Court, which was not perceived as a future stronghold of the politicians who took part in drafting the constitution.

It is interesting to compare the Bulgarian-Romanian experience to the Czech-Slovak one in terms of the effects of constraints on constitutional order and delegation. In all four countries, the constitution was enacted by a newly-elected parliament. However, the pace of the process varied. While in Czechoslovakia (before the country was divided) the elections were preceded by a conciliatory interim government and presidency (the result of what was termed 'the Velvet Revolution'), Bulgaria and Romania lacked such a stage. While in Czechoslovakia the elections resulted in rule by new powers and a clearer picture of the division of political powers to come, in Bulgaria and Romania the process was so swift that the results were 'tentative', with a significant presence of ex-communists (who in Bulgaria actually received the majority of votes). These differences might explain the tendency to a greater separation of powers, or rather more delegation of powers, in Bulgaria and Romania. Politicians will tend to delegate more powers when they feel less certainty about their chances of remaining in power.

In Poland, more than in any other country in this study, constitutional choice was intertwined with post-constitutional choice. Unlike the four countries examined above, elections to a new parliament did not precede the constitutional change. This change began a few years *before* the first free elections and continued after the first elections and then after subsequent ones. In fact, constitutional reforms in Poland preceded the fall of communism. They begun in 1982 with a change of attitude toward the binding nature of the constitution, the introduction of judicial review, and the establishment of a Constitutional Court. This was indeed a phenomenon unique in the Eastern bloc.

We believe that the rather strong form of separation of powers (bicameralism and a strong presidency) and indeed of delegation of powers in Poland can be explained against this background. The initial establishment in 1982 of a Constitutional Court with the power of judicial review can be seen as the Communist regime's attempt to delegate powers in order to remain in power or maintain legitimacy (see Voigt and Salzberger, 2000). The insistence on a strong presidency, with the powers to veto legislation, can be viewed similarly. Fearing to lose powers, both sides – the communists and the opposition – opted to divide powers among several branches of government. After the 1989 elections, in which Solidarity won 99 out of 100 seats in the new Senate and a major share of the seats available according to the round table agreement in the lower house, it was too late to change this basic structure. Thus, although some fine tuning followed in the 1992 interim constitution (also dubbed the 'small constitution'), decreasing the powers of the president and increasing the powers of the executive, for example through the introduction of a constructive vote of no confidence, this basic structure of government in Poland has not been changed. The same is true for the 1997 Constitution.

Because the transition (in terms of the democratisation of the structure of government, not in terms of economic reforms) began later in Hungary than in neighbouring countries, notably Poland, a major constraint on constitutional construction was information on what took place in Poland. The opposition in Hungary did not agree to accept a deal similar to the one agreed upon in Poland, because it saw the materialising powers of Solidarity. Thus, the structure of government agreed upon in Hungary was based less on separating the political powers among various organs and more on a delegation of powers to non-political bodies, such as the Constitutional Court and international organisations. This can be explained in terms of the opposition's realisation that the Hungarian population would face a hard period during economic reforms and that such delegation might help the government remain in power.

Hungary is the only country among the eight we cover in this study in which a new constitution has not yet been enacted. But in fact, Hungary went through a 'constitutional revolution', and this was completed earlier and in much less time than in its neighbouring countries. The Hungarian constitution-makers exploited a 'window of opportunity', a short period in which the Communists remained demoralised and the opposition was not yet seriously divided. In Poland, some members of Solidarity pushed for a similar strategy, but failed.

The last two countries in our study have features significantly different from the other six. In addition to the transition to democracy, Russia also faced a problem of self-definition and the secession of various republics, which also affected an important struggle about the division of powers between the central government and the republics. In addition, Russia is the only country in our study in which physical force was employed to enforce a new constitutional order. Thus, more than in all the countries we previously discussed, the new Russian Constitution reflects the actual balance of the existing powers (between Yeltsin and parliament) at the time of the enactment of the constitution. Yeltsin pushed for an American model of a presidential republic; parliament wanted a continental-style parliamentary democracy. After receiving a vote of confidence in a referendum he called in April 1993, Yeltsin decided to convene a constituent convention to come up with a draft alternative to the one parliament offered. Such a draft was proposed, but parliament rejected it, choosing a constitution-adopting procedure that was totally dependent on parliament itself. In September 1993, Yeltsin dissolved the parliament and, in response, parliament voted to depose Yeltsin.

Subsequently, Yeltsin ordered military forces to attack parliament, suspending the opposition parties, the Constitutional Court, and opposition newspapers. He put his draft to referendum on the same day of the elections to a new legislature in November 1993, and the new constitution was approved by a majority of 58.4 percent.

The new constitution provides for a strong president, who is to be elected by the people and who is given significant executive powers, including the chairing of government meetings and the power to nominate the head of the central bank and constitutional judges (subject to the approval of the Duma). The President can also veto legislation. The procedure for impeachment of the president, as specified by the constitution, is complicated and unlikely to materialise. In the Russian case, therefore, the reasons for the main features of separation of powers differ somewhat from our theory of delegation of powers, which does not take into account the use of physical powers (Voigt and Salzberger, 2000). However, the constitution also creates or reaffirms bodies such as a Constitutional Court and central bank, to which powers are delegated for the reasons of uncertainty, responsibility shift, collective decision-making problems, and other delegational benefits that do fall within the realm of our theory.

The Estonian Constitution has one of the more extensive delegation of powers, especially domestic delegation (e.g. to its Constitutional Court and central bank). This structure can be attributed to the process of constitution-making. Estonia separated from the USSR in 1990. A constituent assembly was formed, comprised of 30 members from the old parliament and 30 members from an interim independent quasi-parliament (Congress of Estonia). In a referendum in 1992, an overwhelming majority approved their final draft, preferring a parliamentary democracy over a presidential one, making Estonia the first former Soviet republic to adopt a constitution. The composition of the constituent assembly, which did not reflect actual powers but was an artificial equal division of seats, brought about this extensive delegation to the non-political institutions of government.

Let us try to generalise and conclude. (A more detailed account of the constitution-making processes in the eight countries is provided in Appendix A.) Normative analysis of constitution-making provides us with strong arguments in favour of separating a constitutional convention or constituent assembly from the ordinary legislature, since one of the aims of a constitution is to place power restrictions on parliament itself (Ostrom 1987; Buchanan 1975). When legislators draft and/or enact a constitution, (1) they will allocate a disproportionately high percentage of time to deciding short-term issues, thus neglecting constitutional issues that are more relevant in the long run; (2) as members of parliament who want to be re-elected, representatives of the constitutional assembly will be less ready to sacrifice the interests of their constituents in favour of the good of the whole nation; and (3) representatives might play an outright power game and support only those proposals that are in the interests of their parties or even only in their personal interests (Mueller 1996, Chap. 21). Despite these strong arguments and the more general normative framework, which views constitutions as a social contract that ought to reflect long-term consensus (Buchanan and Tullock 1962, Rawls 1971), it has been noted that, historically, most constitutional conventions have been constituted from an existing parliament. The countries of Central and Eastern Europe surely are no exception to this rule.

This observation is not surprising. It is not only that an all-purpose assembly might appear to save some time in such periods of radical changes (Mueller, 1996.). Of course the interests of the actors involved in the collective decision-making will make it very difficult to achieve this normative goal. In this sense, the histories of constitution-making in Central and Eastern Europe, as in other places, do not conform with the notion of a constitutional moment (Ackerman 1991). Had politicians and other decision-makers behaved according to the 'constitutional moment' thesis, we would expect to find more constituent assembles that were separated from the legislatures.

We thus believe that the changes in the utility function of politicians predicted by Ackerman's constitutional moment theory do not occur. Periods of increasing uncertainties and lack of information do, however, occur. They affect the choices of the political players. The differences in the constitutions, which were enacted in the early 1990s under similar circumstances after the fall of communism, reflect these uncertainties, among other things. They also reflect informational input from neighbouring countries. Thus, the reason that the opposition in Hungary did not accept proposals for limited democratisation of parliament was its lack of information on the election results in Poland. This information created the expectation of a similar outcome, which resulted in the adoption of a system with a weaker form of the separation of powers. The same reasoning can explain Romania's and Bulgaria's relatively deeper form (though not in comparison with Russia) of separation and delegation of powers as the consequence of election results that were not perceived as revealing the real balance of powers between the communists and the reformers.

SOME INSTITUTIONAL STOCK-TAKING

In this section, we aim to summarise the various constitutional and post-constitutional rules that our eight countries passed in regard to the delegation of powers. Of course, a complete overview is impossible. Regarding domestic delegation, we focus especially on the judiciaries and on central banks and allude to other independent agencies in a third subsection. Possible interdependencies will also be sketched in brief. In regard to international delegation, we focus on possible membership in the European Union, but membership in other organisations, such as the WTO, is also analysed. The last step in this section consists in analysing possible relationships between domestic and international delegation.

Domestic Delegation

Over the last couple of years, an entire cottage industry has evolved to analyse possible relationships between the independence of central banks and inflation rates. Measuring such independence occupies a significant share of this literature, which we survey in section below. In the next section we offer an analogous analysis of the independence of Constitutional Courts, focusing on measuring the courts' independence.

It might seem to make sense to present the established literature (on central banks) first and then proceed to our additions (on Constitutional Courts). We have decided to present our analysis in the reverse order, because in most cases the independence of (constitutional) courts is provided for on the constitutional level, whereas this is not always the case for central banks. Moreover, the independence of central banks can be regarded as a function of the independence of courts. Thus, from a structural and substantive point of view, the discussion of the independence of Constitutional Courts ought to precede the discussion of the independence of central banks.

The constitutional courts

An essential part of every constitutional setup is an enforcement mechanism. Following the two major functions of a constitution – providing for the structure of government and the division of powers of its organs, and protecting individuals from illegal use of government powers – the tasks of constitutional enforcement include monitoring the relations among the state organs and the protection of human rights. In most countries, this enforcement task is assigned to courts. However, one can distinguish between two models used around the world: (1) Countries in which this task is assigned to the general courts system. The federal judiciary in the US may be seen as the most significant example of this model, in which every court can perform judicial review. (2) Countries in which this task is assigned to a special Constitutional Court separated from the general courts system and hierarchy. Most European countries subscribe to this model.

All the emerging democracies in our study, save Estonia, opted for the second model and established special Constitutional Courts. Estonia adopted a system that is closer to the American one. Indirect judicial review in Estonia can be performed by every court and direct judicial review or findings of unconstitutionality by lower courts are deliberated by the National Court, which is the general Supreme Court of the land.[6] Although all the other seven countries adopted the continental model, there are interesting differences in the structure of their Constitutional Courts, these courts' jurisdiction, and the degree of independence of their judges. In what follows, we try to assess the various formal arrangements in the eight countries under scrutiny vis-à-vis the independence of the constitutional enforcement mechanism and its efficacy. We divide this assessment into several components, each of which we give a score ranging from 1 (least independent) to 10 (most independent).

Constitutional vs. post-constitutional arrangement. The independence and efficacy of constitutional enforcement mechanisms or of Constitutional Courts and their ability to serve as a counterweight to the other branches of government are dependent upon the stability and immunity of the definition of the court's powers, its procedures, and the arrangements regarding its operators – the judges. If these arrangements are specified in the constitution itself, we expect a greater degree of independence than in cases where these arrangements are fixed by ordinary law, which is subject to amendment by parliament whenever the latter is dissatisfied with the performance of the court. In the United States Constitution, for example, many structural components regarding the judiciary, the Supreme Court, and its judges are specified in the Constitution. However, the number of judges in the Supreme Court is not specified. This lacuna was well exploited in the 19th century as well as in 1937, when threats to 'pack the Court' through legislation changing the number of its justices were successful in changing the Court's position. This is a good example of the importance of making the arrangement regarding Constitutional Courts part of the constitution itself.

Thus, countries in which these arrangements are part of the constitution and whose constitutions cannot be amended as any other law (i.e. where amendment requires a referendum or a super-majority) will be given the highest score, whereas countries in which the arrangements are a matter of regular statute will be given a lower one.

In Bulgaria (8), the provisions for the Constitutional Court are in the Constitution. Its amendment is possible only by 3/4 vote of the National Assembly. A similar arrangement exists in Slovakia (8) and in the Czech Republic (9), where amendments require a 3/5 majority of parliament. In Poland (8), the provisions are part of the 1997 Constitution, which can be changed by a 2/3 majority. In Romania (9), the fundamental provisions are part of the Constitution, which is very difficult to amend – 2/3 majority in parliament *and* referendum. A more detailed arrangement is provided in a statute.

In Estonia (6), only parts of the arrangement (judicial appointment and independence) are provided for in the constitution. Other parts, including constitutional jurisdiction and procedure of review, are addressed in a special legislation – the *law on constitutional law review procedure 1993*. The constitution can be changed by a majority of parliament members in two separate votes. In Hungary (5), only part of the basic provisions safeguarding the independence of the Constitutional Court are included in the Constitution – the number of judges in the Constitutional Court and their method of election, not including their term of office. However, the Constitution specifies that a statute on the Constitutional Court requires a 2/3 majority of parliament, elevating the court's normative status. In Russia (4), some of the arrangements regarding the Constitutional Court and its judges are fixed in the constitution, together with provisions concerning other courts. However, some significant details were left to legislation, such as the term of constitutional judges. The constitution can be amended by a 2/3 majority of all members of the Duma and a 3/4 majority of all members of the Federation Council (except certain chapters, which require a referendum for amendment).

The power to elect the judges. The procedure of appointment of Constitutional Court judges and the identity of those who have the power to appoint them may have a notable effect on the independence of the court. The Constitutional Court is supposed to protect the citizens from the illegitimate use of powers by the authorities, as well as to settle disputes between the branches of government. Thus, it ought to be as independent as possible from the other branches. The most independent procedure for judicial election is election by professionals (other judges or jurists). The least independent method is selection by one powerful politician (prime minister or a minister of justice). In between, we may find combined arrangements, e.g., appointments made by politicians but from different branches of government or representing different parties.

In Poland (4), the judges of the Constitutional Court are elected by a simple majority of Parliament. In Slovakia (4), they are appointed by the President from a doubled-number list of candidates proposed by the legislature. In Russia (5), the judges are appointed by the Federation Council after recommendation by the President. In the Czech republic (7), the judges are appointed by the President from a list proposed by Parliament, and the President's decision requires the approval of the Senate. In Hungary (8), judges are nominated by a committee of the National Assembly comprising one member of each of the groups of representatives of the parties with seats in the National Assembly. They are elected by a two-thirds majority of the National Assembly. Thus, although the judges are appointed by the legislature, their appointment requires a broad consensus in the legislature. Romania (6) follows the French system, according to which different judges are elected by different institutions: three by the Chamber of Deputies, three by the Senate, three by the President (6). The same method is employed in Bulgaria (7), but there, a third of the judges are elected by their fellow judges in the two Supreme Courts. This increases professional considerations and thus independence from politicians. The other two-thirds of the judges are appointed by Parliament (1/3) and the President (1/3). In Estonia (8), the 17 judges of the National Court are appointed by Parliament upon the recommendation of the President of the Court, who himself is appointed by Parliament upon the nomination of the President. Thus, the majority of judges are appointed on a professional basis (with a significant input from the president of the court) with some political scrutiny. Judicial review is performed by five members, the judicial review chamber within the court.

Judicial Tenure. Judges are most independent if they are appointed for life (or up to a mandatory retirement age) and cannot be removed from office, save by legal procedure. Judges are least independent if they are appointed for a set period, with optional subsequent terms, and where removal from office is a fairly easy process. If judges can run for a second term, their independence in the first term is severely hampered and they will want to be popular among their nominators. Judges who are appointed for a set period and cannot be reappointed are in between. They are more independent than judges who can run for a second term, but less independent than life-tenured judges, because, after the end of their term on the Constitutional Court, they may seek another position contingent on those who elected them. The following coding also takes into account the length of term, which ranges between seven years and life.

In Estonia (10), judges are appointed for life. In Russia (8), Constitutional Court judges are appointed for one term of 12 years (previously, it was a life appointment, and some judges in the Russian Constitutional Court are still governed by the old rule). In the Czech Republic (7), there is one term of ten years; in Bulgaria, Poland, and Romania (6), one term of nine years; and in Slovakia (5), one term of seven years. In Hungary (3), the judges of the Constitutional Court are appointed for a term of nine years with an option for re-election.

The accessibility of the court. Another component of judicial independence is the accessibility of the court and its ability to initiate proceedings. A court that is accessible only to a certain number of members of parliament or other officials will be less effective than a court that is accessible to every citizen who claims that his or her rights have been violated. As we noted before, Estonia (9) is the only country in our sample to adopt the American – general courts – model, and according to this model, constitutional proceedings can be initiated by anyone and in any court. In this sense, the constitutional review in Estonia has the potential to be the most effective among the studied countries. In Hungary (8), Poland (8), and the Slovak (7) and Czech Republics (6), individual citizens can apply to the Constitutional Court in human rights matters. This accessibility is more limited in the Slovak and Czech Republics, where it is not specified by the constitution itself. Access by individuals is partly possible in Russia (5) and is not possible in Bulgaria (3) or Romania (3), where only state organs can initiate proceedings in the Court.

The competence of the court. The last independence indicator for Constitutional Courts is the breadth of competence assigned to them. This is, however, a somewhat tricky variable. At first glance, it might seem that extended competence enhances the independence of courts or that there should be a direct correlation between the extent of powers assigned to a court and its impact. But in fact, from a certain point on, more competence can actually reduce the independence of the court, its perception by the public as a neutral and honest broker, and thus its ability to counterbalance the other branches. In other words, a court that is drawn to participate in political power struggles can lose its reputation and thus its independence and effectiveness. This may be the case with the Russian Constitutional Court, which took sides in the clash of powers between the President and Parliament in the early 1990s.

In all the countries in our study, constitutional review of legislation is the core function of the Constitutional Court. This power probably also includes review of other legislative acts (of lower normative status – either of other organs of central government or of state or local authorities), although only some of the countries (the Czech and Slovak Republics, Estonia, Romania, and Russia) explicitly mention this extended power of review. Romania is the only country in which the review of legislation can be conducted only before the promulgation of the law and in which the decision of the court can be reversed if the law is affirmed again by a two-thirds majority of parliament. Although this is the same majority required to amend the constitution, one can conclude that the judicial review power in Romania is the weakest among the countries we studied. In Russia, judicial review powers also exist in regard to the republics' constitutions (as against the federal constitution) and their agreements with the federation.

A second common power of the Constitutional Courts is to adjudicate conflicts of authority between the various branches of central government and between federal and local authorities. Such powers are provided for in Bulgaria, Hungary, the Czech Republic, Estonia (by post-constitutional legislation), Slovakia, and Russia. The role of deciding on the constitutionality of political parties is granted to the Constitutional Courts in Romania, Bulgaria, the Czech Republic, Poland, and Slovakia. The interpretation of the constitution is listed among the competencies of the courts in Bulgaria, Russia, and Slovakia.

A set of more problematic powers are, on the one hand, the power to review the compatibility of international treaties with the constitution and, on the other hand, the power to review the compatibility of legislation with international law. The variety of the arrangements in this area is especially relevant to our study. It reflects, on the one hand, a component of international delegation – the normative position of international law within the municipal legal system – and, on the other hand, domestic delegation – the extent of powers delegated to a Constitutional Court to review the compatibility of domestic law with international law.

The Czech Republic seems to have the broadest dual delegation in this respect: The Constitutional Court is empowered to invalidate laws that contradict international agreements and to give effect to decisions made by international courts. Thus, the Czech Constitution makes international law superior to domestic law – a far-reaching international delegation – and it delegates enforcement power to the Constitutional Court – a far-reaching domestic delegation. Similar provisions can be found in the Slovak, Polish, and Bulgarian constitutions, without the very significant but rather vague power to take 'measures necessary to effect a decision by an international court that is binding for the Czech Republic if it cannot be effected otherwise' (Art. 87(I) of the Czech Constitution). This is a significant component, because it means that the Czech Constitution not only places international law above domestic law, but also regards the interpretation of international law by international courts as part of international law; this creates a symmetry between its Constitutional Court (whose interpretations of the constitution are binding) and international courts (whose interpretations of international law are binding and made effective through the Constitutional Court).

On the other side of the map, we find the Russian and Estonian arrangements, which empower the Constitutional Court to review the compatibility of international agreement with the constitution, signaling the subordination of international law to domestic law. The Romanian Constitution does not address the jurisdiction of the court to rule on matters connected with international law, and the Hungarian Constitution is also silent about this.

The more tricky powers assigned to Constitutional Courts are: (1) the competence to rule on the constitutionality of parliamentary proceeding, which is granted to the Constitutional Courts in Hungary and Romania; (2) the power to supervise elections, which is specified as Constitutional Court power in Bulgaria, the Czech Republic, and Romania (in regard to presidential election); (3) the power to monitor disciplinary and impeachment procedures against the president, which is provided for in Romania and Russia; and (4) the power to supervise a referendum, in Slovakia and Romania. The Czech Constitution grants powers to the Constitutional Court in all other matter that are not within the jurisdiction of another court, but the Constitutional Court there is also empowered to delegate some of its powers to the administrative court.

Aggregating the various aspects leads to the ranking displayed in table 3. This is, of course, a de jure ranking of Constitutional Courts' competence. The de facto situation might be different.

Summary. The following table summarises our findings of de jure independence:

Table 3: De jure independence of Constitutional Courts

	Constitutional arrangement	Judges election	Tenure	Access	Competence	Sum	Rank
Bulgaria	8	7	6	3	8	32	5
Czech Rep.	9	7	7	6	10	39	2
Estonia	6	8	10	9	8	41	1
Hungary	5	8	3	8	6	30	6
Poland	8	4	6	8	9	35	3
Romania	9	6	6	3	4	28	8
Russia	4	5	8	5	7	29	7
Slovakia	8	4	5	7	9	33	4

What sort of conclusions can be drawn from this table, when we view it vis-à-vis the various constraints on constitution-making and the actual processes of constitution-making in the eight countries included in this study? First, it seems that those countries that were the first to enact a constitution – Bulgaria and Romania – came out with the least independent judiciaries. This is an interesting finding, since we concluded in the previous sections that these countries can be characterised as having a relatively strong form of separation of powers. However, this form applies mainly to the division of powers between the political branches, rather than delegation to non-political ones. A more general lesson might be that one has to distinguish between delegation of powers to politicians and delegation of powers to non-politicians. There might be different reasons for these two forms of delegation.

Second, in the case of the independence of the judiciary, historical legacies can be viewed as an important explanatory factor. The two countries with no such legacy are ranked sixth and seventh in the de jure independence of their Constitutional Courts. Finally, it is interesting to note that the country in which we found the highest degree of judicial independence, or the most extensive delegation, is Estonia. Its constitution was enacted by an ad hoc constituent assembly.

Comparing the independence of central banks

As we have just seen, independent judiciaries, and in particular Constitutional Courts, are in most cases regulated on the constitutional level and can thus be considered within the realm of constitutional choice. In many industrialised countries, central banks do not figure quite as prominently. They often operate on the basis of powers granted by regular legislation. Distinguishing precisely between these levels could prove important, because the de facto independence of post-constitutional independent agencies (such as a central bank) could very well depend on the (de facto) independence of the independent agencies anchored on the constitutional level, such as the judiciary. One of the first steps in describing the role of the newly-created central banks of Central and Eastern Europe, therefore, is to inquire whether they have constitutional or post-constitutional status.

The functions and the institutional structure of the central bank are specified in the constitution in the Czech Republic, Hungary, Estonia, Poland, and Russia (the institutional foundations of the central banks are described in more detail in Appendix B). The Romanian Constitution does not mention the central bank. In Bulgaria and the Slovak Republic, the central bank is mentioned in the constitution, but there are no provisions regarding its functions or institutional setup, and thus we cannot view delegation of power to the central bank as being on the constitutional level in those countries.

Historical legacies also played a role in the processes of writing central bank laws: The Hungarian Central Bank, for example, is organised as a joint-stock company. This can be explained by drawing on the founding of the Bank in 1924, when this organisational setup was a common practice (Kobabe 1999, 136). Similarly, central bank statutes in states that have just regained sovereignty often take their historical predecessors as models, Estonia being a case in point. But historical legacy also played a role in exactly the reverse manner: Slovakia, for example, had never had a central bank, and thus it could design one from scratch. An ad hoc hypothesis could read that, in such cases, more modern statutes can be expected – at least on the books.

Summarising his extensive study on central banks in Central and Eastern Europe, Kobabe (1999, Chap. F) stresses that the safeguarding of the independence of central banks on a constitutional level can be important in case of conflicts with other constitutional organs. He notes that, in case of conflicts, the Polish, the Hungarian, and the Estonian central banks do not have the right to take these conflicts to the Constitutional Court. In Bulgaria and

Romania, there are no constitutional provisions concerning the central banks at all. Government participation in the procedure for nominating members of the decision-making organs of monetary policy is also evaluated critically. Governments participate in this procedure in Hungary, Romania, and Slovakia (Kobabe 1999). The independence of a central bank is also shaped by its relationship to other state organs and those organs' possibilities to influence monetary policy. Should the Czech Central Bank interpret its powers too extensively, this could lead to a reduction of its functional independence (Kobabe 1999, 234). The independence of the Hungarian National Bank is ambivalent because it is organised as a joint-stock company, with the state as the only shareholder. In Poland, the annual report of the central bank requires government approval. In the Czech and Slovak Republics, the bank and the government (co-) determine the budget of the Bank. In Estonia, Parliament even has the function of settling disputes between the organs of the National Bank, implying the possibility that exchange-rate policy decisions are to be taken by Parliament itself. Kobabe notes that price stability is the clearly dominating goal only in Slovakia.

A glance at the sequence in which new constitutions and central bank laws were passed reveals three distinct possibilities: (1) the constitution and the central bank law are passed (almost) simultaneously; (2) the constitution is passed first, followed by the central bank law; (3) the central bank law is first, followed by the constitution. In the first case, it can be expected that the central bank law was part of a larger deal between the various actors involved in the constitution-making process. The second case is the one most in line with our concept of constitutional and post-constitutional choice: Based on a (new) constitution, legislators make post-constitutional choices, e.g., passing the statute of a central bank. The third case is probably the most interesting one: On the basis of an old (or possibly an interim) constitution, the grounds for a new central bank are being laid. Table 4.1 shows that the first case applies to the Czech Republic, Estonia, Romania, and Slovakia, the second to Bulgaria and Russia, and the third to Hungary and Poland.

A national government's commitments to stick to a policy of monetary stability and thus to secure low levels of inflation are not credible. Kydland and Prescott 1977 and Barro and Gordon 1983 have shown that the problem of time inconsistency prevails, i.e. that governments have incentives to announce a certain policy at one point in time and deviate from the announced policy later on, because such deviation promises higher net gains. Since rational subjects anticipate this pattern of behaviour, the inflation level will be higher than it would have been had the government been able to credibly commit itself.

It was long presumed that countries with independent central banks, whose governors were assigned the task of securing monetary stability, would be conducive to low inflation rates. In the early 1990s, various indicators were developed to make that intuition empirically tractable (Grilli, Masciandaro, and Tabellini 1991; Cukierman 1992; Cukierman, Webb, and Neyapti 1991). It turns out that the degree of independence of a central bank is indeed a good indicator of the inflation rate one can expect in a given currency, at least for the industrialised countries.

Very few papers have attempted to apply the indicators designed to measure the independence of central banks to the countries in Central and Eastern Europe. The paper by Loungani and Sheets (1997) is one of them. The authors propose two measures: One is based on Debelle and Fischer (1994), who suggest that central bank independence is composed of 'goal independence' and 'instrument independence', to which Loungani and Sheets (1997) attribute equal weights. Goal independence is ascertained by whether the central bank law stipulates price stability as the central bank's primary macroeconomic objective. 'Instrument independence' is ascertained by an equal weighting of four components: (1) Does the central bank control the 'instruments' of monetary policy? (2) Does the central bank impose any binding legal limit on the direct financing of the government? (3) Is the government allowed to receive any direct financing from the central bank? (4) Is the central bank subject to government directives in the execution of monetary policy? The second index Loungani and Sheets (1997) propose is the 'similarity to the Bundesbank-Index (SIB)'. The Bundesbank is thus taken as the benchmark. The SIB index is made up of nine components that include not only 'goal' and 'instrument' independence but also 'political independence'.[7]

Table 4 specifies the indices for the eight countries of our study. The indices can take any value between 0 and 1, with higher values representing higher degrees of independence.

Table 4: Central Banks' independence

	DF index	SIB index	Constitutional Arrangement	Average	Rank
Bulgaria	0.875	1.000	0.7	0,8583	2
Czech Rep.	0.875	1.000	0.9	0,925	1
Estonia	1.000	0.667	0.8	0,8223	3
Hungary	0.312	0.722	0.7	0,578	7
Poland	0.500	0.611	0.8	0,637	4
Romania	0.500	0.556	0.4	0,4853	8
Russia	0.375	0.500	1.0	0,625	6
Slovakia#	0.875	0.944	0.5	0,773	4

Slovakia is not included in Loungani and Sheets; we present our own calculations here.

Loungani and Sheets (1997) find that the SIB index is a good predictor of the 1993 inflation rate of the countries under consideration, with the R^2 being 0.45.[8] Their study, however, can be criticised on various grounds, the two most obvious ones being the small number of countries (namely 12) analysed and the fact that the inflation rate is based on only one year, which, in addition, was relatively early in transition.[9]

Based on data from 26 formerly socialist economies, Cukierman et al. (2000) find that, for the early stages of liberalisation, central bank independence is unrelated to inflation. But as soon as sufficiently high and sustained levels of liberalisation are reached and variables like price de-controls and wars are controlled for, central bank independence turns out to be negatively and significantly correlated with inflation. The authors ask what factors could possibly explain the variance in legal central bank independence and find that (a) being on the fast track toward EU (and EMU) membership and (b) passing a central bank law late in transition have a positive impact on the chosen level of independence. The problem with the first variable is that it could also reflect (i) geographical proximity to the West or – probably more important – (ii) cultural similarity.

Be that as it may, we can use Loungani and Sheets' two indicators to rank the de jure independence of central banks. But we propose adding the components discussed above: whether the regulation of the bank is by regular legislation or by the constitution, and the substance of this arrangement vis-à-vis the procedure for the appointment of its directors and the reversibility of their decisions (analysis based on Kobabe, 1999). The countries in which the constitution treats fundamental issues regarding the central bank were given a score of 1, from which we deduced whether the substance of the arrangements allow easy reversal of the directors' decisions. The countries in which only the constitution partly regulates the central bank started with a score of 0.7, from which deductions were made accordingly. The one country (Romania) in which central bank regulation is only by statute started with a score of 0.5. The scores are presented in Table 4. The average of the two indices and our additional one results in the ranking of de jure independence found in the rightmost column of table 4.

So far, we have analysed the independence of central banks as domestic delegation. However, the arrangements regarding central banks also have an international delegation dimension. A unique institutional arrangement introduced in Estonia (1992) and Bulgaria (1997) is a good example. This is the currency boards. A currency board can be interpreted as an extreme form of an exchange rate peg: the domestic currency is fixed to an 'anchor currency'. Holders of the domestic currency have the right to exchange their assets against the pegged currency at a fixed rate at any time. Monetary supply is no longer determined by a central bank, but depends on the quantity of reserve assets (usually the peg currency and other foreign currencies, as well as gold). Monetary supply thus directly hinges upon the balance of payments. The establishment of a currency board is almost equivalent to the abdication of a domestic monetary policy. Thus, monetary policy decisions are delegated internationally and made by an organisation beyond the immediate reach of domestic actors, namely those (foreign) central banks that serve as the anchor of the domestic currency.

In addition, one could expect that most of the countries under scrutiny here that want to join the EU would anticipate EU standards for bank independence and other structural and substantial components and that these countries would pass central bank laws in accordance with those standards. Since this issue touches upon the interdependence between domestic and international delegation, it will be dealt with explicitly below (245).

Other domestic delegatee bodies

Most previous stud4ies comparing independent agencies across countries have focused exclusively on comparing central bank independence. This was simply because this was the only agency for which comparable data were available. In this paper, we extended this limited view by offering a simple indicator of the independence of Constitutional Courts. The next step would be to develop indicators for other agencies, such as antitrust offices, etc. The debate on central bank independence suggests the conjecture that the more independent antitrust offices should be able to carry out better competition policies than dependent ones. Such a claim would, however, be very difficult to test empirically. In the case of a central bank, it is fairly easy to operationalise the rate of inflation. No unequivocal measure is readily available for the outcomes or consequences of competition policy.

Empirically, we observe that antitrust offices are much less independent than many central banks. In the US, the (independent) Federal Trade Commission has to cooperate with the Antitrust Division within the Department of Justice. The EU has no antitrust office of its own. In Germany, which prides itself on having an independent *Kartellamt* (antitrust office), the Economics Minister can override its decisions if there is an overwhelming macroeconomic interest. It would still be interesting to have an indicator that evaluates the quality and independence of the various antitrust offices. The only such indicator that has come to our attention is supplied on the Internet by the 'global-competition.com' website, which calls itself 'the site for international competition policy and regulation'. Under the heading 'Rating the Regulators', the performance of 24 competition authorities is compared for speed, expertise, and independence. Unfortunately, none of these authorities is in Central and Eastern Europe.

In the course of a transition from centrally planned to decentrally coordinated economies, competition authorities have a special role to play, at least potentially. Due to the legacies of the past, it is very likely that monopoly suppliers will dominate quite a few markets and that entry barriers for newcomers might be substantial. In such a situation, it seems quite likely that representatives of the ex-monopolists will lobby for special favours like subsidies, but also for exemption from antitrust rules.[10] Normatively speaking, an independent antitrust office would thus appear to be especially important during transition. On the positive analysis level, the composition of the constituent assembly and the legislature can have a major influence on the substance of the institutional arrangement of anti-trust authorities.

Five of the eight constitutions analysed explicitly mention term competition in its economic sense. These are the Bulgarian (Art. 19(2)): 'The state shall establish and guarantee equal legal conditions for economic activity to all citizens and corporate entities by preventing any abuse of a monopoly status and unfair competition and by protecting the consumer'); the Hungarian (Art. 9(2)): 'The Republic of Hungary recognises and supports the right to enterprise and the freedom of competition in the economy'); the Romanian (Art. 134(2)): 'The State must secure: a) a free trade, protection of loyal competition, provision of a favourable framework in order to stimulate and value every factor of production'); the Russian (Art. 34(2)): 'No economic activity aimed at monopolisation or unfair competition shall be allowed'); and the Slovakian (Art. 55(2)): 'The Slovak Republic protects and promotes economic competition. Details will be set out in a law').

It seems safe to argue that competition legislation in Central and Eastern Europe has been heavily influenced by the antitrust rules of the European Union.[11] The agreements that some of the states of Central and Eastern Europe have concluded with the EU usually contain an article stipulating that EU competition policy is to become the norm for the countries' internal legislation. This is quite different from monetary policy institutions, where EU influence was difficult to discern.

Here are some of the institutional features of antitrust authorities. In the Czech Republic, the Chairman of the Office for the Protection of Economic Competition is appointed and (on the government's recommendation) can be dismissed by the President of the Republic. In Estonia, the Office of Competition Control is part of the government and integrated in the Ministry of Finance. The independence of its members was increased with the law reform of 1997, which stipulates that they are nominated for five years and that only a subsequent government can rescind that decision. In Poland, the President of the Office for the Protection of Competition and Consumers is appointed (and can be dismissed) by the Prime Minister. He is subordinate to the Council of Ministers. Poland created a specialised court – the Antimonopoly Court in Warsaw – to which one can apply (further appeal to the Supreme Court is also possible). The Antimonopoly Court often makes use of legal solutions found in the EU. In the view of the AMC's members, not only can this possibility assist in dealing with situations that are not described in detail in the Polish Antitrust legislation, it could also serve to arrive at fundamental definitions on which competition law is based, such as a 'dominant position' (Posluszna and Wiercinski, w.d.). Russia has chosen a different institutional solution: In 1998, it founded an antimonopoly ministry. In the Slovak Republic, a new law is being prepared that is to strengthen the position of the Antimonopoly Office 'and make it one of the more independent state organs'

(Cernejová, w.d.). One interesting aspect of the Slovak solution is that the Antimonopoly Office has a Legislation Division that is responsible for drafting new competition or competition-related laws and for commenting on the drafts of any other laws that could affect competition (Cernejovà, w.d.).

In its annual transition report, the European Bank for Reconstruction and Development has ascertained the quality of the various competition policies. On a scale ranging from 1 to 4+, where 1 indicates the worst possible grade and 4+ means the standard of established Western market economies, the competition policies of our eight case countries were ranked as follows: Bulgaria 2, Czech Republic 3, Estonia 3, Hungary 3, Poland 3, Romania 2, Russian Federation 2, and Slovak Republic 3 (EBRD 1999, 24 f.).

We mentioned in the introduction that we are using a broad concept of the delegation of powers. It would therefore make sense not only to analyse other independent agencies to which governments may have delegated some competence, such as antitrust offices or environmental agencies, but also to analyse direct-democratic elements (because the population at large becomes an actor in its own right) and even to include the independent media. The more independent the media, the more likely it seems that it can play an important role in controlling the government; this could be framed as 'delegation', because the constitution-makers grant others the power to voice critical opinions. Such an analysis is, however, beyond the scope of the present paper.

Interdependencies between domestic delegatee bodies

It is interesting to examine the relationship between the degrees of independence of various delegatee bodies in the same constituency. The possible interrelations between judicial independence and central bank independence are of particular interest. Three conflicting hypotheses can be mentioned in this context.

Based on the observation that judicial independence and central bank independence are usually regulated on different levels of norms – the constitutional vs. the post-constitutional – it almost suggests itself to hypothesise that central bank independence is a function of judicial independence. In addition, one can hypothesise that the existence of one independent delegatee will decrease the costs involved in delegating powers to another independent delegatee. According to this assumption, if the constitution provides for an independent Constitutional Court, the government's costs for delegating powers to an independent bank in the post-constitutional stage will be lower, and thus greater independence is more likely to materialise.

A competing hypothesis is based on the benefits side of the theoretical analysis of the delegation of powers, in particular responsibility shift (Fiorina 1982, see also Salzberger 1993). According to the rationale of this hypothesis, various delegated bodies can be viewed as substitutes. Since one can shift responsibility to various bodies, if there is already an independent delegatee, such as a Constitutional Court, the potential benefits from an additional body will be lower. This would point to a negative correlation between the degree of independence of the Constitutional Court and that of the central bank. However, since the content these two institutions deal with are very different, this substitution effect might be marginal.

A third hypothesis is that there is no correlation between the two, or that such correlation, if it exists, may be a result of a factor different from the delegation framework (e.g., cultural elements). According to this hypothesis, there might be yet another factor explaining both central bank independence and judicial independence. In the context of this paper, this hypothesis might be that the degrees of de jure independence of both the judiciary and the central bank are a function of the composition of the constitutional assembly, the preferences of the actors represented therein, or the rules of aggregating individual preferences in collective decisions.

Our study of only eight countries does not enable a rigorous test of the interrelations between central banks' independence and Constitutional Courts' independence. However, looking at the results in Tables 3 and 4 reveals a pattern of positive correlation between the two, which manifests itself in the fact that the differences in the ranking of the two do not exceed two slots. Countries that are ranked as having the more independent Constitutional Courts are also ranked as having the more independent central banks (the aggregation of the three indices) – the Czech Republic, Estonia, and Poland. Countries that are ranked as having less independent Constitutional Courts also have less independent central banks – Hungary, Romania, and Russia. Bulgaria is ranked number 2 in the central banks independence list and number 5 in the Constitutional Courts table. The indicator for the quality of competition policy, mentioned in the previous section, corresponds to the same pattern, i.e. it tends to correlate positively with the other two independence measures, whereas Slovakia, again, stands as the odd one out.

International Delegation

The constitutional basis for delegating powers to international organisations, or: the level of de jure delegation

Before examining the extent to which governments of Central and Eastern European countries have delegated actual power internationally (de facto delegation), we propose examining the constitutional basis for transferring sovereign rights or competence to a body external to the nation-state as well as examining the status of international law and international agreements within the municipal legal systems. These two indicators can serve as an index of the de jure extent of international delegation. The former can tell us which domestic political institutions are assigned the power to delegate externally. Naturally, different delegating organs – parliament, executive or other – will have different incentives to delegate externally, but more importantly, the identity of the delegator and the process of delegation can indicate how easy it is to delegate internationally. In countries where the government is empowered to bind the legal system by international treaties, the flexibility of delegation is greater than in countries where legislation or constitutional amendment is required to perform such delegation or where such delegation is subject to veto by another branch of government, such as the Constitutional Court.

The second aspect – the normative status of international law within the municipal legal system – is a good indicator for the importance attributed to international delegation. In other words, countries that place international law above their own legislation and that enable their courts to strike down legislation as contradicting international law can be regarded as potentially more extensive international delegators than countries that do not regard international law as superior to their domestic legislation.

Bulgaria, Estonia, and Slovakia seem to have the more flexible international delegation arrangements. In Bulgaria, the competence to delegate internationally is divided between the government and parliament. Some agreements require parliamentary ratification; these include agreements concerning the Republic of Bulgaria's participation in international organisations or international adjudication, agreements containing obligations for the treasury, agreements on human rights, and more. The government has the power to enter into other agreements without the need for further approval. Likewise, in Estonia, the parliament is empowered to ratify or renounce important treaties, among them all the treaties by which the Republic of Estonia joins international organisations or leagues. But other treaties can be made by government decision. In Slovakia, the president is empowered to conclude and ratify international treaties, but he is allowed to delegate this power to the government. Consent by the National Council is needed only for economic and political treaties and treaties whose execution requires legislation.

In Hungary, the power to conclude international treaties is allocated to the president as well as to the government. But if the treaty is of outstanding importance to Hungary's foreign relations, Article 19 of the Constitution stipulates that parliament must ratify it. International treaties that affect matters of national defence must be confirmed by national law and publicly proclaimed.

It is more difficult to delegate powers internationally in the Czech Republic, Poland, Russia, and Romania. In Romania, international treaties are negotiated by the government, concluded by the president, and must be ratified by parliament within 60 days. In the Czech Republic, all branches of government take part in the international delegation of powers. The Czech Constitution allots agenda-setting powers in regard to joining international organisations and signing international treaties to the President, but he may transfer the task of negotiation to the government or, with its approval, to its individual members; this is expressly specified in the constitutional law. The President's decisions require the Prime Minister's signature. He is thus endowed with veto power. Parliament must ratify a greater proportion of international accords than in the countries mentioned above. Such accords include those on human rights and fundamental freedoms, political agreements, economic agreements of a general nature, and agreements whose implementation requires the passage of a law.

Article 90 of the Polish Constitution enables the transfer of certain sovereign rights to an international organisation. The Constitution mentions two possible procedures for the ratification of international agreements: (1) A statute shall be passed by the House of Representatives (Sejm) and by the Senate by a two-thirds majority vote in the presence of at least half of the statutory number of Deputies in each house respectively. (2) A referendum must be held. The Polish President has the competence to ratify or reject international agreements and must notify the House of Representatives (Sejm) and the Senate thereof. Before ratifying an international agreement, he may refer it to the Constitutional Tribunal with a request to adjudicate upon its constitutionality. In other words, the Court has the power to delay ratification and some veto power.

In Russia, international delegation is the exclusive jurisdiction of the Federation, and the president is allocated the power to conduct negotiations and sign international treaties. The Constitutional Court has the power to examine the constitutionality of the treaty. Although the constitution does not mention that the Duma must ratify such a treaty, Article 106 stipulates that if ratification of such an agreement had been conducted by the Duma, the Federation Council must consider it.

The Czech Republic, Bulgaria, and Poland are at the top of the table in regard to the status of international law within the municipal legal system. The Czech Constitutional Court is empowered to invalidate laws that contradict international agreements and to give effect to decisions of international courts. Thus, the Czech Constitution places international law higher than domestic law. In addition, the Court is also empowered to take 'measures necessary to effect a decision by an international court that is binding for the Czech Republic if it cannot be effected otherwise' (Art. 87(I) of the Czech Constitution). This is a significant component, because it means that the Czech Constitution not only places international law above domestic law, but also adopts an arrangement similar to the European Union's direct effect doctrine. It also regards the interpretation of international law by international courts as part of international law. These provisions create symmetry between the Czech Constitutional Court (whose interpretations of the constitution are binding) and international courts (whose interpretations of international law are binding and made effective through the Constitutional Court). These arrangements can be considered the most far-reaching in regard to international delegation.

Article 85 of the Bulgarian Constitution specifies that those 'treaties ratified by the National Assembly may be amended or rejected only by their built-in procedure or in accordance with the universally acknowledged norms of international law'. This clause is far-reaching in terms of our issues. It could mean that the international delegation by ratification of parliament is irreversible, except by the terms of the treaty itself or international law. It also indicates that the normative status of international delegation supersedes regular legislation and requires amendment to the constitution if the international agreement is in conflict with the constitution (as explicitly specified by the second part of the same article). Moreover, the Constitutional Court is granted the powers to strike down new legislation that contradicts international law or agreements that have been ratified by Bulgaria. Thus, the infrastructure for international delegation is indeed very extensive.

In Poland, a ratified international agreement constitutes part of the domestic legal order and is to be applied directly, unless its application depends on the enactment of a statute. Moreover, although they are listed among the sources of the law in Poland (Art. 87 of the Constitution), international agreements are placed after legislation; Article 91 specifies that international law has precedence over statutes if the two cannot be reconciled.

The Estonian Constitution (Art. 123) subordinates all treaties to the Constitution, and if they contradict it they are not to be concluded. However, the same article holds that the treaties are superior to legislation and that, in case of conflict, their provisions are to be applied. The Constitution also empowers the National Court to review the constitutionality of international agreement, but there is no explicit authority to review whether legislation is in conformity with international law.

In the Slovak Republic (according to Art. 11 of the Constitution), international agreements on human rights take precedence over statutes, provided that they guarantee a greater extent of liberties. The relative normative status of other international agreements is not clear. The Constitutional Court has the jurisdiction to review the compatibility of laws with international treaties. Likewise, the Hungarian Constitution states that 'the legal system of the Republic of Hungary accepts the generally recognised principles of international law and shall harmonise the country's domestic law with obligations assumed under international law.' (Art. 7) This can mean the subordination of international legislation and maybe also of the Constitution itself to international law. However, the constitution does not specify how this harmonisation is to be conducted, save that the legislative procedures for harmonisation require a two-thirds majority. It is also silent about enforcement powers. In other words, there is nothing in the constitution about the Constitutional Court's jurisdiction to strike down legislation that contradicts international law.

Russia and Romania are ranked at the bottom of the list in regard to the status of international law within the municipal legal system. Article 15 of the Russian Constitution provides that 'the commonly recognised principles and norms of international law and the international treaties of the Russian Federation shall be a component part of its legal system' and 'if an international treaty of the Russian Federation stipulates other rules than those stipulated by the law, the rules of the international treaty shall apply.' However, no enforcement mechanism is specified, and no explicit jurisdiction is given to the Constitutional Court on the matter, in contrast to its jurisdiction to review the constitutionality of international treaties.

In Romania, treaties ratified by parliament become part of national law. This means that they are subject to the constitution and are also in the same normative level of legislation, i.e. later legislation might take precedent over the international treaty. According to Article 20 of the Romanian Constitution, in case of inconsistencies between international fundamental human rights treaties that Romania has signed, on the one hand, and national law, on the other, international law prevails over national law. However, a possible interpretation of this article is that if the treaty does not concern fundamental human rights and is in conflict with municipal law, the latter takes precedent. The Constitution does not specify enforcement mechanisms, such as review by the Constitutional Court.

The left side of table 5 presents the ranking of the structural foundations of delegation, which can also be viewed as the ranking of the de jure possibilities of international delegation. This ranking is comprised of scores on the two components scrutinised above: (1) constitutional capacity and flexibility of delegation, and (2) the constitutional binding force or normative status (within the national legal systems) of such delegation.

The actual delegation of international powers, or: de facto external delegation

When describing the sequence in which the countries of Central and Eastern Europe have become members of international organisations, thereby delegating power, it must be taken into account that this is not a unilateral decision. To become members, these countries not only have to want to become members; the existing international organisations also have to let them in. The basis on which they are admitted is often the similarity of their legal framework to those of 'more Western' countries. In that sense, one should expect these countries first to ratify a post-Communist constitution and only subsequently to apply to the international organisations. If we look at membership in the Council of Europe – in which safeguarding human rights plays a crucial role – there are two cases in which countries were let in before they had passed a new constitution: Hungary (admitted in November 1990) and Poland (admitted in November 1991). Bulgaria ratified the European Convention on Human Rights in 1992, accepting the optional protocol on civil and political rights. In October 1993, Romania became a member of the Council of Europe.

All of the countries under scrutiny here except Russia have signed so-called 'Europe Agreements' with the EU, providing for a transition period toward customs-free trade while also granting trade advantages exceeding the general GATT standards. Cooperating states set up trade and diplomatic co-operation and prepare for full membership. Russia and the EU have concluded a partnership and cooperation agreement, which does not envisage full membership in the near future. Three of the analysed countries have become NATO members. All of them are members of the WTO except Russia, which is negotiating membership. Some of the countries were members of GATT even before the transition started (Poland became a member in 1967, Romania in 1971, and Hungary in 1973). If one takes membership in various international organisations into account and ranks the countries of the region according to their degree of integration, the ranking from most to least integrated is: (1) Poland, (2) Hungary, (3) the Czech Republic, (4) Romania, (5) Bulgaria, (6) Slovakia, (7) Estonia, and (8) Russia.[12]

Table 5: Extent of integration

	EU time score	Council of EU time score	NATO yes/no	GATT time score	Sum	Integ.Rank
Bulgaria	3	3	4	6	16	5
Czech Rep	3	5	1	4	13	3
Estonia	7	4	4	7	22	7
Hungary	1	1	1	3	6	2
Poland	1	2	1	1	5	1
Romania	3	6	4	2	15	4
Russian Fed.	8	7	4	8	27	8
Slovakia	3	8	4	4	19	6

EU time score indicates the chronological order in which official applications for EU membership were filed (the fastest scoring 1, the second 2, and so forth); Council of EU time score indicates the chronological order in which the countries became members of the Council of Europe; NATO y/n indicates whether the country is a NATO member or not (the coding is 1 for members, and 4 for non-members); GATT time score indicates the chronological order of GATT (WTO) accession. The Sum is the addition of the four individual scores, from which the 'integration rank' is derived.

Summary

In the following table, we summarise our findings about international delegation in the eight countries covered in our study. The left side of the table presents the ranking of the structural foundations of delegation, which can also be viewed as the ranking of the de jure possibilities of international delegation. The right side of the table provides a ranking of the actual prospects of delegation, or the de facto extent of international delegation.

Table 6: Constitutional flexibility for international delegation

	Flexibility of delegation	Status of delegation	De jure delegation rank	Actual delegation*
Bulgaria	6	8	8	4
Czech	4	9	6	6
Estonia	6	7	6	2
Hungary	6	7	6	7
Poland	5	8	6	8
Romania	5	5	1	5
Russia	5	6	2	1
Slovakia	7	7	8	3

For coherence, we reversed the ranking: 8 is the highest delegator, 1 the lowest.

It is clear that there is no full correlation between de jure delegation and de facto delegation. While Hungary, Poland, and the Czech Republic figure as having high levels of both de jure and de facto international delegation, other countries are ranked as having a high de jure status of international delegation, but a low de facto delegation (Bulgaria and Estonia) or as having a low level of de jure delegation and a high level of de facto delegation (Romania); Russia has a low ranking in both indices. A possible and very tentative explanation for these results is that countries in which international delegation is domestically binding and where this delegation also has a high normative status as well as mechanisms of enforcement within the domestic legal system will be more hesitant to join international organisations or bind themselves with international treaties. Be that as it may, one insight of this analysis is that the number of international organisations or treaties to which a country belongs does not provide a complete picture of its level of integration in the international community or of its level of international delegation.

On Possible Interdependencies Between Domestic and International Delegation

Similar to the positive correlation between the levels of delegation to different domestic institutions presented in the previous section, it seems that such correlation also exists between the general levels of de jure domestic delegation and of de jure international delegation. In other words, countries in which the level of domestic delegation – to Constitutional Courts, central banks, or other institutions – is high, also have a high level of international de jure delegation, and vice versa. The Czech Republic, Estonia, and Slovakia feature in the high-level delegation group. Romania and Russia belong to the low-level delegation group. Hungary and Poland are in the middle level of delegation group. Bulgaria is the odd one out: it has the highest level of de jure international delegation and also the highest level of delegation to its central bank, but not to its Constitutional Court or to its competition guardians.

The possible explanation for this tentative finding (tentative because, as mentioned above, the low number of countries in this study does not enable us to examine these interrelations rigorously) can be attributed to our general model of delegation of powers (Voigt and Salzberger 2000). We argue there that delegation of powers would be exercised when the political benefits of such delegation outweigh the political costs. If delegation to one independent body already exists, then the cost involved in delegation to other bodies decreases. Thus, it is more likely that such delegation will occur. Several of the benefits we mention in our theoretical framework (such as responsibility shift and delegation as a tool to remain in power or maintain legitimacy, a tool to expand the public sector, and a tool to solve collective decision-making problems) are not limited to one subject area. They are the result of general features, such as the size of the polity, its electoral system, its legislative process, and more. This can be an additional explanation of the fact that domestic and international delegation are not substitutes, but complementary processes.

CONCLUSIONS AND OUTLOOK

In the introduction, we justified our choice of countries by pointing to a study in which four of them are listed as consolidated democracies (the Czech Republic, Estonia, Hungary, and Poland) and four others as countries in transition both politically and economically (Bulgaria, Romania, Russia, and Slovakia). This division is partially reflected in our subject of analysis – the constitutional and post-constitutional delegation of powers. The Czech Republic and Estonia seem to have the highest level of both international and domestic delegation. Slovakia can be added to this group. Russia and Romania have the lowest levels of both domestic and international delegation. Our tentative findings put Hungary and Poland in a middle group, while Bulgaria seems to have a high level of de jure international delegation as well as a high level of delegation to central bank, but a low level of delegation to a Constitutional Court. An ad hoc hypothesis on Bulgaria's central bank score could be that this is due to the currency board.

These findings tend to support our conjecture that more delegation of powers indicates a thicker approach to liberal democracy, which goes beyond mere majority rule. This conjecture leads directly to the question of correlation and causality. Piazolo (1999) observed that those countries that have been promised full EU membership have developed considerably better than the other transition countries. It is doubtful, however, whether this observation could be made policy-relevant, in the sense that the EU would merely have to promise full membership to effect a boost in credibility as the inevitable result. In other words, it is not clear whether the promise of EU membership was the cause or the result of 'better' development. Our findings also do not fully support the conjecture that the further west the countries are located, the more integrated (with the West) we can expect them to be. Geography might play a crucial role for institutional development, and for political and economic development as well, but the findings indicate it is certainly not the sole factor. The Transition Report of the EBRD recognises regional patterns in development but insists that there are a range of historical and political factors, such as the length of time under central planning, that also play a role (EBRD 1999, 27 f.). We concur.

More than ten years into transition, many questions still appear unanswerable; we have focused here on the newly-passed de jure constitutions, rather than on what they develop to be in reality, i.e. the de facto constitutions. It is probably still too early to ascertain divergences between the two. Yet, it should be possible to come up with hypotheses on the various degrees of divergence: Where constitutions are inherently contradictory, constitutional reality should diverge from the letter of the constitution (see Ordeshook's contribution to this volume). If one accepts the view that constitutions need to be backed by spontaneously arisen institutions (Voigt 1999, Chap. five), one could try to predict divergence by looking at civil society ratings. The higher the ranking, the more costly it will be for the government to renege on the constitution and therefore the less likely this is to occur (*Nations in Transit* regularly reports civil society rankings).

This paper has sought to analyse the choice of rules, i.e. constitutional rules have been *explananda*. We have largely abstained from analysing them as *explanans*. In other words, we have not asked about the welfare effects, the distributional consequences, etc. of alternative constitutional arrangements. More than one paper needs to be written on this issue. We have also abstained from normative analysis. Surely, more than one paper deserves to be written with a normative focus in mind.

APPENDIX A – AN OVERVIEW OF THE CONSTITUTION-MAKING PROCESSES IN THE EIGHT COUNTRIES COVERED BY THIS PAPER

Following are some more details on how and by whom the constitutions in the studied countries were constructed. They are presented in chronological order, i.e. in the order the constitutions were adopted.

Bulgaria

In December 1989, the leading opposition groups in Bulgaria, until then relatively weak, joined forces and founded the Union of Democratic Forces. In January 1990, following demands from this newly-formed power, the National Assembly voted to end the Communist Party's monopoly on political power. However, in parliamentary elections held in June 1990, the Communist (renamed the Bulgarian Socialist) Party won the majority of seats. This was a phenomenon unique among all the transitions in Eastern and Central Europe.[13] It was also a unique background for the adoption of a new constitution – a new parliament governed by the old guard; no round table talks; no referendum, because of fears that this constitution would not be approved. All these components can explain why Bulgaria was the first country in the region to have a new constitution, enacted in July 1991. They can also explain some features of this constitution.

On the one hand, the 1991 Constitution waves the banner of the division of powers, in contrast to the 1971 constitution, which rejected this idea (Ludwikowski 1996, 115). Indeed, despite the fact that the new constitution establishes a regime of parliamentary democracy, the new role of the president is relatively significant.[14] He is to be elected by the people and has the power to veto legislation, a power that can be overridden only by an absolute majority of the National Assembly members. The executive is stronger than in other countries, because the prime minister, who is elected by a simple majority in parliament, can be removed only by an absolute majority, and such a vote of no-confidence can be directed only against the prime minister or the cabinet as a whole, not against an individual minister. The judiciary is also fairly independent, managed by a High Judicial Council, which is responsible for appointments, promotions, and dismissal of judges and which is comprised of the presidents of the supreme courts. A separate administrative court system was also established. On the other hand, some regard this constitution as one of the least liberal constitutions; it bans ethnic parties, for example. The Bulgarian Constitution, like the Romanian one, is influenced more than those of most of the other countries in this study by the French structure of government. This is reflected in the relatively strong presidency and especially in the composition of the Constitutional Court (see page 223 f.).

The second elections after the fall of Communism, which took place in 1991, resulted in a draw between the reformers and the communists. A reform government was formed, but it lacked a majority sufficient to carry out far-reaching reforms. In the elections for president – the first popular elections under to the new constitution – the incumbent president Zehlev, representing the reformers, retained power. In the next general elections in 1995, the communists returned to power.

Summing up, one can definitely point out connections between the political constraints on the constitution-makers and the end result. First, the rapid enactment of a constitution was due to lack of serious round table talks, itself the consequence of the decision to hold elections before ratifying a new constitution; the actual result of these elections was that the new parliament had a Communist majority. Second, the relatively strong form of separation of powers can be attributed to the communists' political calculation that they would not be able to dominate the parliament for long. This can explain the relatively strong presidency. Ironically, the predictions failed: The power of the communists in parliament is still very significant; in contrast, the prediction that a Communist would hold the office of the president proved wrong.

Romania

Ceaucescu was ousted and executed in the last days of 1989. A few days before, a newly-formed body called the Council of the National Salvation Front, comprised of some communists, dissidents, and intellectuals, seized power and announced that it would retain power until democratic elections for parliament and presidency were held in May 1990. In February 1990, this body allowed other parties to participate in the newly-created Provisional Council for National Unity. The National Salvation Front won the May elections (in both houses of parliament, as well as the presidency) by a huge majority.

The NSF's clear majority in all political branches of government enabled it to proceed rapidly with constitution-making, similarly to events in Bulgaria. Unlike Bulgaria, however, the NSF's power allowed it to convene a special constituent assembly to draft the constitution and even to put the constitution to a referendum, which approved the constitution in November 1991. Amendments to the constitution also require popular approval.

The mark of the French system is easily detectable in the Romanian Constitution, as in the Bulgarian one, especially in regard to the composition and powers of the Constitutional Court and the definition of various types of statutes, classified according to their normative status. But unlike in France, the new Constitution enables a two-thirds majority in parliament to reverse the Constitutional Court's decision. This arrangement compels the Constitutional Court to be an active political player – with the opposition submitting all major decisions of parliament to it and thus forcing on it significant involvement in the conduct of legislation; Parliament routinely reverses its decisions (Report of *East European Constitutional Review*, Spring 1995, 22).

Another unique feature of the Romanian Constitution is a bicameralism with no real difference between the two chambers' structure of representation. The president is elected by the people and has more than representational or ceremonial powers. He can, for example, refer legislation to the Constitutional Court before approving it. Legislation, or at least agenda-setting for legislation, is not a monopoly of parliament. 250,000 citizens can initiate legislation, and legislative powers can be delegated to the government.

As in Bulgaria, it seems that the background political circumstances had an effect on constitution-making in regard both to the rapid process and to the degree of separation of powers and delegation of powers. It can be hypothesised that the overwhelming majority in all political institutions of the NSF, which was associated with the old regime, and the rational calculation that this majority would not hold for long induced it to establish a generous delegation of power.

Estonia

Estonia separated from the USSR in 1990. It formed a constituent assembly comprised of 30 members from the old parliament and 30 members from an interim independent quasi-parliament (Congress of Estonia). Their final draft, preferring a parliamentary to a presidential democracy, was approved by overwhelming majority in a referendum in 1992, making Estonia the first former Soviet republic to adopt a constitution.

The Czech and Slovak Republics

Civic Forum was established in 1989 and initiated mass pro-reform protests. These culminated in the resignation of the Communist Party's General Secretary, the Politburo, and the President in what was described as the 'Velvet Revolution'. An interim government of 'national understanding' was formed. The Federal Assembly, still dominated by communists, elected Alexander Dubcek, the 1968 reform Communist leader who was ousted by the Soviets, as Chairman and Vaclav Havel, the leader of the Civic Forum, as the new President.

Against the background of mounting tensions between the Czechs and the Slovaks, it was decided to first elect parliament and than to make a constitution. If the sequence had been reversed, it is possible that the split between the two peoples could have been avoided (Elster, Offe, and Preuss 1998, 71; hereafter cited as 'EOP'). The elections were held in June 1990; Civic Forum and its Slovak counterpart won. Havel asked the interim Prime Minister, Marian Calfa, to form a government, and this government acted rapidly to enact various laws to reform the economy and privatise state property; these reforms widened the gaps between the two republics (Ludwikowski 1996, 165). In the meantime, under Havel's guidance, constitutional reforms were made in a form of amendments to the existing constitution. Among them was the establishment of a Constitutional Court. But these reforms did not culminate in an overall new constitution; this was due to deep and mounting disagreements between the Slovaks and the Czechs and to the requirement of a three fifths majority for such reforms. Not even an attempt to copy the Polish 'small constitution' was successful.

The 1992 elections hammered the last nail in the federation coffin. The Czechs voted for reforms and a unified country. The Slovaks voted to slow economic reforms and for separation. By the end of the year, the two future countries signed a separation agreement and enacted two separate, though similar, constitutions.

The Czech Constitution was enacted by a unicameral assembly, but created a controversial bicameral constitution with a 200-member Chamber of Deputies, elected for four years, and an 81-member Senate, elected for six years. The critics say that the second chamber is unnecessary and prone to influence from far-too-narrow interest groups (Ludwikowski 1996, 172). The president is to be elected by absolute majority of parliament. His formal powers are relatively weak (McGregor 1994), although he and not parliament has the power to appoint the prime minister. A vote of no confidence requires a majority of all parliament members. However, a proposal to institute a constructive vote of no confidence was rejected.

The Slovak Constitution, adopted in September 1992, allows Parliament to elect and remove both the President (by a three fifths majority) and the Prime Minister, as well as individual ministers. The President (and not Parliament) has the power to appoint and to dismiss the Prime Minister, but otherwise his powers are minimal and he is vulnerable to sanctions by Parliament (EOP 101). A vote of no confidence requires a majority of all parliament members.

It is interesting to compare the Czech-Slovak experience with the Bulgarian-Romanian one in terms of the effects of constraints on constitutional order and delegation. In all four countries, a newly-elected post-Communist parliament enacted the constitution. While elections in the Czech and Slovak republics resulted in the rule of new powers and a clearer picture of the division of political powers to come, in Bulgaria and Romania, the results were 'tentative', with a significant presence of ex-communists (who actually received the majority of votes in Bulgaria). These differences might explain the tendency to more separation of powers, or rather more delegation of powers, in Bulgaria and Romania. Politicians will tend to delegate more powers when they feel more uncertain about their chances of remaining in power.

Poland

Constitutional reforms in Poland preceded the fall of Communism. They began in 1982 with a change of attitude toward the binding nature of the constitution, the introduction of judicial review, and the establishment of a Constitutional Court. This was indeed a unique phenomenon in the Eastern bloc (Rapaczynski 1993, Brezezinski 1993). In 1989, following the round table talks between the Communist government and the Solidarity-led opposition, further amendments to the 1952 constitution were introduced. A second house of parliament – a Senate – was established, which was to be elected democratically (unlike the Communist-ruled Seym), and a strong presidency was created, with the power to veto legislation. More amendments came after the 1989 elections, in which Solidarity won 99 out of 100 seats in the new Senate and a major share of the seats available for the opposition in the Seym. The Communists suffered a total defeat. A Solidarity-led government was formed. However, Jaruzelski – a Communist – was elected President.

As a consequence of the further amendments of the constitution, a direct presidential election was held in 1990 and won by Lech Walesa. New elections to a democratic parliament were held in 1991, resulting in a fragmented parliament. These results and, in particular, mounting tension between the two houses of parliament and the President obstructed agreement on a new constitution; not even the procedure for its enactment could be agreed upon. Finally, in 1992, an interim constitution, also dubbed the 'small constitution', was enacted. It dealt only with the structure of government, or the form of separation of powers, decreasing the powers of the president and increasing the powers of the executive, for example, by introducing a constructive vote of no confidence. New parliamentary elections in 1993 brought ex-Communists back to power; their return to power was completed in the presidential elections in 1995, which Kwasniewski, also an ex-Communist, won.

However (and maybe because of the return of Communists to power), a new constitution was enacted in 1997 and approved in a referendum by a majority of 53 per cent from a turnout of 43 per cent. The constitution creates a strong mechanism of checks and balances with a presidential veto and bicameralism. This structure of government brought about the establishment of 16 districts, rather than 12 – the government's proposal (shaped by economic analysis) in 1997. The dynamics of the decision-making on the number of districts is a good example of how institutional setup makes a difference. Had the structure of government involved a weaker separation of powers, it is plausible that the 12 district proposal would have been approved (EECR: 7(3) 1997, 25-27).

The Polish case is an interesting one in terms of constraints on constitutional choice. First, in Poland more than in any other country in this study, constitutional choice was intertwined with post-constitutional choice. Unlike the five countries scrutinised above, elections to a new parliament did not precede the constitutional change. This change began a few years before the first free elections and continued after the first elections and also after subsequent ones. We believe that the rather strong form of separation of powers and indeed delegation of powers can be explained against this background. The initial establishment of a Constitutional Court with the power of judicial review in 1982 can be seen as the Communist regime's attempt to delegate powers in order to remain in power or maintain legitimacy (see Voigt and Salzberger, 2000). The insistence on a strong presidency can be viewed similarly. The Communists and the opposition, both fearing a loss of power, opted to divide powers among several branches of government. Although some fine-tuning followed, the 1997 Constitution did not change this basic structure of government in Poland.

Hungary

Hungary is the only country among the eight we cover in this study that has not yet enacted a new constitution. But in fact, Hungary went through a constitutional revolution, and this was completed earlier and in much shorter time than in the neighbouring countries. The constitutional transition came about through a change of the 1949 Constitution, beginning in 1989 and carried out mainly by the old parliament upon the agreement reached in the round table talks. In fact, only 5 per cent of the original constitution's provisions remained intact. Even the name of the country was changed. The Hungarian constitution-makers exploited a 'window of opportunity', a short period during which the Communists remained demoralised and the opposition was not yet seriously divided. In Poland, some members of Solidarity pushed for a similar strategy, but failed (EOP 1998, 71). The opposition in Hungary, noting the results of the Polish elections, refused a similar deal, in which certain seats would have been reserved for the Communists. An attempt to shift to a presidential regime failed. These amendments were supposed to be temporary, until the enactment of a new constitution.

However, attempts to enact a new constitution in 1994-97 failed to gain the necessary two-thirds majority.

The fact that a non-democratically elected parliament amended the constitution to adjust it to the political changes resulted in a relatively strong presidency and a very strong Constitutional Court.[15] However, Parliament is perceived as the supreme representative of sovereignty, and its powers are the most extensive in the region, including constituent and derived constituent powers and the powers to elect the president and prime minister, the judges of the Constitutional Court, other high judges, the head of the national bank, and other important officials. The strength of the Prime Minister is also notable, since only a constructive no-confidence vote can remove him (EOP 96-7).

In December 1993, the Prime Minister of Hungary died and new elections to Parliament were held, in which the Socialist party won an absolute majority. Minor amendments to the constitution followed, such as the reduction of the number of Constitutional Court judges from 15 to 11. However, plans to enact a new constitution have not been realised.

The case of Hungary adds an interesting perspective to our focus on constraints in the constitutional mechanism. Because the transition in Hungary (in terms of the democratisation of the structure of government, not in terms of economic reforms) began a little later than in some neighbouring countries, notably Poland, one major constraint was information on what took place in Poland. The opposition in Hungary did not agree to a deal like Poland's, because it saw the increasing powers of Solidarity. Thus, the structure of government agreed upon in Hungary is based less on separating political powers between various organs and more on a workable framework of government. However, delegation of powers to non-political bodies, such as the Constitutional Court and international organisations, did take place. This can be explained by the opposition's realisation that the Hungarian population faced a hard period during economic reforms, and that such delegation might help the government remain in power.

Russia

By 1992, the Soviet Union was gone, and Russia faced a serious economic challenge and the need to re-construct the government. Committees of parliament already began drafting a constitution in 1990. The two lines of tension were the federative structure and the status of the different republics and regions, on the one hand, and the division of powers within the federal government, on the other. Yeltsin pushed for an American model of a presidential republic; parliament wanted a continental-style parliamentary democracy. In March 1992, the Constitutional Commission published a compromise draft, which was influenced by the broad de facto powers that the president assumed (relative to the power of parliament). But apparently it did not go far enough with the powers of the president. After receiving a vote of confidence in a referendum he called in April 1993, Yeltsin decided to convene a constitutional convention to propose a draft alternative to the parliament's. Such a draft was proposed, but it was rejected by Parliament, which decided on a procedure to adopt a constitution. This procedure depended completely on Parliament itself, requiring a two-thirds majority. In September 1993, Yeltsin dissolved Parliament and, in response, Parliament voted to depose Yeltsin. Subsequently, Yeltsin ordered military forces to attack Parliament; he also suspended the opposition parties, the Constitutional Court, and opposition newspapers. He put his draft to a referendum on the same day as the elections for a new legislature in November 1993, and the new constitution was approved by a 58.4 per cent majority.

The constitution increased the powers of the federal government in comparison with the different regions (vertical separation of powers). In other words, Russia became more centralised than before. The Constitution also stipulated that it has higher status than the Federation Treaty. But concessions were made in the area of the division of federal powers (vertical separation of powers). The Prime Minister was given more powers, and Yeltsin's plan for an American-style Vice President was abandoned. Still, the new constitution provides for a strong president, who is to be elected by the people and who is given significant executive powers, including the chairing of government meetings and the power to nominate the head of the central bank and constitutional judges (subject to the approval of the Duma). The President can also veto legislation. The procedure for impeaching the President, as specified by the Constitution, is complicated and unlikely to occur (Ludwikowski 1996, 63).

The new Russian Constitution, more than that of all previous countries we have discussed, reflects the actual balance of existing powers (between Yeltsin and Parliament) at the time of the enactment of the Constitution. Indeed, physical force was actually used to bring it about. In this case, therefore, the reasons for major features of the separation of powers differ somewhat from the predictions of our theory of the delegation of powers, which does not take into account the use of physical force (Voigt and Salzberger, 2000). However, the Constitution also creates or reaffirms bodies such as a Constitutional Court and central bank, to which powers are delegated for reasons of uncertainty, responsibility shift, collective decision-making problems, and other delegational benefits that do fall within the realm of our theory.

APPENDIX B: CONSTITUTIONAL PROVISIONS ON CENTRAL BANKS

Bulgaria

Article 84 (8) of the Bulgarian Constitution stipulates that the National Assembly shall elect and dismiss the governor of the Bulgarian National Bank. There is no other mention of the Bank in the Constitution. Bulgaria introduced a currency board on 1 July 1997, making the Deutsche Mark the anchor currency and fixing the Lev at a rate of 1000 to 1 German Mark. A committee of experts appointed by the government chose the anchor currency. In preparing for the currency board, it was necessary to modify the law dealing with the Bulgarian National Bank. A statute (Art. 30) fixed the anchor currency and the exchange rate. By the end of 1998, inflation had fallen to one percent, down from more than 2000 per cent in the first quarter of 1997. After operating for 18 months, the National Bank's reserves had almost quadrupled (from US$ 800 to US$3 billion). The basic interest rate fell from more than 200 per cent to 5.3 per cent by October 1998 (Gulde 1999). The choice of the current monetary regime was made six years after a new constitution was adopted. It can therefore be considered a post-constitutional choice and not part of a package deal including both basic constitutional arrangements and a statute regulating the National Bank.

Czech Republic

The Constitution of the Czech Republic contains a chapter (one article) devoted exclusively to the Czech National Bank. Article 98 names the Czech National Bank the state's central bank and specified currency stability as the Bank's primary, albeit not the only, goal. The Bank's status, jurisdiction, and other details are to be set down by law (Art. 98(2)). Additionally, the Bank is mentioned in an article concerning the functions of the President of the Republic, who is empowered to appoint members of the Czech National Bank Council.

Estonia

Article 111 of the Estonian Constitution lays out the constitutional foundation of the Bank of Estonia. It grants the Bank a monopoly to issue currency and stipulates that the Bank's primary goal is 'the stability of a good national currency'. The Constitution (Art. 65 (7) and (9), Art. 78 (11) and (12)) also lays down procedures for nominating and appointing the members of the Council of the Bank of Estonia. Article 104 of the Constitution specifies some laws that can be adopted or amended only by a majority of all Parliament members (rather than a majority of those present during the vote). These include statutes on the Bank of Estonia.

The Bank of Estonia (Eesti Pank) resumed operations in January 1990, after an interval of 50 years and Estonia's recognition as an independent country. After having gained independence, a working group was founded at the Bank to prepare monetary reform. Soon, the formation of reserves began. Great Britain returned the gold that had belonged to Eesti Pank prior to World War II. Membership in the Bank for International Settlements made reserves deposited there available [UNCLEAR]. In May 1992, the German Mark was selected as an anchor currency. Also in May, the Supreme Council adopted three laws, prepared by Eesti Pank, on banking in Estonia. The monetary reform took place in June 1992, and the Estonian kroon was fixed to the German Mark at a rate of 8 to 1. It has remained unchanged ever since (Eesti Pank 1999).

Hungary

The constitutional basis of the National Bank of Hungary is Article 32 (d) of the Hungarian Constitution. The Constitution makes the National Bank of Hungary responsible for issuing legal tender, maintaining the stable value of the national currency, and regulating the circulation of money. In addition, the article specifies appointment and term procedures. The Bank is organised as a joint-stock company, which is today a very unusual form of organisation of a national bank. This structure can be explained as recourse to the founding of the Bank in 1924, when this organisational setup was common practice (Kobabe 1999, 136). Since the Hungarian state is the sole stockholder, the Bank's independence seems to rest on a fragile foundation.

Poland

The National Bank of Poland is based on Article 227 of the Polish Constitution. It stipulates tasks and goals, as well as the organisational structure of the Bank.

Romania

The Romanian Constitution does not deal with the Romanian National Bank.

Russian Federation

Article 75 of Russia's Constitution mentions the Central Bank of the Russian Federation and the stability of the rouble as the main function of the Bank. The article explicitly states that the Bank is to exercise its powers independently from other bodies of state power.

Slovak Republic

The constitutional foundation of the bank is fragile and deficient: Article 56 of the Constitution states only that the Slovak Republic establishes a bank and that details will be set out in a law.

APPENDIX C: CONSTITUTIONAL PROVISIONS ON INTERNATIONAL DELEGATION

Bulgaria

Article 85 of the Bulgarian Constitution stipulates that the National Assembly 'shall ratify or denounce by law all international instruments that ...'. This article probably means that the competence to delegate internationally is divided between the government and parliament. Some agreements require parliament ratification; these include agreements concerning the Republic of Bulgaria's participation in international organisations or international adjudication, agreements involving obligations for the treasury, agreements on human rights, and more. The same article also specifies that 'treaties ratified by the National Assembly may be amended or denounced only by their built-in procedure or in accordance with the universally acknowledged norms of international law', and that 'the conclusion of an international treaty requiring an amendment to the Constitution shall be preceded by the passage of such an amendment'.

The last two clauses are far-reaching from our point of view. They probably mean that international delegation by parliamentary ratification is irreversible, save by the terms of the treaty itself or international law, and that the normative status of international delegation supersedes regular legislation and requires amendment to the constitution if the international agreement conflicts with the constitution. Moreover, the Constitutional Court is granted the powers to strike down new legislation that contradicts international law or agreements that Bulgaria has ratified (Art. 149 of the Constitution). Thus, the infrastructure for international delegation is very extensive indeed.

Czech Republic

All branches of government take part in the international delegation of powers in the Czech Republic. The Czech Constitution grants the President agenda-setting powers in regard to joining international organisations and signing international treaties. Article 63 of the Constitution stipulates that the President 'negotiates and ratifies international treaties; he may transfer the negotiation of international agreements to the Government or, with its approval, to its individual members, expressly specified in the constitutional law, if it is stipulated so by law.' Presidential decisions require the Premier's signature, who thus holds veto power. Article 49 stipulates that certain international accords require ratification by parliament. These include accords on human rights and fundamental freedoms, political agreements, economic agreements of a general nature, and agreements whose implementation requires passage of a law.

The Czech Constitutional Court is empowered to invalidate laws that contradict international agreements and to implement decisions of international courts. Thus, the Czech Constitution places international law above domestic law. In addition, the Court is empowered to take 'measures necessary to effect a decision by an international court that is binding for the Czech Republic if it cannot be effected otherwise' (Art. 87 (I) of the Czech Constitution). This is a significant component, because it means that the Czech constitution not only places international law above domestic law, but also approaches the European Union's direct effect doctrine and regards the interpretation of international law by international courts as part of international law. These provisions create a symmetry between the Czech Constitutional Court (whose interpretations of the constitution are binding) and international courts (whose interpretations of international law are binding and made effective through the Constitutional Court). Among the countries we have examined, these arrangements can be considered the most far-reaching on international delegation.

Estonia

The Estonian Constitution contains no explicit integration clause. Membership in international organisations is addressed in Chapter IX of the Constitution, titled 'Foreign Relations and Foreign Treaties'. According to Article 121, Parliament ratifies and renounces important treaties, among them all treaties by which the Republic of Estonia joins international organisations or leagues. According to Article 123, all treaties are subordinate to the Constitution and are not to be concluded if they contradict it. However, the same article holds that the treaties supersede legislation and that their provisions are to be applied in case of conflict.

The Constitution empowers the National Court to review the constitutionality of international agreements, but there is no explicit authority to review whether legislation is in conformity with international law.

Hungary

Article 30A and Article 35 of Hungary's Constitution allocate the power to conclude international treaties to the president and the government respectively. But if the treaty is of outstanding importance to Hungary's foreign relations, Article 19 stipulates that parliament has to ratify it. Article 40 (C) stipulates that international treaties that affect matters of national defence must be confirmed by national law and publicly proclaimed. This makes it fairly cumbersome to conduct international delegation.

The Hungarian Constitution states that 'The legal system of the Republic of Hungary accepts the generally recognised principles of international law and shall harmonise the country's domestic law with obligations assumed under international law' (Art 7). This can mean domestic law is subordinated to international law and maybe also to the constitution. However, the Constitution does not specify how this harmonisation is to be carried out, except that the legislative procedures for harmonisation require a two-thirds majority. The Constitution is also silent about enforcement powers. In other words, there is nothing in the Constitution on the Constitutional Court's jurisdiction to strike down legislation that contradicts international law.

Poland

Article 90 of the Polish Constitution enables the transfer of certain sovereign rights to international organisations. The Constitution mentions two possible procedures for ratification of international agreements: (1) A statute can be passed by the House of Representatives (Sejm) by a two-thirds majority vote in the presence of at least half of the statutory number of Deputies, and by the Senate by a two-thirds majority vote in the presence of at least half of the statutory number of Senators. (2) A referendum can be held.

The Polish President has the competence to ratify or reject international agreements and must notify the House of Representatives (Sejm) and the Senate thereof. Before ratifying an international agreement, he may refer it to the Constitutional Tribunal with a request to adjudicate upon its constitutionality (Art. 131). In other words, the Court has the power to delay ratification and some veto power.

A ratified international agreement constitutes part of the domestic legal order and is to be applied directly, unless its application depends on the enactment of a statute. Moreover, it takes precedence over statutes if it cannot be reconciled with the provisions of such statutes (Art. 91), even though international agreements are placed after legislation in the list of sources of the law in Poland (Art 87).

To sum up, although it seems that the Polish Constitution places international law above regular legislation (except for the wording of Art. 87), it holds the Constitution to supersede international law. However, except for the transfer of sovereign powers, the procedure for international delegation is easier than in the other countries examined.

Romania

International treaties are negotiated by the government, concluded by the President, and need to be ratified by Parliament within 60 days (Art. 91). Thus it is relatively difficult to delegate internationally. Treaties ratified by Parliament, however, become part of national law (Art. 11). This means that they are subject to the constitution and are also on the same normative level of legislation, i.e. later legislation might take precedence over the international treaty. Article 20 stipulates that, where international fundamental human rights treaties to which Romania is a party are inconsistent with national law, international law prevails over national law. However, a possible interpretation of this article is that if the treaty does not concern fundamental rights and is in conflict with municipal law, the latter takes precedent. The Constitution does not specify enforcement mechanisms, such as review of the Constitutional Court review.

To sum up, it is relatively complicated to delegate internationally, since the president, government, and parliament all must participate in this process, and such delegation does not enjoy the same high status as in other countries covered by this paper.

Russia

Many provisions of the Russian Constitution refer to international law; these include provisions on human rights, extradition, nationality, and more. Article 79 of the Russian Constitution stipulates that Russia can participate in inter-state associations and delegate some of its powers to them, as long as this does not restrict human or civil rights and liberties or contravene the fundamentals of the constitutional system of the Russian Federation. International delegation is an exclusive jurisdiction of the Federation (Art. 71), and the President has the power to conduct negotiations and sign international treaties (Art. 86). The Constitutional Court has the power to examine the constitutionality of the treaty (Art. 125). Although the Constitution does not mention any requirement for Duma ratification, Article 106 holds that if the Duma has ratified such an agreement, the Federation Council must consider it.

Article 15 provides that 'the commonly recognised principles and norms of international law and the international treaties of the Russian Federation shall be a component part of its legal system' and 'if an international treaty of the Russian Federation stipulates other rules than those stipulated by the law, the rules of the international treaty shall apply'. However no enforcement mechanism is specified, and the Constitutional Court is given no explicit jurisdiction on the matter, in contrast to its jurisdiction to review the constitutionality of international treaties.

Slovak Republic

The Slovak Constitution permits the Slovak Republic to enter into alliance with other states. The right to secession from this alliance, however, cannot be restricted. The decision on entering into an alliance with other states or on secession from this alliance can be made by a constitutional law and a subsequent referendum (Art. 7). The President is empowered to conclude and ratify international treaties (Art. 102 of the Constitution), but he is also allowed to delegate this power to the government. Consent by the National Council is needed for economic and political treaties and treaties that require legislation for their execution (Art. 86).

Article 11 of the Constitution gives international agreements on human rights precedence over statutes, provided that the former guarantee greater liberties. The relative normative status of other international agreements is not clear. The Constitutional Court has the jurisdiction to review the compatibility of laws with international treaties (Art. 125).

NOTES

1   The third category in this survey of 28 ex-Communist countries is countries that are consolidated autocracies and statist economies. These include Tajikistan, Belarus, Bosnia, Uzbekistan, and Turkmenistan.
2   Additionally, separation of powers *à la Montesquieu* can also be distinguished from checks and balances: whereas in the former, each of the government branches is responsible for different functions, in the latter, each branch also performs functions of the other branches, thus having some sort of veto power over the decisions of the other branches.
3   On the question of whether there are systematic relationships between public sessions of the constitutional convention and the rules agreed upon, see Macey (1986), who advances the hypothesis that public deliberations make any obvious use of log-rolling and horse-trading less likely. In this setting, the representatives would at least try to formulate their arguments in terms of the common good.
4   Suppose a government ratifies a set of internationally agreed rules but then does not abide by them and is subsequently sanctioned by the international organization (e.g., via suspension of its membership). It would then be interesting to inquire under what conditions the prestige of the government suffers due to suspension and under what

conditions the prestige of the international organization suffers, i.e. under what conditions the government gets away with it, at least domestically.

5   One can even point to Russia as having one of the more impressive de jure structures of government, with the separation and delegation of powers. But see Ordeshook (1997).

6   The state ombudsman is the initiator of direct judicial review proceedings.

7   Political independence is ascertained by the following questions: (1) Can the executive branch or the parliament dismiss the governor of the central bank if there is conflict regarding monetary policy? (2) Does the central bank governor's term of office exceed the election cycle? (3) Does the term of office of central bank board members exceed the election cycle? (4) Does a government official or representative have a voting seat on the central bank board? (5) Does a government official or representative sit on the central bank board with a veto?

8   We have recalculated their regression, taking Slovakia into account: For 1993, it turns out that the R^2 increases to 0.496. But if one computes the regression for the inflation rates of 1998 and 1999, the results are not convincing: For 1998, the correlation coefficient drops to 0.01 (thus the inflation rate was almost perfectly uncorrelated with SIB). For 1999, it has at least the correct (negative) sign, but its value is not impressive either, namely 0.087. Alternatively, using the Debelle-Fisher index, the results remain virtually unchanged.

9   Radzyner and Riesinger (1997) doubt whether the degree of central bank independence is the major factor in explaining inflation performance in the countries of Central and Eastern Europe. They stress (*ibid.* 60) that, in an environment of economic transformation and stabilisation programs, inflation rates will be determined by a number of factors that are not directly influenced by the central bank, such as price liberalisation and tax reform.

10   More precisely, they might also try to block the introduction of policy competition entirely.

11   Bányaiová, Altheimer, and Gray (w.d.) argue this for the Czech Republic; Sepp and Wrobel (2000) argue this for Estonia; and Posluszana and Wiercinski (w.d.) argue it for Poland.

12   The ranking is somewhat biased against countries that were established only after 1989 (Estonia and Slovakia). This can be one reason for their poor ranking.

13   The reformers, however, managed to push through their presidential candidate who was elected by the new parliament, and the opposition also managed quite quickly to bring down the prime minister. The new prime minister elected by parliament was a politically independent judge.

14   In the Hellman (1996) ranking, the Bulgarian President gets a higher score than, for example, the Hungarian one.

15   McGregor (1994) ranks the Hungarian presidency as the most powerful presidency, based on formal powers. We cannot accept this assessment, since we believe that the presidency in Russia and Poland are stronger.

REFERENCES

Ackerman, B. (1991), *We the people, Vol. 1: Foundations*, Cambridge, Ma.: Belknap.

Arato, Andrew (1995), 'Parliamentary Constitution Making in Hungary', *East European Constitutional Review*, **4** (4): 45-51.

Bach, Stanley and Susan Benda (1995), 'Parliamentary Rules and Judicial Review in Romania', *East European Constitutional Review*, 4 (3), 49-53.

Bányaiová, A. (w.d.), 'Czech Republic – Current developments in competition legislation', http://www.global-competition.com/spl_rpts/ear/czech.htm.

Barro, R.J. and D. Gordon (1983), 'Rules, Discretion, and Reputation in a Positive Model of Monetary Policy', *Journal of Monetary Economics*, 12, 101-121.

Brezezinski, M. (1993), 'Constitutionalism Without Limits', *EECR*, 2 (2), 38.

Buchanan, J. (1975), *The Limits of Liberty – Between Anarchy and Leviathan*, Chicago: University of Chicago Press.

Buchanan, J. and Tullock, G. (1962), *The Calculus of Consent – Logical Foundations of Constitutional Democracy*, Ann Arbor: University of Michigan Press.

Cernejová, A. (w.d.), 'Slovak Republic – Review of antimonopoly practice', http://www.global-competition.com/spl_rpts/ear/slovakia.htm.

Cukierman, A., G. Miller and B. Neyapti (2000), 'Central Bank Reform, Liberalisation and Inflation in Transition Economies – An International Perspective', Tel Aviv University, *Foerder Institute for Economic Research Working Paper* 19.

Dethier, Jean-Jacques, Hafez Ghanem, and Edda Zoli (1999), 'Does Democracy Facilitate Economic Transition? An Empirical Study of Central and Eastern Europe and the former Soviet Union', *Journal of Institutional Innovation, Development and Transition*, 3, 15-30.

Eesti Pank (1999), 'Eesti Pank 1919-1999', http://www.ee/epbe/en/history.html.

Elster, J. (1991), *Arguing and Bargaining in Two Constituent Assemblies*, The Storrs Lectures.

Elster, Jon (1994), 'Constitutional Courts and Central Banks: Suicide Prevention or Suicide Pact?', *East European Constitutional Review*, 3 (3/4), 66-71.

Elster, Jon (1996), 'The Role of Institutional Interest in East European Constitution-Making', *East European Constitutional Review*, 5 (1), 63-5.

Elster, J., Offe, C. and U. Preuss (1998*), Institutional Design in Post-Communist Societies*, Cambridge University Press.

European Bank for Reconstruction and Development (1999), *Transition Report 1999*, London.

Eivind Smith (1995) (ed), *Constitutional Justice Under Old Constitutions,* The Hauge-Kluwer.

Ghosh, A., A.-M. Gulde and H. Wolf (1998), 'Currency Boards: The Ultimate Fix?, *IMF Working Paper*, **98** (8).

Gulde, A.-M. (1999), 'The Role of the Currency Board in Bulgaria's Stabilization', *IMF Policy Discussion Paper*, **99** (3).

Hellman, Joel (1996), 'Constitutions and Economic Reform in Postcommunist Transitions', *East European Constitutional Review*, **5** (1), 46-56.

Hume, D. (1777/1987), *Essays – Moral, Political, and Literary*, ed. and with a Foreword, Notes, and Glossary by Eugene F. Miller, Indianapolis: Liberty Classics.

Karatnycky, A., A. Motyl and B. Shor (1998), *Nations in Transit 1998*, New Brunswick et al.: Transaction Publishers.

Keefer, Phil and David Stasavage (1998), *When Does Delegation Improve Credibility?*, Central Bank Independence and the Separation of Powers, mimeo.

Kirstein, R. and S. Voigt (2000), 'The Violent and the Weak: When Dictators Care About Social Contracts', Center for the Study of Law and Economics, *Discussion Paper*, **2000-2.**

Kydland, F. W. and E. C. Prescott (1977), 'Rules Rather than Discretion: The Inconsistency of the Optimal Plans', *Journal of Political Economy*, 85, 473-91.

Kobabe, Rolf (1999), *Zentralbanken in Osteuropa – Europäische Integration und rechtliche Konvergenz*, Baden-Baden: Nomos.

Levy, B. and P.Spiller (1994), 'The Institutional Foundations of Regulatory Commitment: A Comparative Analysis of Telecommunications Regulation', *Journal of Law, Economics & Organisation*, **10** (2), 201-46.

Loungani, Prakash and Nathan Sheets (1997), 'Central Bank Independence, Inflation, and Growth in Transition Economies', *Journal of Money, Credit, and Banking*, **29** (3), 381-99.

Ludwikowski, R. (1996*), Constitutional-Making in the Region of Former Soviet Dominance,* Durham: Duke University Press.

Macey, J. (1986), 'Promoting public-regarding legislation through statutory interpretation: an interest-group model', *Columbia Law Review*, **86**, 223-68.

McGregor, J. (1994), 'The presidency in East Central Europe', *RFE/RL research report*, **3** (2), 23-31.

McGuire, R. and R. Ohsfeldt (1986), 'An Economic Model of Voting Behaviour over Specific Issues at the Constitutional Convention of 1787', *Journal of Economic History*, **46** (1), 79-111.

McGuire, R. and R. Ohsfeldt, R. (1989a), 'Self-Interest, Agency Theory, and Political Voting Behaviour: The Ratification of the United States Constitution', *American Economic Review*, **79** (1), 219-34.

McGuire, R. and R. Ohsfeldt (1989b), 'Public Choice Analysis and the Ratification of the Constitution' in Grofman, Bernard und Donald Wittman (eds), *The Federalist Papers and the New Institutionalism*, New York: Agathon, pp. 175-204.

Mueller, D. (1996), *Constitutional Democracy*, Oxford: Oxford University Press.

Ordeshook, Peter C. (1997), 'Constitutions for new democracies: Reflections of turmoil or agents of stability?', *Public Choice*, **90**, 55-74.

Ostrom, V. (1987), *The Political Theory of a Compound Republic – A Reconstruction of the Logical Foundations of the American Democracy as Presented in The Federalist*, Lincoln and London: University of Meneska Press.

Piazolo, Daniel (1999), 'Growth Effects of Institutional Change and European Integration', *Economic Systems*, **23** (4), 305-30.

Posluszna, M. and A. Wiercinski (w.d.), 'Poland – Protection of competition and consumers' interests in Poland', http://www.global-competition.com/spl_rpts/ear/poland.htm.

Radzyner, O. and S. Riesinger (1997), 'Central Bank Independence in Transition: Legislation and Reality in Central and Eastern Europe', *Focus on Transition*, **1** (97), 57-91.

Rapaczynski, A. (1993), 'Constitutional Politics in Poland: A Report on the Constitutional Committee of the Polish Parliament' in Dick Howard (ed), *Constitution Making in Eastern Europe*, Woodrow Wilson Center Press, pp. 93-131.

Rawls, J. (1971), *A Theory of Justice*, Cambridge: Belknap.

Salzberger, Eli M. (1993), 'A Positive Analysis of the Doctrine of Separation of Powers, or: Why Do We Have an Independent Judiciary?', *International Review of Law and Economics*, **13**, 349-79.

Schelling, Th. (1960), *The Strategy of Conflict*, Cambridge, MA: Harvard University Press.

Semler, Dwight (1994), 'Focus: The Politics of Central Banking', *East European Constitutional Review*, **3** (3/4), 48-52.

Sepp, J. and M. Wrobel (2000), 'Besonderheiten der Wettbewerbspolitik in einem Transformationsland', *Wirtschaft und Wettbewerb*, **50** (1), 26-44.

Voigt, S. (1999), *Explaining Constitutional Change – A Positive Economics Approach*, Cheltenham: Edward Elgar.

Voigt, S. and E. M. Salzberger (2002), 'Choosing Not to Choose: When Politicians Choose to Delegate Powers', *Kyklos*, **55** (2), 247-268..

Weingast, B. (1993), 'Constitutions as Governance Structures: The Political Foundations of Secure Markets', *Journal of Institutional and Theoretical Economics*, **149** (1), 286-311.

16. Comment

Gerard C. Rowe

SERVANTS OF THE PEOPLE – CONSTITUTIONS AND
STATES FROM A PRINCIPAL-AGENT PERSPECTIVE

1. Introduction

What is the proper relationship between the various actors in the public and
political sector? Who are these actors? How best should one characterise
their roles? How much information about the actions of one actor should be
available to other actors? How much influence should one actor or group of
actors have over another? What rules should regulate these interactions? How
should institutions be structured in order to give effect to these rules? These
are the eternal questions of constitutional law, the law of state organisation
and aspects of administrative law, of political science, of political philosophy, and of public and institutional economics.

Constitutions can fulfil a multitude of functions, among others providing
answers to some of these questions. Constitutions can be more or less detailed in regard to such matters. Any constitution worth its name will regulate
at least the key features of state organisation and governmental structure
which are to apply within the jurisdiction concerned. Where appropriate, the
basis of federal structures and arrangements will also be spelled out. Typically such an instrument will contain some express reference to the relationship
between the state and the citizenry. This might go no further than references
in respect of voting arrangements. Usually, however, – and more importantly
– fundamental rights protection will also be included, thus setting limits on
state action which may infringe or reduce individual freedoms.

There is nothing new in any of this. Lawyers take these constitutional
rules largely at dogmatic face value, albeit sometimes referring to their functions or purposes in generally conceptual, but mostly non-theoretical, terms.
The rules and elements of constitutions to which I have referred do, however,
admit of more overarching conceptualisations or theoretical approaches.

Indeed, the multiplicity of constitutional rules as well as further rules of state organisation found in statutes, subordinate legislation, constitutional conventions and in the rules and practices of procedure can, as others have demonstrated,[1] be drawn within at least one relatively consistent analytical framework which provides useful answers to the questions posed at the outset, namely that of principal-agent theory in economics. This framework highlights not only the sense of particular rules but also the mutually reinforcing or qualifying effects of rules among themselves when taken as a whole. This is a theory which provides a means of making sense of both the institutional structural features of constitutions and state arrangements and of at least some of the basic constitutional human rights protections.

This paper presents some reflections on the questions posed above and related issues from the standpoint of principal-agent theory, and in doing so suggests a framework for considering, for example, a matter such as the appropriate level of independence of various kinds of public organisations (such as central banks). Although the contours of agency theory are generally well-known among economists, they are probably less well-known among lawyers. The paper presents therefore a very brief treatment of the basic features, questions and issues which arise from agency theory. It then proceeds through a number of established features of constitutional law, the law of state organisation and typical institutional arrangements in the public sector, indicating in each case the principal-agent issues which arise, the way in which constitutional and other legal rules and institutional structures typically respond to these issues and how successful these responses seem to be.

Before proceeding, an important qualification or disclaimer is needed here. The application of agency theory to certain institutions and concepts of state organisation should not be interpreted as a rejection of numerous other methods and approaches. This methodology is not an exclusively valid one. Indeed, much of what can be couched in terms of agency theory has certainly already been said by lawyers, political scientists, historians and others within other concepts or theories. An application of agency theory, far from invalidating other methodologies, often suggests more a disciplinary convergence.

2.   Some Basics of Principal-Agent Theory

In economics, agency theory is particularly, but not exclusively, familiar in the context of private business or commercial enterprises. A classic issue arising in that context is that of shareholder control over firm managers, control by the board of directors over the chief executive officer, or control by the chief executive over lower levels in the firm hierarchy. A related issue is the influence of state officials on firms for reasons of public policy. The intersection of legal and economic theory in such a context relates to the general issue of corporate governance. One of the key questions in this context is the contribution of the ambient legal and institutional framework to the optimisation of the complex of agency relationships which exist in and around large commercial organisations. In the present paper the context is different, being shifted to the public sector, but many of the issues and questions remain familiar.

The key idea reflected in agency theory is that, instead of a principal's seeking to achieve desired ends itself, one or more agents will be employed by the principal to do this, or to assist in doing so. Inherent in this, among other things, is the idea that, at least formally, the principal confers a power or competence on the agent to act in its stead, even though in numerous – perhaps the majority of – circumstances the principal engages an agent precisely because the principal is unqualified for or factually incapable of performing the tasks concerned. The principal-agent relation is, at base, a single, *vertical, hierarchical* organisational division.[2] This essentially simple idea becomes immensely complex as tasks multiply, as goals are set which a single individual acting alone could never achieve, as goals emerge which are wholly or partially incompatible, and as tasks become more technically complex and specialised. Then the organisational division moves from a singular vertical one to include both a range of horizontal divisions and, usually, more than one vertical or hierarchical division.[3] The classical organisational pyramid presents this. Between the horizontal elements there may also exist principal-agent relations, but this need not be the case – and indeed from a classical agency perspective would be in fact unexpected – but where they do exists in such a form, they are fundamentally subsidiary or collateral to the primary agency pyramid. Other organisational models, such as the matrix-based organisation, may reduce the number of hierarchical levels where this is seen as desirable, but the key idea can still be identified there.

Agency theory concerns itself with the issue of the form and content of the agency contract and with the conditions under which a contract of a particular kind will come about. Agency theory, at least in its original private business context, points to a number of interlocking elements of, explanations for and problems in organisational rules and institutional arrangements. Among these are the following:

- the issue of the separation of ownership and control, which relates among other things to the question of the distribution of risk and the role and power of management;[4]
- the benefits of specialisation or of expert knowledge and ability;
- the problem of informational asymmetries between principal and agent, i.e. the issue that the agent may possess more information than the principal in relation to the task to be performed[5] and thus may be able to mislead the principal and act to his or her own advantage (so called 'moral hazard');
- the means available for reducing or compensating for such informational asymmetries;
- the problem of task specification (the 'duty statement') and the assessment of an agent's performance;
- the level and quality of control or supervision by the principal of the agent and the mechanisms of incentive, reward and/or correction available to the principal;
- the motivations available for the agent to carry out the task fully and correctly, or at least to apply an effort commensurate with the reward structure;
- the costs to the principal of control over or influence upon the agent,[6] especially in comparison with the benefits which the employment of the agent were meant to achieve;
- the circumstances under which a principal-agent relationship may be wholly or partly reversed, or where it for certain purposes may move in one direction, but simultaneously for other purposes move in the contrary direction
- the contribution which the use of agents may make to reducing transaction costs; and
- the possible role which a market for agents and agent's services may have in the formation and shaping of principal-agent relations.[7]

This is not an exhaustive list of issues relevant to the principal-agent context, but refers to some of the salient concerns. Many of these are as relevant to the agency relationships which arise in the constitutional and state context as to those in the private sector. A number of these points will be referred to again in the course of considering certain typical agency concerns in the public arena.

3. Key Features of State Organisation and Constitutional Arrangements

(a) Introduction – the state as a structure of agency relations and organisational division

Like private organisations, the state as a whole and individual arms and agencies of the state make use of a complex organisational division. A vast range of constitutional arrangements, the organisation of the state and the laws relating to it are concerned precisely with effectuating and utilising the organisational division. Why should this be so? Is it a good thing? Does it a provide a measure of the health of constitutional, political, legal and public affairs? What might be derive through this understanding of state structures in regard to assessment, change and improvement? Can countries in the process of transformation, seeking after new or modified constitutional arrangements, benefit from focussing on the principal-agent model and the organisational division as key features of constitutional and state arrangements?

Let us begin with a consideration of the status quo. Divisions of labour, whether in the public or private context, are employed for many reasons. Where exactly do we find a principal-agent relation and a division of labour in state organisation and constitutional arrangements? Needless to say, countries and legal systems differ from one another, but many of the illustrations which I mention here will be familiar in many systems. It should be noted in passing that not all divisions of labour within the state are principal-agent relationships; this point will need to be revisited later since sometimes there seems to be confusion in the assessment of specific institutional arrangements in this respect. I look first at the idea of the separation of powers, both the tradition 'horizontal' one, and also the vertical ('(quasi-)federal') one. As well I look within the individual elements of the horizontal separation of powers and within a single level of (quasi-)federal arrangements.

(b)   Vertical and horizontal separations of power generally

(i)   The classical separation of powers
A classic organisational division within states is that found in the *separation of powers*, the division of power between legislative, executive and judiciary, in other words the *horizontal* separation of powers well known to lawyers. Between each of these three elements there is, arguably, *no* principal-agent relation, unless perhaps the view is taken, for example, that the administration acts as an agent of the parliament in effectuating legislative commands. This might, without doubt, be a plausible view, especially in the light of a legal doctrine such as the supremacy of parliament. On the other hand, the essence of the separation of powers doctrine tells us that, strictly, the parliament possesses *no* executive (gubernatorial or administrative) competence, so that the administration should not be seen as acting on the basis of a power conferred by the parliament as principal, but rather acting on the basis of a competence derived elsewhere (specifically from the *people as principal*, under the constitution). This is not contradicted by the fundamental concept that the parliament is, in many countries, the only organ of the state which relies on direct democratic legitimation through election, whereas the administration, as a rule, only indirectly obtains a democratic legitimation through parliamentary decision.[8] The proposition might legitimately be seen as qualified, however, by the fact that the executive is given the task of making delegated legislation. In this special case a genuine principal-agent between legislative and executive might be seen to arise.

Even more strongly, however, both under the doctrine of the separation of powers and – at least in most well-functioning western democracies such as Britain, the United States, Germany, Australia or Canada – in reality, the courts cannot plausibly be regarded as agents of either the parliament or the executive (subject to certain minor exceptions). The contradictory view taken by Josselin and Marciano (2000) on this point must be decisively rejected. Their view is that courts such as the United States Supreme Court or the European Court of Justice were originally constituted as agents of the Congress (Josselin and Marciano 2000, 225-226) or, in the case of the European Community the 'member-states...the Commission and the Council' (*ibid.* 227) but have in the course of time exploited their role so as, in effect, to become principals. Apart from not articulating who their agents might now be, this view fails to provide any account of the role of these and similar courts (such as the *Bundesverfassungsgericht*, the High Court of Australia or the Supreme Court of Canada) as part of a larger context of agency relations. Properly understood, both court and parliament are constitutionally established agents of the people, with functions which are deliberately distinct – the separation of powers is a constitutionally effected organisational division – in order to achieve a very specific (and usually highly effective) solution to the recurrent problem of achieving control over agents, through a system of checks and balances. It is precisely in this setting that a decision such as that of the United States Supreme Court in *Marbury* v. *Madison*[9] can be seen not only as a plausible interpretation of an admittedly incomplete agency contract, but indeed in terms of the perennial agency dilemma arguably a necessary one.[10]

It is certainly true, as Josselin and Marciano point out (*ibid.* 222), that the courts of Common Law in Britain did gradually escape the control of their principal, the king. To say, however, that they 'reshaped the setting of the principal-agent relationship to their own advantage' (*ibid.* 222) and, later, that the (existing) 'agency relationship is then at best loosened, at worst reversed' (*ibid.* 229), as though the status quo of an agency relationship is self-justifying, seems a curious, indeed perverse view. A truer account would see that process as an historical development from a non-democratic situation where executive, legislative and judicial power were once all in one hand. This hand was largely the principal from which both parliament and court were gradually able to wrest power (as Josselin and Marciano correctly observe). This process, in which incidentally the common law courts came to the aid of the parliament during the constitutional crisis in the 17th century, was one, however, in which both parliament and ultimately the courts were acting as – or becoming – agents of the people. In other words, a new principal was indeed emerging in both cases, both not the one which Josselin and Marciano identify (court and parliament in their own right), namely the people.[11] Of course it would be naïve to see that historical process as one which single-mindedly sought after this goal. Clearly then, as now, self-serving individual and group interests, which had little to do with such an abstract goal, were the motor for most developments, but the rhetoric was nevertheless often enough itself expressly compatible with this goal. The fact that the resulting separation of powers in Britain is unwritten (and for that reason somewhat less precise and arguably weaker than in those countries where it is embodied in a written constitution) is an historical accident or perhaps attributable to nothing more than a matter of national style. Certainly in countries like Australia, the United States or Germany the constitutionally entrenched doctrine of a balance and sharing of powers is one which was adopted deliberately, precisely because one was aware of the problem of controlling agents endowed with substantial powers (as parliaments and administrations are), even if this awareness was not couched in more recent concepts of principal-agent theory.

(ii) Federalism

A further familiar organisational division is that in federal states between the central and state authorities. Even where there is no formal federalism (such as is found in Germany, the United States, Canada or Australia), many arrangements within supposedly unitary states will echo those in federations, whether through regional or municipal levels of government or administration or comparable structures, which are also typically present in fully fledged federations. The existence of a vertical separation of powers of perhaps as many as four levels of government and administration, on each of which the horizontal separation of powers itself may be either fully of partially represented, is a common phenomenon of state organisation. If we add supranational arrangements, such as the European Community, the number of levels relevant to a particular jurisdiction or geographical region increases further. Add specific-purpose supranational structures such as that of the European Convention of Human Rights, the Interamerican System, or the World Trade Organisation, and further levels of a vertical separation – perhaps better fragmentation – can be identified. Whether such vertical arrangements should be seen as genuine examples of principal-agent relations or whether merely an organisational division without an agency element will perhaps not always be clear. Certainly in most formal federations it may amount to heresy to suggest that the 'lower' level in the federal structure (State, *Land*, Province) is an agent of the federal (central) principal; many proponents of so called 'State's rights' would probably like to see a principal-agent relation in fact in the reverse direction. Nevertheless, it seems clear that, under some circumstances, the central government acts as a principal where, for example, a power to make conditional financial grants to the decentral units is exercised in a federation like the United States or Australia, whereby those units are required to undertake certain tasks (e.g. to pass certain laws or establish certain programs).

Whether the responsibilities of the German *Länder* or the Member States of the European Community to implement legislation of the *Bundestag* or the Council respectively really should be seen as an expression of a principal-agent relation, seems an open question.[12] In many ways, this responsibility looks similar to that of the place of the executive within the horizontal separation of powers (discussed *supra*), where the putative principal in fact has no competence which it can delegate to an agent, the putative agent's competence being derived elsewhere (from another, altogether different principal – here again the people).[13] For example, the German Federal Parliament's power to pass framework legislation which the *Länder* must incorporate and fill out through legislation of their own, and the directive-making power of the Council of the European Community, could be understood in this way, since in neither case would the 'central' legislature itself be competent directly to pass the implementing statutes. Nevertheless such arms-length arrangements do posses principal-agent characteristics of a rather special kind, but these are not unknown in the private commercial context. For example, corporate auditors are almost certainly to be seen as agents of a firm for the preparation of annual accounts or other financial statements. Nevertheless, they may well be formally obliged to do so independent of management influence and, indeed, the management of the firm will often not be legally competent to prepare such statements itself. In these cases, both in the public and in the private examples, we can see indeed the interesting phenomenon of double principals, to whom the agent (the decentralised legislature in the former, the auditors in the latter) owes different duties and for whom a task must be carried out which optimally satisfies competing – but hierarchically organised – goals.

(c) Agency within agencies

It has been asserted *supra* that the separation of powers within democratic constitutions operating under the rule of law involves the establishment of three organs of the state, parliament, judiciary and executive. These three arms can be regarded as top-level agents, not primarily – perhaps not at all (as pointed out *supra*) of one another, but rather as agents of the people. The need to use agents to achieve the goals of a democratic citizenry and to give effect to a democratic constitution seems indeed so obvious that it scarcely needs further explanation. The more complex and populous a society, the more obvious is the need for separate agents for separate tasks, just as can be observed in large private organisations. The need to employ these agents at least partly for mutual control, checks and balances also seems obvious, the greater the scope of competences conferred on each of them. The monopoly of coercion which the state as a whole exercises as the agent of the people quite clearly demands a system whereby this monopoly cannot be abused. The dispersion of power among mutually balancing agents is an effective – possibly the only effective – way to ensure this.

Each of these three agents of the people is nevertheless still confronted with highly complex tasks and, indeed, even with the further need for a dispersion of power to avoid possible abuses. This leads, as can be clearly seen in numerous models of state organisation, constitutional rules and legislation, to further levels of principal-agent relation and/or to further non-agency divisions of labour.

(i)   The legislature

The most obvious organisational division in the legislative sphere is that found in bicameral parliaments. But of course, there too, vast difference exist between systems. The constitution, role, composition and effect of, for example, the German *Bundesrat* is radically different from that of the American Senate in numerous respects. We are not concerned here with the details of these differences. Suffice it to say that almost certainly the distinction between houses in a bicameral system involves no agency relationship. Nevertheless, the division clearly plays a role within a larger principal-agent structure. On the one hand, the existence of two houses, even in non-federal systems, constitutes a splitting of agents' powers, each house being itself an agent of the people, or perhaps a particular subsection of the people (the British House of Lords might be so regarded, at least before its recent reforms, and perhaps still), in effect establishing separate agents for separate principals. The precise rules governing the interactions between the two (or possibly more) agents on behalf of two (possibly intersecting) groups of principals will certainly be the product of historical developments, as one can see from the shifting relationship over time between the House of Commons and the House of Lords in Britain. In recent decades the increasing role of the House of Lords as an investigative body in various areas of public policy might be seen as a particular expression of checks and balances between the two legislative agents, or in respect of the Government, with the benefit of reducing informational asymmetries, and thereby making other agents (the Commons or the Government) more accountable to their own principal (the electorate).

In a federal system, a second chamber on the central level might well reflect a similar agency constellation. In addition, perhaps more importantly, however, such second chambers, like the *Bundesrat*, or the United States' or Australian Senates, have been intentionally designed to reflect a different set of agency relations. The lowers houses can be seen as being legislative agents of the population as a whole, these upper houses either as (qualified) legislative agents of sub-groups of electoral principals (citizens voting directly in each of the states, as in the United States or Australia) or as (qualified) legislative sub-agents of other legislative agents, namely state parliaments (as in the case of the *Bundesrat*). In other words, the exact purpose of the principal-agent relation which is reflected in the creation of a second chamber will vary depending on the specific constitutional rules and the composition and procedures adopted in each country. Here it should also be observed that the formal constitutional rules may not say all that there is to know: Just as is the case in lower houses (see *supra*), the members of such federal upper houses may in practice see themselves less as agents for state-based principals and more as agents of their respective political parties (that is, reflecting the problem of multiple principals).

There are other divisions of labour and possible agency relationships in legislatures apart from those just mentioned. For example, committees are the backbone of virtually all well-functioning parliaments, and can be relatively easily characterised as agents of the house to which they belong. In their procedures, composition and tasks they are indeed usually designed to function just like the particular house itself. They are usually characterised by having a specialised area of focus, special rules for constituting them, rules governing their own powers and procedures (a *Geschäftsordnung* or Rules of Procedure), and – depending on their subject matter and membership – sometimes a special status which almost elevates them beyond the status of the parliament or parliamentary chamber itself; take, for example, the Senate Foreign Relations Committee in the United States, or the recent and previous parliamentary committees of enquiry into party donations in Germany. In these last specific cases, one might see examples in which the principal's control over the agent is somewhat weakened.

The parliamentary committee of enquiry is indeed an example of highly complex agency relations. A parliamentary committee of enquiry can first of all be seen to be an agent of the parliament itself. As already discussed, we know that information asymmetries are an important element of agency relations. The parliamentary committee is itself established mostly to remove or reduce such information asymmetries between the parliament and other bodies. Bodies subject of enquiry, such as the government itself (executive or administration), or persons about to be appointed to judicial office (consider, for example, congressional hearings into nominees for appointment to the US

Supreme Court) or industries or groups which the parliament has regulated or may wish to regulate, may or may not – or to varying degrees – themselves be regarded parliamentary agents. In all such enquiries the parliamentary committee, as an information-gathering agent of the parliament, is likely to come to possess more information than the parliament itself or most of its individual members, thus constituting an information asymmetry of another kind. Beyond that, the individual members of the committee can, for the most part be regarded as agents of their parties or perhaps of particular lobby groups (or both), although the extent to which this is so may well vary depending on the independence of mind and action of individuals. Between the committee as a whole and individual members, or more simply between different members of the committee among themselves, there will be further information asymmetries and, often enough, some will deliberately perpetuate or exacerbate such asymmetries. Clearly the members of such committees provide good examples of agents as the servants of two (or more) masters.

A further example, perhaps even more fundamental to the effective working of democratic parliaments is the organisational division to be found in the role of political parties; in particular, the division between government and opposition parties comes to mind. Here it would seem difficult to see an agency relation between the parliament and any or all of the parties. However, each political party clearly constitutes an agent for a particular group of citizens, and such a function is often either expressly or implicitly acknowledged in constitutional doctrine and arrangements. In addition, elected representatives will act, at least partly, as agents of their own political party.

Even more fundamental is the special agency relationship which exists between a portion of the electorate and a specific elected member of parliament (or perhaps group of members). Such an agency relationship is indeed very special because of the existence of the unrestricted mandate of parliamentarians, subject to the possibility of party influence and discipline. In this regard, the parliamentarian is effectively an agent with three principals: the people as a whole (reflected in the unrestricted mandate), the electors of the relevant district (reflected in the function as a representative) and the party. Many constitutions and parliamentary rules of procedure contain detailed provisions designed to achieve a balance between the demands of these potentially competing principals. The idea of multiple principals is, in fact, a recurring feature of state and constitutional organisation.

(ii)   The judiciary

Within the judicial arm of the state there is a wide variety of court and tribunal types, essentially distinguishable according to subject matter: constitutional, criminal, civil and administrative courts, family courts, industrial and labour courts and tribunals, environmental, land and planning courts, children's courts, valuation courts, taxation and fiscal courts and similar. The European Court of Human Rights provides a supranational example of this type of subject matter specialisation. Then, of course, there are the divisions to be found within a single court. For example, the German Constitutional Court has the two benches (*Senate*), Britain's High Court of Justice has many divisions (bearing historically colourful labels such Queen's Bench, Common Pleas, Chancery (Equity) and the like. Some such divisions represent a subdivision according to subject matter, but not necessarily. It ought also to be noted here that some specialist tribunals are, at least formally, located within the administration and not within the judicial branch, but this is also a matter which varies from jurisdiction to jurisdiction, depending in part on how pedantically the concept of separation of the judicial power is viewed. Beyond such pure divisions based mainly on subject matter, there are, of course, further divisions based on the hierarchies within court systems: chamber magistrates, magistrates courts or lower courts (the German *Amts-gerichte*), local courts, district courts, high courts, courts of appeal, circuit courts, circuit courts of appeal and supreme courts. Specifically named constitutional courts are both specialised in subject matter and part of the hierarchical structure. There is, as well, often a more or less clear organisational division within each court, but this itself will depend on the level of the court and its particular focus and subject matter. Most of the divisions referred to relate not just to subject matter, or to hierarchy for its own sake. Functional divisions are also present, for example the division between judge, jury (*Schöffen*) and, sometimes, expert witnesses (depending on the style of the judicial system as a whole, (broadly) reflecting the difference between inquisitorial or adversarial tribunals) should not be overlooked. Hierarchies are often associated with distinctions between courts of fact and courts of law, courts of review and courts of appeal or – depending on the system – even with differences of capacity, procedure, personnel and effect within one and the same court depending upon whether it can be categorised as dealing with an issue of fact (sometimes also in certain contexts referred to as 'merits') or law, or whether it is addressing a matter of appeal or review.

Despite these complex divisions and subdivisions of court structures, there scarcely seems to be any sense in which they reflect principal-agent relations. It seems entirely appropriate to view courts as a whole as agents of the constitution – and in that sense of the body politic as a principal. Perhaps individual judges might be regarded as agents of the justice system as a whole, but hardly anything more than this. In any other sense, however, it seems decidedly inappropriate to view the courts as agents, given the significance of the value of an independent judiciary. Deep constitutional principles such as the rule of law demand the formal and substantial independence of judges. Such independence stands fundamentally opposed to the idea that, for example, the judge of a lower court be characterised as an agent of a superior court.[14] It can legitimately be said that judges in general, especially those of the highest level of courts, are agents of the people – not, for example, of the parliament or the executive – for the protection of the constitution and the pursuance of constitutional values such as the rule of law and in this regard as exercising a control function towards other constitutional and political agents. The commission given to these judicial agents by their principals can, however, scarcely be specified in much more detail than this (except in the precise rules of the constitution, such as the protection of fundamental rights which are specified there). The judicial agents are given a broad brief (indeed as are the other organs of the state), and the principals do not enjoy in effect rights to instruct them in carrying out their tasks. This could, perhaps, be contrasted with those jurisdictions in which, through plebiscite or referendum – Switzerland is the most obvious, but not sole, example – legislative or executive agents or the people might be given more specific instructions concerning the fulfilment of their commissions.

(iii) The executive

Within the executive branch there are also very important divisions. Even more than those within the judicial branch, these vary considerably from legal system to legal system. The first and most obvious division is that between the political (gubernatorial) leadership and the technical administration, with vast differences between systems. The boundary is set much higher and more firmly, for example, in Germany than is the case in the United States. In the latter system, a change in the political leadership (i.e. in the person of the President) has much more wide-ranging effects on the personnel of the administrative departments than does a change of government in Germany. Wherever this boundary is set, the broad relationship between the political and administrative leadership is one of principal-agent, involving similar complexities to those existing between the directorship of a substantial private corporation and its management.

Even within the highest political leadership, there may be, and usually are, divisions of labour. The German example is useful, being relatively precisely set out in the Basic Law: the 'Federal Government' (*Bundesregierung*) consists legally of three separate entities: the Chancellor, the individual ministers and the collegial organ of the *Bundesregierung*. Among these separately definable elements there is a well established hierarchy. The Chancellor has an overriding competence to define and specify the direction of policy (the *Richtlinienkompetenz*) which binds both decisions of the Cabinet as a whole and of individual ministers, even to the extent of directing a Minister to perform a specific task (and not merely specifying the policy framework within which tasks are to be performed). After this a Minister enjoys the right to exercise authority specifically given to him or her by either the Constitution or a particular statute. Apart from such specific grants of authority, it is decisions of the collegial organ which are decisive below the level of the Chancellor's overriding competence. Finally, the Ministers are free to decide of their own accord in regard to matters which do not fall within decisions made within that hierarchy. In that sense, one can view the Federal Government (on the political level, i.e. above the normal administrative level) as in effect four different organs for various purposes. An interesting detail of this hierarchy is that although the Chancellor can direct Ministers to perform a specific task or function, it is only the Minister who may instruct the administrative officials within his or her own Ministry to carry this task through. Here the Chancellor has no competence.

Needless to say, the detailed structure of ministries and public departments, as reflected in this German example, represents a complex and highly articulated organisational division both horizontally, primarily as regards subject matter, and vertically, as regards responsibility and competence, and sometimes also as regards subject matter. More importantly, we see here also in many of these subdivisions, but not all, a highly complex pattern of agency relationships. This is obvious in the competences of the Chancellor to direct Ministers to perform a specific task. We also see, in the fact that the Chancellor is not legally competent to give instructions to the officials of individual Ministries, that constitutional and legal rules have deliberately sought to avoid the existence of agency relationships in certain circumstances. This issue will be taken up again later.

(iv)   Further divisions and agency relations within the state

It is not possible or desirable to canvass here all the possibilities within state structure which display agency characteristics. One further question of interest though concerns who the principal of the *Bundespräsident* or of the Queen of Great Britain might be. The position of a Head of State can again be seen to reflect a relation where the people act as principal. On one level, at least, this can easily be said: the German Federal President has the job of both representing Germany and its people in many situations both within Germany and abroad. The politically integrative role of the President can also be seen to be one of an agent on behalf of the society as whole – interestingly a task which can almost certainly be accomplished not only better but rather in fact solely through an agent. Systems vary very substantially, obvious in the comparison of the United States or French Presidents on the one hand with the German Chancellor or the British Monarch on the other. In all systems the Head of State itself can delegate certain functions, that is enter into a subagency relation, but the extent to which this can be done varies very greatly. Also, where as in Britain, Germany or Australia the Head of State is largely a symbolic function, a further agency relation arises through the power of the 'active' executive (Prime Minister or Chancellor) to direct the Head of State in the exercise of significant functions (e.g., all acts of the *Bundespräsident*, including speeches or interviews, must be countersigned by the Chancellor or other authorised members of the government (*Gegenzeichnung*) or the general unwritten British constitutional rule, hard-won through the civil war of the 17th Century, that the monarch is to act on and follow the advice of the Prime Minister).

The establishment of special bodies (the nomenclature varies: 'commission', 'agency', 'authority', 'office', 'bureau', '*Amt*') familiar to all systems introduces further forms of principal-agent relations. In particular, the establishment of so called 'independent' authorities, such as prosecutorial agencies, public auditors offices or central banks raises a wide range of issues going to the essence of the organisation of the state and its purposes and functions. Some of these questions will be taken up again *infra*.

4. Agency Theory and the State

Can agency theory really be applied to the state? Is it useful to do so? Its origins in microeconomics and essentially in explicit contractual relationships may suggest that an application to the state is rather wide of the mark, despite the efforts which have been exemplified earlier.[15] Certainly, not all agency scholars have confined it, for example, to explicit contractual relations. Arrow saw, for example, an implicit agency relation between the general public or community and an industrial polluter, where the polluter in effect failed to fulfil the tasks of his principal.[16] In any case, the application of agency theory to the state is by no means new. Niskanen (1971) treated the bureaucracy – or the bureaucrat – as a agent of the politician,[17] although some of his assumptions in that analysis ultimately appear rather exaggerated and have been subject to criticism.[18] More recently, Walsh (1995) has considered the question of the optimal principal-agent arrangements applicable to central bankers for the purposes of inducing socially optimal policy, viewing the bank as an agent of government policy[19] A recent illustration is provided by Bagel's treatment of the issue of administrative reform in Germany from the standpoint of agency theory and information asymmetries.[20] Agency theory has already brought insights to organisational issues primarily in the private sector and also in the public sector. Its potential in regard to the public sector has, I think, not been fully enough explored, and much may be gained from it.

Whereas explicit and negotiated contracts may provide the basis for principal-agent relations in many private and microeconomic settings,[21] this is unlikely to be the case in the agency situations within the state which I have identified. If one wishes to speak of contracts there at all, they might best be regarded as so called contracts of adhesion, 'take it or leave it' contracts which, of course, are very common in, for example, commercial retailing in respect of purchase of goods or in the transport or insurance industries in respects of services (and in the latter at least, also of principal-agent relationships). But where even contracts of adhesion involve explicit contracting, the taking on of a public office involves this only in the sense that, in deciding to take up a task or to be appointed, one knows the rules (of a constitutional or statutory kind) in advance, and explicitly (especially where there is an oath of office) or at least implicitly agrees to be bound by them. This is a rather different route to the specification of the relation of principal and agent and of the duties, responsibilities, competences and liabilities of the agent but, I suggest, nonetheless a valid one.[22]

Equally, much agency literature places a strong emphasis on the aspect of the remuneration or compensation of the agent as part of the incentive structure and control over the agent's activity and behaviour. Here again, some licence seems allowed, if one recognises that there is a wide range of incentive and influencing mechanisms. Once one agrees with Pratt and Zeckhauser that long-term relationships and reputation are to be counted among such mechanisms, the position of many actors within the structure and organisation of the state becomes easy to characterise as one of agency, and it does not then seem difficult to identify particular actors as agents.

This does not, of course, mean that each incentive or control mechanism is simply interchangeable with another, or as effective as another. Indeed it is precisely the importance of reputation among the incentives for agents within the political system that may lead to adverse outcomes for the principal or lead to principals not making the best use of the information available to them from their agents. As Swank (2000) has recently observed,[23] reputational concerns induce policy makers to be secretive, thus exacerbating informational asymmetries and increasing moral hazard, and they tend to ignore expert advice if it conflicts with their own already established and known viewpoint. Findings such as this make very clear that reputation can be an effective element in the overall package of agency incentives and control devices only if threats to reputation are genuine. The political system has historically used reputation as a substitute for the financial rewards which are available in the non-state sector; this is still the case. Without more, however, reputation provides merely a benefit for agents but no device of influence. We have seen very recently, in the course of the scandal concerning the finances of political parties in Germany, that even apparently immense reputational damage may have little or no effect on an agent's behaviour, at least under certain circumstances, bluntly illustrated by ex-Chancellor Kohl. This is arguably a very extreme case, but ought to provide food for thought in regard to agency mechanisms and the effectiveness of control in the state context. Nevertheless, there are numerous examples of failed managers in the private sector who seem to have no difficulty obtaining further engagement and indeed even substantial rewards (if only parting ones) from corporations which they have damaged. In that sense, the agency incentive and control problems on the state level may not be more substantial than those in the private sector (except perhaps that the scope of the damage which an uncorrected agent within the state might cause may be greater).

An important question, however, hanging over the application of the principal-agent paradigm to the state is that of the identity of the *principal or principals*. While it is not necessarily problematic to see a political party as a principal and its individual members as its agents – subject to some further comments below –, perhaps the idea, already stated *supra*, that the 'people' should be regarded as the principal of the Supreme Court or of some other court, of the German Federal President, of the Chancellor, of the Federal Government, of the United States President requires some further attention. My claim is that it is legitimate to identify *notional or ideal principals* in many situations where one can clearly point to the existence of agents within state structures. Indeed, the notional princip*als* may be, and often are, represented and incorporated into the underlying princip*les* of the political, constitutional and legal framework. The principle of democracy, no matter how it might be formulated in a constitutional document (or even in an unwritten constitution such as that in Britain), embodies the idea of government 'of the people, by the people, for the people'. In the declaration of the source of state authority in an expression such as 'We, the people...', one can see the establishment of a collective principal for the many agents of and in the state, from the classic separation of powers and federal or quasi-federal arrangements on down. Even though this perception is in my view legitimate, it should be borne in mind that the 'people' as a principal is a chameleon. Therefore, depending on the process and issue involved, inconsistent instructions may go to the agents.

A problem which is closely associated with the search for the *real* principal in many contexts is that the *tasks* which are allocated to such public agents also must be extrapolated from broad constitutional conceptions and ideals. In other words, the tasks are complex[24] and their definition vague. Thus it becomes difficult both for the agent to know exactly how to satisfy the principal, and even more difficult for the principal to exercise effective control over the agent. Despite this problem, it is equally clear that broadly stated constitutional principles such as that of democracy, rule of law, separation of powers, supremacy of parliament and independence of the judiciary have, over time, become more precise and more closely specified through an extensive practice and jurisprudence, so that problems in the application of agency theory do not seem insurmountable.

Turning to the benefits of an agency-theoretical analysis of relationships in the state, it should be noted that there are certainly alternative explanations for some of the phenomena of state organisation which I have described. Federalist arrangements may be an expression of principal-agent relations, but they are equally or even more an expression of the attempt to avoid jurisdictional spillovers and similar issues; nevertheless in this context principal-agent relations are part of the set of instruments selected to address such issues. In regard to the key features of agency theory analysis mentioned *supra*, state arrangements provide good illustrations. For example, the specialisation of administrative agencies – or indeed of courts – provides the opportunities for reducing uncertainty and increased predictability, subject however to classic risks of insider knowledge and information asymmetries, so that the agents power may grow vis-à-vis the principal.[25] Clark has suggested that in the private sphere the concept of fiduciary duty makes a contribution to reducing agency costs;[26] such duties play a significant, perhaps dominant role in influencing and controlling many agents in the public sector.

5.   Some Specific Issues in an Agency Analysis of the State

(a)   Multiple principals, multiple agents and serial relations

The problem of multiple principals is the problem Goldoni articulated so well in 'The Servant of Two Masters'. Stigler's now famous analysis of regulators and legislators as providers of goods in a political market points to this problem in the state context. Politicians may, on one level at least, be agents of the constitution (of the *polis* as a whole, as already indicated), but at the same time they may be (or appear to be) agents of special interest groups which seek a particular outcome, service or 'product'. The key task of the constitutional and other rules which govern the former of these agency relations and of other institutions or agents, is to seek to ensure that responsibilities under one agency arrangement are not compromised by meeting obligations arising from another. In certain contexts, express legal rules seek to institutionalise precisely this outcome (for example, disqualification or exclusion from holding other offices). Obligations of disclosure of the interests of politicians aim in the same direction, by attempting to remove or reduce informational asymmetries which may engender moral hazard and lead to frustration of the goal sought by the formal principal. The problem of multiple principals can, in fact, be seen in the private sector as well: it is indeed not usually clear whether the chief executive officer is acting as the agent of the board of directors, all shareholders,[27] the majority shareholders or perhaps acting largely (solely?) in its own self interest.

Just as there can be multiple principals, so also there can be multiple agents. Even a single individual may have two (or more) (partly inconsistent) goals, which are to be achieved through two (or more) agents. For example, one may seek to pursue a specific project (by, e.g. seeking to obtain a building approval from the relevant authority or through a specialised tribunal) and at the same time have rather more general goals and values (e.g. the protection of basic rights, such as those to property, which will be protected in, say, the constitutional court). Such goals of a single individual may easily conflict in an immediate situation, where, for example, neighbours take advantage of the guarantee of basic rights in order to attempt to prevent the building project because it interferes with them, rights which the proponent of the project may itself wish to take advantage of in another situation. In other words, for the applicant, there may be a conflict between his or her own short- and long-term goals and values which can be pursued through different agents within the state. Again this is no different from similar problems in the private sector: The chief executive officer of an oil company may instruct one agent (the advertising department) to promote an ecologically friendly company image, and another agent (e.g., the waste disposal division) to reduce its costs to a minimum.

State organisational arrangements are typically pyramidal, involving often lengthy chains of agency relations. This may occur also in private organisations. Some of the rules and structures discussed earlier, such as the separation of powers and the distribution of responsibilities, suggest efforts on the part of constitutional designers to attempt to shorten or break these chains (at least as regards subject matter or type or activity). Alternatively or additionally they may perhaps reflect an attempt to systematise parallel chains of agency responsibility.

(b)   Limits on the creation of agency relations

As has been pointed out, the existence of an organisational division within state organisation should not lead to the view that each unit must necessarily be linked to another by an agency relationship. While it is true that each unit is usually involved in a principal-agent relationship with one or more other units, there are clearly also restrictions on the establishment of agency relations between certain types of units. In addition, certain agents are limited in their ability to become principals to other agents. Such prohibitions are by no means unknown in classical agency relations in firms and private organisations. For example, fiduciary duties including obligations of confidentiality, exclusive dealing arrangements and possibly aspects of insider trading rules, may all possibly restrict the potential for creating agency relationships. Nevertheless, restrictions on the establishment of agency relations seem to play a very important role in the organisation of the state in accordance with certain principles such as the rule of law, separation of powers or federalism. Some restrictions relate to limiting agency relations between specific actors, or placing limits on the creation of agency relations by certain actors.

(i)		Limiting agency relations between specific actors
Under the German Basic Law, municipal authorities enjoy a constitutional guarantee of autonomy (Art. 28 GG). This ensures that in certain spheres their freedom of action cannot be removed, restricted or directed. While the precise content of the guarantee varies over time and cannot be precisely defined, it does entail that municipal government cannot, at least in certain fields, be regarded as merely the agent of the *Land* and that there exists a protection against the removal of certain competences entirely. Local government enjoys then a schizophrenic relationship with both *Land* and Federal government. In respect of some of its activities it is purely the agent of the higher level of government. Here there may still be some limits on the level of control which the central authority can exercise over the performance of tasks assigned to the local level, restricting the central government to examining the legality and appropriateness of an action, but not allowing control over the methodology of carrying it out. In other matters, municipal government may be subject to detailed direction of how it should perform given tasks, although such direction may find its limit at the point where the minimum constitutional protection of local government cuts in, for example in respect of its internal organisational autonomy.

A further example from the German context is the guarantee of *Länder* autonomy vis-à-vis the central State within the framework of the 'federation principle' contained within the Basic Law. This can act as a brake on the creation of a principal-agent relation between the central government and the *Länder*. Here again, this is rather schizophrenic. The very extensive competences of the Federal Parliament to enact framework legislation which the *Länder* are obliged to fill out through their own legislation clearly reflects a type of principal-agent relation, similar to that existing between the European Community and the Member States in regard to Community directives, as observed *supra*. In both cases there are enforcement procedures devoted not primarily to the method of satisfying the obligation but to considering the legal adequacy and conformity of the measures adopted (in Germany, the *Bundesaufsicht*). Again within the German structure, the *Länder* clearly occupy an agency role in regard to the administration of federal law in numerous spheres where the federal Parliament has exclusive legislative authority. Here too, the supervision is restricted to scrutiny of the legal conformity with the relevant statute (*Bundesaufsicht*). In certain other spheres the agency relation takes on a different character when the Länder carry out tasks specifically commissioned by the Federal Government (*Bundesauftragsverwaltung*). In respect of these tasks the Federal authorities may, under certain circumstances, also direct the Länder as to how the task is to be conducted (*Weisungsgebundenheit*).

(ii)   Limits on the creation of agency relations by certain actors

Restrictions on becoming a principal. Sometimes state actors are obliged to carry out the tasks allocated to them and are themselves not permitted to employ agents to perform the tasks for them. One classic formulation of such a rule can be found in the Latin maxim, *delegatus non potest delegare* (a delegate may not sub-delegate). I have already alluded to the central problem of the control of agents and the desire and need that they act in the interests of the principal. This issue becomes particularly crucial where the coercive power of the state may be being exercised. It has already been pointed out that that the mechanisms of influence and control within state structures may be often less direct and decisive than those in private organisations, relying heavily on the role of reputation rather than on financial incentives. Thus we have seen a certain centralisation of responsibility and liability, which concentrates (or should concentrate) the effect on an individual's reputation. The well-known (but often disregarded) concept of 'ministerial responsibility' reflects the idea of the principal's taking responsibility for the agent's errors (perhaps precisely because the principal allocated tasks to the agent in the first place), even though this means of control is admittedly weak. The rule against sub-delegation is an attempt to strengthens this methodology of control by establishing a special rule for contexts where the mere attribution of responsibility for an eventual error does not suffice. In other words, the risks associated with lack of control over agents are intended to be excluded completely.

Restrictions on becoming an agent or on the competences of agents. A number of rules or structure have already been referred to which impose limits on the freedom of an actor within state institutions to become an agent, or at least to become an agent of a particular kind. The unrestricted mandate of elected politicians, for example, in effect prevents a parliamentarian from being bound to act or vote in a certain way (apart from the effects of party discipline). Rules concerning the disqualification criteria for public office holders, in particular rules concerning secret commissions, bribes and the like have a similar function. Another type of restriction arises from limits on the competences of agents. Such limits are clearly present in the case of the strict separation of powers. A further example is provided by the concept of 'caretaker government' during an election campaign or following a lost election (until the new government can be sworn into office).

(iii)   How much control over agents is allowed within state organisation?
How much freedom may or should an agent be able to claim? Is it still legitimate to assert that there is an agency relationship, if the principal can not only direct an agent to perform a task but also to instruct the agent as to how it is to be carried out. As has already been mentioned above, the relationship between, for example central (*Land*) government and municipal government in Germany is characterised by two relatively distinct types of supervisory competence, legal supervision and content supervision. Which of these applies in any given case is a function of the subject matter, the formulation of the enabling act and whether the degree of supervision would amount to an interference with the guarantee of municipal autonomy under the Basic Law. Again, the representatives of the *Länder* in the *Bundesrat* are capable of being fully directed in their voting decisions by the government of the *Land* which they represent. Are they still meaningfully described as agents when their capacity for independent action has, in effect, been reduced to zero?

In the case of so called independent agencies, such as those referred to earlier, other questions concerning the extent of control arise. It has been made clear that numerous agency relations have been specifically structured (or even disallowed) under constitutional and other rules in order to avoid some of the classic problems of control over agents, or to achieve effective control, especially in the light of the danger and costs associated with the allocation of state powers. Such powers are, not always but often, more comprehensive and therefore more subject to the risk of abuse than the powers of private organisations. The latter are, as well, usually subject to ultimate supervision by state authority, even if in some circumstances this may be difficult; arms of the state can be subject only to other arms of the state to the extent that this is specifically provided for or understood as part of the constitutional order. In certain situations it is clearly desirable that certain constitutional agents not be subject to the possibility of day to day interference in the exercise of their functions. The courts provide a good example of this, and this is achieved by the principle of judicial independence and separation of powers, such that the parliament can intervene only via the form of a legislative amendment, the executive hardly at all. In the case of other authorities for which a certain level of independence from day to day political interference might be desirable, there still remains the issue as to whether, within the complex patterns of state organisation complete independence is either possible or desirable. There seems to be no compelling reason, for example, why 'independent' regulatory boards or authorities should be free from supervisory control through the courts, at least in regard to the legality of their activity and behaviour. The same can also be said of state financial organisations, such as central banks.[28]

6. Conclusions

In conclusion, it is important to say that (aspects of) agency theory have been applied here primarily to *organisational divisions, boundaries and structures* within the state. This by no means exhausts the potential for the application of this theory to the state. There are certainly many other aspects of state organisation which could also bear the application of agency theory, some of which I have fleetingly mentioned (e.g. the nature of constraints on state actors which arise from constitutional rules such as those concerning basic rights, or the sanctions available for controlling or influencing different types of agents).

In many respects the quality of constitutional arrangements and state organisation might be judged by the nature of the organisational divisions and the structure of principal-agent relations within the state. It is banal to observe that without the independence of the judiciary the observance of the rule of law and the security of democracy is at risk. We do not need agency theory to tell us this. Perhaps, however, the role of the courts as part of the control and incentive mechanism in regard to other agents (whether generally of the constitution or the people, or more particularly of specific organs within the more detailed framework of state institutions) can underline this point and, by expressing it in a different way, give it new life.

An application of principles of agency-theory may provide insights in respect of the far-reaching changes which have been made for the provision of public services. The extensive privatisation and deregulation which have occurred in numerous systems world-wide over the past 20 years provide ample opportunity for a consideration of the standard questions with which agency theory has been always been concerned: control and influence by the principal, the problem of informational asymmetries between principal and agent (adverse selection), and the problem of moral hazard. In many ways, however, such rearrangements involve just the replacement of at least implicit principal-agent relations with explicit ones, in the form of explicit contracts.[29] The central question is whether the substitute agency arrangement achieves more or less than the previous one. As a rule it is not the case that a completely different concept is being employed. Both those who are in favour of such a change in a given case, and those who oppose it, ought to be aware of this. This would contribute usefully to making the discussion somewhat more dispassionate and less ideological. An interesting illustration is provided in regard to the problem of information asymmetry. Feld and Kirchgässner (2000) have recently concluded that direct democracy, such as in the Swiss example, may provide incentives for citizens – our principals – to collect more information or be better informed.[30] From the perspective of agency theory, this might be seen as a two-edged sword. On the one hand, direct democracy may indeed reduce information asymmetries between principals and agents. On the other hand, one of the key reasons that agents – politicians – are employed in the political process is precisely to reduce social and individual costs of information gathering and dissemination, and of transactions and negotiations (just as in the private sector). In that sense it would seem at least incautious to regard direct democratic methods as a solution to agency problems (except to the extent that one might be said to be simply abolishing the agency relation altogether!).

More generally, incentive and control mechanisms as understood within agency theory as fundamental elements of efficient and effective organisational arrangements. This is equally true of measures for reducing informational asymmetries. In the light of the current neoliberal vogue, which has as one of its consequences the calling into question of many long-accepted features of sound state practice and arrangements, it is seems useful to be able to rely on a generally ideologically neutral concept such as agency theory to support arguments for increased – not decreased – availability of information for and from government (such as through freedom of information legislation), of increased – not reduced – opportunities for access by citizens to bureaucratic procedures and decision-making, and for sufficient resourcing and support for elements within the state apparatus which ensure that controls on agents – checks and balances – are adequate and effective. The recent German party donation affair referred to *supra* provides an outstanding example of where an agent (a party) has completely departed from the tasks set by its principal, and where incentive and control mechanisms clearly failed. If this occurred within the firms owned by some of the anonymous – and possibly illegal – donors, it would be regarded as grossly inefficient. So it is within principal-agent arrangements within the state.

NOTES

1   See, e.g. Josselin and Marciano (2000); Merville and Osborne (1990); Witt (1992).
2   It should be pointed out here that not all divisions of labour reflect this kind of principal-agent relation, except perhaps to the extent that, for different purposes, both A and B are both principals and agents: In respect of one task, A is B's principal, in respect of another task B is A's principal.
3   The simplest variant here is that of one principal and numerous agents with different specialisations, that is, one essential hierarchical organisational division, and numerous horizontal divisions of labour. The latter need display no agency relation; this could be said to be the case in the horizontal division of powers in the state (see *infra*).
4   See Fama (1980, 290-292).
5   This is sometimes referred to as 'adverse selection', although the term seems ultimately more suited to the insurance context.
6   See Jensen and Meckling (1976) on agency cost and mechanisms for reducing them; they emphasise the role of the legal franework among other elements in the setting of these costs.
7   See Fama (1980, 296ff.).
8   This must, of course, be qualified in respect of countries with a directly elected executive head, such as France or the United States, so that two branches within the separation of powers achieves direct democratic legitimacy, the administration, however, only in respect of its highest officer (expanded somewhat in a few systems, usually restricted to local government, where a collective executive may be directly elected).
9   5 U. S. (1 Cranch) 137, 2. L.Ed.2d 60 (1803).
10 It should be observed that the additional proposition by Josselin and Marciano (2000) that the decision of the US Supreme Court in *Erie, Lackawann Railroad* Co. v. *Tompkins* 304 US 64, to the effect that there was no federal common law, reinforced its own power, misses the point completely that the court thereby restricted both its own powers and those of all federal courts vis-à-vis state courts, and suggests that the authors do not understand the meaning of the concept of common law. The Court's decision strengthens in particular

the position of the Supreme Courts of each of the states in respect of matters of (state) common law.

11 It is true that, in discussing historical developments Josselin and Marciano (2000) do refer to the people as a 'new principal' (p. 224), but fail to articulate the consequences of this for constitutional structures in more detail. In particular, their proposition, quoting Madison, that the people 'could alter constitutions as they pleased' (p. 224), needs careful qualification, both in respect of special rules concerning amendment or, in the case of certain other constitutions such as the German Basic Law, elements which are regarded as unalterable.

12 The over-simplified but confusing construction of a principal-agent relationship within the European Community presented by Josselin and Marciano (2000, 227), fails to state precisely in respect of what tasks, based on what competences and on granting what powers these agency relations were established.

13 In this regard, one can agree with Josselin and Marciano's (2000) conclusion concerning the emergence of a strong federal level in the United States (p. 224).

14 The only possible exception to the proposition that, within judicial institutions, no principal-agents relations are to be found (or at least in principle unacceptable), is that legal representatives acting before the court are sometimes regarded as agents of the courts in relation their role and position. This view must, however be regarded cautiously and subject to strict limits.

15 Note 1 *supra*.

16 Arrow (1985, 39). I myself have some difficulty in being convinced that this is appropriately characterised as an agency relation (in contrast to the relationship between the public and the environmental regulatory authority), but Arrow's example nevertheless clearly shows that he sees no need for explicit contracts.

17 William A. Niskanen Jr. (1971).

18 E.g., that the bureaucrat is a monopolist and that the politician (state) has no choice ('take it or leave it'situation); see Bagel (1999, 5) including further refs.

19 Walsh (1995).

20 Bagel (1999).

21 Clark says that in corporations this is anyway not the case (1985, 59).

22 It should be noted that Clark (1985, 71) allows for reliance on the notion of implict contracts, but counsels caution in so doing.

23 Swank (2000).

24 See e.g. Bagel (1999, 14).

25 See e.g. Josselin and Marciano (2000, 222), concerning the growth of specialised knowledge in the development of the common law courts in England.

26 Clark (1985, 71ff.).

27 Clark says no (1985, 56-59).

28 See, e.g. Fabian Amtenbrink (1999); de Haan and Eijffinger (2000).

29 See, e.g. Wallerath (1997).

30 Feld and Kirchgässner (2000).

REFERENCES

Amtenbrink, Fabian (1999), *The democratic accountability of Central Banks – A comparative study of the European Central Bank,* Oxford: Hart.

Arrow, Kenneth J. (1985), 'The Economics of Agency', in John W. Pratt and Richard J. Zeckhauser, *Principals and Agents – The Structure of Business,* Boston: Harvard Business School Press, pp. 37-51.

Bagel, Ida (1999*), Die Verwaltungsreform aus vertragstheoretischer Perspektive,* Berichte aus der Volkswirtschaft, Aaachen: Shaker Verlag.

Clark, Robert C. (1985), 'Agency Costs versus Fiduciary Duties', in John W. Pratt and Richard I. Zeckhauser, *Principals and Agents – The Structure of Business,* Boston: Harvard Business School Press, pp. 55-79.

de Haan, Jakob and Sylvester C. W. Eijffinger (2000), 'The Democratic Accountability of the European Central Bank – A Comment on Two Fairy-tales', *Journal of Common Market Studies,* **38**, 393-407.

Fama, E. F. (1980), 'Agency Problems and the Theory of the Firm', *Journal of Political Economy,* **88**, 288-307.

Feld, Lars P. and Gebhard Kirchgässner (2000), 'Direct Democracy, Political Culture, and the Outcome of Economic Policy – A Report on the Swiss Experience', *European of Journal Political Economy,* **16**, 287-306.

Jensen, M. C. and W. H. Meckling (1976), 'Theory of the Firm – Managerial Behaviour, Agency Costs and Ownership Structure', *Journal of Financial Economics,* **3**, 305-360.

Josselin, Jean-Michel and Alain Marciano (2000), 'Displacing your Principal – Two Historical Cases Studies of Some Interest for the Constitutional Future of Europe', *European Journal of Economics,* **10**, 217-233.

Merville, Larry J. and Dale K. Osborne (1990), 'Constitutional Democracy and the Theory of Agency', *Constitional Political Economy,* **1**, 21-47.

Niskanen, William A. Jr. (1971), *Bureaucracy and Representative Government,* Chicago: Aldine-Atherton.

Swank Otto H. (2000), 'Policy Advice, Secrecy, and Reputational Concerns', *European Journal of Political Economy,* **16**, 257-271.

Wallerath, Maximilan (1997), 'Kontraktmanagement und Zielvereinbarungen als Instrument der Verwaltungsmodernisierungen', *Die Öffentliche Verwaltung,* 57-67.

Walsh, Carl E. (1995), 'Optimal Contracts for Central Bankers', *American Economic Review,* **85**, 150–167.

Witt, Ulrich (1992), 'The Emergence of the Protective Agency and the Constitutional Dilemma', *Constitutional Political Economy*, **3**, 255-266.

17. Constitutionalism Beyond the Nation State

Dieter Grimm

Until recently it was indubitable that constitutions refer to the state. They had been invented for two purposes. One was to subject public power, which had existed out of its own right or had been legitimised by divine right before, to the consent of the governed. The other one was to legalise and thereby to limit public power, which, before, had been the source of law without being itself subjected to law. Hence the constitution had two functions: the regulation of public power – this is the rule-of-law-element of modern constitutionalism; and the legitimisation of public power by popular consent – this is the democratic element of modern constitutionalism. Constitutions could fulfil these functions only when they emanated not from the state, but from the people, and when they ranked higher than the laws emanating from the state, so that government acts could claim legitimacy only when performed on the basis and within the framework of the constitution.

Public power, in turn, used to be state power. Both terms had become synonymous by the time when modern constitutionalism took shape. This had not always been the case. In former times, public power was fragmented. A number of independent public powers coexisted, referring to persons, not to a territory. Many of them were exercised as an annex to a status which would now be called private, such as land ownership. This was also true for the princes who differed from other authorities only in the number and range of the public powers (prerogatives) they held. It was the necessity of ending the religious civil wars of the sixteenth and seventeenth century and of restoring peace that brought forth a concentration of the scattered public powers in the hands of the princes. Two notions, inexistent before, now characterise the new situation. One is 'sovereignty', meaning that there is a higher and impermeable public power over a territory and its inhabitants from which all other powers derive. The other is 'state', describing the holder of this power. Hence, it was the concentration of public power which constituted the state, and public power was state power.

The concentration of the scattered prerogatives into one public power was the precondition of the constitution, understood as a single normative document designed to regulate the establishment and exercise of government. The fact that the new constitutions immediately started out to divide the single public power among various branches of government did not imply by any means a return to the old system. Separation of powers leaves the existence of one single and highest public power untouched. It operates, not on the level of power of the state, but on the level of power within the state. In view of the experience of monarchical absolutism, its exercise is organised in such a way that the abuse of public power becomes unlikely. No branch of government disposes of public power in total. Each branch possesses only a share of public power which belongs to the state as such and is limited to the territory of the state.

Public power always included the right to self-limitation. The constitution itself is an internal self-limitation of power. Likewise, external self-limitations are possible. Here the means are not constitutions, but treaties. States can bind themselves mutually by way of treaty. Treaties are governed by public international law. In order to acquire internally binding force they must be transformed into domestic law. Without such a transformation, treaties bind the state in its external relations, but do not create rights or obligations within the state. Thus, no foreign or international power had the right to exercise public power within another state. Under such circumstances the question of extending the achievement of constitutionalism beyond the state did not arise. There was a dualism of internally effective domestic law and externally effective public international law, but nothing in between.

Things changed with the founding of the European Communities. For the first time, states agreed to transfer sovereignty rights to a supranational entity. That entity's law has direct effect within the Member States and trumps domestic law. That broke up the old dualism between domestic law and international law. Community law stems from an independent source and claims priority even over the Member States' constitutions. Still, the new entity cannot be called a state. On the one hand, it has too many sovereignty rights to be just one international organisation among others. On the other hand, it does not possess enough sovereignty rights to form a state. In particular, the European Union lacks the capability of determining its own legal foundations, the so-called primary Community law. The Member States retain this right, and they exercise it – not by way of legislation but by concluding international treaties. Still, the founding of the European Communities had the effect that state and public power were no longer identical. They fell apart. In its wake, it soon became clear that the demand for regulation was not bound to the state, but had to follow public power when the benefits of constitutionalism were to be preserved. What was in need of being legitimised and limited was not the state as such, but only in so far as public power was concentrated there.

Yet, the European Communities never lacked such regulation. They were created by international treaty. That treaty did not restrict itself to bringing forth a new political entity, free to determine its own organisation and activities. The treaty defined the purpose and the competencies of the Community, established its organs, regulated the recruitment of agents operating within the organs, limited their powers, named the instruments the organs were allowed to use in order to carry out their task, regulated the procedures to be observed and contained provisions on the relationship between the Community and the Member States and, to a certain extent, also the relationship vis-à-vis its citizens. All these are provisions which nation states enshrine in their constitutions. The treaty also functions as higher law of the Community. The Community derives its power from the treaty. Acts of Community organs are only legitimate when performed on the basis and within the limits of the treaty, and the organs themselves have no right to change or amend the legal foundations according to which they operate.

All this taken into account, one can conclude that the treaties fulfil the function which, within the nation states is fulfilled by the constitution. For this reason, it is not without justification that scholars of European Community law early began to call the Treaty of Rome the constitution of the European Community. This statement contrasts, however, with the growing demand for a European Constitution in the public discourse. Suggested as early as 1984 by the European Parliament, the constitution is meanwhile on the agenda of national governments and the European Convention as well. Both positions apparently contradict each other. Either the treaties are the constitution of the European Community. In this case, one can discuss improvements of that constitution, but – since there is one already – it does not make sense to call for one. Or the treaties are not a constitution. In this case, it is possible to argue that the Community should have one.

Yet, the contradiction disappears, and both positions gain a relative justification when the two basic elements of modern constitutionalism are taken into account, the rule-of-law-element which is fully developed in the European Union, and the democratic element which is still underdeveloped. In other words: the treaties have all necessary elements of a constitution but one: They do not emanate from or are attributable to the people as the ultimate source of legitimate public power. Rather, it is the Member States which created the Union and retain the power to amend or abolish its legal foundations. They continue to be the so-called 'masters of the treaties'. Whereas nation states give themselves a constitution, the European Union receives its constitution from outside. Democratic constitutions are the result of auto-determination of a society as to the mode and form of its political unity. The present 'constitution' of the European Union is hetero-determined.

To be sure, we know of constitutions that were adopted by the members of a newly created political entity by way of treaty. Still, this is not the same. In those cases, the treaty was only the origin of the constitution, the way in which the constitution was brought forth. But with the conclusion of the treaty its character as treaty was consumed. The decisions about the future mode and form were handed over to the political entity itself. From that moment on, it determined its own fate. The founding states, when they remain in existence, may retain a share in these decisions, but not in their capacity as 'masters' of the constitution, but as members of an organ of the newly founded state. In the European Union the Member States are also represented in an organ, the Council. But the Council neither has nor participates in constitution-making power. That power still belongs to the states as such and requires unanimity.

Hetero-determination, therefore is the only element that separates the treaty from the constitution. The 'pouvoir constituant' is not handed over from the original founders to the society of the new foundation; rather, it remains with the founders. The source of public power in the European Union are not the European citizens, but the Member States. For this reason, it is only logical that the European Parliament is not the central organ of the Union. The Council is the central organ. If the demand for a European constitution means more than making the treaties look like a constitution or reforming the institutions of the Union, the consequence is to add the missing element.

Decisions of this breadth should be taken in view of the consequences. The immediate consequence of adopting a constitution in the full sense, i.e. adding the only missing element that separates the treaties from a constitution, would turn the European Union from a confederation into a state. For it is this element that makes the difference between the Union and a state: self-determination on the mode and form of the political unity which is characteristic for the state, and hetero-determination as far as the legal foundations are concerned, which is characteristic for a confederation. The question of a European constitution in the true sense of the word therefore is the question of a European federal state. Whoever wants a European constitution should know that he or she will get a European state. Hence, everything depends on the answer to the question whether a European state would be desirable or not.

Since the European constitution is demanded in the name of democracy, the first test of desirability is, whether the European Union would be more democratic after its full constitutionalisation than before. Here, much depends on the understanding of democracy, to be more precise: on a more formal or a more substantial understanding of democracy. No doubt, the European Union could be construed according to the model of national democracies with an elected parliament which – different from the present one – would be the central legitimising organ, with all the functions national parliaments have. The Council would be a sort of a second chamber of the parliament. The Commission might act as European government, and perhaps there might even be a European president.

However, it is doubtful whether this would, at the same time, enhance democracy in a substantive understanding. The doubts stem from the fact that well functioning democracies cannot be established on the level of state organs alone. A democratic organisational structure is, of course, indispensable for democracy. It is not sufficient though. The democratic state has societal preconditions. It must be based on a societal substructure which enables a constant feedback between the sovereign and its representatives. Only such a structure creates real, not merely formal accountability. What needs to be in place is the existence of intermediate forces between state and society, such as political parties, interest groups, citizens' movements etc. All these do not, or hardly, exist at the European level. It is not difficult to predict a change as soon as the European Union turns into a state. But there is a further precondition of well-functioning democracies: They are in need of a society which is capable of communicating about their own concerns in a discursive manner. A democratic process in lack of such discourse is hardly democratic at all.

Discourses of that sort can be found in nation-states, not in the European Union. There are no European communication-media, there is no true transnational European public discourse, and there is no European general public. All this is, however, the indispensable precondition of democratic constitutionalism. Rather, fifteen nations discuss European matters in national perspective only. European discourse does exist at the level of experts and of representatives of strong and organised interests, but does not extend beyond this sphere. Yet, democracy is not a matter of elites, but of society as a whole. It is true that one should not underestimate the knock-off effect of state institutions being ahead of societal conditions. But in the European Union with, at present, a population of 370 million, divided among fifteen member states with eleven languages of which everyone is a minority language, the conditions are particularly unfavourable. Switzerland, the United States, also India and South Africa are no proof to the contrary.

It is, therefore, likely that the European Union, after its full constitutionalisation and transformation into a state, would for quite some time be a self-supporting institution farther away from its societal basis than now. Therefore, the basic decisions should, for the time being, remain where they can be democratically controlled and accounted for: on the member-state level. At the same time, the legal foundation of the Union should remain a treaty, rather than become a constitution. All the necessary reforms of the European institutions are not affected by this difference. None of them depends on the transformation of a treaty into a constitution. Everything can take effect within the framework of a treaty. A European constitution in the full sense of the word is unlikely to bridge the gap between institutions and society. The legitimacy brought forth by a constitution would to a large degree be a fictitious one, much more than is the case within nation states.

This is but one reason to refrain from fully constituionalising the European Union and thereby turning it into a state. There is still another one. The European Union is the most important political innovation of the past century. It was an ingenious idea to preserve the traditional units and allow them at the same time a close cooperation under conditions where many problems can no longer be effectively solved within the national frame. At the same time it avoids the shortcomings of international organisations, mainly with respect to the enforcement of rules and to the adjudication of conflicts. The European Union has not yet been copied, but it seems highly attractive for other parts of the world. It is a model for the future. It does not render the state superfluous. But it gives the state a new role in a changing world order. Constitutionalisation of the Union in the full sense of the term would sacrifice the very features that make the Union so innovative and attractive.

In this sense, one can conclude, on the one hand, that the constitution in its full meaning is bound to the state and cannot be transferred to entities like the European Union without altering their nature. But this does not mean, on the other hand, that supranational political bodies like the Union are barred from the benefits of modern constitutionalism. As far as the rule-of-law-element is concerned – government of laws and not of men – it is entirely applicable to the Union. But it does not depend on adopting a European constitution. The treaties fulfil this function as a quasi-constitution. The democratic element is more complicated to deal with. The Union can hardly be democratised without a continuing responsibility of the Member States. This makes a shared democracy necessary for which the treaties are the adequate legal basis. A constitution would reduce rather than enhance democracy.

18. Comment

Anne van Aaken[1]

It is a great honour to be asked to comment on Dieter Grimm. In summary, Grimm's main points are the following[2] Grimm agrees with scholars of Positive Constitutional Economics that the EU has not yet a constitution. Why so? The European Treaties are treaties between member states not a constitution legitimated by the people themselves.[3] Grimm then asks his crucial normative questions: Do we want a European constitution and under what circumstances it is advisable to have one? Grimm denies the desirability of a European constitution for the moment. He argues as follows: Due to a lack of a common language, there is no European political communication and discourse through European media. Lacking a genuine European political public and therefore democratic control, a constitution legitimised by the people would therefore be an imaginary resp. feint constitution creating institutions without democratic backing.

I take Dieter Grimms' arguments very serious, as indeed the lack of public control due to a lack of a European public would provoke the danger of feint legitimisation through constitutionalism. Political loyalties have indeed remained mainly national. Even though there exists a single European Parliament, one cannot yet talk of a single European electorate with which it can connect. Most important EU decisions require unanimity among the member-states. Few, if any, such decisions would survive 15 referendums in 15 countries – and in more still, if the EU further expands. Given the chance, German voters might well have rejected the Maastricht treaty in 1993, torpedoing the Euro before its launch. A referendum on whether to adopt the new currency has divided Denmark. A referendum on enlargement might produce a 'no' vote in Germany now; the same might happen in Austria. Hence the rising enthusiasm among some governments for a European constitution, as a more manageable way to bolster the EU's legitimacy. They think it could give the Union a public face that voters liked and trusted.[4] Opinion polls suggest the EU public likes the idea, too.

Nevertheless, considering the example of Switzerland, I would like to put forward another hypothesis. I would like to answer Grimm's normative question otherwise: Yes, there should be a constitution beyond the nation-state in Europe. To make my point, I would like to stress three main arguments.

(1) History has known nations by will (Willensnation), which lack one common language resp. common culture or identity. Switzerland is the best self-declared example of this type. A short survey of Swiss constitutional history and comparisons of identities in EU and Switzerland thus helps to highlight what I view as the two crucial questions in the current debate about the EU's future path: what are necessary conditions for the identity of a nation and what kind of identity is ex ante necessary for a constitution?

(2) My second argument focusses on the further question of what kind of institutional balances and fine-tuning are necessary for legitimating constitutionalism in a nation of will characterised by linguistic and cultural diversity. I do agree with Dieter Grimm that 'unification' or centralisation in one form or another needs to be counterbalanced through more democratic participation. Unification on the one hand requires enhanced control of political agents by their principals on the other. An efficient form of this might be a double legitimisation both by the member states and the citizens of these member states, as it is the case in Switzerland.

(3) My third argument will be that constitutions as symbols function through formation of preferences in the long run. If at the time the constitution is promulgated, we would find a nation of will, we might, after a while and assuming widespread acceptance, a nation of identity! This third argument goes against a basic assumption of the neoclassical economic approach to the subject matter, as economist normally take preferences as given. This premise might not be advisable for subjects as Constitutions in transition or constitutions for supranational bodies as the EU.[5]

I would like to develop my arguments following Peter Häberle, who has considered the Swiss example as a model for Europe[6], thereby stressing the institutional arrangements, which could lead to a stable state. Having lived for quite a while in Switzerland myself, I will provide some arguments why I do want to take the Swiss constitution as a role model for a European constitution. Reading Swiss constitutional history[7] is almost like reading EU history – though until now the latter is not a *constitutional* history. Switzerland has had a constitution in addition to those of the *nation-states* of the cantons. As already mentioned, Switzerland in its own self-perception is a nation of will, not of culture or language. Switzerland with a population of about 6.5 million people has four official languages, making the often cited problem of the European languages seem exaggerated, as the ratio of people to languages is much better in the EU (eleven official languages and about 375 million people).[8] Despite all this, Dieter Grimm takes Switzerland as an example not be compared to the EU, as in his view there had been a national identity before the arrive of constitutionalism in Switzerland – a hypothesis, I would like to shed critical light on by giving a short survey of Swiss constitutional history.

In 1291 there was the Rütli-Oath, an agreement of defense aid, by which the cantons pledged mutual assistance against all outside enemies. This pact was the foundation of a Swiss Confederation. The cantons as nation-states remained to be part of the Holy Roman Empire. There was neither a Swiss nationality nor free movement of people or goods. The heads of nation met in irregular periods. In the westfelic peace of 1648 the cantons/states became independent from the Holy Roman Empire. The then 13 cantons of the Helvetic Association had no central government; each had its own army; religious antagonisms still prevailed; the rural cantons were suspicious of the towns; and the small cantons were jealous of the larger ones.

In 1798 Napoleon decreed a Constitution for Switzerland, which was similar to the French Constitution: Switzerland was built as a centralised state with a Swiss nationality (Art. 19) and free movement of goods and persons. The cantons lost their status as states, the power to tax was centralised and all cantons got equal status (which had not been the case before). The result was war and discontent between the former states.

Therefore, a second, federalist Constitution was promulgated in 1802 which gave independence and the power to tax back to the states. A referendum was held on the constitution, employing a dubious scheme: abstentions were counted as approvals. When the result was counted, out of a total ballot of 330.000 citizens, 92.000 had rejected, 72.000 had approved the constitution. However, given 167.000 abstentions, the constitution was declared the new law of the land. Maybe that 'trick' is worth considering for an EU-Constitution?! In the end, that constitution never came into force because of the prevailing civil war. When the Mediation Act by Napoleon that reinforced federalist structures had disappeared with himself, its place was taken by a new Federal Pact that once again established Switzerland as a confederation of sovereign states united only for common defense and the maintenance of internal order. The formulation and execution of a united foreign policy, however, remained impossible. In addition, the Swiss were separated by legal barriers because each canton had its own laws, currency, postal service, weights and measures, and army. The right to reside freely in any one canton had also ended with the Mediation Act, and therefore the inhabitants of each canton regarded the inhabitants of the other cantons as nationals of different countries. Furthermore, civil liberties were almost nonexistent, and religious differences reappeared.

Until 1848 there were several movements for a Swiss union. As within Germany, the reason was primarily an ideological one; i.e. the efforts were driven by liberal, not primarily national motives. In 1845, the deep religious and political divisions led to the formation of a separatist defensive league of Roman Catholic cantons known as the Sonderbund (special Union), comprising Lucerne, Uri, Schwyz, Unterwalden, Zug, Fribourg, and Valais. In July 1847 the Diet, representing the other cantons, declared the Sonderbund to be incompatible with the Federal Pact and demanded its dissolution. A civil war broke out that lasted for only 25 days and resulted in a victory for the forces of the confederation. Fortunately, few lives were lost, making reconciliation relatively easy.

A new constitution, modelled after that of the United States, was established in 1848 and modified in 1874. This constitution can be considered the first free unification of Switzerland. It defined the political organisation that exists today. The members of the Rütli-Oath became a nation. An important problem nevertheless arose which has relevance for today's discussion of a European Constitution: how could the contract be transformed into a constitution? By the majority, of the citizens or the majority of the cantons? Finally, the cantons decided that either the governments of the cantons or the citizens could vote, just as cantons decided. The Constitution was approved not by unanimity but by the majority of cantons (about 75 per cent). This procedure might serve as a model for the introduction of a European Constitution.

The constitution maintained that every law needed a double majority in parliament, which meant that for every law the two chambers had (and have) to agree: by that way the double majority of cantons and people was to be secured. Sovereignty was divided among the cantons and the federal state. Representatives to the federal government were elected by the two chambers of parliament, therefore requiring the majority of the country's population and of the cantons, thereby providing national representation for the small cantons. This sounds familiar to the European ear.[9] A common foreign policy was finally made possible, but the federal army was still organised by the cantons. This is again what we can observe in the EU today. Law, e.g. the law of obligations, was harmonised only for economic purposes (up to now twenty-six codes of civil procedure coexist). In addition, the federation now regulated customs, currency, weights and measures, and the postal service. Harmonisation in the economic sphere has already long been institutionalised in the European Community. The Swiss federation also provided for the protection of the rights and liberties of all citizens and for the promotion of the national welfare, but the competence nevertheless remained with the cantons. Every citizen of a canton was also citizen of Switzerland, which is still the case and is similar to the situation within the EU. Free residence was permitted, but only for those having the means of sustaining a life. Again, we find the same in the EU, based on the articles of free movement[10] of employees[11] and the articles on free residence[12] and free movement of services.[13] There was a waiting period for the right to vote in cantons, but it was capped to a maximum of two years.

There were two total revisions of the constitution in 1874 and 1995. Interestingly, in 1874 the new constitution contained more centralising elements while at the same time giving more direct democratic rights which still exist today. Switzerland became a semi-direct democracy. It is important for my second argument to notice that there seems to exist a balance between centralisation and (direct-democratic) democratisation in Switzerland. To me this also seems a possibility for Europe.

There is one more interesting feature of constitutional history in Switzerland concerning the language problem. Originally, German, French and Italian were official languages. In 1938 a fourth official language (räteromanisch) was introduced by an overwhelming double majority of cantons and people in a constitutional referendum. Its publicly formulated motivation was to provide against the tendencies of centralism in Germany and Italy.[14] Switzerland explicitly stated its self-understanding as a multi-cultural and multilingual state! The 'language problem' is still fiercely discussed in Switzerland, especially in connection with the problem of identity and a common political public.[15] Another characteristic of Swiss political life is that Swiss citizens identify more with their cantons than with Switzerland. The fear of dissolution and loss of national cohesion of the Confederation is still latent and became acute with the referendum in 1992 which rejected the membership in the European Economic Area, in which the French cantons and citizens voted 'yes', but the majority of the German part 'no'.[16]

Concluding, Switzerland is very conscious of the fragility of the institutional balance necessary for upholding the Swiss Confederation. This fact is mostly forgotten by external observers. I would like to mention some characteristical institutions, which – at least in Switzerland – help to sustain the nation and might further thinking on how a European Constitution should be drafted to achieve legitimisation and stability in Europe:

(1) Elements of direct democracy on all levels of government (newly discussed is the direct election of the Bundesrat (members of federal government);

(2) strong federalism with strong emphasis on cultural federalism for municipal and cantonal entities;

(3) a strong tradition of basic rights with a strong tradition of private law;

(4) freedom of languages as a group right;

(5) competition of constitutions on the level of the cantons.

To restate the three arguments I put forward above: Switzerland shows that there is a possibility even for a linguistically and cultural diverse area to become a nation of will and might therefore figure as an example for a European Constitution. Concerning the first point: the nation of will, it is interesting to look at public opinion polling: Already now a majority of citizens of the European Union feels attached to the European Union,[17] and 38 per cent agree that there is a cultural identity shared by all Europeans.[18] In all member-states the majority of people support the membership in the European Union (even in GB), especially the younger ones and the educated ones.[19] Also a majority of people in the EU (even though the desired speed varies from country to country) wish for the EU unification process to progress faster than what they perceive it to be.[20] Those are conditions which are supposedly better than in Switzerland in 1848 after its civil war.

This leads to my second point: the institutional balance of a European Constitution. Here again it is interesting to look at opinion polls. The European parliament is the institution of Europe which is viewed as most trustworthy (53 per cent), with the Court of Justice and the Commission in the second and third place respectively.[21] The European Parliament is also the institution with the most direct democratic legitimisation. It therefore provides most control of the agents by their principals. But of course other democratic institutions can be imagined. As the example of Switzerland suggests, there needs to be an institutionally supported balance between unification and division of powers in a horizontal and vertical way, embracing direct democratic participation and a strong emphasis on basic rights. It also presupposes tolerance and respect for regional or national linguistic and cultural peculiarities, giving self-governance not only to nations and regions but also to municipalities.

Could there be a European polity and public discourse, as requested by Dieter Grimm? In my view, the introduction of a constitution by a double majority vote of the nation-states and the citizens themselves is a fine possibility of legitimisation, as it might initiate a political identity. Concerning the problem of communication, again Switzerland can serve as an example: There, English as *lingua franca* is already well established. It could also serve that purpose in Europe as a whole as nearly half of the citizens of the European Union speak it.[22] This way, just as in Switzerland, where the political public is also divided through language and cultural lines, a political public could nevertheless emerge by controlling its agents on several levels. A constitution could be the beginning of a united Europe legitimised by the citizens of Europe, and could work as a symbol for a European identity – if the institutions are designed with care and keep in mind the crucial importance of building trust, I dare say that there is a good chance for a legitimate constitution.

NOTES

1   Humboldt-Universität zu Berlin, Juristische Fakultät, Lehrstuhl Prof. Dr. Dr. Christian Kirchner; Unter den Linden 6, 10099 Berlin; Tel: 030–2093-3317; Email: anne. van.aaken@rewi.hu-berlin.de.

2   See also Grimm, D. (1995), 'Does Europe need a Constitution?', *European Law Journal*, 1, 282ff. Grimm D. (1996/97), *Vertrag oder Verfassung. Zur Neuordnung der Europäischen Union*, in Grimm, D., R. Jochimsen, F. W. Scharpf and J. J. Hesse (eds), Baden-Baden: Nomos, pp. 9-31.

3   This conclusion does not change by the summit of Nice, as the procedures of legitimization by citizens are unchanged, if one abstracts from the change of the voting procedures or co-decisionmaking. See http://www.presidence-europe.fr for information about the Summit and the Treaty of Nice. See also The Economist of 14 December 2000: 'So that's all agreed, then' with the new and old voting allocation in the Council of ministers in proportion to the population. An EU with more members will necessarily mean that each individual country will have less sway. This matters because so many of the EU's decisions are now made by majority voting, which cannot be thwarted by national vetoes. Even before

Nice, more than 80% of EU decisions were made this way. As a result, the question of how a majority is constituted assumes crucial importance. Under the old system, small countries had more votes in the Council of Ministers, in proportion to their populations, than larger ones; that privilege, though still preserved, has now been somewhat watered down. All the big countries' voting weights have increased at the expense of small countries. Forming a majority will require clearing several hurdles. In the enlarged EU, with different countries having different numbers of votes, 74.6 per cent of those votes will be needed to form a 'qualified majority'. This means that a coalition of three big countries plus one small one will be enough to block a qualified majority. Another form of blocking minority is one that requires a check that any decision has the backing of countries representing 62 per cent of the total population of the enlarged EU. As the Economist states: 'It is safe to say that few of the 'citizens of Europe' will understand this system, meaning that at least one of the aims of the Nice summit – to bring Europe 'closer to the people' by making European decision – making clearer – has not been achieved.'

4   The Economist of 7 September 2000: 'The public uninterest'.

5   See the round up discussion by Christian Kirchner.

6   See Häberle, P. (1991/1992), "Werkstatt Schweiz': Verfassungspolitik im Blick auf das künftige Gesamteuropa", *Jahrbuch des öffentlichen Rechts der Gegenwart,* Tübingen: Siebeck/Mohr. Neue Folge, **40**, 167-173.

7   See for a survey of Swiss history: www.Britannica.com, for a survey of Swiss constitutional history: Aubert, J.F. (1996), 'Geschichtliche Einführung', in Aubert; Eichenberger; Müller; Rhinow, Schindler (eds), *Kommentar zur Bundesverfassung der Schweizerischen Eidgenossenschaft,* Basel et al.: Helbing& Lichtenhahn, Rz. 2-273.

8   See for a Survey of languages spoken in the EU and knowledge of foreign languages: Eurobarometer 52 (1999), Point 6, especially Fig. 6.1, 6.2, 6.3. at www.eurobarometer.com.

9   See the Treaty of Nice at: http://www.presidence-europe.fr.

10   Free residence is defined as the right of all citizens of the member-states to reside in another member-state, work under the same conditions as the national citizens and stay there, under conditions stated by the commission, for retirement. See Groeben, Thiesing, Ehlermann (1997), 'Kommentar zum EU-/EG Vertrag', Vor Art. 48-50, Rz. 1 EGV.

11   Art. 39ff TEC.

12   Art. 43ff TEC.

13   Art. 49ff TEC.

14   See BBl. 1937 Vol. II Nr. 1 and BBl. 1968 Vol. I Nr. 23.

15   See e.g. *Swiss Political Science Review* 2000 with various articles about the language policy. I could myself experience in the council of the economic and social science faculty at the bilingual University of Fribourg that the equilibrium between the French and the German speaking parts of the faculty is fragile. Nevertheless, everybody is aware of the problem, which means also that every member could speak his or her native language and everybody else was expected to understand. If there were foreign visitors, english normally became the common language.

16   See e.g. Köppel, Th. (1994), 'Droht ein Verlust der nationalen Kohäsion?', http://www.fsk. ethz.ch/publ/bulletin/ bulle_94/b94_koep.htm.

17   *The Economist* of 23 October 1999, 17.

18   Eurobarometer 52 (1999), Fig. 1.8.

19   Eurobarometer 52 (1999), Fig. 3.2. and comment thereby.

20   Eurobarometer 52 (1999), Fig. 3.7a and 3.7b.

21   Eurobarometer 52 (1999), Fig. 3.9a.

22   Eurobarometer 52 (1999), Fig. 6.2 and 6.3.

19. Constitutions in Transition

Christian Kirchner

Whereas in most countries of the world constitutions are supposedly stable frameworks for state and society, this is not the case in so-called transition economies, namely those in Central and Eastern Europe. Constitutions serve as means of accomplishing the transition process and they are products of this process as well. Their function should be to stabilise the reform process in which democracy and market economy are the corner stones.

The transition process poses a challenge to constitutional economics, because this discipline can no longer just theoretically approach its subject but it should give answers to practical questions. And there is a threat for every social theory when its answers can be tested in real life. Central and Eastern Europe has been viewed by a group of researches (Chicago group) as a kind of laboratory. But such a laboratory only is of any use if there are clear hypotheses to be tested. It is necessary to clarify the methodological approach in order to be able to learn from the process of constitution building in Central and Eastern Europe.

The workshop 'Constitutions in Transition' has tried to shed new light on that process of constitution building in Central and Eastern Europe by choosing an interdisciplinary approach, in which economists, social scientists and lawyers have presented their questions, their approaches and their answers. The papers discussed have focused on general problems like the 'relationship between state and economy', 'flexibility vs. stability', 'sub-optimal rules', 'constitutionalism beyond the nation state' and the question 'What belongs in a Constitution?' On the other hand practical experiences in countries like Russia, Poland, Bulgaria have been brought into play. Altogether the endeavour of the workshop was to reflect practical experiences in the light of various methodological approaches.

The difficult task of a general commentator and the round up discussion then is to find some 'results' of that attempt to blend different issues and approaches. In the light of the complexity of the subject and the multiplicity of methodological approaches this appears to be sisyphus task. It can only be managed if the general comment views the whole spectacle from a given perspective. I shall choose the perspective of constitutional economics which tries to understand constitutions as symbiotic collective decisions of citizens. In order to gain mutual benefits these citizens accept a set of binding common rules. The citizens – including the politicians and even judges – are supposedly selfish, opportunistic. They cannot accomplish the common good by trying to become better human beings but by developing rules which serve as incentives and constraints and channel social activities in a way that mutual benefits can be gained.

In a transition period such an endeavour may mean to proceed from one suboptimal set of rules to another suboptimal set of rules; but it is essential that the new set of rules better serves the interests of the citizens than the old one. Progress is relative. Constitutions are but one device amongst others to foster the common good. In constitutional economics this common good cannot be defined theoretically but is the product of the process of the collective decision making process which is to reflect the preferences of the citizens. Legitimacy rests upon the consent of citizens and not on the accomplishment of theoretically defined general goals.

For the constitutional issue of the transition process in Central and Eastern Europe this means that solutions should be in accordance with the preferences of citizens of those countries and not just reflecting so-called western value patterns.

The point raised in this context was the potential use of paternalism. Should a constitution in a given point of time reflect the existing preferences of citizens or should a constitution be instrumentalized in order to form the preferences of citizens in the future. One of the advantages of the interdisciplinary approach of the workshop has been the fact that it opened up the scenario not being bound by the economic approach which views preferences as given and then asks how institutional changes affect the process of social interaction. In a time sequence a constitution may be seen as a major factor in shaping preference structures in the future. This has led to the general observation that the constitution-building process is not a search for a static optimum but rather a search path from one disequilibrium to another, a learning process. Such a learning process implies universal factors which might be easily transferred from one country to another; but on the other hand there are a number of national factors. From an economic perspective this phenomenon can be understood as a certain path dependence of national developments. Or one may understand the constitution building process as a national learning process borrowing theoretical elements and experiences from outside.

The starting point of a constitutional discussion in transition economies is the new definition of the role of the state vis-a-vis the 'economy', i.e. the private sphere. From a constitutional economics perspective it is evident that there cannot be markets without rules. The role of constitutionalism is to define the necessary prerequisites of a functioning market. 'But even the most perfect market economy needs a number of institutions in the sense of behaviour-constraining rules and organisations ensuring that these rules function properly. Core elements of a well-functioning market system are secure private property rights, freedom of trade and freedom of contracts, hard budget constraints, clear liability obligations, and stable money' (chapter 3). In order to make sure that these prerequisites are given a 'strong state' is needed. The constitutional task is to frame constitutional rules in a way that they form the fundament of these fundamental legal principles. The role of the constitution then is a purely functional one, like in the ordo-liberal concept. The message is a normative one, without asking the question of how these constitutional rules may be brought into play, how they may be legitimised by the consent of the citizens.

The issue of protection of shareholder and creditor rights in transition economies (chapter 5) seems to be rather a subject not being in the centre of the constitutional debate of transitions economies. But it is interesting to note that the message of the analysis is rather essential for the constitutional discussion: If the absence of effective legal institutions makes the wonderful transplants of governance structures imported from western models unworkable, it is the general legal framework which matters. And this general legal framework is laid down in the constitution, not in a constitution in the books but in the constitution in action. If such constitution in action does not work this bacillus infects other legal constructs as well. Constitutions matter! Legal contracts not imbedded in a functioning constitutional framework are dysfunctional.

To what degree should the constitutional framework in transitional economies be flexible? Should it rather provide stability or not? The question as such cannot be answered. The discussion must be inconclusive. If we start with a given political culture of the constituency, we may then move towards a provisional constitutional framework. The end might be to bring about a pluralistic and liberal culture. But then we are confronted with the question of how to establish in the long run a constitution guaranteeing the rule of law and at the same time a liberal culture. The difficulty of such an approach trying to provide a stable framework for the rule of law and a liberal culture – viewed from a constitutional economics point of view – is that we try to postulate certain goals without asking the question whether or not they are reflecting the preferences of the citizens. If we pose the question of stability and flexibility in a context of constitutional economics and we accept that changes of preference structure are a function of the working of constitutions we have to admit that the dichotomy of flexibility vs. stability is a wrong choice; we rather should look into the process of constitutional change which is reflecting a learning process; not only the knowledge about the real working of constitutions is improved but the preference structures of citizens are changed by the working of existing constitutions. The real issue then is, whether or not given constitutions may serve as a stabilising factor and simultaneously change the preferences of citizens who are in charge of promulgating the next constitution.

Realising that constitutions cannot but produce suboptimal solutions the question arises whether economics might provide criteria for optimal rules. Alexander Blankenagel's paper clearly showed that optimal rules are beyond the reach of constitution building. But the question remains open whether even in such a context it is worthwhile to look for mutual gains to be accomplished by constitutional rules. The example of retroactivity of rules shows that it might well be the case that refined rules may be superior to simple answers.

When constitutions are drafted the question arises what belongs in a constitution. The issue at stake is that alternative problem solutions exist. Constitutional solutions may be rather authoritative, if power is vested in constitutional courts to decide on political questions. There is a substitution between solutions legitimised by means of constitutions and decisions of constitutional courts and decisions legitimised by the ordinary political process. The argument for a minimal constitution goes along with the idea that essential political decisions of a given community should be rather handed over to the political process and not to be hidden under the camouflage of a constitutional decision.

Constitutions might be the result of a law-making process in which the participating actors are aware that they decide on far-reaching problems of societal framing. These actors are then supposedly focusing on the longterm effects of such decisions taking into account the longterm preferences of the constituency. But it might well be the case that every-day-political problems are shaping the context of constitutional decision making. The case of the constitution of Bulgaria has been an example of the working of short-term political decision making which then has found its way into a constitution which has a long-term influence. These effects may be viewed in the Hayekian mode as unintended consequences of intentional decisions. But if we look into the functions of a working constitution we find out that it does not matter too much what have been the motives behind the process of constitution building. What matters is the real impact of the resulting constitution.

Constitutions are a necessary prerequisite of functioning markets in transition economies. The interdependence between the constitutional devices and the necessary framework of a market economy may be much more complicated than just formulating the basic legal rules for a functioning market economy (see chapter 3). The process of maintaining a plurality of concepts and political options and nonetheless of attaining functioning solutions of governing coalitions is a prerequisite of an open society which is then a necessary prerequisite for making markets. This is a functional approach and should not be overburdened by a normative theory which tries to balance three goals: political, economic and social justice.

'Constitutions in transition' means that a high degree of uncertainty prevails in the countries at stake about the constitutional developments in the future. Constitutions have been used as stabilising devices which should defend the 'progress' of the transition process towards democracy and market economy against potential threats in the future. Such threats may easily come from the citizens themselves voting for populist parties not in favour of the new values. Thus constitutions in transition are more or less characterised by a certain degree of paternalism. This goes beyond the attempt to influence the preference structure of citizens as mentioned above. Rather it leads to a certain preference for so-called non-majoritarian institutions like constitutional courts and central banks. Delegation of power to these institutions may be rationalised as a kind of safeguard against future temptations to change the whole constitutional structure in the legislative process. The distrust in majoritarian rules may be seen as the motor of delegation of power to non-majoritarian institutions. They may serve as a kind of anchor. The legitimatisation problem cannot be simply solved by stating that the delegation process as such confers powers from democratically legitimised institutions to these non-majoritarian institutions. The legitimisation of the latter ones can only be grounded in the constitutional decision as such. It is interesting to note what a central role these non-majoritarian institutions play in countries of Central and Eastern Europe. The comparative analysis of eight countries (in chapter 15) sheds new light on the actual importance of this constitutional device (without discussing the potential legitimisation gaps in a longer perspective). The example of the role of the Hungarian constitutional court in interpreting the Hungarian constitution may be seen as a two-step approach of constitution building. The drafters of the constitution are content to write an incomplete contract and leave it to the constitutional court to develop this contract according to the new problems arising in the transition process. There are many similarities to the problem of longterm contracts in international trade using arbitration clauses in order to adapt these contracts to changing circumstances. But again the problem has to be solved of how to supervise the supervisors, of how to legitimise non-majoritarian institutions in the long run.

The other anchor used by constitutions in transition is another delegation device: delegation to supranational or international institutions. Where delegation to national institutions may be revoked in the future if a deficit of legitimisation becomes evident this does not work easily in case of 'external delegation'. The issue of 'sovereignty' is at stake. In a constitutional economics perspective this means that the constituency is not a fixed one but may change over time. Delegation to supranational and international bodies means that a group of actors, i.e. the national constituency, decides to form a subgroup of a broader constituency. The result is vertical delegation of powers. For the transition countries this vertical delegation of powers serves as a very strong anchor; it works under the assumption that the new values laid down in national constitutions may be better protected if these constitutions are imbedded in an international or supranational context in which these values are supposedly shared.

The problem of legitimising political power is the one problem when constitutionalism is extended beyond the nation state. If a supranational constitution means the formation of a state this might lead to ficticious legitimacy. The constitutional economics issue then is whether the problems of principal-agency-problems can be solved better in a supranational constitution than in the common treaty situation. But then new forms of participation of citizens on different levels seem to be necessary.

Looking into the various distinct problems of constitutions in transition a workshop in constitutional economics automatically is confronted with the problem whether there are universally accepted constitutional principles (chapter 11). This question should not be mixed up with the problem of just transferring western constitutional solutions to the countries of Central and Eastern Europe. The problem rather goes to the heart of economic theory as such. Is the economic model a universal one? Today we are quite confident that allocation of resources via the market mechanism is not different in different countries and regions of the world. The myth of a specific Japanese market economy – to take this as an example – has vanished. But when it comes to the application of the toolbox of economics to the organisation of society by means of constitutions we are less confident that our assumptions – used by economics – are universal. We are confronted with the cultural factor which cannot be easily put into economic models. If different cultural factors in different countries lead to different constitutional solutions we have to give up the idea of universally applied principles. One may try to solve the problem by sticking to universally applicable assumptions but modifying them from country to country according to the national culture. Or one may try to modify the model of rational man. A third solution could be to broaden the definition of relevant institutions. There are not only formal rules, but informal rules or conventions (Boscheck[1]) which serve as institutions as well (Lachmann: implicit institutions). Those informal rules and conventions are path dependent; they are a kind of specific collective investment. If this is true the distinction between preferences and constraints may be blurred. If a national constituency may be characterised as well by its specific investment in implicit institutions and by its specific set of preference structures both factors have to be taken into account in the constitution building process. The problem is aggravated if one accepts that preference structures as such may change over time. The inherent problems cannot be solved when we are looking for optimal constitutions. We are rather inclined to view the constitution building process as a learning process in which as well preference structures and implicit institutions will change over time. This does not mean that we have to give up the endeavour of an economic analysis of that process. But we should be careful to distinguish between a comparative analysis in a given period and a longterm vertical analysis. Whereas the first kind of analysis may make full use of the conventional toolbox of economics, the latter one becomes highly speculative. What is needed is a better understanding of implicit institutions and preference changes.

'Constitutions in transition' if taken seriously as a research topic of constitutional economics leads to 'constitutional economics in transition'. It has been a proved to be a wise concept of the organisers of this workshop not to confine the discussion to experts of constitutional economics but to invite the neighbouring disciplines which may well add a lot to 'constitutional economics in transition'.

NOTE

1   Boscheck, Ralf (2002), *Market Drive and Governance*, London: Routledge.

Index

accessibility of constitutional courts 242
accountability of representation 141–4
Ackerman, B. 21
adaptation of constitutional law 89–90
administrative jurisdiction 38–9
Africa, South, transition from apartheid 76
agency theory 288–91
   and the state 291–313
Althusius, J. 41
amendment of constitutions 8–9
anthropology and constitution building 199–200
antitrust offices 251–3
apartheid transition, South Africa 76
Arrow, K.J. 303
association of interests, scheme of representation 141–2, 144

Bagel, I. 303
balanced regulations, US 145–6
Barro, R.J. 45, 47, 247
basic values and commitments 11–14
Ben-Gurion, D. 14
Bentham, J. 23
Beresovsy 45
Berger, P.L. 27
Berkowitz, D. 73
bicameral parliaments
   agency relationships 296–7
   in heterarchies 148
Bills of Rights 9–11, 18
Boettke, P.J. 64

Bönker, F. 50
Bork, R. 24–5
Bourdieu, P. 140
Britain, separation of powers 293
Buchanan, J.M. 28–9
Bulgaria
   central bank 246–50, 273
   constitution-making 115–26, 232–3, 264–6
   constitutional court 240, 241
   constitutional legacy 231–2
   economic competition 251–2
   international delegation 255, 257, 259–62, 275–6

central banks
   constitutional provisions 273–5
   independence 246–50
      and judicial independence 253–4
Central European countries
   constitutional legacies 231–7
   constitutions 96–7, 114–26, 333–40
   delegation of powers 222–31
   market economy 133–4
   see also individual countries
China, transition to market economy 35–6, 55
citizens, and rule-making 30
Clark, R.C. 306
coercive power of state 38–9
communism
   as constitutional constraint 223, 228–9
   failure of 37, 188–90